THE FIRST COMBAT BOMB WING

THE FIRST COMBAT BOMB WING IN WORLD WAR II

RON MACKAY

Schiffer Publishing Ltd

4880 Lower Valley Road • Atglen, PA 19310

Library of Congress Control Number: 2014948007

Printed in China.
ISBN: 978-0-7643-4375-9

We are interested in hearing from authors with book ideas on related topics.

Published by Schiffer Publishing Ltd.
4880 Lower Valley Road
Atglen, PA 19310
Phone: (610) 593-1777
FAX: (610) 593-2002
E-mail: Info@schifferbooks.com.
Visit our web site at: www.schifferbooks.com
Please write for a free catalog.
This book may be purchased
from the publisher.
Try your bookstore first.

Photograph Credits

Mike Bailey
David Crow
Alan Dann
Richard "Doc" Hecker
Vic Jenkins
Kevin Wilson

Contents

Chapter One—Groping in the Dark 6

Chapter Two—Into the Enemy Heartland 14

Chapter Three—Spring to Summer Expansion (April/June 1943) 24

Chapter Four—Full stride for *Blitz Week* (July 1943) 42

Chapter Five—Darkening Horizons 54

Chapter Six—Full Combat Bomb Wing Status (September 1943) 70

Chapter Seven—“Black October” 83

Chapter Eight –Winter Doldrums (November 1943/January 1944) 97

Chapter Nine –Blow for Blow (February/March 1944) 119

Chapter Ten—Enter the 398BG 139

Chapter Eleven—“D-Day has Come....” 157

Chapter Twelve—Oil and Transportation Strangulation 177

Chapter Thirteen—Air Supremacy in Place 193

Chapter Fourteen—En Route to Victory 209

Chapter Fifteen—“Killing the Cow” 221

Appendix 233

Color Photo Gallery 234

Index 241

Chapter One
Groping in the Dark

In the course of the near 1,000 days of the USAAF's Daylight Offensive—from early 1944 onward—the pace of progress advanced from one of stuttering and sometimes negative "progress" with minimal human and logistical resources on hand to an all-out onslaught, with regular launching of over 1,000 bombers and similar scale fighter escorts. The latter provision was only properly addressed from late 1943 onwards, prior to which the B-17s and B-24s had to fend for themselves on missions extending deep into the Third Reich; they not only suffered swinging casualties in the process, but had seen mooted the likely cancellation of the Offensive in its current form.

The concept of daylight precision bombardment of an adversary's industrial and military resources had been an article of faith with the USAAC authorities well prior to America's entry into the twentieth century's second major conflict, which unlike its 1914-18 predecessor was truly global in scale. The creation of the VIII Bomber Command, in February 1942, was made with the very laudable intention of cutting the heart out of Hitler's (and later Mussolini's) ill-gained Empires. This was to be achieved not by defeating their military forces on the battlefield, but rather by destroying the industrial resources that produced the materials with which to conduct their ever-nefarious campaigns. (To paraphrase the commentator in the original *Memphis Belle* film: "We seek out his production factories—pin-points on the European map that spell rubber, oil, steel, etc.—the greater menace behind the Nazi lust for conquest....")

The campaign's inaugural mission involved just eighteen B-17s of the 97BG, six bombers of which formed a diversion for the twelve who struck (achieving a marginal degree of accuracy) marshalling yards at Rouen, France. Fighter opposition was minimal, but the bombers' heavy armament in conjunction with tight formation flying was confidently expected to see off any assaults, regardless of their weight or endurance. General Ira Eaker (CG VIII BC) tactfully commented: "One swallow doesn't make a summer" in his post-mission report. However, it would be many months before he would be able to amass anything approaching a "flock" of that specie's aeronautical counterparts. In addition, the *Jagdwaffe* pilots, having steadily taken the measure of their Trans-Atlantic adversaries, would introduce tactics to put the "self-defending bomber" concept firmly on the back foot.

While the three groups on hand during the offensive's initial phase in August and September were experiencing a staccato pace of operations—with British weather playing no small part in the process—no less than four more groups were in transit to the UK and assignment to the 1st Bombardment

Wing (1BW). The 303BG, 305BG, and 306BG Ground Echelons were on hand during the latter month, having settled in at Molesworth, Grafton Underwood, and Thurleigh, which would feature as their permanent respective bases during WWII, other than for the 305BG, which would only move to Chelveston during December.

Wray's Warriors

The fourth acolyte group was the 91BG, whose personnel, led by Col. Stanley T. Wray, ultimately found themselves at Kimbolton. The Trans-Atlantic crossing had been duly achieved by the crews, although the weather conditions during the first week of October proved ever-daunting; in spite of this, an almost perfect delivery of bombers was achieved. The tragic exception was 41-24451/LL: E, bearing Capt. Dale Dasselle's team, as well as a group Flight surgeon; foggy conditions over Northern Ireland led to a crash that only two crewmembers survived.

The assigned airfield was a wartime utility creation similar to the other three aforementioned locations, with T2 metal-constructed hangars and Nissen huts. The Air Echelons (for other than Thurleigh) only arrived during October, with the 91BG crews landing first, between the 10th and 17th. The prospect of making do with the surrounding facilities probably disappointed the combat crews arriving up to the 14th at least, but an unbelievable transformation was already being initiated by Col. Wray—which was seemingly totally unauthorized as well. The current state of the runways was regarded as not being up to regularly handling heavily-laden bombers, and steps were on hand to carry out the necessary strengthening work. In the meantime (so the story goes), the Col. searched around for a temporary "home" for his group. Kimbolton lies fairly close to Bassingbourn, a prewar RAF permanent base with brick-built hangars and support buildings and —even better—steam-heated brick accommodations.

The airfield was reportedly unoccupied when Col. Wray chanced upon it. Consequently, he lost no time in initiating the personnel's transfer to this comparative "paradise" in terms of facilities. When higher authority heard of Wray's action, he was summoned and given a hard time. However, no further action in terms of reversing the transfer was taken and the ensuing thirty months of operational duties of the group would be conducted from the "hijacked" expanse of Bassingbourn!

Another anecdote suggests that B/Gen. Longfellow had referred Wray in the direction of Bassingbourn just 24 hours prior to his inspection of the airfield, so his reported annoyance with the Col.'s extremely prompt act of transfer the very next day appears to be open to question. Further clashing with Wray's seemingly precipitate act is the existence of an official VIIIBC document (General Order No. 26/19 October 1942) that sanctions the group's retrospective transfer on the 16th and the reverse transfer from Bassingbourn to Kimbolton for the 17BG, a medium-bomber unit.

Of course, Wray must have been aware of the fact that once Kimbolton's runways were brought up to heavy bomber standards, his unit was going to be brought back there. A more plausible reason for the group's subsequent retention of the new airfield was that the VIIIBC hierarchy regarded the time and effort involved in a second transfer as impinging unnecessarily upon the group's operational ability, especially at a time when the offensive required maximum effort from the Command's currently marginal strength in aircraft and crews.

VIIIBC Structure in 1942

The presence, up to November, of nine groups within Gen. Eaker's Command—seven B-17 and two B-24 units—gave the sadly short-lived hope of a reasonably large striking force; the gross availability of between 300 and 350 bombers with a supporting number of combat crews, when allowing for the perceived wastage factor of non-operational machines, as well as a degree of MIA aircraft, still indicated an ability to dispatch three-figure numbers on any mission. However, a notable stumbling block arose in terms of overall USAAF strategy within Allied plans when Operation *Torch* was proposed.

The operation involved the invasion of Morocco and Algeria in NW Africa and, part of the aerial support provision called for several command units to be sent out from Britain. Among this contingent were the B-17s of the 97BG and 301BG, the latter having only crossed the Atlantic during late August. These groups flew their final missions on 21 October and 8 November, respectively, and by late November, were deploying southward; they would become permanent elements of first the African-based 12USAAF and then the Italian-based 15USAAF. Eaker's current operational strength was further reduced by the 92BG's withdrawal between October and the following May and employment in a training role.

Another deleterious factor at this stage of operations lay in the relative lack of support equipment with which to maintain full operational status on each airfield. The build-up of the necessary supplies proved to be painfully protracted, with more supposedly being diverted towards the 97BG and 301BG than was arriving in East Anglia. The still-punishing U-Boat offensive against the Atlantic convoys was likely adding to the problem in this respect, since much of the bulkier items had to be transported by sea and were being lost in the process.

Of the six remaining groups on hand as November was entered, only the 93BG and 306BG had gone operational several weeks previous. Now, on the 7th of the month, came the call to battle for four groups that included the 91BG. The target was U-Boat facilities at Brest, on France's Atlantic coast, and one of four major ports utilized by the *Kriegsmarine* submariners. What Churchill later described as the only thing that caused him the most sleepless nights—namely the U-Boat threat—was biting into the ranks of the Allied convoys with frightening effect.

Any measure, however effective in countering the threat, was now to include the RAF and USAAF "Heavies," who were to be regularly employed in bombing the U-Boat lairs. The presence of multi-foot thick concrete enclosures for the "Rattlesnakes of the Ocean" would make these impervious to all but the RAF's aerodynamic duo of 12,000-lb "Tallboy" and 22,000-lb "Grand Slam" weapons, let alone the USAAF's 2,000-lb standard bomb; at least a measure of punishment could be administered to the surrounding facilities and might even involve snaring a U-Boat as it arrived or departed.

Combat Initiation

The fourteen Bassingbourn crews alerted were duly briefed and headed for their aircraft, each bearing ten 500-lb bombs. Assembly first by unit and then by link-up with the 306BG—its partner in the 101PCBW (Provisional Combat Bomb Wing)—was effected, but by the time the bomb run was in progress, only eight group crews were still on hand. The reported cause for some of the "aborts" was the freezing-up of machine gun mechanisms; the tendency to over-apply oil when cleaning the weapons may well have been the reason for this defensive failure, but whatever the facts, the overall group firepower was now seriously reduced. However, *Jagdwaffe* reaction was surprisingly muted, despite ample warning of the formations' presence and direction, and the eight crews gaining mission credit arrived back at base to end what was the first of 340 credited missions over the ensuing thirty months.

Abbeville/Drucat airfield was targeted next day, but only eleven of the sixteen dispatched B-17s completed their bomb runs. This diversionary run was followed 24 hours later by the first foray against St. Nazaire's pens, with just one "abortion" occurring. What was rightly known as "Flak City" for its ferocious flak barrage directly or indirectly cost the 306BG three crews, but Bassingbourn's ranks remained inviolate, both on this occasion and during return visits on the 14th and 17th, although the first occasion witnessed a diversion from similar facilities at La Pallice after the Primary was found to be cloud-blanketed.

The first St. Nazaire mission had involved the group and other VIIIBC elements in an experiment that was particularly fraught with danger and surely contributed to the 306BG's aforementioned punishment. The target approach by the two B-17 units was made at 7,500ft before climbing to a still low altitude of 10,000ft. Meanwhile, the 44th and 93rd BG B-24s came in at 18,000ft. The hope that the higher-flying groups would distract the flak gunners' attention away from their B-17 contemporaries was not realized; in the circumstances, it was surprising that the Bassingbourn ranks was not similarly shorn of bombers, although heavy damage was applied to some airframes and serious injuries, including one fatality, were incurred. The relative absence of enemy fighters was an added blessing for the survivors, and as it transpired, the experiment was never repeated.

Although the 91BG's ranks were left inviolate on the St. Nazaire mission, one aircraft provided an early example regarding the inherent strength of the B-17's airframe. A flak shell struck home around the waist window area and severely weakened the fuselage of 41-24050/DF: E **Quitchurbitchin;** in spite of this, the aircraft was kept aloft as far as SW England, where it was put down on an RAF airfield. Repair crews sent from Bassingbourn then brought the bomber back to operational condition just in time for participation in a mission to St. Nazaire.

The continuing inviolability from aircraft loss lasted almost to the month's end. The sixth completed mission on the 18th saw La Pallice attacked albeit with just eight out of seventeen B-17s still on hand. A mid-air collision between 41-24453/LG: O **Mizpah-The Bearded Beauty** and 41-24499/LG: P **Fury** thankfully left both bombers airborne, although the latter was declared "salvage" after Maj. Zienowicz brought off a crash landing, while **Mizpah** was landed at RNAS Yeovilton by Lt. Hardin. (Sadly, the Major's remaining life span was measured in days). Then, four days later, St. Nazaire was due to receive its latest baptism of fire, but the ever-pernicious weather patterns over Europe saw solid cloud cloak the Primary from all but a handful of B-17s; the 2,000-lb bombs nestling in the 91BG's contingent of ten were hauled back to England.

Reality Strikes Home

The 91BG's eighth mission would witness its fourth effort against St. Nazaire, with ten crews forming part of a 58-strong VIIIBC force provided by five of the six available groups. To date, a number of crewmembers had been injured, with at least one fatality, but the MIA fate had been avoided by all participants. Rendezvous with the other groups was thwarted by the weather; worse still was the fact that the dispatched number was down to half. In spite of this, the miniscule and dangerously isolated force headed southwest. This number was then reduced to four when 41-24479/LG: R **Sad Sack**, flown by Capt. Tom B. McCormick, with Maj. Victor Zienowicz (323BS CO), turned back with engine problems, never to be seen again.

The truncated formation, having reached the Brest Peninsula, found their efforts to unload on the Primary or any alternate source to be in vain. Worse still was the appearance of FW190 elements from JG2 who descended upon the B-17s. The ensuing air battle was brief, but resulted in one MIA casualty. Capt. Duane Jones's **Pandora's Box**, also bearing Maj. Harold Smelser (324BS CO), lost two engines to fighter strikes and inevitably began to fall behind. Smelser was seen to wave away the other B-17s, whose pilots naturally but ill-advisedly also reduced speed. The harsh principle that "a crippled plane is expendable but all other crews' obligation was to retain the formation integrity" was rightly if self-sacrificially applied by Smelser. When last seen, 41-24503/DF: E was gamely plugging onward, but in a descent. As with the other MIA B-17, that was the last seen of bomber or crew, their last resting place the Atlantic or the English Channel.

On return, Lt. Charles B. Cliburn, although wounded, managed to land his badly shot-up bomber, this being the first of several combat incidents for the 324BS pilot, who was also the sole arrival back at Bassingbourn. **Quitchurbitchin** (41-24505/DF: E) had been badly shot-up, with one cannon shell penetrating the cockpit and wounding Cliburn and Lt. Clyde DeBaum (CP), the latter seriously. Debaum's seat was taken by Lt. Phil Palmer (B), and the B-17, by then low, held on course despite suffering rudder and elevator trim tab failure. The safe return was later followed by a DFC award to Cliburn, while the B-17 was destined to languish for many months before being restored to full combat status. This "original" veteran's final mission occurred on 31 December 1943, and she was transferred out the following March for relegation to training duties.

The group's combat martyrdom was still incomplete, because a third bomber (41-24506/DF: G **The Shifless Skunk**), flown by Lt. Nathan N Corman (KIA), crashed during an emergency landing at Leavesden, near Watford; half of the crew were killed instantly or died of their injuries. The fourth returnee diverted into RAF Chivenor, which was Capt. Ken Wallick's machine. So the seal had been truly broken in terms of technical and human casualties, with the two MIA crews' fate destined to be duplicated on 195 further occasions, albeit not always with the same 100% loss of personnel.

The punishment handed out by JG2's pilots during this latest assault on St. Nazaire coincided with a change in tactics that was in turn initiated by Hptm. Egon Mayer, *III Gruppe Kommandeur*, and was one that promised increasing grief for the VIIIBC crews. He reportedly deduced that the forward defensive provision on both the USAAF heavy bomber designs was much more fragmented in comparison with their lateral and rear-functioning armament. The scant time span in which to land strikes from this angle was more than compensated for by the feeble and dispersed nature of the flexible gun mountings within the currently-available B-17F and B-24D nose compartments, while the top turret weapons were only partially capable of taking on such thrusts. The effect of gunfire penetrating the forward fuselage could and would result in pilots, navigators, and bombardiers being killed or incapacitated. And so it was that this key deficiency in the "self-defending bomber" theory would steadily erode the prospects of the VIIIBC gaining its targets and returning with acceptable loss scales over the coming months.

Closing off the Year

The loss of twenty-one MIA airmen, among whom were two squadron COs, was a sharp rebuff that surely left a sense of depression. The personnel would have time to reflect upon the situation, since nearly two weeks would elapse before the next "alert" resulted in a mission. The late autumn weather intruded upon the launching of the bombers, and it was 6 December before an industrial plant at Lille (NE France) was targeted by 43 out of 85 dispatched B-17s, of which all but four of the 22-strong group contingent unloaded upon the Primary.

The mission was destined to be followed by a mere three more during the month—exactly half the November figure—and reflecting the offensive's frustrating scale of build up. Not only were dispatched numbers of bombers almost always less than three figures, but added to this was the fact that the intention to strike at Germany's industrial heart was currently on hold, since the targets to date were all located outside the Third Reich's territory.

All four 1BW groups went out to Rouen/Sotteville's marshalling yards (12th), with all but the 306BG returning intact. A further eight days elapsed before the bombers again headed out in harm's way, and for the last occasion in several months, a three-figure number of B-17s and B-24s were dispatched to bomb Romilly-sur-Seine airfield, SE of Paris. This was a target that with most others was well beyond the range of escort cover, a fact that the *Jagdwaffe* took advantage of, although the overall effect was fairly marginal—three out of the 72 crews gaining mission "credit" did not return.

The 91BG's seventeen aircraft was four short by the bomb run, but only two were affected by mechanical problems. Scarcely had the Allied escorts withdrawn when a sizeable body of fighters commenced a protracted series of attacks upon the bombers. A head-on run saw one fighter land lethal strikes upon 41-24432/LL: F/E **Danellen,** flown by Lt. Dan W. Corson. The B-17 began a descent that culminated in a spinning action and terminal impact near Vascoceuil, with one survivor among the nine-man crew. A second 401BS bomber (41-24452/E, in Lt. Robert S. English's charge) was culled from the formation and came down in the region around Rouen; the pilot was one of three fatalities, as well as being declared MIA (indicating his body was never recovered), leaving seven crewmembers as POWs.

The losses were a third of overall 1BW MIA casualties, but could have been further increased after the Lead B-17, flown by Capt. Ken Wallick, suffered damage that resulted in the landing gear drooping; the resultant drag saw the bomber falling inexorably back and seemingly easy prey for the fighters. Lt. Bruce Barton now broke the sacred rule of "group integrity" to ease back and provide defensive support. The subsequent mini-conflict witnessed both B-17s surviving.

On the other hand, although Wallick managed to make it back to base with his **Rose O'Day** (41-24512/LG: N**)**, the greater degree of punishment landed on Barton's 41-24439/LG: Q **Chief Sly**, which included the loss of one engine among a range of disabled equipment that ended with the bomber barely gaining the south coast of England before crash landing near Fletching. Lt. Paul Burnett (N) was badly wounded, but was the sole crewmember so affected. As for the B-17, its combat days were over and it was subsequently recovered and "cannibalized."

The combat crews were now under less illusion regarding the hard and uncertain road ahead, even although four MIA losses in eleven missions seemed to promise a sound basis for completing their operational tours of duty; such odds would steadily decrease in the weeks and months to come. The penultimate day of 1942 marginally reinforced the loss of operational innocence when the latest thrust against the U-Boat offensive was directed at Lorient.

The 1BW dispatch of 77 crews was down by a quarter on the bomb run, since the 306BG had almost totally "aborted" the mission during Assembly, with the single exception ironically ending up MIA. Lt. William Bloodgood's crew had brought 41-24449/LL: **Short Snorter** over the Atlantic and today were again on board. The regular fighter assaults were pressed home on either side of the bomb run that this crew completed. As the homeward course was taken, up the latest foray by the *Jagdwaffe* resulted in mortal damage that included the firing-up of No. 3 engine. Shortly after the bomber blew apart, and although several crew were reported as deploying their parachutes, they likely joined their hapless colleagues in the frigid Atlantic waters now being traversed by the formation. Capt. Cliborn brought his B-17 back with only nine crewmembers still alive. The tenth was Maj. Meyers (401BS CO), who was killed during a head-on fighter attack.

Comment

The VIIIBC's operational record between 17 August and the year's end was, on the face of it, unimpressive in general. The numbers dispatched had rarely exceeded upwards of 100, while the range of target categories was small, with locations falling into the strategic bracket proving marginal at best. German soil was yet to be flown over, although the initial effort in this respect was not too distant. The lack of even medium-range escorts indicated that the bombers would have to depend upon their armament when the Spitfires and soon P-47s were forced to leave their charges to their own devices. Moreover, although losses to date had been due to flak as much as the *Jagdwaffe*, its already battle-tested pilots were beginning to get the measure of the *Viermots* (four-engine aircraft) in a manner that boded ill for the USAAF crews. Egon Meyer's November 23rd experiment over St. Nazaire had planted the seeds of disaster for escort-free penetrations of the Nazi hinterland.

Bassingbourn's distinctive extension to a normal British layout is seen at top right. The tree-lined avenue holding several dispersal pans lies on the far side of A10. The five brick construction "Type C" hangars for what is a prewar Expansion Base form an arc at the bottom of the picture.

This "shot" of an anonymous mechanic reportedly attempting to warm his hands on a mobile generator out on a mist-shrouded and soaking-wet dispersal amply depicts the conditions under which the ground crews had to operate while ensuring the highest state of B-17 operational readiness and therefore security for the combat crews.

The hazy atmosphere in this Nissen hut aptly sums up the overall atmosphere within the VIII Bomber Command during its initial spell of operations in 1942/43. Officer on the left is attempting to maintain some form of heat from the infamous "pot-bellied" stove. His colleague is probably cleaning up prior to venturing off the base to seek whatever pleasures are available in the surrounding countryside.

The Lead P-47 in an Element commences the "peel off" procedure after entering the circuit at Bassingbourn. B-17F in foreground is 41-24459, a 401BS aircraft named Hellsappopin that was finally MIA over Bremen on 17 April 1943, when half of Lt. John Wilson's (KIA) crew shared its fate.

A Mk. IX Spitfire from No. 302 (Polish) Squadron tucks in close to a 91BG B-17F. The otherwise superbly performing Supermarine design suffered from very short operational range due to its equally limited fuel capacity. Medium Green blotching on aileron surfaces was common on B-17s during 1942/43.

A major impediment in the setting up of an airfield anywhere in Britain was mud. These two airmen are busy removing as much of the cloying mess from their boots using their spades, but the liquid surface will still provide an unwelcome slick when they enter their billet or any other building.

Ancient and modern at Bassingbourn. The horse-drawn cart ambling casually across the front of a 91BG dispersal provides an almost weird contrast with what is a current 'state of the art" implement of aerial combat.

The assistance provided by the RAF during the formative stage of the VIIIBC's life span was as comprehensive as possible. In this instance, the gesticulating fire crew staff at Bassingbourn are standing on and around two Fordson WOT1 3-ton 6 x 4-wheel vehicles.

The almost casual disposition of these packing cases on the mist-shrouded airfield belonging to one of the "pioneer" 1BW groups in the winter of 1942/43 speaks eloquently of the organized chaos surrounding the creation of the VIII Bomber Command's operational structure.

On 18 November 1942, Lt. Hardin's crew survived a mid-air collision with their B-17F 41-24453/LG: O Mizpah – The Bearded Beauty, the bomber diverting into the Royal Navy airfield at Yeovilton. The crew are here seen flanking two RN officers; the group "original" aircraft survived operations until the Schweinfurt mission on 17 August 1943.

Chapter Two

Into the Enemy Heartland

Continued Winter of Discontent

The anticipated expansion of VIIIBC, far from being realized, was not only continuing to be delayed, but the resources of men and material needed to even maintain the current level of operational effectiveness were badly strained. The Allies were engaged all over the globe and the Command's claim upon priority treatment was almost certainly "in the pipeline," as it were. The battle of the Atlantic and the land campaigns in North Africa and the Pacific were either poised on a knife edge or barely swinging in the Allies' favor. Then, sizeable supplies had to be diverted to assist the Soviet forces in their still-desperate struggle on the Eastern Front. Small wonder that the England-based units were expected to currently soldier on with what was on hand.

The perceived general lack of success with the Campaign was also drawing heavy criticism from several quarters, both military and political, within the Anglo/American camp. Churchill was a leading figure in the latter category, suggesting that the Command switch over to join RAF Bomber Command in its nocturnally-directed offensive. Gen. Eaker was going to have to utilize all his verbal skills at the forthcoming Casablanca Conference to dissuade the British Premier from pursuing his aims.

"Flak City Again"

The new year (1943) was two days old before the first evening "Alert" for the next day was announced. St. Nazaire's pens were targeted by all four 1BW groups, along with the 2BW's 44BG. The still-critical Atlantic Conflict merited the American crews' continued attention and today would be the first of nine assaults spread between this location, Brest, and Lorient up to late June.

Col. Curtis LeMay (305BG CO) was a superb innovator who was credited with several tactical measures in respect of the Command's operational procedures. A key element in formation flying was the ability to not only hold tight formation, but to do so in a manner that permitted maximum defensive gunfire without impinging upon surrounding bombers. Until recently, the groups had not flown any formation pattern that satisfied these twin requirements. In addition, the crews had been only maintaining a steady course immediately prior to bombing, an action that ironically militated against any guarantee of accurate bombing, given the need to set up the Norden bombsights properly. The fear of flak was reportedly the primary reason behind this mass maneuver.

Lemay calculated that a steady bomb run would result in no material increase in losses, while his proposal for the groups to stagger their Elements vertically and laterally would further minimize the flak threat, as well as satisfy the defensive fire requirement. He further suggested that a Lead Bombardier in each group should set up his bombsight and the other bombardiers release upon his signal. Today's mission was certainly the first time the 305BG was recorded as putting these theories into practice and it seems likely that the other groups applied the same principles.

The clear weather conditions for once provided a perfect sight of the target, although the destructive effect of the mix of 1,000- and 2,000-lb bombs was going to have no effect against the pens or their predatory occupants. The JG2 fighters were present in numbers and, between their efforts and the flak gunners, seven crews were culled from the seventy-two B-17s. **Panhandle Dogie** was the second group bomber to bear this title, the first one (41-24570 /OR:) having been "written off" following the 91BG's second mission. Lt. Bill Anderson, who had flown the "original" B-17 over the Atlantic, was allocated a new bomber on 14 December, upon which he bestowed the same name, but 42-5084's luck ran out in the target area, along with the pilot and all but one of the other nine crewmembers, when flak strikes resulted in it exploding.

The staccato pace of missions experienced to date continued during January, when just three more were launched. Lille was visited ten days later, when industrial plants were struck by 64 out of the 72 assigned crews; in Bassingbourn's case, ten out of 13 bombers gained mission "credit," while the escorts kept the Luftwaffe largely at bay, although three B-17s from other groups were lost. The frustration of weather-cancelled missions was again visited upon the Command with the same time period experienced before a run to Lorient was completed.

Once again, the group returned without material loss over Europe, although Lt. Philip Fischer had one crewmember killed by flak and was forced to crash land 41-24504 /DF: D **The Sad Sack** at Great Horwood. This "original" B-17 was initially treated to regular "cannibal" treatment for use by other bombers, but was finally brought back to operational status by M/Sgt. Roberts's team; she was fated to receive a thorough pounding that very same day (22 March), but was again returned to combat status and finally returned stateside in early 1944.

Operational Sea Change

In the superbly understated 1948 film "Twelve O-clock High," which depicts the early fortunes of VIIIBC, there is a scene where Gregory Peck, having delivered his preliminary Briefing remarks, continues: "And now—for the first time...," only to be interrupted by Hugh Marlowe standing up and softly uttering the single telling word, "Germany!" The same reaction, perhaps not as dramatically pitched but equally heartfelt, must have penetrated the minds of the crews assembled for Briefing in the early hours of 27 January 1943. They were embarking on the first full stage of bringing home to the Nazis the folly of declaring war on the USA and by extension adding to the already sizeable opposition to their dreams of European domination demonstrated by Britain and the Commonwealth, as well as Soviet Russia.

Vegesack, on the western fringe of Bremen, held important ship and U-Boat construction yards and was chosen as the Primary, while Wilhelmshaven's huge naval base, situated on Germany's North Sea coastline (some 30 miles NW) was the Secondary. All six groups dispatched an average of fifteen crews, but by the time target approach was made the cloud cover was becoming ever-thicker, albeit not totally solid. The decision was taken to switch to the Secondary, and although a smoke screen was issuing forth that partially obscured the area, the bulk of the 91BG at least released their loads.

Part or all of the other three B-17 units held their loads as the formations turned for home and finally dropped on Emden's naval facilities due west of the Secondary, as did two Bassingbourn crews. The relative lack of fighter opposition was puzzling if gratifying for the participants; three bombers had gone down—one to a mid-air collision—but this low loss scale was unlikely to be maintained as deeper thrusts into Germany were initiated.

February Fortunes

Wilhelmshaven had been the 91BG's sixteenth completed mission, in the course of which just six crews had gone MIA. This was a tally that in crude terms compared relatively well with the other 1BW units' experience, with 13 (303BG) and 11 (306BG) being their respective tallies and four MIA casualties for the 305BG. Now that the VIIIBC had broken its combat "duck" over Germany, the prospect of further regular thrusts into the Third Reich seemed good, but in the ensuing two months, the majority of targets would still involve locations within Nazi-occupied countries; in addition, the German targets, with the exception of Hamm, would tend to be found on the western fringes of the Third Reich.

Gen. Hap Arnold (CG, USAAF) was growing increasingly impatient with the seeming lack of progress evinced by Gen. Eaker's Command in making effective inroads on Germany's ability to wage the conflict. Eaker could in turn point to the paucity of material and human resources currently being directed his way; his difficulties were further added to by adverse weather patterns casting up a genuine stumbling block in successfully prosecuting the offensive. As it was, the pace of operations would not pick up significantly until 1943 was nearing its end, with double figures of monthly missions the exception. Although VIIIBC's overall unit strength would increase threefold by the summer, this logistical improvement would be balanced by equally increasing and ultimately swinging loss rates in bombers and their crews.

A mission to Hamm's marshalling yards NE of the Ruehr was initiated (2nd) but recalled over the North Sea, only to be reinstated two days later. This time round, the full 1BW force crossed into Europe, but was confronted by ever-higher and solid cloud banks that thwarted any attempt to strike the Primary. As on 27 January, the 1BW finally headed for Emden, but the

305BG alone is not recorded as bombing even the Secondary, although it lost one of two MIA crews in a mid-air collision with a fighter.

Three further crews were culled from the ranks of the 303BG and 91BG. Bassingbourn's duo of casualties were incurred on the way home, as the gunners fought back against the *Jagdwaffe,* whose ranks included Bf110 and Ju88 "twins"—almost certainly *Nachtjagd* (night fighter) machines pressed into day service—as well as single-engine fighters. **Pennsylvania Polka** (41-24544/OR:O/L) was the latest "original" bomber to feel the lethal sting of the enemy as the group was skirting the north Dutch coastline and the western end of the Frisian island chain. Lt. Bobrow's (KIA) charge was seen to be lagging and finally suffered a catastrophic series of strikes that ignited an engine; she disappeared into a cloud bank and finally descended into the North Sea waters to leave no survivors among the ten airmen. Her companion in misfortune, also a group "original" and fellow-squadron B-17, was 41-24589/OR: R **Texas Bronco**. However, Lt. Eugene B. Ellis's (POW) crew suffered a far better scale of individual fortune, since just two out of the ten airmen failed to survive the fighter assaults that culminated with a crash landing on Terschelling Island, directly north of the Ijsselmeer, then known as the Zuiderzee.

This day coincided with the planned dispatch to the States of Lt. Jack Crumm and crew, who had just completed their eleventh mission in 41-24490/DF: C **Jack the Ripper**. The reason for doing so was for the airmen to collaborate in the production of an official handbook that utilized their combat experience for the benefit of future acolyte crews joining the VIIIBC's ranks. Their combat days were now over, but the B-17 would soldier on until 22 February 1944, before going MIA, when it was reportedly the group's last "original" bomber to be consumed in combat.

It was mid-February before a marginal flurry in operational activity arose with three daily missions flown, although the B-17 and B-24 BWs each only participated in two. The first (14th) intended once again to strike at Hamm's marshalling yards and was completed as far as NW Holland when abandonment was made in the face of increasingly adverse weather conditions; at least all 74 B-17s returned safely. The 2BW crews struck Dunkirk, France, the next day, after which the 1BW again took up the cudgels—but not against German targets. Instead, the latest assault upon St. Nazaire was launched and completed by the early afternoon. However, a 10% MIA tally was incurred by the 65 attacking bombers with a further two among the original 89 briefed crews suffering a mid-air collision over the English coast.

A new slant on fighter countermeasures was noted by some Bassingbourn airmen this day, when clusters of objects dropped from above onto the bombers burst with red and white smoke plumes; the conclusion at debriefing was that the intention was to damage or destroy the B-17s and B-24s through the use of time-fused fragmentation bombs. Plans to drop full-sized bombs were well in hand and, for example, would be deployed by JG11, based in NW Germany; the use of rockets was another forthcoming and patently unpleasant countermeasure.

The number ten, in respect of breaks enforced or otherwise between missions, again arose, with the bombers only getting aloft and heading out on the 26th for Bremen in full twin-BW force. This target's temporary respite from assault was sustained thanks to weather and, as on 27 January, it was Wilhelmshaven's ill fortune to be focused upon as a Target of Opportunity by two-thirds of the 93 dispatched crews. The *Jagdwaffe* was again in evidence and, between its pilots and the flak, seven B-17s became MIA statistics. Once again, a duo of 91BG crews was among this figure.

It was the 401BS' turn to lose out on both occasions. The first involved yet another group "original," 41-24447/LL: H **Kickapoo**, the title alluding to the "Hooch" brew in the "L'il Abner" comic strip. Capt. John Swais had flown the bomber for the majority of the ten missions completed to date; the aircraft was still on hand as the formations headed home over the North Sea, but was last seen with one engine smoking as it turned back toward the east. No further sight of aircraft nor crew was ever realized, so the North Sea almost certainly swallowed up both.

The same tragically anonymous fate awaited all ten in Lt. Beman E. Smith's team on board **Short Snorter II** (42-5362/LL: F). The bomber had been observed to similarly turn back as the formation was leaving the Frisian Island chain behind, but clearly never survived the attempt to regain solid ground, even if enemy-controlled, with mechanical failure or fighter interception being alternative causes for their tragic failure.

Eighteen crews were rousted out of bed less than 24 hours later for the final monthly mission briefed for the latest chapter in the VIIIBC's participation against the U-Boat campaign. In this instance, Brest's facilities were targeted by both BWs, with 60 out of 79 crews releasing upon the Primary. The fighter opposition must have been patchy, since no MIA casualties were incurred, even though the flak barrage was assessed as "intense." An insidious factor in high-altitude flying related to the physical discomfort visited upon the airmen. A principal and ever-threatening aspect of operational flying concerned frostbite, which took its toll despite the presence of heated suit and glove equipment. On return from the previous day's mission, no less than nineteen group personnel were treated for this malign condition that could and did regularly result in amputation of the affected limbs.

"Recall. . .What Recall?"

VIIIBC's efforts to strike the marshalling yards at Hamm were finally realized on 4 March, but of the original 1BW force of 71, less than a quarter got through to the Primary and, furthermore, did so in blatant disregard of Standing Procedures. What transpired brings to mind a second excerpt from "Twelve O'clock High" that was probably based upon this mission's events.

Gregory Peck's attempt to dispel the "jinx" atmosphere surrounding the 918BG has him seemingly disregarding the "recall" signal dispatched at the behest of the Commanding General—played by Millard Mitchell—and responded to by all other groups. Mitchell, frustrated by the lack of response, goes down to the airfield in time to see all aircraft joining the circuit. When Peck emerges from his B-17 to praise the group's conduct, Mitchell tersely says: "Fine, Frank—but what about the Recall?" to which Peck responds innocently: "Recall—what recall?"

On 4 March, Maj. Paul Fishburne headed out as Lead for twenty B-17s, among whose number was 42-5225/OR: S **Stormy Weather**, flown by Lt. George Birdsong; in fact, this was the Lt.'s second bomber today, as his regular B-17 42-5077/OR: T **Delta Rebel No. 2** had developed problems after take-off, whereupon Birdsong had promptly landed and transferred the crew to OR: S! The chill winter weather soon cast up ever-heavier contrail patterns from the formations, but it was the cloud build-up constituting several deep layers that likely decided the two 101PCBW groups to seek an alternate target that evolved into shipyards at Rotterdam.

The 306BG had meanwhile "aborted" the mission, but the 91BG, positioned in the rear, sailed blithely onward towards the Primary. Fishburne subsequently claimed that the restricted visibility created by the combined contrails and a haze over the North Sea prevented him from realizing the extent of the overall force's disintegration. By the time visibility improved, the group was well into Holland and he kept on course; in so deciding, he unconsciously adopted the RAF tradition of "Press on regardless."

Fortune initially favored the lethally isolated unit, whose numbers were now down to sixteen. The *Jagdwaffe*'s response was not initiated until the bombers were heading in over the Dutch/German border, but from then the fight was on. One of the first bombers to be punished was **Stormy Weather**, whose title would return to haunt the crew; strikes set oxygen bottles up front on fire, but these were promptly extinguished. The group bored on and finally reached the target, where strings of 1,000-lb bombs were accurately delivered. As the group turned for home, the gunners braced themselves for further prolonged assaults that commenced almost immediately and with the first lethal effect.

Lt. Henderson's (KIA) 42-5370/DF: K was set upon and summarily dispatched with the loss of nine out of the ten-man crew. Lt. Birdsong was wounded, along with his copilot, and the B-17 wallowed inexorably out of formation. Although one eye was badly affected, Birdsong, as he later recollected, then managed to hold position with two other straggling bombers, but the defensive efforts of this impromptu Element were to come to naught. First 41-24549/OR: Q **Stupen-Taket** exploded following a fighter thrust from a broadside angle that left just two of Capt. Martin W. McCarthy's (KIA) crew alive. (A separate account by Lt. J. R. Bell (N) states the pilot ordered the nine surviving crewmembers to bail out, with the B-17 crashing scant miles north of Hamm.)

The third B-17 was **Rose O'Day** (41-24512/LG: N), flown by Lt. Ralph Felton; this aircraft staggered on until the group was over the Ijsselmeer. Then, with No. 2 engine on fire, Felton gave the order to bail out, but was killed as he went to exit the forward hatch. Sgt. Bob Paul (ROG) watched his colleagues float down into the water, where they almost certainly drowned or died of exposure, other than Lt. Hal Kious (CP), who was fished out by a boat crew. A third crewmember was the sole other survivor.

The beleaguered group formation was holding up well, despite being reduced by almost one-quarter as the Dutch coast approached and was traversed. A fourth casualty was being set up at this point, as **Excalibur** (41-24464/DF: J) gamely held course for home, despite lagging behind on reduced power. The loss of a third engine finally decided that the sole option was to "ditch," and Lts. Brill and Lowry did so in an exemplary manner that left all ten crewmembers alive, despite the high-running seas and the B-17 breaking in two.

It was then that disaster struck, as a prolonged period passed before the life rafts were extracted and inflated. During that time, both pilots and Sgt. Morgan (BT) were swept away to their deaths. The seven others clambered aboard and spent several chilly hours prior to rescue by a Royal Navy minesweeper. The DSC awards to the pilots would be of scant comfort to their families.

Four B-17s had been lost, but **Stormy Weather** was fortunate not to add to this figure. The B-17 was shot up and knocked out of formation by the first of many successive fighter passes. Both pilots received serious injuries, with one of Lt. Birdsong's eyes temporarily blinded and the copilot so incapacitated by his wounds that he sagged out of his seat with the pain and slipped forward and down to jam the controls. Birdsong managed to regain some control through operation of the trim tabs, but he had to call up Sgt. Remmell (Eng.), who, with a second crewmember's help, extracted the copilot and took him back to the radio room.

The B-17 managed to catch up with two other stragglers comprised of the McCarthy and Felton-flown bombers, but all too soon **Stormy Weather** was again on her own, following the demise of its temporary Element contemporaries. With little chance of survival at altitude, Birdsong decided to "head for the deck" and eased the bomber into a dive. His battered charge continued to be pursued all the way down and for some time after levelling off close to the ground, but the final attacks still left her in flight. The navigator had suffered a bad head wound, but retained enough concentration to provide a course homeward.

The bombs were still aboard and their volatile RDX content provided no guarantee that they would remain inert during a landing, even with the safety pins reinserted. An offer to bail out over England was rejected, but a further shock awaited the crew on landing—the brakes failed, leaving the pilots with little option but to attempt a ground-loop maneuver. As it was, the B-17 over-shot the runway, cutting through a fence and having its momentum finally halted by of all things, a manure heap!

The ramifications of the action, or rather maligned action, in pure operational terms, could have led to severe consequences for the Major. As it was, the matter was seemingly shelved and, in fact, the group received a Distinguished Unit Citation (DUC). However, the fact that this was awarded after WWII clearly indicates the USAAF hierarchy's desire at the time to hush up the incident. (The same scenario would be acted out by the 95BG an exact calendar year later, when the group would push on alone in an arguably even more suicidal and prolonged solo run further east to Berlin.) As for Maj. Fishburne, far from being officially pilloried for his action, he was instead awarded a DFC for his perceived leadership the following month.

Marginal Operational Advance

The operational travails of VIIIBC were still some way from being rectified, but the prime reason for its existence had recently been reconfirmed following the Casablanca Conference in January. Gen. Eaker attended and put the argument for the Daylight Offensive's continuance to the still-sceptical Winston Churchill by citing several key advantages within his seven-point submission, one of which was reportedly pitched in a deliberate, if unconsciously emotive, manner. He asserted that a joint Bombing Offensive with the Americans by day and the RAF by night meant that in effect, "We could bomb the Devils round the clock." Whether Eaker actually pitched his words in this manner or not, the romantically-inclined Churchill, although hedging his bets, subsequently made a statement to this effect as part of his speech to the members of the House of Commons, who now granted continued support for USAAF daylight operations.

Hamm witnessed the beginning of an enhanced run of missions (nine), a figure that was barely satisfactory in terms of pressuring the enemy, but nevertheless was double January's and February's equivalent total. The statistic did conceal the fact that only two German-based targets would be included, both of which supplemented the Allied counter-strikes against the U-Boat threat by falling into the "strategic" category.

Prior to this mission, the bombers completed four missions over France, the first of which was Lorient (6th), followed by Rouen's marshalling yards three days later. Another three-day gap intervened before a return to Rouen was followed 24 hours later by similar rail facilities at Amiens being struck. No group losses in aircraft were realized over this period and, indeed, just five crews were listed as MIA, although there were several "operational" incidents involving crash landings, etc.

Vegesack's U-Boat production yards had originally been targeted on 27 January, when weather conditions forced a switch to Wilhelmshaven. A second attempt on 26 February was similarly thwarted, but conditions on 18 March promised a successful penetration. All but four of the 103 crews sent out encountered little or no visibility problems in laying their bomb loads onto the Primary, while the defenses claimed only two bombers.

The relative success at Vegesack whetted "Pinetree"'s appetite for more, but it was a further 96 hours before the latest mission was successfully launched, when U-Boat production facilities at Wilhelmshaven were the focus. The 91BG had experienced no losses since Hamm, but the Grim Reaper was always hovering around and struck today. The B-17 in question was 42-29659/DF: **Liberty Bell**, whose presence with the group was barely seven days old. In addition, Capt. H. C. McClellen's crew were actually from the 92BG, which was still non-operational and serving on detachment to the 91BG. The 21-strong group force was bypassing Helgoland Island when it encountered the latest aerial threat.

This took the form of a bomb released by a Bf109 and time-fused. The enemy pilot's aim was tragically accurate, as the weapon's explosion was close enough to excise part or all of one wing. The luckless crew stood little or no chance of bailing out of their violently gyrating charge that slammed into the North Sea; even if they had, their fate would almost certainly have been death by drowning or exposure. (Oblt Heinz Knoke, a JG11 *Staffelkapitaen*, described the bombing incident in his book *I Flew for the Fuehrer*; he further stated that he had previously proposed to and been granted permission by higher authority to initiate this operational action.)

Lt. Charles Cliburn was piloting **Sad Sack**, which had just been brought back to operational status, and now he was personally confronted with yet another crisis as the homeward route was commenced; an engine "blew up" and caused the airframe to vibrate viciously. Worse still was the loss of speed that inexorably left the bomber straggling and potentially easy prey for the fighters, three of whom descended upon the B-17. Their efforts were successfully countered by brilliant maneuvering, but the enemy's eventual withdrawal was still no guarantee of survival; a second engine on the same side now went "out," leaving **Sad Sack** on the verge of stalling out. The asymmetric angle of flight was surely adding to the pressure on both pilots, but fortune did not desert them and safe landfall and a landing were finally achieved.

Only two missions would now be flown prior to the month end, beginning with the 28th, when both BWs were sent to strike at a by-now familiar location, as well as one that had witnessed the Campaign's birth—the marshalling yards of Rouen/Sotteville. There was never any security from loss when completing a mission, regardless of the distance to and from the target. Rouen lies not far from the Channel coast, but the pilots of either JG2 or JG26—both *Geschwadern* featuring well over two full years of operational experience—were ever on hand to take advantage, especially when escort cover was absent.

Only the 1BW completed the run, despite weather conditions that forced the B-24 groups to "abort." All but eleven of the 81 B-17s got through despite heavy cloud cover with a single loss; the 91BG featured in both negative categories, since seven of the "aborts" and the single MIA came from its ranks. The fighter assaults that commenced on the inward route finally culled 42-29537/DF: L from the ranks; the stricken bomber descended into the Channel waters close to the French coast, with Lt. John A. Coen and most of his crew killed in the process.

The construction of ships was a "strategic" activity and was the object for the final March mission. The Dutch port of Rotterdam possessed such yards and was targeted by all units on the 30th. However, an even greater percentage of crews that included all twenty from Bassingbourn failed to bomb and four crews were MIA—an unsatisfactory result all round. (The ability to utilize "Bombing Through Overcast" [BTO] equipment was nearly six months distant; meanwhile, Mother Nature "cooperated" with the enemy in denying the bomber crews unfettered or even partial visual access to their targets.)

Sixteen crews had so far been declared MIA in the course of 30 completed missions, while a further number of individuals had been killed or seriously injured. Thirty-four B-17s and crews had formed the original cadre, so the statistical chance of completing a combat tour still seemed quite positive. It is somewhat ironic that the initial statutory number of missions (25) had only recently been implemented by the authorities; even more ironic was that the chance of tour completion would steadily decrease until by mid-summer there would be, as one acerbic individual asserted, "just as sound a chance of surviving deep-seated cancer as winning through one's combat tour!"

LG: O/41-24453 bears the field modification—in this case increased to two .5 forward-firing weapons—in a rectangular cut-out. The original left hand circular mounting for a .3 caliber weapon can be seen level with the revised mounting. The Plexiglas frame was prone to cracking should a .5 gun be mounted into these apertures.

The overall logistical supply situation for VIII Bomber Command would remain critical from the inception of the Daylight Offensive until well into 1943. Here at Bassingbourn, a complete B-17 inner wing section is being hoisted from an RAF specialist loader known as the "Queen Mary."

Cpl. Billie Navalle is applying the finishing touches to the artwork for Dame Satan. The B-17F arrived at Bassingbourn in January 1943 and served with the 322BS. She is seen early on with five mission "bombs" and survived until 17 August, when she went down while being flown by Lt. Jack Hargis and crew.

Sgt. Joe Harlick was a camera specialist involved with repairs assigned to the 324BS who added to his technical skills by assembling a collection of photographs covering all aspects of group operations that was retained by him after WWII, as well as being utilized by numerous authors on the 8USAAF. He is holding a flak fragment found inside this strike camera adjacent to the lens.

The three groups of four bombs lined up in front of a group B-17F indicate that these are 500-lb weapons. The internal layout of the Fortress bomb bay allowed for the carriage of twelve bombs of this caliber. The maximum internal load of 6,000lbs led to the B-24 personnel acidly describing the B-17 as a "four-engine medium bomber."

Col. Stanley Wray, the 91BG's first CO, is seen consulting his watch up in the control tower at Bassingbourn. The photo appears to be taken during the hours of darkness, thereby suggesting a mission start-up is in progress; take-off was regularly commenced when daylight was barely appearing.

A leaden winter sky forms the backcloth for a B-17F just returned from the mission of 26 February to Wilhelmshaven, when all seventeen 91BG crews reaching the Primary returned safely. The fuel truck has already "hooked up" its hose to the starboard inner tank even as the crew are milling around the rear fuselage prior to heading for debriefing.

Royal Flush! transferred from the 303BG to the 91BG and commenced operations in January 1943. She bears the typical restricted markings applied to 8AF bombers up to mid-1943 that were limited to code letters and serial; the national insignia bears no bars outline and is "dulled down" in this instance. The B-17F was finally lost on 22 June, although all on Lt. Fountain's crew survived her "ditching" to end up as POWs.

Personnel from the Armament Section at Bassingbourn are applying their skills to the maintenance of a row of machine guns. The need for these defensive weapons to be in unconditional operating status was a prime necessity for combat crew survival.

This picture was probably taken after graduation at Bombardier School. Bob Black (standing right), with his wife Louise, is seen with Lts. Dick Harland (standing) and Bob Ball. All three will arrive in England, with Bob Black part of Lt. Manchester's 381BG crew, only to lose his life on 8 October over Bremen. The fates of the others are unconfirmed, although a Robert E. Ball (B) was a POW from 42-29857/LL: J Jolly Roger on 12 August 1943.

Stormy Weather (42-5225/OR: S) was extremely fortunate to bring herself and Lt. Birdsong's crew back to Bassingbourn on 4 March 1943. She overshot the runway to grind to a halt in a manure pile, where she was liberally doused with fire retardant foam. Brought back to combat status, she was renamed V-Packette and fought on until 17 August, when she was downed, along with all but one on Lt. Von Der Heyde's team.

Stric-Nine was assigned to the 323BS on 7 March. Points of note are the Medium Green color for the fin center section, a regular feature on camouflaged B-17s, and the addition of a navigator's astrodome. This B-17F soldiered on until a failed "ditching" in the English Channel on 17 July claimed Lt. Forsblad and all but two of the other nine airmen on board.

Col. Wray (middle) poses with several of the 91BG's senior- and middle-ranked staff. Officer second from right is identified as Maj. Paul Fishburne, who led the group formation on 4 March 1943, when it alone penetrated to the Primary of Hamm's marshalling yards, an action that earned the group a DUC—but only promulgated after WWII.

Sgts Eldon Lapp (left) and Bill KIng are seen posing, probably in their regular B-17F Invasion II. The stationary propeller seen through the port waist windows confirms a ground 'shot' as does Sgt King's gloveless hands - no way to operate at high altitude! The ammunition feed-covers are a point of note. Both men became POWs as did all ten on Lt. Oscar O-Neill's team on 17 April 1943.

Chapter Three

Spring to Summer Expansion (April/June 1943)

Out of Winter's Shadow

April 1943 was to prove a month of sharp contrasts for the VIIIBC. The six groups on hand were still going to have to soldier on without further unit reinforcement, while the number of missions flown (four) would be a frustrating regression compared to March. The quartet of assaults would feature a double occurrence of back-to-back daily efforts, the final one of which would result in by far the heaviest rebuff for the 101PCBW, in particular.

The re-emergence of three-figure numbers in dispatched crews commencing on 31 March was continued during three of the four monthly missions and would presage a notable expansion, as the Command began to receive several acolyte units during May. The 1BW alone was sent out on the 4th to another "strategic" target, this time located in the French capital.

The Renault vehicle manufacturer had seen its facilities at Billancourt turned over to producing equipment for the Germans following France's collapse in June 1940. The greater majority of the five hundred 1,000-lb bombs borne by 97 B-17s rained down upon the Primary to cause a sizeable degree of damage, although the heavy production machinery's ability to absorb much punishment resulted in production being resumed fairly quickly. The defenses in turn took down four bombers.

Twenty hours later, both BWs were aloft and setting out for the Belgian city of Antwerp with 79 B-17s and 25 B-24s. An almost diametrically opposite scenario was to arise compared to the previous day. The ERLA aircraft production facility was located in the Mortsel district of the city, so the risk of civilian casualties was potentially high. Whereas the bomb loads deposited at Billancourt had largely landed within the target, despite its siting within the boundaries of Paris, today's result was a tragic dispersal that consumed the properties and lives of many Belgians and elicited an official complaint from the Belgian Ambassador to the USA. The propaganda value of the incident to the enemy was immediate if not long lasting, although some within that occupied country's population must have remained soured with their Ally's perceived careless conduct.

Yet another extended period of non-operations occurred between the 6th and 15th, to be followed by the second bout of 48-hour mission activity. It was back to countering the U-Boat threat (16th) when Lorient and Brest were targeted respectively by the B-17s and B-24s. The latter force was not only frustrated by smoke screens, but lost three crews out of four overall. A better measure of success, at least in terms of releasing upon the Primary, awaited the 59 crews completing the mission out of 83 dispatched, Bassingbourn having 13 out of 21 in this positive category. This was the fourth mission free of loss for the group, but, as ever, Fortune was about to desert its combat crews, with the 401BS being the principal sufferer.

Holocaust over Bremen

Bremen was one of the Nazis' principal industrial cities, and among the various production plants was one devoted to producing the Fw190—arguably the major component in the *Jagdwaffe's* armory. Kurt Tank's creation was a superb overall performer matching current designs within the Anglo/American fighter commands. The margin of advantage, even when it was pitted against the equally superb Mk. IX Spitfire, was as much dependent upon the pilots' performance as their mounts. The P-47 was probably out-performed in horizontal or climbing maneuvers, but could match its adversary by adopting dive-and-zoom tactics. Any measure to at least slow down FW production would be welcomed by the bomber crews, in particular.

What was the largest force to date (115) was duly assembled and headed out over the North Sea. On the way over, an enemy aircraft was sighted and its presence was later put forward as a reason for the then-forthcoming Luftwaffe ambush, the assumption being that the crew had radioed in the force's details. True or not, the Germans would have had ample time, having picked out the radar screen "traces" that confirmed the American bombers' approach and accordingly making their fighter dispositions. There was no guarantee as to the exact target in order to concentrate a large counter-force, but there were sufficient fighter resources to provide a fairly comprehensive "screen" in order to make some form of contact with their adversaries. As it was, the bombers' progress remained unhindered until they were tracing in between the Frisian Island chain and the Primary.

III/JG54 *Gruenherz* (Green Hearts) had not long transferred from the Eastern Front and was up on its first sortie from Oldenburg—a location directly west of and close to the Primary— along with elements of JG11. Both sets of pilots were battle-hardened veterans, although the former naturally lacked the techniques for high-altitude combat, the aerial battles in the East being low-level by comparison. This being true, they would still play their part in the ensuing attrition borne by the 101PCBW, flying in the van of the overall bomber formation. Moreover, the groups were reportedly strung out in line as the bomb run was commenced and therefore even more vulnerable than when linked up within each PCBW.

The first indication of fighter assault was the ever-startling, multi-fighter approach from head-on and in waves. What was to become known as the "12 o-clock high" attacking run and was destined to pay grim dividends in downed bombers and their crews had handed a major advantage to the *Jagdwaffe*. The forward defensive firepower of both USAAF "heavies" was dangerously limited in order to cope with the enemy.

The top turret twin mounts were adequate, but all other current weaponry "up front" was primarily single-mounted and flexible; they were also manned by the bombardier and navigator, but only when this duo were not otherwise occupied. Some B-17s had jury-rigged single or double mounts in the upper nose Plexiglas, but the latter arrangement was made at the sacrifice of the bombsight, there being no overall space for both. Thus did the air battle into and out of Bremen become one that evolved sharply in the defenders' favor.

The 401BS was flying Low squadron, a position that was the least protected in terms of any overall group structure. Although the 91BG had the largest PCBW sub-force (32), the 401BS initially only had eight crews on station, of which five were destined not to return; the other three crews had all "aborted" the mission, an unconsciously fortunate act on this day, at least.

Invasion 2nd (42-5070/LL: A) was on her 18th mission and in the hands of an equally veteran crew led by Capt. Oscar O'Neill. The constant hail of fire from Bf110s and Ju88s, as well as the single-engine fighters, steadily took its toll on this bomber. Shortly before the bomb run was completed, O'Neill's charge was observed having the forward fuselage and inner wings wreathed in flames. It was a miracle that all ten airmen cleared their doomed B-17, which tumbled to earth close to Oldenburg, leaving its erstwhile occupants facing POW treatment.

Hellsapoppin (41-24459/LL: B) was the longest-serving squadron B-17 operating today, but the "original" machine was "heading for the last round up," as the assaults were maintained even during the bomb run, with flak adding its telling weight. Lt. John W. Wilson's crew likely completed their run, but their aircraft was quickly taken down, with the crash site listed at Bruchhausen, close to the SE fringe of Bremen; the pilot and all four gunners in the rear did not survive.

The Low squadron's decimation proceeded apace with four further losses. **Short Snorter III** (42-5337/LL: J) bore an arguably unfortunate name, since her two predecessors had both gone down with no survivors among the twenty airmen concerned. Sure enough, the run of misfortune recurred here when the nine-mission B-17F bearing Lt. Nathan Lindsey's crew on their eighth mission was brought down at an undisclosed location. Lindsay and six out of the other nine were listed as MIA, suggesting either a violent aerial explosion or a watery grave. Of the other three, two were captured and one was listed as KIA, to confirm his body was found.

A B-17F with an even shorter time at Bassingbourn was 42-5291/LL: D **Rain of Terror**, which had only arrived on 25 March. On board were Lt. Robert B. Walker and crew, all but two of whom escaped alive before their bomber plunged into the ground. The fifth squadron casualty was 42-5172/LL: Z **Thunderbird**, which had only been assigned the day after **Rain of Terror** and now was on its fourth mission. The bomber was seen to be burning as all but the pilots safely exited to float down near Bruchhausen, where **Hellsapoppin** descended. However, the actual crash site for the B-17F, after it disintegrated in mid-air, was further west at Harpstedt, several miles from Bremen's SW fringe. Lts. Harold Beasley and Walter McCain were killed during their charge's violent demise, their bodies later discovered among the wreckage.

The 401BS' suffering today was completed when 42-29547.LL: G **The Sky Wolf II** was taken out. However, her crew, led by Lt. Nicholas Stoffel, were on secondment from the 92BG. The circumstances of when and where its loss occurred remain unclear, but Stoffel at least ended up a POW.

The Aftermath

If the 91BG's punishment was heavy, then that inflicted on its companion PCBW group was extremely severe. No less than ten crews would never again join the circuit over Thurleigh out of the 29 that had lifted off scant hours previous. It was furthermore a supreme (if not a gratefully accepted) irony for the 303BG and 305BG, flying in trail to the 101PCBW, that their ranks remained intact throughout the entire mission. Why the *Jagdwaffe* units had stayed their hand remained a mystery, while the flak barrage was also wholly ineffective in terms of bringing down any of the 102PCBW bombers.

However, the overall effect upon the Command's airmen was to emphasize the burgeoning striking power of their aerial adversaries, with no signs of the situation being even stabilized, let alone swinging back in the Americans' favor. A social reaction to the day's stunning events occurred the same evening at Bassingbourn. A party had been previously arranged for the 17th, and although it went ahead, some of the attendees who had clearly survived the debacle over Bremen proceeded to "let off steam" in a manner that was very much unappreciated by their superiors.

An indicator that the logistical situation in respect of bomber replacement was improving arose following the Bremen mission; the MIA shortfall for the 91BG was made up within 48 hours and for the 306BG within three days. By the month's end, overall assigned strength within the 1BW would be 166 (128 operational), compared to equivalent statistics for February (117/70) and March (154/111). This steady advance was furthermore soon to be noticeably expanded with the arrival of three groups during May, as well as the 92BG's return to combat status. The latter situation was unknown to the personnel currently on hand to prosecute the Offensive, however.

In the event, the 17 April mission signalled the end, enforced or otherwise, to further immediate operations by VIIIBC. This ever-frustrating block to pressuring the Nazi empire was felt by the senior staff at "Pinetree," but this was even more the case for the combat crews; any delay in progression towards completing the now specifically ordained total of 25 missions was psychologically and sometimes even physically inhibiting.

May 1943

Structural Changes

During May, the 1BW structure was expanded from two to three PCBWs to reflect the arrival of the new units. While the 103PCBW accommodated the 379BG and by month's end the recently-arrived 384BG, its third component was the 303BG, which was transferred out of the 102PCBW. Meanwhile, the 306BG moved to the 102PCBW and the 92BG was added to form the second trio of groups, along with the resident 305BG. Finally, the 91BG was joined by the 351BG within the 101PCBW, but the equivalent expansion to a three-group entity would await the imminent arrival of the 381BG, which would occur during June. Thus was the framework for the Combat Bomb Wings set in place that would replace the PCBW titles on 13 September.

The "switchback" pace of monthly operations recurred during May, when double April's effort of four was achieved. However, the mission spread swung sharply from almost daily frequency in the middle of May to a seven–day gap during its latter stages. There was also an even divide between targets in Germany and the Occupied Counties, with U-Boat production largely involved in the former instance, although two aircraft plants in France and Belgium were also on the target agenda to reinforce the "strategic" aspect of operations.

By this stage of the Battle of the Atlantic, the odds had just begun to tilt in favor of the Allied naval and air forces, and within weeks Admiral Doenitz, the enemy U-Boat Commander, would acknowledge this by withdrawing his wolf packs; by the time he resumed the Offensive, the Allies would continue to hold the upper hand, and in time would squeeze the life out of their opponents' operational efforts. In the meantime, the aerial assault against bases and production resources continued apace.

St. Nazaire was targeted on the 1st, but the bombing results were disappointing, with over half 1BW's force of 78 failing to strike the Primary, a failure that involved all but two from the group. Worse still was the poor navigation effort on the way back that placed the 101PCBW over the port of Brest, whose gunners threw up their usual lethal flak screen and brought down or fatally damaged three Thurleigh B-17s. The 91BG force of twenty broke left upon witnessing the incident; although avoiding the danger from flak, in so doing it exposed itself to the undivided attention of the *Jagdwaffe*.

The first pass saw 41-24547/OR: P **Vertigo** absorb strikes around the cockpit that killed Lt. Robert Rand and injured Maj. Maurice Rosener, a squadron CO from the 94BG that was temporarily based at Bassingbourn prior to operating as an element of the 4th Bomb Wing. The No. 2 engine was set on fire and the bomber slumped out and down. The intercom was disabled, so no warning of the intention to "ditch" and for crash positions to be adopted could be made. As it was, the heavy running sea, although safely negotiated, ensured that the aircraft was quickly submerged. In that all-too-brief period, the eight airmen still alive nevertheless succeeded in breaking out the dinghies, but three were swept away and drowned, leaving five of their colleagues drifting towards inevitable capture. And so another group "original" B-17F had joined its veteran companions in oblivion.

Alone No More

Much better results were realized on the 4th, when an aero-engine plant in Antwerp was saturated with over 320 1,000-lb explosives; this time round there was no material destruction to surrounding civilian property as occurred one month previous and all crews returned safely. Unbeknownst to the 1BW personnel and their 2BW contemporaries was that today's mission constituted the last time they would be bearing the entire weight of the Campaign upon their operational "shoulders." The initial cadre of three groups (94BG, 95BG, and 96BG) constituting the nucleus of the 4BW were now present in England and poised to commence operations. Also on hand were the latest 1BW-assigned units: the 351BG based at Polebrook and the 379BG that was allocated—Kimbolton! Finally, due to resume active operations from Alconbury was the 92BG.

That day duly arrived on the 13th, when the 4BW attacked St. Omer/Longuenesse airfield in NE France, housing elements of JG26, and the 351BG was allocated St. Omer/Rouge airfield, while the 1BW headed towards the Avion-Potez aircraft production factory at Meaulte in the same region. Fully 90% of the main force attackers unloaded upon the Primary at a cost of three crews; any satisfaction with the bombing results must have been tempered on return to Bassingbourn, however, because two of the losses were from the group, both involving the 323BS.

Vulgar Virgin (42029642/OR: L) was yet another recent arrival on 16 March that had flown just several missions to date. Now the initial fighter attacks that came in soon after crossing in over the enemy coast set the aircraft on fire, which then described a circular maneuver as it was falling away; seconds later it exploded, killing Lt. Lawrence J. Stark and seven of the crew, as well as an official photographer. Lt. Biggs (KIA) and crew in 42-5406/OR: were the other team failing to run the enemy's defensive gauntlet, five of the other nine airmen sharing their pilot's fate after fighter gunfire downed its prey.

A 24-hour break ensued before the 1BW crews were awakened and briefed for a run to Kiel's shipyards. The four veteran groups were supplemented by the presence of the 92BG, albeit with a marginal force of seven, this being the first mission for the group since early October. The number of "original" B-17s on hand at Bassingbourn had inexorably shrunk as losses mounted, and now another one was removed from group establishment in the shape of 41-24481/LG: M **Hells Angels**. Lt. William Broley's charge survived the outward leg and appears to have gained the North Sea coastline on return. By then the ailing bomber had one engine "out" and was flying at minimum altitude when it finally faded out of sight; its permanent disappearance was clearly due to a crash or failed "ditching" that in either case consumed all on board.

Wilhelmshaven and Emden were listed the next day for assault by the 1BW and 4BW, respectively, but whereas the acolyte Wing, along with the 351BG, managed to gain access to its Primary at the cost of a single Polebrook crew, its experienced partner was thwarted in its primary intention and ended up releasing upon the fortified island of Helgoland and Wangerooge, in the Frisian island chain, to which those not returning were added five crews MIA.

Upwards of 200 VIIIBC crews had participated in the 13 May mission; this level of availability was now being maintained and would expand noticeably before the end of the month. On the 17th, VIIIBC dispatched its forces on the latest direct assault against the U-boats. The two B-17 BWs headed for Lorient, with the 2BW going further south to Bordeaux. Just under 80% of the 159 bombers released on Lorient, with the same percentage doing so for the 91BG (19 out of 24).

Forty-eight hours later, the strategic aspect to the Battle of the Atlantic was resumed with construction yards at Kiel and Flensburg allotted to the 1BW and 4BW. The 351BG now linked up directly for the first time with the other five groups attacking the former Primary. The defenders were active as ever, and for the second mission in succession took down four 305BG B-17s out of six losses in total.

Yet another 91BG "original" bomber was destined for oblivion, being 41-24483/LG: U **Spirit of Alcohol**. On board Lt. Ed Baxley's aircraft was a British correspondent who was rewarded with death in his bid to report the action, as a fighter pumped its fire into the B-17F. The crippled machine, with one engine "out," managed to gain access to another formation after dropping out, but was again assailed over the target and fell to its destruction in the Bay of Kiel. Six of the ten-man crew, including the pilot, successfully bailed out.

To date, the group had witnessed 27 crews declared MIA in the course of 39 missions, but the odds against survival had steadily begun to rise over the past ten missions, with eleven among the grim tally having been claimed in that spell compared to sixteen during the previous 29. The Bremen mission had been a major factor in this equation, of course; on the other hand, 27 had been completed without direct loss in combat out of the overall mission figure.

Another Rebuff

The loss statistic was about to be given another unpleasant hike akin to that borne over Bremen as the crews assembled for briefing on 21 May. The target was Wilhelmshaven's U-boat construction yards, and a hot reception could be guaranteed from the defenders—but just how hot a reception was looming for the group that was 1BW Lead? The Initial Point had been reached before the fighter assaults reportedly began, but the tardy response was to prove no consolation for four crews, three of which were flying 324BS B-17s.

Desperate Journey (42-3052/DF: Z) was on its twelfth mission with Lt. Norbert Koll's (KIA) team, but the fire started in the bomb bay by fighter strikes proved uncontrollable and the bomber fell to its destruction near Wittmundhafen; one officer and one Enlisted man alone survived. Lt. Phillip Fischer had brought 41-24515/DF: H **Marie Jane** across the Atlantic the previous September, but bomber and pilot were destined to be united in death along with everybody else on board. The aircraft completed its bomb run and the formation had regained the North Sea when the latest fighter thrust sent it down to a terminal fate.

A third squadron loss involved 42-5857/DF: J, in Lt. John H Miller's hands; all four officers along with two others failed to survive their bomber's final descent close to Schortens. DF: Z and DF: J both came down west of the Primary and the sole 323BS casualty's last resting place was in the same area at Warnsath. At least the fatality rate was not nearly as severe—except for engineer S/Sgt. J. O. Wing, who was the unlucky exception—with Lt. Norman Retchin (P) and the remainder of the crew safely evacuating 42-29657/OR: X.

"Sweating out the mission" was the apt term for the ground support personnel's mind set, since they were helpless to influence the course of the air battles and could only hope that their best efforts had provided the combat crews with fully functioning aircraft. Therefore, the sight of seventeen B-17s orbiting the airfield circuit instead of 21 must have left those on the ground with gnawing doubts that were sadly confirmed for the four ground crew teams concerned after time subsequently ran out for the MIA crews to be accounted for elsewhere. This scenario was a common feature of operations at USAAF airfields during the Offensive's entire course.

What was to be the penultimate strike against the U-boats' operational lairs in France was dispatched on the 29th. The seven groups within 1BW sent out 169 crews between them, of which 147 struck the target at a cost of eight MIA crews; the 379BG, on its inaugural run, contributed three to the figure. A new and short-lived defensive feature for the Command was the operational presence of eight YB40s. These airframes possessed supplementary armament in the form of turrets under the nose and mounted around the radio room and were intended as "shotgun guards" for the bomber stream. Ironically, their heavier all-up-weight (AUW) reduced their top speed compared to their charges, especially after "bombs away," resulting in an unnecessary slowdown of the formations' progress!

Polebrook's early Fortunes

The 351BG entered the combat lists on 13 May, although the mission was abandoned on the way over the Channel to St. Omer/Rouge airfield. This group was the first unit of four over the ensuing weeks to be assigned to the 1BW. Formed in October 1942 under the command of Col. William A. Hatcher, Jr., the assigned personnel trained at Biggs, Texas, then Pueblo, Colorado, from where the combat crews departed overseas on 1 April and the support personal during mid-month.

Among the aviator's number was a 42-year old individual bearing Captain's bars who was no professional or even "citizen soldier" Serviceman. This was the Hollywood actor Clark Gable, whose perceived function was to direct the completion of a documentary film on aerial gunnery training. Combat flying was very much a young man's game, but "America's Sweetheart," as he once acidly described himself, would not be found wanting in completing a run of at least five missions in the course of filming.

Polebrook was one of several VIIIBC bases located NW of Bassingbourn, and the fortunes of both groups would be intertwined over the next six months, since the 351BG was now assigned as an element of the 101PCBW in place of the 306BG. The combat crews had a taste of tragedy even before flying their first mission. A formation practice was being concluded when Maj. Keith Birlem's (508BS CO) 42-29865/YB: collided with Capt. Roy Snipes piloting 42-29491/RQ: over the airfield; none of the twenty airmen on board survived after both B-17s came down just outside the airfield perimeter.

The first briefed mission occurred on 13 May, but the intention to attack St. Omer/Fort Rouge airfield in NE France was "aborted" on the way over. The failure was not repeated next day, when eighteen crews joined the 4BW's 96BG in a strike on Courtrai airfield in Belgium (Wevelgem airfield, close to Courtrai and home for III/JG26 at this date, is quoted by a leading author on JG26 as the actual target). The bomb loads thoroughly carpeted the Primary, rendering it untenable for immediate operations. Several hours later, only sixteen B-17s were back on their Polebrook dispersals, illustrating there were no "easy" missions, even a short range one as generally granted to most new groups.

The group was in Lead position, but 42-29859/YU: H **The Annihilator** absorbed terminal strikes from a fighter flown by Hptm. Johannes Naumann (6/JG26 *Staffelkapitaen*) during the bomb run. Capt. William P. Forsythe (510BS CO) became the second Senior Staff member to be lost inside a week, but at least he ended up a POW, as did seven of the other nine, leaving their bomber to impact near Dadizeele. The second loss involved Forsythe's No. 3 in the Lead element; 42-29862/YB: H, flown by Lt. Clifford J. McCoy, appears to have been downed on the way home. The flak guns of 2/Res. *Abteilung* 252 based near Ostend claimed the bomber, which exploded with one of the crew killed in the process; the shattered remains fell at Stene. (Again, there is an apparent conflict regarding the victor, since the same leading author credits the loss to Ltn. Radener NW of Antwerp; however, this pilot is only recorded as gaining a *Herausschuss* [i.e., a separation of his victim from the formation], so the likelihood is that the now isolated B-17 then became easy pickings for flak gunners.)

Maj. Burns (Deputy Group CO) headed nineteen crews for a mission to Emden that again was a joint effort, albeit with the 4BW's full complement. The port of Emden was squarely struck and the formations headed back past the eastern fringe of the Frisian Island chain. Lt. Joseph A. Meli, Jr.'s 42-3173/DS: R **Spareball** was lagging below and behind the formation, and thus easy prey for several Bf109s who dispatched the cripple into the sea, a fate that was shared by all ten occupants.

The trickle of losses continued on the next mission (19th) regarding two crews, although the latter incident only involved one airman. Over the target at Kiel, flak struck home against 42-29701/TU: B **In the Mood** and the bomber began a steady but inexorable descent that was believed to have ended with its falling into the Baltic. Lt. Robert W. Mansfield (P) was one of only three survivors, with only one body out of the other seven ever recovered.

The single fatality occurred in a cruelly needless manner on 42-29852/ DS: V **Fireball**. A flak strike that disabled the rear oxygen system resulted in T/Sgt. Lewis T. Baker, among several personnel, becoming disoriented. His attempt to bail out only resulted in his parachute snagging the rear door and retaining his body against the fuselage exterior. By the time crewmembers coming back to render assistance realized the hapless airman's situation and hauled him back in he had expired from the combination of anoxia and exposure to the slipstream—yet another of hundreds of aerial victims from other than enemy action during WWII.

The Kiel run was the first time the 351BG was directly integrated into the 1BW, which was its operational assignment. On the 21st, the group formed up with the 91BG, but in sharp contrast to its fellow unit that lost four B-17s, came back unscathed, although only two-thirds of the 19 crews bombed. Eight days later, the Wing was over St. Nazaire and returned less one crew out of 46 dispatched. The unfortunate exception was **The Concho Clipper** (42-29838/RQ: U), piloted by a Lt. with the surely confusing first name of Colonel J. Russell, Jr.!

The flak shell that impacted around the bomb bay blew away the ball turret with S/ Sgt. Nathannie Bader inside, while the blast also killed both waist gunners. Fire caught hold, and with two engines disabled the quickly isolated bomber stood little chance against the circling Fw190s. Six of the seven remaining airmen bailed out of the B-17 after it was levelled off and the "abandon" order was issued, but T/Sgt. James F. Welk (ROG) was killed at some stage. Their bomber's remains impacted near Vannes, while Lt. Stealey (N) was very fortunate to survive 1) being blown out of the exploding aircraft, 2) his descent under a badly ripped canopy, and 3) a subsequent immersion in the sea, from where he was fished out by French civilians, having suffered serious injury.

Eunuch Status for "Eightball"

The original CO of Polebrook's 511BS was Clinton F. Ball, who decided that the word "Ball" be included in all the squadron aircraft titles, beginning with his own **Linda Ball**, named for his daughter. During the Wilhelmshaven mission (21st), 42-3136/DS: **Eightball** experienced ultimately irreversible problems with its No. 2 propeller, which finally detached itself just as the landing run was under way. The blades sliced into the nose compartment and mangled much of the fuselage skin that bore the **Eightball** artwork. Hauled away for repair, a neat surgical job was carried out using a section from another bomber, in this instance actually a 306BG machine declared "salvage." Once back on its dispersal during June, a revised name was applied that accurately reflected the sardonic humor prevalent among military circles—**No Balls at All!**

The final May mission had witnessed another increase in 1BW active operational strength to seven groups, with the 379BG having linked up with the 303BG within the 103PCBW. In addition, an eighth group (384BG) had commenced its Air Component's arrival at Grafton Underwood (also sardonically known as "Grafton Under-mud") on the 25th, with the ground support elements currently traversing the Atlantic waters; the unit was to become part of the aforementioned PCBW. However, VIIIBC's overall strength of twelve operational groups was reduced to ten by the end of the month with the departure to North Africa of the 44BG and 93BG's B-24s for participation in the planned strike against Rumanian oil-fields at Ploesti. Even so, the opportunity to regularly strike the enemy with sizeable forces was on the cards as June was entered.

June 1943

As with May's experience, a similar frustrating delay in initiating operations during June now arose, with fully ten days wasted before the crews completed a run. On the 11th, all seven groups went out on what was the latest attack against U-Boat production at Wilhelmshaven. The flak barrage, coupled with fighter attacks, downed seven bombers, with the luckless 379BG bearing all but one of the casualties. Then, 48 hours later, it was the turn of yards at Bremen (probably Vegesack) to be hammered. The ill fortune associated with the date struck home against four crews in all, half from the 101PCBW.

The 101PCBW had just crossed in over the enemy coast when a Polebrook B-17 turned back; this was Lt. Willard T. Forrest's 42-5814/YB: B, the 508BS bomber having developed problems. The situation became increasingly critical and culminated with a "ditching," from which only eight airmen emerged alive to drift in their dinghies for some eight hours. The proximity to Mid-summer's Day provided enough daylight for a combination of an ASR Launch and a RAF Walrus amphibian to effect the rescue. The aircraft was first on the scene and landed despite a fairly high-running sea, but this factor coupled with what was an overloaded machine prevented take-off, despite several attempts.

A rendezvous with the launch was subsequently made as the Walrus taxied ponderously west and transfer to the former unit was duly carried out. A second 351BG crew went down in the target area after 42-5815/RQ: Q developed progressive failure in three engines, whether due to flak or fighters is unclear. Brake, NW of Bremen, was close to where the B-17 came down; three on Lt. Robert W. Jackson's crew were killed, but the pilot was among the seven now facing captivity.

"Memphis Belle"—the (True) Movie!

The WWII documentary that utilized Capt. Robert Morgan's "original" B17F as well as its crew has entered the film archives of the conflict as a classic example of a well-presented and reportedly successful bid to raise the American public's awareness of the Bombing Offensive. At the same time, the script pulled no punches in casting up the material and even more so the human cost of the Offensive, unlike the equivalent film material emanating from British sources that was more inclined to eschew much if any reference to the casualty factor.

Hollywood Director William Wyler had taken up the matter following the request from Washington and duly arrived in Britain in early 1943. The choice of

Bassingbourn for the project may have been accidental, although its superior "permanent" facilities compared to the "tin shack" equivalent enjoyed by the other groups may have swayed the film team's decision. Certainly, several B-17s from these units were as combat-tested as anything the 91BG possessed, to scotch any impression that "The Ragged Irregulars" were special in this primary sense.

The search for a specific crew if not also their aircraft finally settled upon "Belle" and the stage was set for filming to commence. However, although Wyler had brought along a team of cameramen, he was not content to remain ground-bound himself. His courage was not in any doubt; on the other hand, his specific presence on the aircraft was not always welcomed, since he was inclined when taking film from the waist windows, for example, to intrude seriously upon the gunners' proper rendering of their weapons' fire power.

Further inhibitions created by the film crew's inclusion were that they placed extra demand upon the finite oxygen supplies and inevitably added to restricting the crew's movements within the fuselage. There was also the risk, given their normal and total insulation from the pressures of combat, that their reactions in the event of an emergency—especially if a bail out became necessary —could add even further to the burden placed upon their combat crew colleagues in ensuring safe evacuation for all on board. Filming culminated with the farewell ceremony for the B-17 and her crew at Bovingdon attended by Gens. Eaker (GC 8VIIIBC) and Devers, following which both departed for the States on 9 June, there to commence a nationwide Bond drive tour.

The finished product released during the winter of 1943/44 embodied a basic but natural contradiction regarding the "Belle's" quoted 25th and final mission. This was presented as the run to Wilhelmshaven on 21 May 1943; in actual fact, that was her 24th mission, with the 25th actually completed eight days later over the U-Boat facilities at the French port of St. Nazaire. The film script's seemingly unjustified amendment has to be viewed from a joint propaganda and diplomatic angle, with the VIIIBC crews seen as directly striking at a source within the Third Reich's boundaries. Conversely, it would not have sat so well with the American Public's mind set to present the bomber's operational career as having culminated over an Ally's territory, whatever the true facts were. (The heading reference to the 1943 film being "true" is not intended as a sharp rebuff to the 1989 Hollywood follow up. Although there were scenes therein that rendered the makers open to criticism, the aim appears not to have been to repeat the single-mission format; rather, it was an attempt to show the mission as a microcosm of what could and did beset many crews over the course of their combat tour. It must also be acknowledged that the film was for general public consumption, as opposed to indulging the small percentage of the public interested or immersed in the history of WWII.)

Mid-Summer Strike

The vagaries of weather patterns over Britain and the northern European continent again cast their negative shadow upon the Offensive for a further eight days, so it was the 22nd before the next mission went out. In the meantime, the final operational touches were being managed by the personnel of the latest group to be assigned to the 1BW: the 381BG led by L/Col. Joseph J. Nazzaro, a future Four-Star General and CG of the postwar Strategic Air Command.

Established at the turn of 1942, the group had completed its Phase Training at Pyote, Texas, and Pueblo, Colorado. Overseas movement was begun and completed between late May and early June, the Air Component arriving at Ridgewell, in Essex via Bovingdon, on 9 June. The 101PCBW now had its full, three-group complement. Over at Grafton Underwood, the 384BG was also ready to fly its first mission, along with the 381BG, both units intended to provide a diversion for the main strike force.

Today's plan was for a full-blooded assault upon what was a key source for synthetic rubber production, the plant being at Huels/Recklinghausen, on the NW fringe of the Ruehr industrial zone. Both BWs were assigned and provided 235 crews spread between ten groups and an extra sub-force, the latter being a Composite 303/379BG entity. The target's location promised a strong reaction from the *Jagdwaffe* in particular, especially given the strategic nature of the Primary. The Ridgewell and Grafton Underwood crews were to provide the required diversion, in this case a run to Antwerp under strong USAAF and RAF escort cover.

At Bassingbourn, 22 crews were assembled in the Briefing room with their third Group CO present: L/Col. Baskin R. Lawrence, who had assumed command on 23 May from L/Col. William M Reid, who had himself replaced Col. Wray at the end of April, when the latter transferred to HQ, 1BW. (Three days later, Lawrence would give way to L/Col. Clemens Wurzbach.) Over at Polebrook, one less in crew number was attending the equivalent Briefing. By the day's end, six teams would be missing from the Mess halls at either airfield, although one would return almost intact some days later, albeit without their B-17, which was now nestled under the North Sea.

The Huels attackers' inward course would cross the North Sea to Holland before bending SE towards the Primary; the Antwerp-directed diversion was hopefully going to keep the Germans confused as to the Americans' intention and at least delay concentration upon the main force if nothing more resulted out of the action. Full stream Assembly was made without incident in relatively clear conditions and the formations bored on over the sea and into Holland without much interference from the Germans. The diversionary mission further south was experiencing problems in Assembly; moreover, it would face a personal struggle with JG26 in the process.

The initial contact with the *Jagdwaffe* emerged as the main force was well inside Dutch territory. The bomber crews' defensive measures were as ever no more than adequate in terms of individual or corporate concentration when set against the superior concentrated firepower mounted within the solid structural platform of each fighter's wings. The assaults grew ever fiercer and all too soon gaps began to appear within the bomber ranks.

Regarding the 91BG, it already appears to have been short two B-17s as the bomb run began, but problems were mounting for several other crews. Bocholt lies some 30 miles NW of the Primary, and it was at Bungern, just SE of the aforementioned location, that 42-29998 /DF: J crashed with all but two on Lt. Joseph E. Slattery's (KIA) team killed in its loss. Wulfen, between Bocholt and Dorsten, was where fighter attacks brought down 42-29526/LL: A **Mary Ruth**. The fatality scale within Lt. Kenneth L. Brown's crew was diametrically opposite (two), with all eight others bailing out safely.

Royal Flush (42-5132/LL: E) was by now a 32-mission veteran, having originally been with the 303BG before transfer. Lt. Marcell E. Fountain's crew were allotted a No. 3 position in the Low squadron that was an ever-vulnerable one in terms of exposure to assault. According to Lt. Maury Herman (N), the B-17 took flak strikes as the group passed over—instead of to the north of—the confluence of the Ruehr and Rhine rivers as briefed in order to avoid heavy flak concentrations at that point. One engine had to be "feathered," while power loss was experienced on a second. The bomb run was nevertheless completed in spite of the inevitable struggle to maintain formation. Worse was to ensue with this bomber as the group rallied for the homeward course.

Lt. Buster Peek's 42-29797/LL: Y **Old Ironsides** had lost an engine shortly before the IP, but was holding station. Also on hand was 42-5789/LG: X **Golden Bear** with Lt. Paul D. Kahl and crew. Shortly after the bomb run was completed, Kahl's charge was observed with both starboard engines "out" and an inevitable loss of speed and height. The apprehending of all ten airmen near Muenster, roughly 25 miles NE of the Primary, confirms that the B-17 came down soon after this final sighting.

Royal Flush's pilots were similarly falling behind, but still held course for home, albeit with a steady loss of height that was barely 2,000ft by the time the Rhine was being crossed, this despite jettisoning all surplus equipment. Lts. Fountain and Oscar Dietering kept their faltering aircraft aloft until near Brugge, Belgium, at which stage the bail out bell was rung. All ten jumped safely, but Sgt. Thomas A. Stephens (ROG) tragically died from unknown causes while a POW in late July 1944.

Old Ironsides' short operational career, commenced on 18 May, was nearing its end, but the pilot still struggled on despite fighter attacks knocking out a second motor on the now-straggling bomber. It was amazing that the assaults not only were not terminal, but that the B-17 managed to gain the open expanse of the North Sea. Fortune then partially deserted the crew, because the aircraft's condition forced Peek to carry out a "ditching"; the ever-risky action was successfully completed, leaving ten airmen alive, but then tragedy struck when Sgt. Evert Lingberg (TG) drowned after drifting away.

The B-17 had only just returned to combat status after losing most of its starboard stabilizer to a bomb dropped by another group bomber on 13 June. Capt. Weitzenfeld had managed to bring his charge out of a dive and bring her back to Bassingbourn. Lt. Peek's luck would run out on 31 August over the English Channel, however. (This crew formed the centerpiece for the first chapter in the WWII official account of the VIIIBC's initial year of combat entitled *Target Germany*—a fine, understated record of that combat period. The sole difference was that the crew's experience on the Huels mission stated only *eight* airmen survived the "ditching" incident.)

Eleven more B-17s were lost from the Main force, among which was 42-29826/YB: R. Fighter-inflicted damage either before or after "bombs away" culminated in Lt. Leo P. Turgeon bailing out his crew close to the border with Germany and the abandoned B-17 finally coming down near Beek. Back at Huels, the degree of destruction to the factory initially appeared to be severe. In fact, full production would be resumed within several weeks, something that a goodly number of staff would never realize. These were individuals who had gone outside to gaze at what they took to be an approaching Luftwaffe formation; by the time they realized their error, they were caught up in the initial wave of bombing that took their lives.

Supernumerary Experience

Tex McCrary was a prominent newspaper correspondent who had already flown on several missions with the 91BG, including the controversial run to Hamm (4 March). He joined Lt. Jim Smith's crew for today's mission, as ever well aware that as a supernumerary he was taking up space as well as oxygen capacity. In addition, he had just returned from an overnight visit to London and barely managed to collect his gear and scramble on board; also, the combination of a hangover and lack of a breakfast promised an uncomfortable ride at best.

The initial mood of disinterest bordering on resentment among the crew regarding his presence gradually disappeared. McCrary noted how Smith's voice, once the fighter attacks commenced, went from an almost monotone level to one of staccato and almost juvenile pitch as he alerted the gunners to particular attackers and their approach. **Our Gang** remained personally inviolate from attention until the group was on the bomb run; then, the left inner wing was struck and was quickly followed by another hit in the same area that set the wing on fire.

The correspondent's reaction was not so much apprehension as fury that he was caught up in a situation that could be terminal; he was in the radio room at this time and the calm reaction of the ROG steadied his mind set, added to which the fire, which gained and faded in intensity several times, almost miraculously faded out after several minutes. (The strike probably set the rubber surround to a fuel tank ablaze and the slipstream's force was almost certainly the reason for the flames being extinguished.)

Meanwhile, the physical state of his stomach that had steadily deteriorated finally reached breaking point following the latest sharp evasive maneuver that cast an ammunition box into his midriff; he barely made it to the bomb bay and tore off his oxygen mask before vomiting violently several times. Once back in his mask, he resumed taking the series of pictures that formed the prime reason for his presence on board. The attacks finally over, he was called up into the cockpit by Smith, who proffered a cigar to him that he quietly refused.

On talking over the mission, McCrary raised the matter of the fire, to which the pilot responded by saying that had he been aware of the severity, it "might have made him sound nervous," and had this been communicated to the crew via his tone of voice it would not have been a good thing. McCrary later felt that Smith's comment aptly summarized the average combat crewman's reaction in battle, namely one of controlled apprehension.

Diversion Fortunes

The two acolyte groups for the Antwerp sortie dispatched forty-two crews in all, with the twenty from Grafton Underwood in the Lead. The process of Assembly and course as far as the Kent coast passed off in order, but then the situation deteriorated at this stage; the allotted fighter escort screen did not make rendezvous with their charges. The risk of severe punishment to what was a small force had to be balanced against the denial of diversionary assistance to the Main force in the event of "aborting" the mission. The decision was quickly taken to head onwards into the enemy hinterland.

The unprotected formation experienced a trouble-free passage over the Channel and had flown most of the route to the Primary—an aircraft production plant—when the first JG26 Fw190s, with their *Kommodore*, Maj. "Pips" Priller, in the lead, swept in with stunning force from twelve o'clock. Although strikes were inflicted through the bombers' ranks, no immediate losses were experienced, although several began to lag behind or below.

The bomb run was successfully completed, although the 384BG Lead bombardier (Capt. Bonnett) deliberately undershot, with the result that only a proportion of the bomb loads fell onto the target. His action was reportedly due to concern that civilian housing adjoining the far borders of the Primary might have been otherwise affected—if the report is correct, he probably did so after being briefed regarding the "friendly fire" debacle of 5 April.

The 381BG followed up with a sound bombing result and both groups rallied for home. It was then that fighters from II/JG26, headed by its *Kommandeur*, Hptm. "Wutz" Galland (Adolf's younger surviving brother), made their presence felt, this time with terminal effect for several crews. The bombers were over the Scheldt Estuary when their ranks were quickly depleted. Lt. Robert J. Oblinski's (POW) 42-30076/JD: V exploded and the shattered remains spiralled down onto the Dutch island of South-Beveland on the estuary's northern shore; the pilot and five out of his nine colleagues survived. Soon after, 42-5853/SO: U, flown by Lt Frederick O. Disney, was brought down, along with seven of its occupants, six of whose bodies subsequently washed up on the Belgian coast.

The same attrition rate was borne by the 381BG, beginning with Lt. Earl R. Horr's 42-30016/VE: M **Iron Gut Gert**. The pilot, who wryly made postwar claims of ½ mission completion to his veteran contemporaries at reunions, got out and down alive after gunfire administered the final blow to the already flak-afflicted B-17. The other crewmembers also jumped prior to the bomber's crash at Hoek, near Terneuzen, but one tragically drowned and his corpse was later found, while a second's body was never recovered.

The 533BS' 42-30021/OQ: G was shot down into the estuarial waters, the excision of part or all of one wing throwing the B-17 into violent gyrations that probably held most of the crew in position until final impact. Seven bodies out of the eight dead airmen on Lt. John L. Martin's (KIA) crew were recovered, with the two survivors treading a path to a Stalag. A pursuing Fw190 was reported as following its prey into the water thanks to the gunners' final desperate burst of fire, but in fact JG26 losses were recorded as due to the escorts.

Fortune and the Brave

The belated arrival of the escorts occurred around this time and with the JG26 elements engaged and put under pressure in their turn, the bomber crews settled down for an unhindered passage back to base—all but two from the 381BG, that is. 42-9984/OQ: **Devils Angel**'s and 42-3226/OQ: S **Little Chuck**'s return to friendly soil bordered on the miraculous, even if the final result was the "scrapping" of both airframes and the death of one crewmember.

The former bomber was piloted by Lt. Martin Shenk, and his B-17's problems developed fully on the return route around the time his element leader, Lt. Martin, was downed. The oxygen system was disabled, among other damage, and the aircraft fell below and behind. Sgts. Brinton (WG) and Sloan (TG) were wounded, but the latter stuck to his position, while T/Sgt. Sinclair (ROG) responded by administering First Aid to Brinton. Meanwhile, Shenk and Lt. Bill Grant swung their charge in violent maneuvers against the persistent fighter assaults that finally ended with them escaping their tormentors' clutches.

One engine had already gone "out" and now a second followed suit as the wallowing B-17 wended its torturously slow course back to England. This was finally achieved, but the failure of the landing gear to deploy as the airfield at Framlingham was approached resulted in a crash landing that all ten crewmembers immediately survived. Unfortunately, Sgt. Brinton's injuries proved fatal seven days later, despite his receiving blood transfusions. The B-17 was adjudged too badly damaged for other than "salvage" action. T/Sgt. Sinclair, who was also wounded during the mission, later received the Silver Star.

Little Chuck's martyrdom was more extended and severe, since it had commenced on the bomb run when No. 2 engine was knocked out. Lt. Inman Jobe's bomber veered out of formation and was promptly set upon. Lt. Larry Potenza's inability to discharge the bomb load added to the critical situation, while loss of another engine forced the pilots to operate the elevators and even the automatic pilot in order to maintain flight. The aircraft's end seemed imminent, but as the Scheldt estuary was nearly overflown, the appearance of P-47s and RAF Typhoons relaxed the immediate pressures. The bomb load was finally released and all surplus equipment jettisoned, but a crash landing became mandatory as the Kent shoreline passed underneath.

The final stroke of luck for the crew—if not their aircraft—now arose as the B-17 was set down. Its skidding onrush was barely reduced in pace when a concrete post loomed up directly ahead. The resultant contact, which could have caused major or total destruction of the airframe, was miraculously restricted to the complete excision of one wing, the obstacle having sliced through the wing/fuselage structure at that point! All ten airmen gratefully emerged from the intact fuselage to reflect upon this final stroke of Fortune in surviving the mission. **Little Chuck** was only fit for salvage, but at least brought her occupants back safely.

Twenty Ridgewell personnel were MIA, but this was not the full extent of the casualties for the group's combat initiation. To the forthcoming death of Sgt. Brinton was added the loss of S/Sgt. Arnold Lorick, a gunner on Lt. Hedin's 533BS team who had been killed at his post—a terminal fate that unknowingly lay just three weeks distant for the pilot and five other crewmembers.

No Safety Anywhere

Gen. "Monk" Hunter (CG VIII Fighter Command) had flown with the 381BG in 42-30024/OQ: A, piloted by Lt. Doug Winters. Next morning, the group was preparing for the mission to an airfield at Bernay St. Martin, France. Some sixteen ground crew were clustered around this B-17, carrying out maintenance and bomb loading duties while the Enlisted complement of the crew assigned to fly it were busy inside. Lt. Paul E. Tull (B) was also busy in the adjoining 42-29992/OQ: J's nose compartment.

Just after 1100 hours, there was a fairly muted explosion, followed nearly a minute later by a second greater percussive blast centered at OQ:A's dispersal. Where a multi-ton bomber had squatted was instantly converted into a scene of total devastation, with the airframe reduced to scattered fragments within a shallow crater. None of the 22 personnel in her immediate presence had survived and some bodies were totally eviscerated. Also dead was Lt. Tull thanks to a metal fragment, one of many that reduced OQ: J to "salvage" status.

The cause of the tragedy was later assumed to have been due to a bomb dropping onto the ground following orders to change the type of weaponry. Ground crew were just as exposed to injury and death as the combat crews, albeit in less comprehensive circumstances, but no headlines were made by such incidents compared to events "up aloft"; the effect upon families and relatives was equally stunning, however. The subsequent mission was ironically "scrubbed" on the way out due to adverse weather.

Two days elapsed before the bombers headed out again, this time with the intention of attacking Hamburg, an intention that was again thwarted by weather. Alternative targets on Wangerooge Island and a convoy proved rather minimal substitutes; on the other hand, the defenses were fully on hand to inflict fifteen casualties among the 197 crews dispatched, including six from the seemingly "jinxed" 379BG. One B-17 from the 101PCBW failed to return to Ridgewell; 42-30027/OQ: E was shot down into the sea between the mainland and Langeoog, in the Frisian Island chain. Three bodies later washed up, but all others on Lt. Robert K. Schrader's team joined the horrendous total of airmen whose names would adorn "Walls of the Missing" in postwar U.S. military cemeteries.

Three further June missions were to be launched, but all would be to France, with only one fully completed. All three PCBWs were out on the 26th, but Mother Nature again cast up unfavorable conditions that saw the greater bulk of the force assigned to Villacoublay airfield failing to bomb; the two groups assigned to Triqueville airfield did bomb, but must have enjoyed good visibility. During the Campaign, Allied bomber crews were adjured from bombing targets in Occupied countries for fear of inflicting casualties among the populations; however, this rule was often disregarded during 1944/45, although the advent of "blind bombing" equipment by then probably provided a reason, however justified, for such rule relaxation.

St. Nazaire's Lethal Adieu

During the VIIIBC's near eleven months of operations, the major U-Boat lairs on the French Atlantic coast had been a regular feature on Briefing room maps, but 28 June 1943 witnessed the final run to this region and this target category. St. Nazaire had gained a particular defensive reputation as "flak city" and its gunners, who were apprehensively treated as "post graduates" in their deadly art, were supported by the pilots of JG2. The 101st and 102nd PCBW were assigned the duty of taking out the port's lock gate system, unconsciously following up on the 1942 success gained during a British Commando raid; this was centered around an ex-U.S. Navy destroyer packed with explosives and rammed against the dry dock gates that had completely immobilized the largest European complex of its type for the rest of WWII and several years after.

The flak was as thick as ever during the bomb run and soon found its mark on at least three Polebrook B-17s. All four engines on 42-29817/YB: D were fired up by strikes, leaving Lt. William C. King (MIA) with little option but to call for a bail out. Unfortunately, the sea was below, into which all ten descended and the rescue efforts of French fishermen only secured four living personnel. TU: D/42-29843 was similarly flak-afflicted, but its final demise was due to fighters that caught the isolated B-17 and sent it into the sea; the survival rate was little better at five out of ten from Lt. John M. Moss's crew, the pilot being among the survivors.

The third flak victim was another 510BS machine (42-29887/TU: K), although Lt.

Derward R. Copeland (POW) managed to keep his charge aloft for some time on the return leg before it descended on Belle-Ile; three Enlisted men lost their lives at some stage with the others soon rounded up by the Germans. The final loss was started in an unfortunate manner when slipstream effect caused **High Ball** (42-29847/DS: T) to fall below the formation. Before Lt. Robert W. Adams could pull back up with the others his aircraft was assailed by fighters, whose strikes set No. 3 engine on fire and killed three gunners. The fatally-crippled bomber was abandoned near Muzillac, but one of the remaining seven on board also failed to survive; in sharp contrast, two among the six to reach the ground alive even managed to evade capture.

Thunderbird /Marnita No. 2 (42-5724/LG: T) had replaced its predecessor lost on the 17 April Bremen run and had just returned to operational status following damage sustained over Huels (22 June). Now, Lt. Edward T. Brodnax, Jr. and John C. Kaufman, Jr. were fighting to hold the bomber aloft after flak struck home. The course homewards was maintained with increasing difficulty that culminated in all but S/Sgt. James F. Wright bailing out close to the French coastline. Once again, the waters of the Channel claimed seven among this tally through drowning or exposure, despite the efforts of local boatmen to come to their rescue. The seas around Britain are rarely more than moderate in temperature even in summer, while the airmen's heavy flight clothing was often a dangerous impediment in sustaining an adequate degree of buoyancy for the individual concerned. These five losses constituted the total for the 1BW today.

Next day's overall mission was split between airfields at Villacoublay and Triqueville (1BW) and Le Mans (4BW) with an extreme result in failure and success. The latter Wing won through to its Primary that also included the town's marshalling yards. No such luck attended the 1BW's efforts, since a solid undercast was encountered at both locations. The mid-point of 1943 had now been reached and the expectation of regularly punishing Germany's industry was still in its formative stage of achievement. The days of striking as much at the geographic periphery of the Nazi empire as in its heartland were not yet behind the combat crews, but the ensuing two months at least would witness a distinct switch in favor of the latter.

Ominous signs that the *Jagdwaffe* in particular was mounting a burgeoning threat to the Offensive in the form of unsustainable bomber losses could not be discounted, even by the most avid supporters of the "self-defending bomber" theory. The available Allied escort designs were incapable of accompanying their charges much beyond the coastal fringes of Western Europe. This was a situation that would only marginally advance when drop tanks were fitted to the P-47, while the arrival of the P-38 in the autumn would provide some comfort in longer-range cover. Meanwhile, the bomber crews' individual and corporate salvation would continue to primarily rest in the hands of their own gunners—sadly, with sharply diminishing success throughout these interim few months.

Gable is among the smaller group gathered around the tail compartment of Delta Rebel No. 2. The actor actually came over to England with the 351BG, with whom he would complete some of his five-mission tally while producing the documentary Combat America.

Lt. "Red" Cliburn (P) is talking to a 324BS contemporary, Lt. Jim Verinis (CP). The latter was to gain permanent "fame" as copilot to Lt. Bob Morgan in the documentary film Memphis Belle; however, he was not a regular member on this specific crew and was actually an airplane commander for his first 19 missions.

Lt. Robert Rand's crew pose alongside 41-24547/OR: P Vertigo, which bears eight mission symbols. This picture was taken on 14 April, but seventeen days later, the B-17 lay submerged off the French seaport of Brest; a "ditching" by the same crew resulted in Rand and four others out of the ten-man complement losing their lives.

Capt. Oscar O'Neill chats with Cardinal Spellman, New York's Catholic Prelate (left), and Capt. Hall (Group Catholic Chaplain) prior to the 5 April 1943 mission. Twelve days later, O'Neill's crew would be involuntary "guests" of the enemy following the loss of their B-17F Invasion II (42-5070/LL: A), one of six 91 BG losses over Bremen.

Clark Gable poses near Delta Rebel No. 2's port "waist gate" during his visit to the 91BG. Although he flew five missions during his involvement with Combat America, a gunnery training documentary filmed during the summer of 1943, the actor never did so aboard a group B-17.

Capt. Morgan is seen shaking hands with Belle's ground crew, although the number present seems too large; the presence of Sgt. Giambrone on the right does support the official caption's contention, however. The occasion is believed to be the stateside departure of the B-17F along with Morgan's crew, with Lt. Verinis standing on the left.

Capt. Cliburn and Lt. Clyde DeBaum (CP) are seen in the cockpit of Bad Penny (41-24480/DF: C/B) on 5 May 1943. Clyde assumed command of the crew following his pilot's departure stateside and also completed his combat tour. Although plagued by a series of mechanical failures added to battle damage, the "original" B-17F ended up being relegated to non-operational duties later in May that culminated in salvage action during October 1944.

Several members of Capt. Bob Morgan's crew inspect their B-17's artwork. Morgan is on the right, next to Lt. Verinis (CP), while Crew Chief Joe Giambrone (on the step ladder) applies the 25th mission symbol to the veteran bomber.

Three....two....one...hack! The briefing is over and all personnel set their watches. The officer on the left is Lt. James M. Smith (324BS pilot), whose Spaniel mascot is partially visible on the table. Jim's crew featured in several pictures with Our Gang (42-5609/DF: G), although it was not reportedly their regularly assigned bomber.

Queen Elizabeth was not only a pillar of strength to King George VI, but was also a fine conversationalist. Here, she talks to three ground crewmembers during the visit to inspect Memphis Belle and Capt. Morgan's crew. The airmen still seem ill at ease in response to what was a formal occasion in their eyes.

Delta Rebel No. 2 was a group "original" who was named by her regular pilot, Lt. George Birdsong. Here, she is receiving her "coming of age" bomb symbol following her 21st recorded mission.

Delta Rebel No. 2 (42-5077/OR: T) is receiving a comprehensive examination of all four Wright Cyclones. However, the presence of nine ground crewmembers suggests a publicity picture, since individual maintenance teams rarely exceeded four in number.

The American WWI "Ace" Eddie Rickenbacker visited Polebrook on 28 July 1943. To his right is Col. Hatcher, who sports the almost obligatory sunglasses favored by many USAAF airmen in England, regardless of whether it was sunny or clouded over, as appears to be the case here.

The formal hand-over of the RAF airfield at Polebrook to the 351BG occurred on 28 June 1943. An RAF Squadron Leader hands over the documentation to Col. Hatcher, who still bears the insignia of a L/Col.; most group COs only attained full Colonel status after arrival overseas.

The strain of combat is temporarily behind Lt. Baird's (2nd from right) crew as they sit for debriefing on 28 June 1943. The officer on the far side of the S2 is Capt. Don Sheeler. He would become 322BS CO from 16 July '43 until 25 April '44 and end up the final 91BG CO with Lt.Col. rank.

Hurry up and wait! The 91BG's mission readiness on 19 May 1943 appears to have been delayed, judging by the bomber line-up and several combat personnel standing or laying around. The national insignia on the wings have been "dulled down" and lack the bars added the following July.

The inherent aerodynamic stability of the B-17 is amply demonstrated here. On 13 June 1943, a bomb excised virtually all of 42-29797/LL: Y Old Ironsides' starboard stabilizer. Capt. Weitzenfeld managed to pull the bomber out of its errant descent and land back at Bassingbourn. Nine days later, Lt. Buster Peek successfully "ditched" it in the North Sea.

B/Gen. "Monk" Hunter (CG, VIII Fighter Command), having flown with the 381BG on the group's inaugural mission on 22 June 1943, is now deep in discussion with several officers following the mission's completion.

Lts. Cos (right) and Lundy are seen by Oklahoma Okie, posing with the recently introduced flak suits produced by Britain's Wilkinson-Sword Co. Cos's equipment has a "turtleback" lower section, but no backing due to the pilot's seat being armored.

Maj. Aycock (324BS CO) makes notes sitting on his Jeep, while up in the cockpit of 42-5069/DF: G Our Gang is Lt. Jim Smith. The B-17F sports sixteen mission symbols. This bomber operated from late December until 17 August 1943, when it was MIA, although all on Lt. Bill Wheeler's crew survived as POWs.

Shot of Lt. Jim Smith with his crew and his Spaniel mascot "Skippy" is probably taken the same day. Absence of a Division triangle on the fin of the background B-17 indicates the date was prior to July 1943, when the geometrical design was introduced on the fins and starboard upper wings of 1st Bomb Wing aircraft.

Lt. Baltrusaitus (left) holds a discussion with Lt. Fred Nudell (532BS Engineer), Capt Murrey (S2), and L/Col. Leland Fiegel (Deputy Group CO). Baltrusaius's crew survived their combat tour, while Fiegel transferred to command the 93BG from 9 August until September 1944. Date is 10 July 1943.

His combat tour completed, Capt. Birdsong acknowledges his and the crew's debt to Delta Rebel No. 2 by "awarding" a DFC to the equally veteran B-17F that had successfully borne the airmen on many missions. The crew's good fortune would not be shared by the bomber, which would go down during the following 12 August run to the Ruehr.

"The strain is over and now the men can think of going home." Lt. George Birdsong (right) parades with his 323BS crew in front of their regular B-17F on 16 June 1943, following the completion of their combat tour. Delta Rebel No. 2 would not enjoy the same good fortune, as she would be lost the following 12 August.

Chapter Four

Full stride for *Blitz Week* (July 1943)

Lead-up to *Blitz Week*

The latter part of July 1943 was destined to be an unpleasant one for one Axis dictator (Hitler) and arguably a worse individual experience for his Italian partner in crime, Mussolini, who would be deposed and imprisoned. The Nazi autocrat had recently seen the slaughter of his infantry and armored units during the Battle of Kursk, on the Eastern Front, and would now witness further pressure upon his nation's industrial resources thanks to a sustained offensive conducted by the VIIIIBC during the final week.

Gen. Eaker had thirteen B-17 groups at his disposal on 1 July, the latest addition being the 100BG, assigned to the 4BW and operational from 25 June. The current absence of the 2BW's B-24s in North Africa would last until the end of August, but in the meantime, the 4BW would have an expanded strength of seven groups. Only four missions would be flown up to the 23rd, however, and all but one would be limited to French targets.

The first would occur on a date of historical and emotional import to Americans, namely Independence Day. The French had assisted the then-British-controlled Colonialists to gain their independence in 1783, so it was of some symbolic justice that today's mission would directly demonstrate the USA's intention to ultimately rid France, among other suppressed European nations, of the Nazi yoke.

The 101PCBW was one of two 1BW sub-forces to target an airfield at Caen, Normandy; 121 crews went out, of which 107 gained the target at a cost of four B-17s, one of which was a Ridgewell aircraft. Lt. Olaf Ballinger's 42-29928/OQ: W was the aircraft in question, and Lt. John Carah (CP) recalled how fighter gunfire raked the fuselage during the bomb run. Both waist and the ball turret gunner were killed and further assaults after the aircraft was culled from the formation jammed the elevators and forced it into an ever-steeper climb.

Unable to correct the malfunction, the pilot rang the bail out bell, to which six crewmembers responded in time; Lt. George W. Williams (B) was the unlucky exception, having spilled his pack and emerging far too close to the ground to save himself—an unlikely act anyway, since the bombs were still on board and their resultant violent explosion would have probably consumed him.

John Carah buried his chute and, using his compass, headed south, but after several hours on the move decided to ask for help at some houses, hoping that the occupants were friendly. His lack of French forced him to resort to sign language that fortunately worked, with a woman responding to his knock. From there on he was in Resistance hands, whose personnel initially transferred him SE towards Switzerland before redirecting him towards Spain. Previous to this switch—for which he volunteered—and while at one location near Frangy, his party was captured by German and Vichy police, only to be freed by a Resistance counterattack! His bid for freedom ultimately succeeded in early 1944, as also proved to be the case for Lt. Ballinger.

Three airfields in France were designated for assault after a five-day gap in operations. A location at Caen, a town that would be a pivotal site during the Battle for Normandy, went to the 101st and 102nd PCBWs, but only the former sub-force released upon the Primary, the other three groups finding it "socked in." The *Jagdwaffe* was on hand as usual, but only managed three "kills," one of which was a 91BG machine. **Stric-Nine** (42-29475/ OR: R) survived the Bremen run on 17 April, when it was knocked out of formation but came through the punishment inflicted by several pursuing Fw109s. Now it was in the hands of Lt. Leland E. Forsblad, whose crew was largely fated not to enjoy the same fortune as experienced by their contemporaries three months previous. One of a series of head-on attacks cast the B-17 out of place and it exploded several miles distant from the French coast. Forsblad and Lt. John Bennett alone survived the blast, as well as being deposited into the Channel, from where they were extracted by French fishermen.

Georgia Rebel (42-3217/MS: T) was nearly lost on one mission without direct enemy intervention. A life raft hatch inadvertently opened and the dinghy swept back, lodging itself against the vertical fin. The resultant vibration from the unwelcome "aerofoil" also broke up the airflow and caused an incipient and initially uncontrollable downward motion for Lts. Osce V. Jones (P) and Melvin R. Hecker (CP). The latter immediately vacated his seat and went back to the waist window, alongside which the lines securing the dinghy to the hatch were streaming.

His first attempts to pull at the lines were thwarted by the slipstream, but the stratagem of wrapping the lines around the machine gun mounting and hauling upon them finally resulted in the raft being detached, thus freeing the control surfaces and permitting the B-17 to be brought back into formation. This was none too soon, since fighters were on the attack and would almost certainly have added the potentially straggling bomber to their "kill" list had Hecker not promptly succeeded in his effort. This 381BG B-17F would make history of a kind on 24 July.

Extremes of Combat Fortune

Four days after the Caen mission, the VIIIBC launched its latest force on a date that held as much significance for the French as the 4th of July for the Americans. The French Revolution of 1789 that culminated in the nation becoming a republic has always been commemorated on 14 July—Bastille Day. For the second occasion in the month, the American combat crews were about to strike another blow on behalf of all the democracies with another three French airfields as their targets.

The 101PCBW was allotted Amiens/ Glisy, with 20 out of the 64 B-17s coming from Ridgewell. Thirty individuals among the personnel being briefed there would have no inkling of how the harsh vagaries of operations was soon to affect sixteen of them terminally, with the remaining fourteen surviving in circumstances that should have seen them similarly consumed.

Lt. Charles E. Hedin's 42-3223/VP: R **Red Hot Riding Hood** was circling east of Bury St. Edmunds with the other bombers when No. 3 engine caught fire, followed almost immediately by the B-17 exploding. All officers bar Lt. Frank Cappel (B) were killed, along with half the Enlisted man complement, while the remains fell just off the airfield perimeter of Rattlesden, future home for the 447BG. Frank never regained any memory of what had transpired and was permanently grounded, followed by a 1944 discharge from the Service. Later examination of No. 3's master cylinder rod confirmed it fractured; this malfunction led to a swift progressive disintegration of the engine, then the wing and finally the overall airframe.

The nineteen other crews maintained formation and, with one exception, got through to unload upon the Primary. Whether or not the exception failing to unload was Lt. Robert L. Holdom's 42-30011/MS: R **Widget** is unclear, as were the circumstances under which it was lost; as it was, all ten on board were lost after their bomber crashed at Berck-Plage, on the Channel coast. The three groups rallied off the target and headed for home under steady *Jagdwaffe* assault, primarily head-on. Lts. Edwin R. Manchester (P) and Robert L. Weniger (CP) were holding course within the Ridgewell formation when, as the latter noted, two Fw190s approached in a "balls to the wall" attack run.

The leader broke left in a "split-S" maneuver so close that Sgt. Arthur L. Tucker yelled: "He nearly took my guns with him!" The wingman, who was reported at debriefing as probably being dead or in a vengeful mood, was similarly rolling, but one wing smashed into his intended victim between the fuselage and No. 3 engine. His propeller became detached and slashed into the upper wing surface, causing an oil gusher from No. 4's oil tank, while wing fragments and one of his cannon barrels lodged in the bomb bay. The right stabilizer and elevator were also noticeably damaged.

Given these horrendous circumstances, it was a miracle that the collision did not bring down 42-3211/MS: O **TS** (Initials officially standing for "Texas State," Bob Weniger's birthplace, but actually meaning "Tough S...!"). The massive impact did stall the B-17, and it took a magnificent piece of cooperative pilotage to prevent her developing a spinning attitude and then to bring her back into level flight, albeit well below the relative safety of the group formation.

No. 4 engine had to be switched off and full power applied to the inboard motors as the lone bomber was eased into a steady glide in order to keep it aloft. Electrical power to the top turret was "out," a serious defensive failing should fighters appear—which they duly did. However, it was flak that proved the first obstacle when the Channel coast was looming. The subsequent flurry of shells could only be marginally countered by gently maneuvering the B-17, and although many more holes were added to the already well-shredded airframe, luck was still on the crew's side.

The coastline of France was slipping by when the first call of "bandits" was made. The ball turret was also inoperable and Sgt. Wade McCook (TG) had one of his guns jam as the B-17's restricted fire power promised an outcome in favor of the attackers. However, the very timely appearance of 78FG P-47s led by Capt. Jack London (The VIIIFC's first Ace.) momentarily saved the day for the embattled bomber crew as they brought **TS** in towards the SE English coast.

Manston's Emergency Airfield was finally reached, but not before the pilots faced a daunting task of threading their way through barrage balloon cables as the aircraft steadily lost height. Once over the airfield, a flap-less, wheels up landing was smoothly accomplished—only for an RAF officer to later inform the crew that they had unknowingly chosen a location free from mines previously sown against a Nazi invasion. Having come through this ordeal, Fortune would still deal cruelly with six of the crew the following 8 October.

The first monthly strike against two separate German-based targets (17th) proved abortive, with a fraction of the 331 twin-Wing force bombing Targets of Opportunity or the aircraft industry in Amsterdam. One crew alone was left behind on the Continent, with a second from the 351BG ending up in the North Sea. This was Lt. William F. Peters's 42-29872 /DS: W **Snow Ball**, which had No. 4 engine set on fire and No. 1 damaged with the propeller "running away"; further strikes up front killed Lt. Fred M. Wattles (N). Most defensive armament was knocked out, but the sustained fighter assaults did not bring the B-17 down, although they unknowingly sealed her fate.

A "ditching" became the only option, and this action was successfully accomplished. One dinghy could only be partially inflated, but the nine airmen managed to utilize this as well as the intact one; the evacuation was hasty in the extreme, because the aircraft's momentum was barely at an end when it began to sink and it was completely submerged inside one or two minutes. Two RAF Walrus amphibians subsequently turned up in sequence into which the airmen were bundled, but the condition of the sea prevented take-off and recourse was made to call up two ASR Launches whose crews took over; the Walruses were still unable to get off and had to taxi all the way back to Great Yarmouth.

Another week would elapse before meteorological reports of a prolonged period of clear weather over central Europe would lead to the launching of a sustained assault against a range of target categories, all but one of which was located within the Third Reich's boundaries. What would be forever known as *Blitz Week* in USAAF circles was duly commenced on 24 July.

Northerly Diversion

To date, the VIIIBC's targets outside Germany itself had involved those based in France and the Low Countries. On the morning of 24 July, the crews gazed upon the Briefing maps, whose course ribbons angled sharply upwards to settle upon Heroya and Trondheim, on the coast of Norway. The former Primary was allotted to the 1BW and featured the newly-completed Nordisk Lettmetal aluminium production plant at Heroya, on the southeastern coastline between Oslo and Kristiansand.

Georgia Rebel (42-3217/MS: T) was being piloted by Lts. Osce V. Jones and George B. Mackintosh; the latter officer had headed the 535BS "Model crew" during training in the States. Today, this duo of "original" officers was unknowingly about to set a trend for B-17s and B-24s whose crews felt unable to risk a return over the North Sea, thanks either to structural damage and/or badly injured crewmembers whose survival could not be guaranteed prior to attaining British shores. In addition, their ultimate fate was incarceration at the same Stalag and within weeks of each other's final mission during 1944.

This mission also featured the introduction of an enhanced method of Assembly in overcast conditions through the medium of "splasher" beacons, or British medium frequency radio stations. However, the facility appears to have only been used on the 24th by the 1BW, while the 4BW went out at low level and only climbed to bombing altitude when on the target approach. (Col. "Bud" Peaslee, 384BG CO, states in the book *Heritage of Valor* that the 1BW also adopted the same procedure, which—if correct—would appear to render the beacons' availability unnecessary.)

The enemy defenses were seemingly caught flat-footed by the Command's switch away from central Europe, as well as the operational tactics deployed. At Heroya, the formations encountered minimal flak barrage and the resultant series of bomb patterns left the factory with little ability to carry out production for many months, if at all. All but one of the 167 crews completing the bomb run remained unscathed and turned for home, the exception being **Georgia Rebel**.

The B-17 was unfortunate enough to absorb flak damage to the extent that the pilots regarded it as too severe to get their charge back to England. A short distance to the east of the target was the neutral territory of Sweden, towards which the bomber was now pointed. Matters must have been critical, because once this primary goal was achieved the aircraft was headed in towards a fir-tree-fringed clearing for a crash landing at Vannacka. The presence of a solid wooden pole directly in its path could have caused a serious problem, but **Rebel**'s momentum fortunately came to a halt with the pole straddling the gap between the No. 2 engine and cockpit!

None of the ten crewmembers were injured and they clambered out to be greeted by a crowd of local people, after which the police arrived to first interrogate, then arrange their transportation elsewhere. And so were interned the first of dozens of USAAF aircraft, along with some RAF contemporaries and their crews. A good proportion of the airmen were actually repatriated to Britain during WWII; this option was subsequently taken up by MS: T's ten occupants, most if not all of whom resumed combat operations.

Return to Combat Reality

The Heroya mission had indeed proved to be an almost perfect "milk run" in terms of loss, but any illusion that this pattern would be repeated next day was swiftly quelled at Briefing for the 101st and 103rd PCBW personnel when the map ribbons were seen to stretch out to Hamburg. Two Primaries were selected, with the Kloeckner aircraft engine plant assigned to the former sub-force that dispatched 64 bombers. During the previous night, RAF Bomber Command had dealt a smashing blow to the city, the first of several assaults over the ensuing few nights and whose smoking aftermath would unfortunately cast up basically insoluble visual problems for its VIIIBC partner's bombardiers.

Problems during Assembly for the 381BG first of all led to two complete Elements that included the designated CO "aborting," followed by the remaining crews finding themselves isolated from their High group position with the PCBW and unable to make up the gap prior to the target. On approach to Hamburg, all three group COs must have almost been shocked by the extent of the smoke pall created from over 700 bomb loads that was hovering above the city and in the 101PCBW's case had totally shrouded the Kloeckner plant.

The 91BG's Lead bombardier hastily switched his attention onto dock facilities west of the Primary that included the Howaldswerke construction yard, where bomb loads were deposited with some effect; the 351BG then followed suit. In the meantime, Capt. Shackley, acting as CO, cut to the right of the other two groups' briefed withdrawal course in the hope of linking up, a course of action that proved fruitless; he also ordered his crews to hold their bombs for (hopefully) a Target of Opportunity, an alternative intention that would subsequently be fulfilled.

By this stage, the *Jagdwaffe* was intervening in some numbers, and along with Hamburg's ever-fierce flak barrage was beginning to bite into the B-17s' ranks, with fifteen—a third of whom would stem from the 101PCBW—joining the MIA list. Flak certainly caused the initial stage of deterioration for Lt. Marshal L. Pilert's 42-29813/DF: B1. All attempts to hold formation by diving into the Lead and Low squadron ranks failed and with the fighters engaging the overall formation, the straggling B-17 was soon fastened onto. The pilots nevertheless held course for home until the scale of attrition persuaded Pilert into lowering the landing gear prior to bailing out the crew—an action that saw the fighters desisting in their assaults but circling around to ensure nobody remained on board.

Surprisingly, only one member was lost, albeit in tragic circumstances. The ball turret gunner (Sgt. Warren A. Haynes) had not worn his parachute harness while operating his position due to its discomfort and he could not find it on emerging. A last desperate bid for survival consisted of the pilot pulling the rip cord on his parachute (a seat pack unit) and tying some of its lines around his companion before collecting up the chute and jumping out the rear hatch. The slipstream immediately caught the parachute whose lines snagged the stabilizer, whereupon those lines attached to the hapless gunner came free and he fell to his death.

Pilert should have suffered the fate of being "hung up" and either dragged to his death or killed by anoxia and/or exposure. However, the parachute's "hang up" must have been brief in duration, apart from which neither canopy nor lines could have been adversely affected and he duly drifted down to a safe landing and ultimate delivery to a *Stalag*. The B-17's crash site was at Heide, in between Hamburg and the coast, whose railroad facilities would feel the weight of Ridgewell's bombs.

The sole Polebrook loss was made in similar circumstances to Pilert's machine. Flak over the city adversely affected the progress of 42-3272/DS: M **Captains Ball**, which was left with No. 3 engine smoking and faltering. Lt. Edwin S. Boyd (POW) also tried to remain within the formation, but an inexorable drift out of position coupled with loss of altitude witnessed persistent fighter gunfire that finally sent the aircraft into a dive, culminating in its crashing east of Hamburg with six fatalities out of the ten on board.

Ridgewell's Tribulations

The 381BG would return three crews short, beginning with Lt. Jack H. Owen's team flying in **Sad Sack** (42-29976/VE: Q). A flak strike between Nos. 3 and 4 tore up the wing interior and set the fuel tank on fire. Both engines were switched off and "feathered" as the bomber wallowed back out of position and was given hostile attention by several fighters. The overall situation once again persuaded the pilot that it was time to bail out before the B-17 exploded and he duly "roller coastered" his charge in order to provide a physical indication to the crew that they should jump; this was a standing arrangement should the intercom ever be disabled and prevent any bail out order being heard.

The ten airmen drifted down between Hamburg and Heide, with Jack, having survived a 20mm strike on the windshield, then finding himself falling at a dangerously accelerated rate due to having opened his parachute too soon and ripping out several panels in the process. Fortunately, he reached the ground with no more than a strained groin from his harness tightening up due to the parachute's opening shock.

A second 532BS crew that felt the lethal bite of the flak gunners was led by Lt. William R. Moore in 42-30013/VE: E **Lethal Lady**, a sadly apt title in negative terms for four of her occupants. Lt. Phil P. Dreiseszun (N) recalled that the crippled bomber managed to hold course for some distance. Then, as the latest turn was being made by the formation, the B-17 swung out to one side; before it could be eased back into position a head-on thrust by one or more fighters blasted the forward area.

Lt. James B. Houck (B) suffered a dreadful chest wound from a 20mm shell that defied all of Phil's frantic attempts to staunch the resultant blood flow, but the injury scale was such that the officer's life span was measured in minutes if not seconds, and he ended up one of the four fatalities; he reportedly went down inside the bomber, along with Sgt. John M. Watkins, Jr. (TG). Also killed were Lt. Dale G. Wende (CP) and Sgt. Joseph G. Kralick (WG).

Phil managed to evacuate the doomed B-17, but his parachute was badly shot up. The result was that he descended at such a rate that the impact with the ground knocked him unconscious. He later came to with the weight of a German soldier on him, the latter being in the process of searching what he probably took to be a corpse. He must have received a shock when the "body" reared up, throwing him to one side! The bomber's crash site is quoted as the Bay of Neustadt, NE of Hamburg. Since the Rally point for the bombers was some distance to the SW between the city and Bad Oldesloe, it appears that the dying machine lumbered on for several minutes prior to expiring following its abandonment.

The 532BS was further fated to provide the final casualty as the formation was tracking homeward. Prior to departing enemy territory, the group zeroed in on the small town of Heide and its railroad junction, upon which the surviving bomb loads were dumped. Still on hand at this stage were Capt. Joseph E. Alexander and crew in 42-30153/VE:, which had suffered serious damage to two engines but was still plugging away. The heavy vibration set up by the malfunctioning motors reached a stage where the risk of not making it across the sea forced Alexander to turn back, since the enemy coast was almost invisible.

The single B-17 was picked up by fighters who did not fire, but positioned themselves around their reluctant "guest." One pilot closed in and indicated that Alexander should follow him, thus indicating an intention to get the B-17 down onto an airfield. The pilots had no intention of actually landing their charge; instead, when on approach to the indicated airfield at Aurich, they stretched their flight to well beyond the runway and onto an open area seemingly bounded by woods. This stratagem worked to the extent that a crash landing was safely made.

However, the hoped-for escape into the trees from where an admittedly unlikely bid to evade capture by "heading south for France" could commence ended just as abruptly. As the pilot and Sgt. George Orin remained momentarily behind and prepared the B-17 for destruction by fire, the others came running back to say the treeline possessed a huge fenced-off camp! The arrival of civilians followed by a dog and his handler guard proved the farcical conclusion to the escape bid.

Hamburg Again

The opening phase in what was to be forever known as the Battle of Hamburg would be viewed as a largely RAF Bomber Command conducted campaign. As it transpired, the VIIIBC's contribution would realize some material increase in effective striking power when its second mission was launched just twenty-four hours later; the visual conditions would be little improved, a situation that militated against accurate bombing, although it was the existence of a burgeoning smoke screen that created the problem on the 26th more so than the after effect of the nocturnal assaults.

The possibility of losses equalling if not surpassing the previous mission must have been on everyone's mind, but two factors would appear to have stayed the hands of the aerial defenders. First of all, a mixed 1/4BW force was dispatched to Hannover, well to the SE of Hamburg, and it seems the bulk of *Jagdwaffe* attention was focused upon this sub-force of six groups, which lost nearly one-seventh of the 121 bombers dispatched. Although fighters did appear as the Hamburg-bound formations crossed in over the coast to utilize the same IP, these did not press home their attacks with any ferocity or effect.

A second benefit was realized against the flak gunners. Unlike 24 hours before, the four groups out of the six that had been sent (the 379BG and 384BG had "aborted" at different points on the way over) were operating at a higher altitude. Not only that, but there was no material time span between the two PCBW sub-force bomb runs that would have permitted an enhanced degree of separate concentration by the flak batteries the day before. The lone 303BG from the 103PCBW had closed up with the other groups and all four, having again been thwarted from striking the same pair of Primaries, turned their attention to the Howaldswerke U-boat construction yard and the area around the Neuhoff power station.

Having deposited around 120 tons of explosives and incendiaries with variable results, the formations now commenced the homeward route, consisting of a protracted curve to starboard. The southerly withdrawal involved a longer time over German soil, but the action might well have thrown the fighters off the scent, at least momentarily. As it was, only one of the B-17s was fated to remain behind on land with a second forced to "ditch," both being from Bassingbourn.

The 324BS' **Nitemare** (42-3031/DF: F) was the more unlucky example regarding the crew of Lt. James Rendall (POW), who were on their fifth mission in this B-17. The flak gunners landed strikes that sent it plummeting towards the ground. It was finally pulled out of this terminal attitude, but was now hopelessly isolated in altitude and distance and ripe for fighter attack. However, the pilots managed to get as far as the region south of Oldenburg, a distance of some 70 miles from the target, before their B-17 was latched onto by several fighters. The further punishment handed out soon induced a bail out order that nine of the ten responded to; Sgt. John Monohan (ROG) was seriously injured and fated to be on board when the aircraft crashed at Rotenburg. Two further crewmembers were "shot while attempting to escape," according to German records, and a fourth airman also failed to survive in unknown circumstances.

Suspended Sentence for Some

Lt. Jack Hargis was piloting 42-3119/LG: M—reputedly titled **Frisco Jinny**—and both B-17 and her crew were relative newcomers to the 91BG; the ten airmen were completing their third mission on board this bomber. The target had been safely traversed, as had the homeward course, but matters turned critical when an attempt to switch between fuel tanks failed, leaving the pilots with little choice but to "ditch." The initial contact with the sea witnessed the ball turret impacting, casting the airframe back into the air prior to final immersion. However, all ten airmen were aboard the two dinghies within the few minutes before the bomber sank, having broken in two thanks to a fracture occurring around the area of the ball turret.

An ASR Hudson and two Spitfire escorts were soon overhead, followed by a pair of Walrus amphibians who landed safely. The process of picking the airmen out of their dinghies and into the aircraft was finally achieved, but in that time the sea surface condition that had permitted a landing deteriorated to the extent that all efforts to take to the air again were not only thwarted, but resulted in structural damage to one of the Walrus' tail. Once again, an extended sea voyage in a wallowing airframe was the fate of ten more Americans, although the final stage for the airmen was made in less discomfort and time afloat aboard a rendezvousing ASR Launch! Sadly, the pilot and Sgt. Starr A. Tucker (BT) had only cheated the Grim Reaper by 22 days, both losing their lives during the costly mission to Schweinfurt.

Blitz Week Part Two

To date, a total of 44 crews had entered the MIA lists and marginally more than this figure would also succumb during the three remaining missions of *Blitz Week*. The daily punishment handed out by the Command over the previous three days was not extended into the fourth, but the respite granted the Nazi industrial infrastructure lasted just 24 hours before resumption on the 28th. This time round, both BWs were destined to make the deepest penetration to date into Germany.

The anticipated defensive effort was to be realized in a prolonged and severe manner by the 4BW, which would lose fifteen crews out of a force that witnessed barely one-quarter of its strength making bombing runs either at the Fw190 plant at Oschersleben (Primary) or over Targets of Opportunity. Although the 1BW's percentage of mission-credited crews was little better while striking at the Fieseler aircraft plant in Kassel, 100 miles east of the Ruehr, the loss of seven crews MIA could be deemed a more moderate rebuff in crude statistical terms at least, although the 303BG suffered three crash landings on return to England.

The twin major target categories assaulted to date involved aircraft production and ship construction, the latter with an accent upon U-boat hulls and engines. Kiel, north of Hamburg, with its sizeable shipyards, was now due its third pounding within two months by the 1BW. Two of the three Wings struck the Primary, with the 103PCBW unloading upon Targets of Opportunity. The 101PCBW did not contribute to the overall total of six crews declared MIA, but one Ridgewell crew had a tough homeward experience.

Whaletail (42-3221/GD: E) had progressively lost power in three of her engines and was barely eased down into a wheat field near Thetford by Capt. Arthur F. Briggs and Lt. William Wroblicka. The extended skidding groove formed by the crash landing did not apparently please the farmer who, on arriving at the site, remonstrated Bill regarding the destruction of his crop. In turn, the farmer was reminded politely if firmly by Bill of the reason for the emergency and the fact that the crew were fighting for his nation's survival as well as their own—crop or no crop. Bill's time at Ridgewell, along with several of his crew flying this mission, was to end abruptly on 12 August; however, he and Lt. Lester Schneider (B) would survive as POWs, while two others would forfeit their lives.

Finis to *Blitz Week*

The string of daily missions over five of the past six days had inevitably placed an increasing strain upon the Command's material and human resources that could not currently permit operations to be indefinitely maintained. Therefore, what proved to be the final mission for *Blitz Week* (30th) would bring a measure of relief for the crews—destined to extend over a twelve-day period—in its wake. Both Wings were tasked with striking at separate aircraft production sources in Kassel, with the Fieseler complex located in the city's Bettenhausen district again going to the 1BW and 4BW, albeit without participation of the 102PCBW in the former sub-force's case. The target's extended distance east of the Ruehr promised a prolonged exposure to the defenders' counter-thrusts extending over several hours.

The 101PCBW's brief immunity from aircraft loss during *Blitz Week* was ended to the tune of three, although these casualties were sustained on the homeward route following a successful bomb run by the bulk of the 119 dispatched crews. In fact, the luckless trio of B-17s managed to reach Dutch territory before expiring. The 381BG's latest loss involved 42-3100/VE: A1 bearing Maj. Robert F. Post (532BS CO), as well as Lt. Gordon W. Humason's crew.

Flak-inflicted damage was added to by fighter gunfire, and by the time friendly soil near Appeldoorn was reached, the pilots brought off a successful crash landing out of which six survivors emerged; of the four others who had opted to bail out, S/Sgt. Walter J. Anderson (WG) alone failed to survive after he tragically impacted with the tail while jumping. However, barely had the B-17 ground to a halt when it was strafed by at least one fighter, causing severe injuries to the Major that included the loss of an eye and a broken leg; this was a scale of suffering that resulted in his repatriation to the States during 1944.

Four days previous, Bassingbourn had surrendered two bombers, and now a second pair were destined to follow suit, both from the 323BS. **Man O War** (41-24399/OR: V) was the first of three similar-titled group B-17s and the oldest "original" aircraft still operational at Bassingbourn. Her final demise at the hands of two fighters was matched in cruel circumstances by no less than six crewmembers of Lt. Keene McCammon's team. Eight airmen jumped clear, but the fighters then made firing passes that probably killed five, while a sixth had his canopy so riddled that his precipitate descent culminated in a fatal impact with a cottage roof's internal structure. Both pilots survived their descent near Opijen, where the bomber crashed and where the bodies of the dead airmen are still buried.

Whereas **Man O War** had completed nearly ten months duty with the group, 42-29916 /OR: L's operational presence with the group only extended between 7 June and today's mission. The large-scale fighter assaults experienced during the withdrawal stage finally caught up with the B-17 as the Dutch coast was none too distant, at which point the bomber was straggling. Two gunners were killed, but all others among Lt. Bob Miles's crew managed to bail out before **Yankee Dandy** went to her doom at Berkel-Zoetermeer, near Rotterdam.

Comment

The assault upon Kassel (30th) signalled the practical completion of *Blitz Week*. A reasonable degree of damage, if not wholesale destruction, had been achieved in the course of the string of six missions. However, the dispersal of the overall VIIIBC strength to more than one target inevitably reduced the punishment handed out to each Primary; in addition, the explosive content of even the largest transportable USAAF bomb (2,000lbs) was not generally up to inflicting a permanent degree of destruction to much of the heavy manufacturing equipment.

A secondary limitation related to the Command's technical and human resources. Eighty-eight bombers, along with the bulk of their crews, were MIA, with a sizeable number of returnees either "written off" after crash landings or requiring varied degrees of repair. The scale of replacement in both these operational aspects was not yet matching up in a manner that would be the norm, and even better than the norm to be realized during the following winter and spring. It was time to draw an operational breath, but a special mission's imminent launch was probably an equally pressing influence upon this particular act of retrenchment—the ball bearing factories of Schweinfurt that were selected to await the full might of the Bomb Wing.

"Winding up" the "Rookies"

A favorite trick indulged in by veteran combat crewmembers to test the spirit and resolve of "newcomers" was to call on them shortly after their arrival and prior to their commencing operations. The following account of one such encounter was noted by Sgt. John Comer from Lt. Carqudeville's 533BS crew immediately after arrival at Ridgewell in late July. He and his fellow crewmembers had already been made aware of the current loss factor among the personnel by the squadron authorities, but what transpired as the veterans entered their billet later in the day was a further perceived jolt to their already uncertain morale. First of all, when they answered the question on Lt. Carqueville's high altitude formation experience—none and not much in any form—there was a feigned expression of deep regret directed their way. A throw-away remark that they might win through their first mission—even if some twenty crews had been lost in seven days (In itself a current exaggeration.)—was a second spirit dampener. The suggestion that the fighters went after bombers failing to hold tight formation, a situation Comer's pilot was clearly perceived to be likely to face, just added to the gloom. Then, the veterans firmly scotched the notion that return gunfire was of any material benefit in holding off the aerial assaults.

The penultimate element in the "winding up" session was when the veterans pointed to several of the billet bunks in which some of Carqueville's crew's predecessors had slept and the very lurid fates these individuals had allegedly met. The final twist came when one veteran asked Sgt. Balmore what jacket size he wore, the inference being that the item, if suitable, would soon be available, since he (Balmore) would soon become an MIA statistic along with his fellow crewmembers! Comer was a more mature individual at around 33 years of age, but even he felt the psychological pressure. As it was, a few weeks later he and his now combat-experienced colleagues would freely indulge in the same tactics—at a stage in VIIIBC's fortunes when the chances of survival for any airmen, experienced or otherwise, were arguably at their lowest level to date.

The pristine condition of these additional dispersal pans within the 534BS section of Ridgewell contrast sharply with the oil-stained original examples. This picture was taken prior to July, judging by the bar-less national insignias, as well as the absence of the 1st Bomb Wing (and later Bomb/Air Division) triangle symbols on the lower and central B-17s.

A line up of Enlisted men and officers is preparing to participate in an awards ceremony. The B-17F in the background bears the artwork applied to both sides of the nose compartment of Memphis Belle. This picture was taken no earlier than late April, judging by the tree foliage.

Lt. Jack Hargis (left, front) poses with his crew, including Lt. Ted Winslow (right, front) and Sgt. Gerold Tucker (left, standing), on 13 July 1943. Thirteen days later, they would survive the "ditching" of 42-3119/LG: M in the North Sea.

Lt. George B. Mackintosh (left) holds the attention of Capt. Osce V. Jones. Both were 535BS pilots, and on 24 July 1943, shared the dubious "honor" of diverting into Sweden off the Heroya mission, the first American "heavy" bomber to seek sanctuary in that neutral country. Both returned to Ridgewell but ended up POWs on 20 March and 28 April 1944, respectively.

This mid-summer 1943 scene at Bassingbourn demonstrates how the original use of RAF vehicles during the first months of operations as exemplified by the 6x4 Fordson truck in the foreground, which has now been supplemented by USAAF equipment, such as the "Cletrac" towing unit, as well as the crane-bearing vehicle directly behind.

Bob Hope is accompanied by Tony Romano during a visit to Bassingbourn on 7 July 1943. Hope did not confine himself to tours within Britain during WWII, choosing to travel to operational Theaters as widespread as North Africa and the Aleutians.

The fortunes of these four "original" 535BS officers would reflect the fortunes of combat crews. Lt. Edwin Frost (L) and Bill Cormany (2nd left) would end up as POWs. Lt. Melvin Hecker (2nd right) would come through his operational tour, as would Lt. Becker. At least all four survived the experience, unlike over 400 of their group contemporaries.

A 4 x 4 bomb carrier vehicle is parked by 42-5845/GD: A Whaletail II, a squadron "original" B-17F. She was one of a Lockheed-Vega batch that featured reversed location cheek gun panels; the port side fitting was also unframed and bulged at the front to permit the weapon's enhanced forward angle deployment.

These 7th Station Complement airmen are (L-R): Rudy Ramirez, Frank Hoffman, Jesse Wilson, Ed Hawkins, Frank Pine, and Bill Frye. Rudy worked with the Gas decontamination Section and recalled his most fraught experience was being "co-opted" with the Fire Section to fight the fire that destroyed fuel and ammunition-laden 42-39906/MS: X on 15 April 1944.

This YB-40 "Gunship," originally one of the number assigned to the 92BG, was transferred to Bassingbourn on 22 July 1943. The bomber (41-5741) joined the 401BS (LL: Y), but reportedly did not fly any missions prior to a stateside transfer during the following November.

Hells Belles/42-30157/OR: P's brief combat career of less than two months ended with this overshoot into the countryside on 30 July. Damage to the hydraulic system incurred on the outward leg was the primary cause of the incident. The scale of damage rendered the B-17F liable for salvage action, while almost all of her crew, led by Lt. Von der Heyde, had but eighteen days to live.

Many of the ground support personnel's functions were repetitive if not humdrum, but vital in their perfect execution. These two 91BG airmen are testing the wiring in electric suits for the combat crews. The failure of any part of the heated clothing could and often did inflict physical discomfort and even serious injury to the combat crewmember so affected.

Memphis Belle is seen during its PR tour of the USA—a world away from the stresses of aerial combat over Nazi-occupied Europe. The white-domed structure in the far right is probably the Capitol Building in Washington, D.C. Inscriptions above (and more faintly) below the serial probably relate to the 25 missions flown by the veteran B-17F.

The original squadron code letters issued to three of the four sub-units at Ridgewell were changed in the summer of 1943. This 535BS B-17F is TS (standing for Tough S…!) and the PL letters were changed to MS. Lt. Manchester's crew survived a mid-air collision with a Fw190 on 14 July 1943 while manning TS; a crash landing at Manston saw the bomber "written off" group records.

Chapter Five

Darkening Horizons

The Lure

The possibility of bringing about a foreshortening of the conflict through the use of air power was naturally always on the Allied planners' minds. One aspect of this eminently desirable goal focused on inflicting lasting destruction to industrial "bottleneck" resources, such as fuel and transportation. Germany had no natural oil complexes and relied upon imports from other locations, such as Ploesti in Rumania, supported by internal production of synthetic oil supplies. Transportation was perceived as a weakness, in that destruction particularly of the rail network would seriously hinder the movement of all forms of military equipment. As it was, the U.S. planners currently had their minds set towards ball bearings, a basic but vital item in permitting the efficient function of much manufacturing equipment and the material turned out therefrom.

Schweinfurt, in northern Bavaria, possessed several bearing production plants and its destruction was regarded as placing an inordinate strain upon German industry. In effect the enemy's industrial base would literally "grind to a halt," and with it the means to continue prosecuting the conflict. However, what was forgotten or ignored in examining this "quick fix" was 1) the presence of similar plants at Stuttgart and also in France and 2) the fact that supplies were relatively easily imported from Switzerland and Sweden. Nevertheless, planning for a mission was already on hand as August commenced.

Costly Failure

In spite of the fact that daylight hours were currently still near their peak—especially with the use of the Double British summertime extension—the VIIIBC's bombers remained firmly wedded to their dispersals for twelve days following the Kassel mission. Only on the 12th did they finally rise up unhindered by either technical or weather limitations over England and head out toward *Festung Europa*. Whereas less than 200 between both BWs had been dispatched on 30 July, the equivalent figure for a joint strike against Gelsenkirchen, in the Ruehr, was well over 300.

Mother Nature had clearly relented regarding Assembly and departure of the formations, but she revealed her quixotic mind set as enemy airspace was penetrated by casting up increasing cloud layers that finally intruded upon bombing the selected Primary or Primaries. Both BWs were forced to spread their nets wider in search of Targets of Opportunity, with locations in neighboring Bochum and Recklinghausen picked out among others.

The *Jagdwaffe* had ample warning of the B-17s' incursions and its pilots' assaults directly inflicted casualties among all 1BW groups other than the 351BG, although one crew ended up with their bomber being "written off." In addition, of the 25 crews MIA overall, all but two came from the Wing's formations, even though the 4BW's formations had spent an equal time over the Ruehr. The 103PCBW came off the worst, with ten crews taken down, although statistics would have counted for nothing among those crews circling Bassingbourn and Ridgewell several hours later, their ranks having been shorn of four and three B-17s, respectively.

Two of the 91BG casualties appear to have been incurred as the original 22-strong formation—now reduced to fifteen—was approaching the Dutch/German border south of Nijmegen. Lt. Jerold Kethley named 42-5787/OR: U **Billie K** after his wife, and both bomber and her team had been on hand since March, being well into their combat tour in the crew's case. The initial fighter assault had seriously damaged the bomber to the extent that refuge was sought in a following formation, but to no avail. When last seen, it was still under control, but subsequently descended near Goch. Fortunately, by then, all ten crewmembers had vacated their aircraft and floated down into captivity.

Wesel lies on the Rhine, and it was here that a group "original" B-17 commenced upon her involuntary "exit." **Delta Rebel No. 2** (42-5077/OR: T) had been brought over by Lt. George Birdsong's crew, and apart from featuring in a photo shoot with Clark Gable, it was also reportedly ahead of **Memphis Belle** in completing her 25-mission run. Her original crew had now completed their combat tour and Lt. Robert Thompson was piloting the 30-plus mission aircraft.

The initial fighter pass set her on fire and further attacks killed one gunner and indirectly sealed the fate of a second, whose parachute caught fire as he jumped. Two further gunners, who were seriously wounded, failed to clear the doomed bomber before she slammed into the ground at Horde, close to Dortmund on the Ruehr's NE fringe. OR: T's agony must have been fairly prolonged, as the distance between Wesel and Dortmund is around 40 miles.

Formation flying in heavy bombers during WWII was never easy. This was especially the case under operational conditions, with often overladen airframes whose controls did not always respond to emergency situations. Two 401BS B-17s were fated to impact with each other, although the terminal effect on one was delayed until it was out over the North Sea. As for 42-29587/LL: J **Jolly Roger**, its four-month sojourn at Bassingbourn was also closed, but it staggered along, losing altitude and height until near Schmidheim, due west of Ahrweiler, where Lt. Robert Heller brought off a crash landing with all but one crewmember ultimately surviving; the exception was Sgt. Thomas G. Price, who succumbed to his wounds in hospital some days later.

The spread of 91BG losses between the NW and SW fringes of the Ruehr lends some credence to how the 101PCBW at least was wending an extended arcing flight path while searching out suitable targets. The impression is reinforced by what happened to the 381BG's casualties. To date, Ridgewell had suffered the loss of fourteen B-17s MIA or "written off" on return and now that figure would extend to seventeen.

Lt. Bill Wroblicka was on board **Whaletail** when it crash landed on the 29 July run to Kiel; also on board that day were five or six of his regular crew. Now, as the group was skirting the southern fringe of the Ruehr, the latest fighter pass landed strikes that fatally crippled 42-29954/GD: D **Devils Angel** and killed the four gunners in the rear. Bill and the five survivors bailed out, leaving their bomber to crash at Hemmerich, NW of Bonn.

The 535BS's 42-29950/MS: N **Forget Me Not** bore a title that was to prove unfortunate for this and at least one other similar-named squadron B-17. Lt. Fred G. Evans was in charge, but he and four others were lost after strikes set the aircraft on fire and disabled two engines. The crash site at Rheurdt, on the NW edge of the Ruehr, suggests the loss was realized after the group had diverted from the Primary, roughly 20 miles to the NE of where MS: N descended. The 532BS' share in the losses involved 42-5847. VE: T **Margie Mae**, one of a Lockheed-Vega production batch with the "cheek gun" window frames reversed. The crew, headed by Lt. Theodore L. Moon, fared the best in terms of survival rate (ten) after the B-17 was set on fire and abandoned.

Nearly There

The other 91BG bomber involved in the collision with **Jolly Roger** was 42-3162/LL: A **Buccaneer**, which sustained heavy damage to its top central fin. The aircraft had transferred from the 94BG in April, but today ended her operational career, although not immediately after the impact. Lt. Talmidge G. Wilson managed to maintain control, though dropping down and back. A homeward course was held, but barely was the enemy coast out of sight when the North Sea claimed its latest victim, albeit only the B-17. Having safely "ditched," all ten airmen evacuated safely into the dinghies, but it then proved to be a worrying experience for them that spanned the ensuing night before rescue appeared in the form of a German vessel.

The 351BG's contingent of 21 was reduced by a third in terms of crews gaining mission "credit," but none of its bombers failed to return. However, only 20 remained on full combat status that evening. A flak strike on 42-29874/TU: J **El Conquistador** had disabled No. 2 engine with the almost inevitable loss of speed and therefore distance from the formation. Immediately latched onto by fighters, further damage was rendered to two more engines and Sgt. Edward W. Hanninger (TG) was killed and others wounded.

In spite of this, Lt. Jose J. Garcia not only kept on for home, but finally escaped from his tormentors' clutches. The North Sea was safely negotiated, but as soon as the English coast appeared the pilots made for the first available airfield (Leiston), where the B-17 was crash landed. The crew survived the experience, but not their charge, which was subsequently declared "salvage."

Lead-up to Disaster

The Schweinfurt strike was part of a multi-force assault upon several targets, but the final draft was not decided on until at least the 14th; this was after one postponement (10th). The second draft would have seen both VIIIBC BWs combining to strike Schweinfurt there and back. The final draft now had the 4BW flying to the Messerschmitt factory at Regensburg and heading on to North Africa; the 1BW would follow shortly after to attack Schweinfurt before heading back to England. That was the theory, but what transpired in practice was an extremely qualified disaster for the latter sub-force and a lesser-qualified success for the former.

In the interim period between 12 and 17 August, the Command's crews went out twice to France and the Low Countries, with the 1BW dispatching all nine groups with variable results. For instance, on the first occasion, the 91BG ended up bombing the Dutch port of Flushing, whereas 381BG records indicate the Primary as a location in Brussels. Amiens and Poix airfields were also struck, but there were no MIA losses. Next day, 171 of the 180 crews sent out struck the Primary (Lt Bourget airfield), but this time round four bombers were lost.

However, the single 91BG casualty only involved the B-17, although enemy airspace was not penetrated. **All American** (42-3213/OR: M) was another 4BW reassignment that arrived during May. An internal explosion disabled the No. 1 and 2 engine control cables, so Lt. Eldon J. Smith immediately commenced a gentle turn towards the English coast that was just several miles distant when the pilots were forced into a "ditching." Once again, Fate was kind to all ten airmen and they scrambled into their dinghies, from which they were soon plucked by an ASR Launch.

Anniversary Mission Background

On 17 August 1942, the VIIIBC entered combat with its "Heavy Brigade" in the form of the 97BG's twelve-strong force of B-17s backed by a six-plane diversionary sub-force. The pioneer group had long debarked to North Africa, but exactly one year later, the England-based Command, whose unit establishment was currently sixteen times greater, was about to embark upon a twin-mission strike that, if successful in one specific aspect, was expected to administer at least a long-term if not an immediate critical blow to Nazi Germany's industrial production capacity.

The seven-group force provided by the 4BW was briefed to attack the Messerschmitt production factory at Regensburg, but instead of reversing course would head on towards airfields in North Africa. Behind them, within a short time span, would appear the 1BW's nine groups, whose two Task Forces would be extended to six units each, the extra three being Composite in nature. Having attacked Schweinfurt, the formations would return home. The basic intention behind these maneuvers was to force the *Jagdwaffe* to dissipate its overall strength, thereby limiting the strike effect against either bomber stream—an ever-vital factor in individual and corporate survival for the American crews, who would be largely dependent upon their gunners alone to see them safely through the extended period over hostile territory.

Operational Setback

The extended distance over which the 4BW would have to fly compared to its 1BW contemporary necessitated a take-off time early enough for the bombers to reach North Africa before darkness descended. However, the personnel woken up on 17 August must have wondered if the mission would ever be launched, because the fine clear conditions experienced over the previous day or so had perversely given way to a solid fog extending over much of East Anglia.

The dilemma facing Gen. Anderson (CG VIIIBC) only really emerged when, having delayed the 4BW launch at least once, he then acceded to B/Gen. LeMay's (CG, 4BW) assurance that his groups could safely negotiate even these elementary weather conditions. However, no similar action was reportedly deemed to be safe to attempt at this time in the mind of LeMay's 1BW contemporary, B/Gen. Robert Williams. Thus, the separate dispatch of the Regensburg-bound groups basically destroyed the concept of blunting the enemy fighter's counter strokes as envisaged within the overall mission plan. To make an analogy with the sport of tennis, this was really advantage *Jagdwaffe*!

The Growing Pressure

The crews, having been briefed, then went out to their aircraft, into which they would climb and debark over a several hour period. Over at Bassingbourn, the journalist and war correspondent Tex McCrary, who had flown the 22 June mission to Huels, now prepared to accompany Lt. Bill Wheeler's crew in **Our Gang**. The general reception from the airmen varied between guarded and almost overtly hostile, in addition to which the suspicion began to grow in his mind that they were not going to come through today, basing this judgment (somewhat illogically) on their nervous wisecracks among one another.

He could not conceive of a reason to cancel without presenting himself as a coward in his own mind as much as in the minds of the combat crews, so when he was formally ordered to remain on the ground by a senior staff member, his conscience was basically salved. Much later that day, the soft words "Hello, Luck" addressed to Tex by an Intelligence officer aptly summed up the good fortune granted by his being "grounded" on this occasion.

The superstitions affecting most crew members' minds came into play among Jack Hargis's team as they prepared to take **Dame Satan** into action. The squadron CO, linking up with the crew at their dispersal to announce the latest delay in take-off, glanced at the B-17's artwork and remarked: "One good thing about this Dame—she always comes back," causing Lt. Ted Winslow (N) to feel an icy chill down his back accompanying the unspoken thought *I wish he had not said that*; this premonition of disaster was to be fully realized within a few hours.

The frustrations of the Bassingbourn crews were similarly expressed at Ridgewell and Polebrook. Twenty-six B-17s were ready for dispatch from the 381BG-occupied airfield, with a further twenty-eight fully laden bombers squatting on their dispersals at the latter base. S/Sgt. Ken Stone was ball turret gunner on Lt. Marvin Lord's 532BS team, and unlike so many of his colleagues seemed to have overcome any sense of apprehension, since he was quite able to eat a couple of Spam sandwiches brought out by truck to their dispersal! It was as well he had no forewarning of the depredations soon to be wrought upon the group, otherwise his appetite would have surely been badly blunted.

The 101PCBW would be Lead for the overall 1BW formation with the 91BG up front. Col. Clemens Wurzbach (Group CO) would have Col. William Gross in the right seat as Commander for what was the forward Task Force, while Gen. Williams would fly copilot to Capt. Weitzenfeld. However, the 351BG would actually fly Lead for the second trio of groups within the Force, while its place within the 101PCBW would be taken by a Composite group comprised of single squadrons from the 91BG, 351BG, and 381BG flying the Low position. A similar six-group structure following behind would be led by Col. Howard M. Turner.

The Ambuscade Awaits

The series of delays in launching the mission not only played upon the airmen's nerves, but more ominously, now permitted more than ample opportunity for the *Jagdwaffe* units who were either stationed on or had previously been redeployed to airfields well within striking distance of the 4BW's inward course. Having taken on the Regensburg force and inflicted a sound measure of destruction before returning to their temporary airfields, they were still mainly on hand when the first indications followed by growing confirmation of the 1BW's approach along the same route was established. The distance between the point at which the P-47 escorts would reach their endurance limit and the Primary ensured that the bombers would have the undisturbed attention of their aerial tormentors extending over a three-hour period at least—set point, *Jagdwaffe*!

Off at Last

Having been wakened early in the morning, the several hours spanning the original briefing and the revised take-off times meant that it was reaching toward mid-day (1120 hours) before the first Elements lifted off to commence the ever-laborious act of Assembly. The German monitoring service soon gathered the initial evidence of such an action in spite of strict radio silence, but could not yet be certain of their adversaries' precise intention. However, it would be at least two hours before the enemy would find themselves forced to decide the disposition of their fighters; time enough for the various *Gruppen* currently tackling the 4BW to be on hand for this second incursion.

Assembly went off without any problem, although a 4% "abort" figure was realized up to the point of traversing the North Sea; no replacements were on hand, but two of the crews turning back actually took off again and linked up with the stream that now encompassed 222 B-17s. The 101PCBW's original sub-force of 115 included 24 from Bassingbourn, one of whose number was Lt. Eugene Lockhart's 42-3043/LL: B **Hitler's Gremlins**, the crew's regular B-17. The pilot had flown the first-ever VIIIBC mission on August 17, 1942, but had then been wounded and was not long back on combat status. A supercharger failure on one engine should have resulted in an "abort," but he pressed onward, despite facing the likelihood of fuel starvation thanks to the other engines being boosted and soaking up reserves at a faster rate.

Progress as far as the Belgian hinterland passed off uneventfully and the lead formation approached the border with Germany around Eupen. The initial escort force of Spitfires had given way to their P-47 cousins, having encountered and thwarted the efforts of the *Jagdwaffe* to get through their screen. However, only the group assigned to Turner's Task Force made the rendezvous, leaving Gross's formations uncovered. As it was, a looming "fly in the ointment" regarding the bomb run had already been created.

Col. Gross, having apparently observed a cloud layer directly ahead of his formations, decided to lower altitude by several thousand feet. One definite and one problematical complication thus ensued from this action. First, Turner's Task Force encountered no such natural obstruction and remained at the briefed altitude; this would result in bunching up when Gross resumed the same altitude prior to the bomb run. Second, it is likely that the 4FG assigned to escort the first Task Force rendezvoused at the briefed altitude and therefore did not make visual contact with the then lower-positioned B-17s.

"Here they come - Twelve O O'clock High"

The absence of any escort cover at this point ensured that the first thrusts to be delivered by the *Jagdwaffe* would all too soon begin to have an effect on the bombers. This was to prove especially deleterious for the forward section of the Task Force, upon whose ranks the fighter thrusts would continue to be directed. By the time the crews were back over the North Sea, the three groups concerned were destined to be shorn of twenty-three B-17s, a figure that was to constitute almost two-thirds of the 1BW's final MIA casualty figure.

Lt. Don Von der Heyde's team in 42-5225/OR: S **Stormy Weather** included a replacement navigator, Lt. Edgar Yelle, who had only arrived at Bassingbourn scant hours previous. This B-17 had barely survived the Hamm mission of 4 March while bearing Lt. Birdsong's crew, but her combat career was brutally concluded during the initial series of assaults. The entire wing outboard of No. 2 engine was sheared off by cannon shells and the aircraft immediately began to spin. Only Yelle and Lt. Walter Brown (B) managed to either fight off the centrifugal forces or were ejected into mid-air when the airframe disintegrated, their eight fellow airmen going down with the bomber NW of Leopoldsburg, Belgium. (Yelle's scant combat career both plumbed the depths by lasting less than 30 minutes and subsequently reached its zenith due to his evading capture and ultimately returning to England via Resistance links.)

The 91BG had commenced its attrition rate for today, but it was the 381BG, flying in the Low position, upon which the enemy now mainly directed its lethal attention, culling no less than five of the six ensuing bombers from the group formation after entering German airspace south of Aachen. Lt. Neil H. Wright's 534BS "original" crew were on their eleventh mission, but the fighter-inflicted damage to their 42-30028/GD: H **Sweet Le Lani** forced its abandonment around the Dueren area; its terminal fate was fortunately not shared by its ten occupants. The 533BS suffered a loss at Pesch, near Bad Muenstereifel, where 42-33092/VP: T **Strato Sam** fell to earth. Only Lt. Kenneth E. Robinson (B) from among F/O James C. Hudson's team failed to exit the bomber.

All four squadrons would share in the losses, and now it was the 532BS' turn to surrender 42-30140/VE: V **King Malfunction II** to the airborne executioners. Capt. Robert E. Nelson was squadron operations officer and flew every fourth mission in this capacity. The eleven-man crew was led by Lt. Jack B. Painter, but their progress towards the Primary was brought to an abrupt halt SE of Bad Muenstereifel. The pilots had attempted to extinguish the fire-stricken No. 1 and 2 engines by diving, but when this failed the bail out order was given.

Ten airmen jumped, but the pilot was still on board when his B-17 impacted at Esch; whether he was already dead or trapped by centrifugal force remains unclear. The area where the crew descended was well distant from the Belgian or Luxembourg borders, so the prospect of evading capture seemed extremely poor. However, Bob Nelson and Sgt. Raymond Genz (TG) were about to buck the trend of ending up POWs in these circumstances.

Game, Set, and Match in Tactics

The approach of the fighters from directly ahead and slightly above had been paying increasing dividends over the past few months, but the "kill" rate on the anniversary mission through use of this tactic was to be far ahead of anything to date. The B-17's flexible guns "up front" could only be realistically operated regularly by the bombardier, since his colleague had to maintain some form of flight log. The top turret and ball turret gunners, especially the latter, were able to gain but fleeting sights of their adversaries, while the waist and tail gunners were similarly restricted to short, hastily-aimed bursts of fire as the fighters swept past at high speed. The fighters' close-packed armament mounted in a solid wing structure and forward engine cowling could by contrast deliver a lethal weight of gunfire upon the larger outline of the bombers.

"Run for Home"—Odds Against

The chances of a crew regaining England by attempting a solo run from deep in enemy territory were never high, especially with the presence of sizeable fighter forces, as well as the ground-based barrier posed by innumerable flak batteries. Nevertheless, no less than four crews would commence walking this aerial "tightrope" even before the formations had reached a point SE of Koblenz.

The first among this number involved the 534BS' Lt. Weldon Simpson in 42-30245/GD: L **Lucky Lady**; Oostmalle, due east of Antwerp, was where the shot up bomber descended with the pilot the sole fatality. Lt. Hamden Forkner's 42-3227/GD: G soon followed suit after No. 1 and 2 engines were disabled with the former on fire, but the pilots, after back-tracking from south of Aachen and into Belgium, ultimately established the situation as hopeless and all on board jumped clear. In addition, Forkner, along with three of his crew and one from Simpson's team, succeeded in swelling the ranks of Allied evaders. The B-17 came down at Teuven, north of Diest, not far from the Von der Heyde bomber's location.

Stupntakit (42-29559/OR: Q) had replaced its squadron predecessor **Stupen-Taket** in early March. Lt. Charles A. Bennett's aircraft was Lead for the Low squadron, but was turned for home within minutes of its 381BG companions in misfortune after being knocked out of formation. The battle against pursuing fighters also ended near Diest (Langdorp), where the bomber exploded, although seven of the crew survived, of which the pilot and two other airmen gained the bonus of evading capture.

Lt. Jack A. Hargis and crew had survived a "ditching" on 26 July and were now on board **Dame Satan**. The formations were south of Koblenz when strikes on No. 2 engine caused a power loss and inevitable drift-back in speed and altitude; even jettisoning the bomb load availed the pilots nothing, so the decision was taken to reverse course. With well over 200 miles to go before crossing out of enemy territory, it was amazing that the bulk of the distance was completed, despite one brief series of fighter passes that had no effect.

Sadly, the odds finally proved insuperable as the B-17 was skirting Brussels to the south when a single fighter's fusillade riddled the airframe and sent it into a steady dive. All ten airmen jumped, but parachute failure led to the deaths of Hargis and Sgt. Starr A. Tucker (BT); a diametrically opposite fate awaited four of the other eight, since they ended up in Resistance hands. Lt. Winslow (N), the officer who had reacted with foreboding to the pre-mission comment about this B-17 "always coming back," was also sheltered by the Belgians, but ended up two months later in *Gestapo* hands following his betrayal.

The Attrition Rate Intensifies

The forced withdrawal of **Dame Satan** from the 91BG's ranks raised the overall loss figure to twenty, the bulk of which had been borne by the 101PCBW. It had proven difficult enough to even ward off the worst effects of the *Jagdwaffe* with a full strength bomber force. Now the absence of twenty B-17s further reduced the defensive screens by an average of twelve machine guns per aircraft. The twelve additional losses included four from Bassingbourn, two from Ridgewell, and two Polebrook casualties, with one of the latter flying with the group formation in the1st Task Force's second wave.

Lt. Arlyn E. Weieneth was piloting aptly-named **Frank's Nightmare**—42-5437 /LL: H, because the errant B-17 had "aborted" nearly one-third of its missions to date. Now the nightmare scenario really struck home, because not only did the bomber fall close to Dueren, but none of the ten airmen survived the grim incident. Koblenz lay eastward when 41-24453/LG: O **The Bearded Beauty-Mizpah** suffered heavy punishment around the cockpit that almost certainly killed Lts. Everett L. Kenner (P) and George M. Bryan (CP); the final crash site at Mayen left half of the ten-man crew still alive.

Not long after, Lt. Bill Wheeler's 42-5069/LL: G **Our Gang**, in which War Correspondent Tex McCrary had been due to fly before being officially "grounded," was fatally crippled, to be abandoned by all ten crewmembers prior to piling into the ground at St. Goar on the Rhine. The final 91BG casualty at this inward stage was **Chief Sly II** (42-5139 /LG: V), piloted by Lt. Joel W. Gatewood. The latest fighter pass landed solid strikes up front that killed or fatally injured three airmen and set the No. 3 and 4 engines ablaze. The bomber fell out of its No. 2 slot in the High squadron and clearly veered to the left, crossing over the Rhine to its northern bank and finally crashing SW of Wiesbaden; only six crewmembers got out alive, but two were subsequently killed, either by bad landings or thanks to "summary treatment" at the hands of civilians or military personnel.

The latest duo of Ridgewell losses was more spread out geographically. Lt. Challon P. Atkinson had charge of 42-29983/VP: X **Iris**, which had begun to slip back out of formation due to reduced engine power. With one engine showing signs of being on fire the bail out bell was rung, to which some crewmembers responded, but the order was cancelled by the pilot, who then put his bomber into a gliding turn to try and extinguish the flames, after which a homeward course was set. Fighters took up pursuit of the B-17 now on half power, but did not press their assaults; rather, they seemed to be awaiting the imminent crash of their quarry, rather than adding the finishing touches to her dispatch, according to Sgt. Peter Katsarelis (WG).

As it was, the end came near Kesseling when the pilot again rang the bell, to which all still on board reacted. However, Atkinson and Sgt. James C. McGoldrick (BT) did not survive, the gunner having gone out in response to the first bell. What had been the crew's 13th mission had lived up to this numerical indication of ill fortune. Some of Lt. Reinhard M. King's crew were flying the same numbered mission while none had less than ten to their credit. Bad Schwalbach, SW of Wiesbaden, was where fighter assaults finally dispatched 42-29978/GD: F **Hells Angels**, which was by then bereft of all ten airmen.

Polebrook's Tithe

The 351BG's primary formation was Lead for the 1st Task Force's second wave, whose overall strength was to be diminished by just six B-17s during the course of the mission. Allocated the No. 6 position within the Lead squadron was 42-29839/ TU: C **Cherokee Girl** in the hands of Lt. Helmuth F. Hansen. The crew were within five missions of completing their combat tour, but what was the "coming of age" example was to end in arbitrary failure. A burst of cannon shells set the B-17 on fire, precipitating a call for bail out to be issued.

The pilot and all but one of his nine colleagues jumped clear near Mayen, SE of Koblenz. The tragically unfortunate exception was Sgt. Tuite H. A. Ambrose, whose parachute pack was burned by the flames and who presumably could not find a replacement pack. Meanwhile, flying the "slot" position at the rear of the 101PCBW Composite Group's High squadron was 42-5812/DS: O **Cannon Ball**. It is likely that it was already down at Bad Ems, east of Koblenz, having been previously abandoned by Lt. Max A. Pinkerton and his crew following terminal damage from fighter gunfire.

Target Approach

The PCBW had now borne sixteen of the twenty-three casualties ultimately suffered and had two more added to the negative tally even before the IP was reached. Lt. Anthony G. Arcaro found his 41-24524/ OR: O **Eagle's Wrath** allocated No. 6 in the 91BG's Low squadron and particularly vulnerable to attack. Five crews from the group formation were already gone as the final leg to the IP was being negotiated when a *Schwarm* (foursome) of fighters approaching from 8 o'clock landed their concentrated fire on the bomber.

A fierce fire in the nose compartment and an inoperable intercom forced the pilot to dispatch a crewmember to pass the bail out order further back. Then, having waited several minutes to ensure as far as possible that all the crew had been alerted, he managed to dive out through the fire-encircled nose hatch. Sgt. Delmar Karch (ROG), having been thwarted from going out through the bomb bay that was ablaze, hoisted himself backwards onto his radio hatch rim before releasing his hold; amazingly, he avoided impacting the vertical fin and floated down to captivity with his seven still-living colleagues. (Lt. Harry K. Warner had suffered serious injuries to which he later succumbed on the ground.) As for OR: O, her eleven-month sojourn with the group ended violently near Gelnhausen.

The Great Speckled Bird (41-24527/DF: Y) had served the 401BS prior to transfer into the 324BS. An "original" contemporary of **Eagles Wrath**, she was bearing Lt. Bill Munger's crew, but the steady punishment handed out to her—including the apparent crippling of both inboard engines when last observed—forced a bail out that all ten airmen carried out in good order. The abandoned B-17, which had been threatening to slip into an uncontrollable spiral when still manned, then did so and impacted several miles east of Aschaffenburg.

Failure

The overall results arising from the 1BW's assault on Schweinfurt were to prove very poor, but two key alterations—one in planning and one in tactics—probably contributed to this. First, the lengthy delay in starting out resulted in a change of approach from the original IP situated to the east of the three Primaries, which featured distinct ground references to one west of the target that in contrast was largely bereft of such guidance for the navigators. Second, and probably even more of a cause of failure, was the earlier decision of Gen. Gross to lower his Task Force's altitude over Belgium and later bring it back up to bombing altitude. This was an act that now dangerously foreshortened the distance between his and Col. Turner's Task Force; the result was that some units in the latter sub-force ended up having to maneuver in a manner that saw them having to make bomb runs from other than the briefed direction.

Post-mission reconnaissance reports indicated that of the 184 B-17s still retaining their loads at "bombs away," only a small proportion had managed to direct them onto any of their assigned Primaries. The remainder had landed concentrations in a shallow arc around the southern fringe of Schweinfurt, with the village of Oberdorf (to the SW) receiving the attention of one, although this was within ½ mile of the VFK No. 1 plant. In addition, several groups having found their Primaries obscured had followed the briefed alternative in such circumstances of releasing upon Schweinfurt itself.

The first wave's failure was the most inexplicable, because not only was their progress unhindered by the following formations, but visibility was totally free from smoke clouds resulting from the bomb concentrations that would steadily block out sighting of the Primaries for the ensuing waves of attackers. It had been bad enough to lose twenty-four crews up to this point, but adding what was a huge scale of bombing deficiency must have struck a severe blow to the personnel's morale.

The Long Retreat

Up to now, it had almost solely been the *Jagdwaffe* who had administered fatal punishment, but the flak gunners could not be discounted from the defensive effort. The flak provision at Schweinfurt was at least adequate in terms of strength and placed its mark directly upon one bomber during the 381BG's bomb run. The loads had been released and the group was banking to port for the Rally point when a shell impacted between No. 3 and 4 engines on 42-29731/VE: **Moorde-Fidite**. Lt. Bill Lockhart (B) was getting up from his bomb sight when a shell fragment struck his face and lodged behind his left eye. The full extent of the pain did not emerge until later, such was the shock of the injury. With both engines "out," the chances of even making a run towards Switzerland soon vanished and Lt. Leo I. Jarvis ordered his crew out, all ten floating down safely. As for their B-17, it came to earth at Ebrath.

Another group bomber had probably already been added to the unit loss tally at this time. Fighter gunfire had lanced into 42-3220/MS: M **Damfino** and the fatally affected B-17 tumbled to destruction at Marksteinach, several miles east of the target, albeit without any of Lt. Harry M. Smith's team; Lt. Lloyd W. Qwinn (B) later recalled that he was so busy firing his gun that he had to be physically shaken by Lt. John P. Noonan (N) before becoming aware of what was happening, only to feel an illogical sense of having to leave his post regardless of the aircraft's terminal state!

The defeated formations—defeated in terms of successfully thwarting the defenders' countermeasures, as well as landing a crippling blow upon Schweinfurt's industrial capacity—straightened out north of the target, ready for more sustained hostile attention without Allied escort cover. With at least an hour's flight time until that desperately-needed support would be on hand, the prospect for further depredation loomed large.

In fact, just ten more B-17s would either go down over Europe or end up under the North Sea, this number being spread between the four sub-forces. The *Jagdwaffe* pilots did take two B-17s down, one of which was already flak-damaged as the bombers left the target area, while a third crew dropping out and attempting a "home run" at low level got as far as French territory before luck ran out. Thereafter, just one crew was culled from the overall force before the Belgian/German border was overflown.

Several crews, in their stricken bombers, were desperately attempting to maintain some form of contact with the formations. One among this number was the 381BG's 42-3225/MS: V **Chug-a-lug-Lulu**. Lt. Lorin C. Disbrow's "original" charge was suffering engine problems and bearing the badly-wounded Lt. David R. Jones (N). As the formation was approaching the briefed rendezvous point with the P-47s, the crews was greeted by the unwelcome sight of Fw190s from II/JG26.

By now, Disbrow's bomber was several thousand feet below the group and therefore easy pickings for a *Schwarm* of fighters. The anticipatory joy of gaining fighter cover and returning to base felt by Lt. Allen J. Chapin (CP) changed stunningly into the realization "I was now certain we would never make it back." And so it now proved, as gunfire riddled the bomber, which came down near Tongeron, Belgium. All ten airmen reached the ground alive, of which four or five evaded capture.

The Casualty List is Completed

Bassingbourn, Polebrook, and Ridgewell's blood debt in aircraft and crews lost over the Continent had now been indulged, but the Fates had not finished with three B-17s from the last two groups, only one of which would deliver its occupants onto dry land. The first of this trio was the 91BG's **Hitler's Gremlins** (42-3043/LL: B), in Lt. Eugene M. Lockhart's hands. Flak-incurred damage had plagued the B-17's progress from an early stage of the inward route.

Its position as second Element leader in the Composite group's Low squadron was nevertheless retained until the enemy coastline was looming. It was at this point that engine power loss caused the bomber to begin a steady descent, culminating in a "ditching" that all ten airmen emerged from to gain access to the dinghies. An RAF Walrus subsequently arrived, but the attempted take-off once again ended in failure and S/Ldr. Grace was forced to laboriously "taxi" his amphibian back to Ramsgate over an extended time span.

"Hanging On"

F/O George R. Darrow (532BS) was flying his 13th mission, but his crew were relative novices, with an average of just three missions under their belts. George was originally copilot to Lt. Marvin Lord, but had recently been granted his own team. Today's run to Schweinfurt would cast up all the ill fortune connected with the number 13, however. Their B-17F (42-29735/VE:) was flying in the Low squadron, and all too soon the initial fighter passes landed a damaging strike on No. 2 engine. The diminished degree of power soon had its negative effect upon the pilots' ability to hold formation; although Lt. Darrow gave thought to dropping down "on the deck" for a solo run home, he soon passed it up. (The several 1BW crews who had taken up this option all failed in their bids.)

The isolated B-17 inevitably attracted the fighters' attention, but with his 22nd birthday 24 hours distant, Darrow was determined to present the enemy with a hard contest. Head-on assaults saw the bomber held on a steady course until the last moment before being maneuvered out of the bullet and shell stream; when the fighters altered their approach to a six o'clock angle, the B-17 was put into a roller coaster maneuver. The tactics worked, but it is likely the *Jagdwaffe* pilots in question were probably none too experienced; by comparison, the chances of an *Experte* failing to register lethal strikes would have been minimal, to say the least. As it was, the crew were still airborne and heading east as the overall aerial assault upon the 1BW waned and temporarily faded out.

The group was still in sight as the IP was over-flown, but the pilots now took up a more direct course for the target in order to catch the formation as it banked to port following the bomb run. The release of the 6,000-lb bomb load now provided better prospect for maintaining contact with the formation for the run back. Even so, the increase in engine power necessary to do so threw up the reverse danger of consuming too much fuel. Fortune still favored Lt. Darrow's crew, in that the fighters did not land lethal strikes on the airframe, but the scale of damage made itself felt further as the Dutch coast was barely being crossed; it was then that No. 4 engine's propeller stuttered to a halt as the motor finally failed. The B-17 now steadily lost altitude, but remained free from fighter attention, due in no small measure to the presence of several Spitfires as later reported by the crew.

Any prospect of reaching friendly soil on the remaining two engines diminished when first one, then the other ground to a halt. Only partial flap was employed, since a full open position was dependent upon power fed by the now-defunct engines; the crew were ordered to "ditching" stations in the radio room, where Sgt. Jack Kaufman was busy sending out Morse signals to back up the Spitfire pilots' "fix" reports to the ASR Service. The sea surface was relatively smooth and the B-17 was safely slid into the water.

The life raft hatch toggles were pulled, but only one emerged in inflated condition, into which six of the crew scrambled. The other raft was pulled out of its stowage by Sgt. Baker and he spent a few minutes literally tearing the cover off in order to reach the CO_2 bottle operating lanyard, a task that succeeded. During this time, the B-17 had sunk and the pilots, having exited via their cockpit windows, were floating around in the none-too-warm sea along with Baker and a fourth crewmember; the quartet were more than glad to clamber aboard their flimsy "boat." The ensuing hour or so before the welcome sight of an ASR Launch appeared on the horizon was passed in an apprehensive mood by the ten wet and hungry airmen, since they had no guarantee as to when or even if their rescue would end in success. Once on board the RAF vessel, their flight gear was removed and they donned replacement gear that included thick white pullovers that were a hallmark of the ASR's clothing provisions. The RAF skipper then directed the Launch towards Ramsgate, from where the crew were driven the short distance to RAF Manston. Here, they were royally fed and remained overnight before a 381BG aircraft appeared in the circuit. It was none other than 42-29789/VE: O **Big Time Operator**—the B-17F on which Lt. Darrow had flown as copilot to Lt. Lord, who furthermore was at the controls on this occasion! Lt. Darrow had not only won through to his 22nd birthday, but would go on to complete his combat tour.

Summary

The Anniversary mission's hoped-for success was far from equalled by events. The immediately successful 4BW effort over Regensburg proved to be of a temporary nature, with much of the production plant brought back into service within weeks. This contrasted with the 1BW's almost total failure over Schweinfurt. Even worse was the huge scale of aircraft and crew loss: sixty B-17s MIA, along with all but 118 of the 601 airmen, the exceptions being those rescued from "ditched" bombers (80) and on a variable time scale the majority of those evading immediate capture (38).

The "self defending bomber" supporters were now firmly on the back foot regarding perpetuating the theory in practice. However, the operational requirements to bring and maintain Germany's industry under the hammer of the VIIIBC's strength, coupled to the lack of any long-range, let alone effective, escort cover, augured badly for the bomber crews' survival prospects. They would be expected to continue probing deep into the aerial "bandit Country" for the foreseeable future whenever the U.S. authorities deemed it necessary.

A Minor "Disaster"

Although the bulk of the 1BW groups had returned from Schweinfurt with low loss rates—in the 306BG's case none at all—the call to arms 48 hours later witnessed only that unit and three of the remaining eight groups dispatching anything like a full strength force. Battle damage had clearly left its mark in terms of serviceable B-17s, and in the case of the 101PCBW, the twin factors of this limitation coupled with MIA casualties meant that a combined figure of just 24 bombers were ready to go. The 1BW force of 125 was assigned the Dutch airfields at Gilze-Rijen and Flushing, with a token 4BW formation striking Woensdrecht airfield. The short distance to the Primaries promised a "milk run" mission with escort cover for the entire duration.

Problems for the Gilze-Rijen attackers during Assembly ended with the Composite group, comprising the 384BG and 379BG, not only failing to do so, but being reduced to just eight B-17s from Kimbolton's sixteen dispatched crews. This sub-unit then succeeded in joining the 101PCBW sub-force, which assumed Lead for the 1BW; following behind were the twenty crews from Molesworth.

This truncated formation headed out over the North Sea and finally commenced its bomb run, but this did not go on schedule. First of all, only the 351BG and 379BG elements actually released their loads and the Lead sub-force made a 360 degree circle, ready for a second try by the 91BG and 381BG. Their loads were successfully released, but the extremely poor scale of accurate strikes visited upon the target by the other two sub-formations was barely exceeded in quality following this second run. Worse still, the scattering of loads outside the airfield resulted in many Dutch civilian casualties.

The sole MIA casualty borne by the Ridgewell contingent was 42-3101/VP:, bearing some of Lt. Orlando Koenig's crew who had formed the 535BS "Model" crew at Pyote, Texas. Flak had previously damaged the B-17 around No. 3 engine, causing fuel to commence leaking, and the formations had turned for home when a fighter pass from between 9 and 11 o'clock landed strikes that ended with the right inner fuel tank catching fire. Eyewitnesses described how it appeared to be under control as it detached itself in a right-hand curve and opined at debriefing that there would have been no reason to suppose all ten crewmembers would not get out.

Lt. Len Spivey (N) had been part of the "Model" crew and recalled that almost as soon as the fire caught hold and he had reported dense smoke in his compartment to his pilot, the latter had said "Bail out!"; Len queried his remark, only to have it sharply confirmed, whereupon he and Lt. Edward T. O'Loughlin moved to the escape hatch. They were joined there by Koenig and all three followed one another out for a safe descent. Lt. Joe Mangarpan (CP) and two of the Enlisted complement also jumped clear, but the remaining quartet of gunners went down with the B-17, which crashed SW of Rotterdam at Oud-Rozenburg. (A Dutch eyewitness described how he saw one outer wing section sagging but remained attached by the main spar before becoming completely severed during the bomber's subsequent and violent spinning motion; it is likely that the four victims were pinned in place until the final impact. He also stated that he witnessed six parachutes deploying, a figure tallying with the number of survivors from 42-3101.)

Continued Retrenchment

The twelve remaining days of August witnessed not only a continued reduced rate in missions flown (three), but also a concentration upon targets within France. The first strike was launched on the 24th against Villacoublay airfield in SW Paris, but only the 101st and 102nd PCBWs participated, with the 103PCBW acting in a diversionary role. The overall force of 146 B-17s reflected a steady if unspectacular drift towards a regular level of operational strength as existed up to the Schweinfurt mission.

Three days later, all nine groups went out for a short run to the Pas de Calais, with only Bassingbourn and Ridgewell's contingents of thirteen and ten still well below normal group strength. The existence of unusual "ski site" structures around the town of Watten was the reason for what was the first in many attacks upon the launch pads for the infamous V-1 "Doodlebug" pilotless bomb extending over the next twelve months. Just over 80% bombed the Primary at a cost of single crews from four groups. One of these was Polebrook's 42-29716/YB: A **Fast Woman**, which was reportedly fatally damaged by fighter gunfire; fire caught hold and the resultant explosion dispatched the airframe down at Villers-sur-Simon, roughly 30 miles SE of Watten. Lt. William J. Suit (P) was killed, along with two others, but two of the seven survivors ended up in Resistance hands.

"Luck of the Combat Draw"

The latest several-day lapse in operations ended on the 31st, when Amiens/Glisy airfield near Rouen was targeted as a Target of Opportunity following failure to gain access to the briefed Primary (an airfield at Romilly). Three crews were officially declared MIA, but just one was claimed by the defenders, the other two being consumed due to one operational hazard ever likely to arise in formation flying, namely collision.

Lt. Buster Peek and eight of his crew had survived a "ditching" on 22 June, and now the veteran pilot was in charge of 42-29816/LL: K **Eager Beaver**. As the group was crossing out over the English Channel coast, Lt. Richard H. Rodman maneuvered his 41-24523/OR: N **Snooks** to take up a formation position on the far side of where Peek's B-17 was located. The former bomber's lateral path took it too close to its companion aircraft and the resultant collision chopped the tail section off **Eager Beaver**, sending the main portion into an uncontrollable spiral.

Sgt. Charles E. Allen (TG) recalled hearing the impact, and on peering up saw the other B-17 almost on top of them. He grabbed at his pack, but what he naturally assumed was an intact airframe now went into a spin, and it was some time before he successfully fought off the centrifugal forces to reach and snap it on. Failing to release his door, he worked his way forward, only to discover on passing the tail wheel that the main fuselage was gone and the mangled metal at the point of separation prevented any further movement ahead.

He frantically resumed hammering on his door and got it open, but then ended up having to struggle his way out into mid-air, fortunately with more than sufficient height to deploy his parachute and drift down into the Channel; even then, he was fortunate that none of the falling wreckage intruded upon his more gentle descent. An ASR Launch was fortunately in the immediate vicinity to fish him out, but once immersed in the sea he still had a tense if brief struggle to release the parachute, whose billowing canopy was dragging him along away from the Launch. He had unknowingly become the sole survivor between the twenty airmen involved, as **Snooks** also delivered her entire human content to their deaths in the Channel's waters.

The group's torment was not yet at an end, however. Flak struck home against Lt. Jess D. Rogers's B-17 **Patty Gremlin Jr.** (42-29973/LG: Q) over Amiens/Glisy, causing the bomber to lose speed and altitude. Three of the crew tragically took up the option of bailing out over the Channel after the pilot indicated the bomber would unlikely regain friendly shores and drowned. Nor was Fate any kinder to Rogers and four of the other airmen; the B-17 did get back over the Channel, but the crash landing in a forested area near Polegate went tragically wrong when the airframe burst into flames. Three severely-burnt crew members scrambled clear, one of whom—T/Sgt. Paul M. Kelly (Eng.)—subsequently died from his critical condition.

This 91 BG "original" (B-17F 41-24527/Y) served in turn with the 401BS and 324BS. The unusual mission log layout totals 24; the name change from The Sky Wolf to its displayed record occurred in July, but the bomber was fated to go down with Lt. Munger's crew on 17 August while en route to Schweinfurt.

This picture is likely posed for the cameraman, but still highlights the problems of manning a waist gun, especially when wearing a flak suit weighing around 20lbs. Maintaining a firm footing with a cascade of cartridge cases littering the floor would have increased the difficulty in handling the weapon; canvas bags attached to the ejection slot subsequently cured the situation.

A crowd of ground personnel at Bassingbourn are inspecting the damage to V-Packette's stabilizer back from a mission on 26 June. Aircraft partially concealed by the men is an RAF Short Stirling, one of the trio of four-engine "heavies" operated by Bomber Command. All but two on Lt. Von Der Heyde's crew would die in 42-5335/OR: S on 17 August.

This picture of 42-3227/GD: G was taken between early July 1943—when the triangular 1BW insignia was applied to the fins and starboard upper wings—and 17 August, when it went down with Lt. Hamden Forkner's crew. The No. 1 engine is detached and positioned on a workbench located on the thoroughly oil-stained dispersal's forward rim.

Close aerial view of the Station HQ structure at Ridgewell. The two large Nissen huts house the administrative staff, while the flat-roofed building is the Operations block. This site was cleared and now contains a small housing estate.

A large number of non-Tokyo tank B-17Fs were transferred from the 4th BW to the 1st BW, including 42-3106, which joined Maj. Ball's squadron at Polebrook as YB: M. On 13 August, a power failure shortly after take-off ended with her being "bellied in." Damage was sufficient for salvage action, much to the squadron crew's happiness, as she was regarded as a "clunker" in terms of overall performance! (Slide)

Lt. Eugene M. Lockhart and crew, seen here by Hitler's Gremlin, had flown their first mission on this B-17F. Two days after this picture was taken (15 August), the same team successfully "ditched" this bomber on return from Schweinfurt.

A cheerful pose is struck by some of the crew led by Lt. Donald Von der Heyde, but Fate would prove to be cruelly unkind. On 17 August, the majority would die when their B-17F spun violently and disintegrated after suffering fighter-inflicted punishment on the way to Schweinfurt.

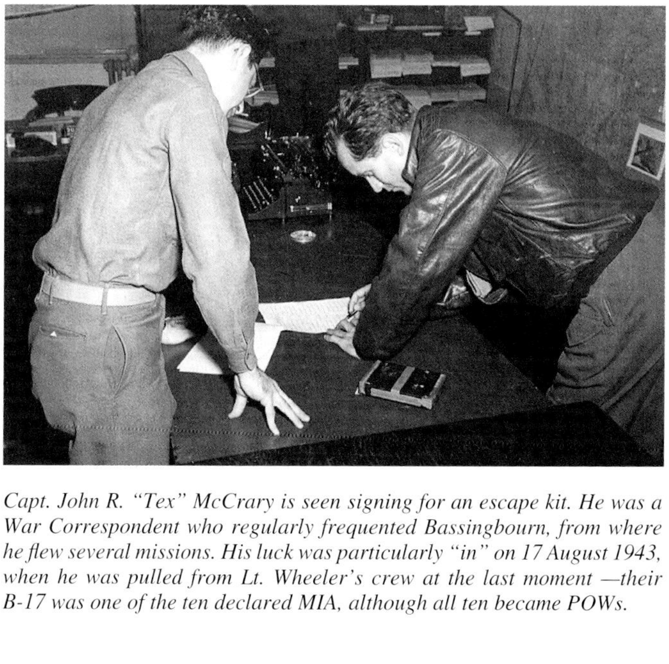

Capt. John R. "Tex" McCrary is seen signing for an escape kit. He was a War Correspondent who regularly frequented Bassingbourn, from where he flew several missions. His luck was particularly "in" on 17 August 1943, when he was pulled from Lt. Wheeler's crew at the last moment —their B-17 was one of the ten declared MIA, although all ten became POWs.

A group of 381BG mechanics have just installed a replacement fuel tank in this B-17's starboard wing. Tasks such as these required skill and involved back-breaking effort, as well as being time consuming.

An anonymous bombardier manning the twin machine gun mounted in the center of the nose Plexiglas has little protection from fighter gunfire although what is probably an armored plate is located below the weapon. B-17s with this fitting were sometimes positioned on the flanks of a squadron or group. The presence of the ammunition box ensures the absence of a bombsight.

The erect frame of Col. Joseph J. Nazzaro festooned in flight gear is seen walking along the passage way to Ridgewell's Briefing room. The Colonel was the group's first CO between its inception at Pyote in January 1943 and the following December, when he was assigned to 8AF HQ.

The crew headed by Lt. Jess D. Rogers is snapped in a relaxed fashion, but Fate was to be cruelly unkind to eight among their number, including the pilot. On 31 August 1943, they were killed during an attempted crash landing on return from a mission to Romilly-sur-Seine airfield. The B-17 concerned was 42-29973/LG: Q Patty Gremlin Jnr.

This mobile Control Caravan with its distinctive checkered exterior is part of the 381BG ground equipment establishment. The adapted B-17 nose cone with the bombardier's optical flat detached was a feature on many such vehicles in USAAF service.

This is a view of the main road leading down from the southern hangar at Ridgewell. The contrast with Bassingbourn's permanent pattern buildings is notable. Here the structures are a temporary mix of Nissen huts and Maycrete buildings, within which personnel comfort was decidedly marginal, compared to the generally steam-heated facilities enjoyed by 91BG personnel!

The duties of the ground crews, apart from operating outdoors in the often unpredictable East Anglian climate, were also often onerous albeit vital in execution. Here several airmen are inserting cartridges in proper order within a belt as the man in the foreground winds the completed unit into its ammunition box, ensuring the belt is properly aligned and therefore less likely to jam while its attendant weapon is firing.

Chapter Six

Full Combat Bomb Wing Status (September 1943)

September 1943 was to witness the final upgrading of the three sub-forces within the VIIIBC. To date, the prefix "Provisional" had applied to each CBW within the 1st, 2nd, and 4th Bomb Wings. From 13 September, that word would be dropped and the reduced term CBW, denoting "Combat Bomb Wing," would apply until VE-Day. In addition, the three-figure numerals would give way to single or double numbers. In the case of the 101PCBW, the title was now fully amended to the 1st CBW.

The pace of operations for the Command would proceed similarly to that of August with just eleven missions, of which all but two were confined to sources outside the Third Reich. One of the latter runs would furthermore result in a debacle both in terms of success over the target and the scale of casualties. The first, on the 2nd, saw a "recall" signal issued to the full 1BW force as it was heading out to attack airfields in NW France, the reason being that regular annoyance of visual bombing, heavy cloud; electronic aids for carrying out visually-restricted bombing were soon to be made available to the Command, but in the meantime, the bombing of targets in Occupied Europe was forbidden in other than clear conditions.

The fourth anniversary of WWII's inception for Britain (3rd) had 168 crews briefed to attack an air depot at Romilly-sur-Seine, E of Paris, of which 140 struck either the Primary or two alternative airfield locations. The 101PCBW unloaded on the Primary and returned just one B-17 short, the unfortunate exception being an acolyte crew from the 381BG. However, among its ranks were two airmen who definitely did not fall into this category, since they were group "originals" seconded to fly with Lt. Benjamin Zum's team. T/Sgt. Edwin R. Myers (ROG) had served with Lt. Chapman in the 535BS, while Sgt. Charles F. Bang (BT) was another crew veteran with one more mission (11) than Eddie. It was a puzzle to their contemporaries why both were assigned to this crew, but orders are orders and had to be obeyed.

Ed Myers was later to recall that the pilots had difficulty in holding formation with 42-29789/VE: O **Big Time Operator** (normally Lt. Lord's 532BS B-17), but the fact that it was only Zum's second mission probably explained this. The aircraft gained the target, but soon after was taken down by fighter assault, with ten parachutes reported blossoming out prior to the bomber piling in near Provins, west of the target. Only nine airmen survived, with the fate of Lt. Luther C. Clark (B) the sad exception. Not all ended up in enemy hands, however.

Fiasco over Stuttgart

The city of Stuttgart, located in SW Germany, was an important industrial location, among whose industries was ball bearing production. The distance to be flown equalled that of Schweinfurt and promised a hot and prolonged reception from the *Jagdwaffe*, but the decision was taken on the 5th to dispatch both B-17 Bomb Wings in this direction on the morrow. The overall Air Commander was Gen. Travis, and the manner in which he conducted the mission arguably added to the projected mission's overall failure. In addition, the loss scale was destined to approach that of 17 August.

Over 330 crews were briefed and set out, with the 101PCBW contributing sixty in total. The relatively sound weather conditions during the initial mission stage began to deteriorate into an ever-increasing level of cloud cover. By the time the leading formations were on final approach to the target, the visibility was so reduced that Travis ordered a 360 degree maneuver hoping to achieve a second and successful bomb run, a hope that was not fulfilled. The alternative of seeking Targets of Opportunity was signalled and adhered to with very varied results.

The formations had naturally come under *Jagdwaffe* scrutiny for most of the inward leg, but an equal if more insidious threat to many of the crews' survival chances lay in the matter of fuel reserves, or rather, the distinct possibility of not retaining enough to regain English shores. The original B-17s had not been equipped with the extra outer wing tanks that were introduced on recent production blocks. The extended distance to the target, coupled with the double bomb run, now witnessed the older examples of the Boeing design being left with dangerously reduced fuel capacity as they headed back northwards.

Varied Fortunes

The sixteen-strong Bassingbourn force was reduced by one even before reaching the Primary. Lt. Elwood Arp had charge of 42-5763/LL: F **Bomb-Boogie**, but the group was barely 15 minutes into northern France when fighter strikes damaged the B-17 sufficiently for it to fall behind. Thus isolated, it was finished off, but not before all on board bailed out near Lille, with the aircraft coming down at Mons-en-Pevele, south of the city. Arp and three of the other nine evaded capture, although Lt. Nathan Weltmann (N) was subsequently captured three months later.

This aircraft loss was the first of four borne by Bassingbourn, although the tally was largely not matched by crew loss. As it was, a total of six further B-17s from the Wing would be "written off" in one way or another, but none would actually go down over enemy soil. On the other hand, a critical fuel situation seems to have been the common thread that linked all six incidents.

The Channel waters off the Sussex coastline beckoned for two of the remaining 91BG bombers. The first of these was 41-24497/LG: F, following the complete draining of all the fuel tanks soon after departing the French coast. The ASR Service was promptly on hand to pick up all ten airmen, who emerged from the incident shaken but free of serious injury. The same good fortune only partially came the way of the other "ditched" machine, 42-29540 /OR: P flown by Lt. Lloyd S. Schaper. The mercifully flat calm water permitted the same chance of the airframe withstanding the impact. However, the time interval between striking the water and the B-17 disappearing beneath the surface was less than 60 seconds. Not only was this an insufficient period for the dinghy hatches to be accessed, but of the ten crewmembers forced to rely on their Mae Wests to support them, only seven were still alive when an ASR Launch reached the site.

A pair of Polebrook crews followed suit, beginning with Capt. Richard E. Hathaway's 42-29684/RQ: T, which he put down when still well out into the Channel. The other "ditching" involved **Foul Ball** (42-3150/ DS:Q), piloted by Lt. Clarence F. Norris, who like the two 91BG bombers got as far as the coast off Beachy Head, so close in fact that the ten crewmembers swam ashore.

One of the final pair of B-17s ending up as "salvage" was **Connecticut Yankee** (42-2970/DF: C), a nine-month veteran assigned to the 91BG with nearly forty missions to her credit. Lt. William G. Pegram managed to get as far as the coastline before all four engines were starved of fuel. The resultant crash landing was severe enough for "Category E" action to be taken on the 10th, but all ten crewmembers survived for the time being; sadly, in the case of Pegram and two of his colleagues, all were KIA exactly three weeks later. The B-17's Polebrook companion in misfortune was 42-29841/RQ: V **Shady Lady**, which was deposited on its belly further east at New Romney by Lt. Robert M. Spika, again with no fatalities or serious injury to the crew.

Luck

Lt. Paul Gleichauf's 533BS crew bemoaned their luck after their regular B-17 was declared unserviceable and they were reassigned to what T/Sgt. John Comer (Eng.) said was regarded throughout the 381BG as the unit's "jinx ship," namely 42-5846/MS: X **Tinkertoy**. At this stage of its combat career, only one crewmember flying his first mission had actually been killed on board, but presumably the reputation was strengthened by numbers of wounded personnel, although group records tend to discount this factor. The B-17 was one of the older models bereft of "Tokyo tanks" with which to have a comfortable fuel reserve while undertaking such a deep penetration mission, a factor that only increased the sense of incipient doom pervading the atmosphere.

An even greater problem was the limited oxygen tank capacity that was threatening to reach exhaustion level well before the group cleared enemy soil and reduced altitude to a natural breathing level; the fact that a slow leak in part of the system was discovered when already inside enemy territory, but with the bulk of the mission still ahead, really added to the tension. Comer had brought along several portable oxygen bottles, but these had to be utilized with great care, given their maximum capacity of 30 minutes. Finally, three "hung up" bombs impeded retaining formation position without applying increased power and therefore fuel consumption.

A gradual altitude loss by the force gave them renewed hope of a safe return, but the fuel tanks were running dry as the English coast loomed up. A frantic search for an airfield finally ended over a small RAF fighter airfield, where they landed to receive good hospitality; having had enough fuel pumped into the tanks, they then resumed their flight back to Ridgewell the same evening. Lt. Carl Shutting (N) would by then have been in a marginally more personable state as far as the crew were concerned.

During the mission, Lt. John Purus (B), being afflicted by a severe attack of recurring diarrhoea, had utilized an ammunition box as a toilet and, having evacuated his body, left the box on the compartment floor. Soon after, Sgt. Nicholas Abramo (BT), who had been ordered into the nose compartment after his turret's oxygen system failed, was becoming steadily more anoxic as he was moving forward; he managed to stumble down into the nose, where he collided with the navigator, knocking him down and into the box, whose still-fluid mass cascaded all over Lt. Shutting's flight gear!

Capt. Dexter Lishon was piloting his regular mount 42-5845/GD: A **Whaletail II**, a companion to **Tinkertoy** off the same Lockheed-Vega production line and one whose ultimate fate would parallel that of the Gleichauf-crewed machine the following 20 December. His crew's experience was similar in struggling back against rapidly dwindling fuel reserves. Both B-17s had been lightened as much as possible once the Channel coast was approaching, but it was fortunate that an airfield near Ashford came on hand just in time.

Comment

The Stuttgart mission had cost VIIIBC exactly 75% of its aircraft compared to Schweinfurt. As it was, there was an important difference in relating each statistic to the other. The vast bulk of airmen lost on 17 August had gone down over Europe, with most in turn being permanently lost for further operations thanks to their capture. Contrast this with the fact that although 45 B-17s had been lost today, a far greater percentage of the crews concerned had returned safely and were available to resume combat operations immediately, or as soon as they recovered from injury. In effect, aircraft were immeasurably more expendable in operational terms compared to their human operators.

A total of twelve 1BW B-17s would "ditch" on 6 September. Several accounts of this mission aspect—including one previously used by the author—have asserted that all but either two or four of the 120 airmen concerned survived their involuntary immersion, the exceptions having been already killed in action. The Schaper incident tends to contradict this, however. A further anomaly lies in the fact that one B-17 from the 4BW also successfully "ditched" along with its ten-man crew, so increasing the overall human tally to 130.

On into September

The Allied military authorities had decided upon a "decoy" operation over NE France code-named Operation *Starkey* launched during August. The intention was to deceive the enemy into thinking that an allied invasion via the beaches of the Pas de Calais coastal strip was imminent, hence the concentration of the VIIIBC bombers over the entire region during the month and into September. On the 7th, all three "Heavy" BWs attacked a series of airfields, while the B-26s of the 3BW went after coastal defenses at Boulogne. Lille/Nord was targeted by the 351BG and 381BG alone, with all 37 crews returning safely.

The mini-surge in operations did not last, however, because it was six days later before what was now the 1st Bomb Division again dispatched a five-group force as part of an overall Command strike against French targets. A Target of Opportunity comprising Romilly-sur-Seine's air depot was struck with no MIA casualties. Yet, as 42-29825/DS: Z **Meat Ball** was on her final approach to Polebrook, Maj. James T. Stewart found his path barred by another B-17 that forced him to "abort" the landing run. As he circled and straightened out for a second approach, his B-17 suffered progressive engine failure while yet another encroaching B-17 forced a second "abort." Now on half power, Stewart still managed a circuit and line-up before the remaining duo of engines quit. The resultant crash at Lutton split the fuselage in half, but fortunately no crewmember was lost in the incident; **Meat Ball**'s fate in contrast was confirmed as "salvage."

Operational Adaptation

The mission on the 15th witnessed the external carriage of 1,000-lb bombs mounted on racks adjacent to the fuselage on selected aircraft. This experiment was short-lived and was only put into practice for relatively short-range missions. This adaptation unconsciously highlighted a main weakness of the B-17 (and to a certain extent the B-24), namely the inability to carry a really sizeable bomb load internally. In the case of the Boeing design, its internal capacity never exceeded 6,000lbs, in addition to which neither bomber could internally mount an individual missile exceeding 2,000lbs.

The destruction created by the USAAF's heavy bombers during the Offensive reached a notable level of success, but arguably could have been even more effective had the B-17 and B-24 been able to match their RAF contemporaries' greater carrying capacity—especially the Lancaster's 18,000lbs. Conversely, it is regrettable that RAF Bomber Command could not practically venture upon regular daylight operations until after D-Day, when escort provision was sound, if not quite comprehensive. Its bombers' poor defensive armament and relative lack of tight formation flying techniques would have seen its crews suffer equally if not more so had they attempted to emulate the American experiment of "self defense"—an experiment that was currently upon its last legs at this stage of the aerial battle.

The nineteen-strong 351BG formation discovered during the return from Romilly that the extra drag of their externally-mounted bombs had pushed fuel limits to such a dangerously low level that seven crews diverted into airfields, rather than risk running dry before reaching Polebrook. Lt. Jack Omohundro, flying 42-3140/RQ: P **Patty Ann II**, maintained course for home, but was still well short when he lost first one inboard, then the other inboard engine.

A three-searchlight pattern indicated an airfield was desperately headed for, but his first landing approach was met by a barrage of red warning flares. He managed to hold off and complete a circle before heading in again, only to see the reason for the flares in the form of a Stirling bomber at the runway end ready to take off. He somehow diverted to one side and put his charge down on the grass—only to discover on stopping that the bomber was surrounded by several rows of gliders at what was RAF Wratting Common! The initially hostile reaction encountered by the crew became more relaxed when the emergency action was explained.

All but the 92BG went out on the 16th to strike port facilities at Nantes and an adjacent airfield at Chateau Bougon. The latter target was reportedly attacked by the 91BG and 381BG, with the former listed unit returning one short of the nineteen dispatched. It is not clear whether 42-3079/OR: X was culled from the formation by flak or fighters, but its demise was only matched by S/ Sgt. Thomas S. Bone (WG) following a complete bail out of Lt. Eldon J. Smith's crew; the gunner was unfortunate enough to drift down into the Loire estuary, whose waters claimed his life.

The relative short-range mission on the 16th had still cost the 1BD eleven out of 137 crews gaining "credit," proving the fact that there were no guaranteed "milk runs," as easy missions in the ETO were labelled by the crews. Seven days later, a return mission to Nantes by the 1st and 40th CBWs ironically cast up this ever-hoped-for situation, because no MIA casualties were sustained. On the other hand, the loss of two B-17s (one during Assembly and one on return), that claimed the lives of thirteen of the twenty airmen involved, highlighted the constant danger faced by all when in the vicinity of or on board what was an unpredictably volatile airframe.

No Celluloid "Hero"

One of the two Nantes-bound missions for the 351BG resulted in the culmination of a combat tour for an internationally famous individual. The man concerned was not only a "supernumerary" in terms of combat availability, but was moreover, at 43 years old, way above the upper limits for even indulging in this function. He was Clark Gable who, in contrast to some of his Hollywood contemporaries destined to portray the American fighting man—particularly one postwar "celluloid hero"—had put his life on the line, as opposed to sitting in safety on film sets.

He had enlisted in August 1942 as a Private, and his commission awarded the following October had to be earned, instead of being automatically promulgated. Gen. Arnold then utilized his skills in promoting a gunnery instruction film intended for recruitment purposes. After passing Gunnery School he was assigned to the Polebrook group, with whom he arrived in England. Even then his activities could have been confined to non-operational flights, but this was not to be the case.

Gable settled in at the airfield, where he shared the relatively Spartan living conditions with the personnel, thereby eschewing offers to live elsewhere in greatly-improved accommodation as befitted his film star status. Although he visited several airfields during the course of his spell within the VIIIBC, the first of his five missions occurred on 4 May, but not from Polebrook; instead, he travelled to nearby Molesworth, where he joined the then Capt. (Later L/Col.) Bill Calhoun, who led the 303BG to Antwerp.

The other four missions were flown out of Polebrook and entailed runs to Courtrai (Belgium), Gelsenkirchen in the Ruehr, Heroya (Norway), and finally Nantes (France). There were detractors who later asserted that Gable had only participated in "milk run" missions, but this was a simplistic view, since 1) there was no guarantee of safety at any time on any mission and 2) the Gelsenkirchen and Heroya runs were at least well within the ambit of sustained fighter assault.

On 5 November 1943, the actor and his small team of cameramen were flown back to the States, where they then commenced to edit the thousands of feet of film into a viable 50-minute documentary, "Combat America." That was duly released during 1944. Although not as compelling in its emotional appeal as its "Memphis Belle" contemporary, the offering still provided a sound impression of the pros and cons of combat operations and the part the gunners were playing in carrying the Offensive to an ultimately successful conclusion.

After WWII, Gable said that his greatest fear in flying his missions that earned him the Air Medal was of being captured alive and exploited by Dr. Goebbels's fiendishly efficient Propaganda Ministry. His superb portrayal of the "hard-nosed" Gen. Casey Dennis in the 1949 film "Command Decision," which dealt with the strategic aspect of 8AF operations, was probably enhanced by his wartime presence with the "Mighty 8th."

Month End Attrition

Two back-to-back missions on 26/27 September closed off the Command's account, but the intended run to a target in Paris for the 1CBW alone was abandoned over the French coast thanks to adverse weather. Then what transpired as only the second run into Germany during the month was launched next morning, with the port of Emden selected for assault.

The *Jagdwaffe* was up and ready, with its pilots snapping away at the 300-strong force as the bombers closed in on the Primary. A pass at the 91BG shortly before "bombs away" ended with fire catching hold on one inboard engine and the central fuselage on 42-30624/LG: Q. Lt. Cleo C. Struble ordered the bomb load to be jettisoned as the B-17 began to sag out of the air and presumably called for a bail out; half the crew were dangling under their parachutes when the bomber exploded, depositing its remains east of the city, with all four officers and one Enlisted man either being killed instantly or later succumbing to injury.

Three weeks prior to this mission, Lt. Bill Pegram's crew had emerged unscathed from a crash landing on the Channel coast after running out of fuel. Now, the pilot and seven of his regular crew were heading in towards the target on board 42-3111/ DF: AI **Local Girl**, a June transfer from the 95BG. The bomb run was over and a turn for home under way when the B-17's progress was brutally halted by fighter strikes that disabled No. 2 engine and set the fuel tanks ablaze.

As the B-17 approached Delfzyl, Holland, located on the western fringe of the Ems estuary and in direct line with Emden, the wing spar was finally weakened so badly that it gave way, causing the bomber to be cast into a spin. Only Pegram and Sgt. Belvin J. Peters were seemingly still on board, and both went down with the aircraft. Sadly, four of the other eight landed in the coastal waters: only Lt. Norman C. Eatinger (B) emerged alive, and his survival was only thanks to a Dutchman who came to his rescue as he struggled in his heavy flight gear.

Rebels Revenge (42-29750/OR: L) enjoyed an even shorter spell on combat operations than **Local Girl**, having only arrived on 24 August. Her title alluded to taking up where her predecessor and long-term veteran B-17 **Delta Rebel No. 2** had closed out its combat career over Gelsenkirchen on 12 August. Whereas the latter aircraft had put in over 30 missions before her demise, OR: L was only making her fourth combat run, which would be her last.

Lt. John M. Perritt was at the controls, but could do little or nothing to prevent the bomber being mortally battered by the fighters around the same time as **Local Girl**. The B-17 staggered onward for several minutes before heading inexorably down towards the North Sea near Langeoog, within the eastern section of the Frisian Island chain. Perritt and seven of the crew did not survive the incident and only the bodies of the pilot and Lt. Frank O. Rolfe (N) were ever recovered.

Comment

The VIII BC's constant and often thwarted battle with the elements during its first full year of operations had finally persuaded the USAAF authorities that the laudable, but now clearly fallible principle of Precision Bombardment would have to be at least partially sacrificed. RAF Bomber Command had been operating the first of several electronic devices utilizing centimetric wave signals with which to at least identify a briefed target city. Code-named *H2S*, it was a basic plan-position indicator that provided an outline of the geographic features passing beneath the bomber, with land and water displaying as light/dark screen images to the navigator.

The Emden mission had witnessed the Americans' initial use of the equipment, which had been given the revised title *H2X*. In the months ahead, a version produced by Massachusetts Institute of Technology (MIT) in the States would feature a refined 3-cm wavelength set. Even so, the bald truth was that the use of *H2X*, along with the future utilization of other electronic devices, inevitably promised that what was deemed "Bombing through Overcast" strikes would result in a general degradation in bombing accuracy compared to visual target sighting.

Three Pathfinder Force (PFF) B-17s from the recently-formed specialist 482BG were on hand over Emden, of which only the one assigned to the 1BD still had an operable *H2X* set during the bomb run; the following two CBWs dropped on the smoke markers released by the Lead CBW. As it was, post-mission reconnaissance photos suggested no more than a general concentration within the target zone. On the other hand, regular pressure was henceforth maintained upon German morale, if not always upon the nation's industrial resources, in a manner almost totally lacking to date.

Evader

The last reference to St. Edwin R. Myers (ROG) in this chapter goes back to 3 September, when he was among the members of Lt. Zum's crew that jumped over France following their B-17's loss. Ed and his fellow veteran member of Lt. Chapman's "original" team had been seconded to this crew, who were only on their second mission. However, Sgt. Bang's misfortune in quickly ending up a POW was destined not to be matched by his equally combat-tested colleague.

Ed floated down into a field in which a group of farmers were working. As he disengaged his harness, he noted the men gesticulating to him in a manner that suggested he conceal himself within a nearby copse. He took up the suggestion, little knowing that this would be the start of 48 hours without further assistance; in that time, he sighted individuals who largely just passed by, the exception being two young children who came up to him. In his frustration at being left on his own he almost made a fatal mistake.

He attempted to communicate with the children, but despite having no knowledge of French or German nevertheless illogically uttered one word—"Ja"—whereupon his "visitors" fled! It was as well that this detail did not filter back to the local Resistance; had it done so, he almost certainly would have been summarily disposed of on the grounds that he was a Nazi or *Milice* (French fascist) infiltrator, notwithstanding that he had been seen landing by parachute.

He had bailed out on Friday, and by Sunday decided he would have to take the initiative in seeking assistance that so far had not materialized. It was now that fortune really rode on his shoulders. Despite all the strictures concerning what not to do in these parlous circumstances that had been outlined in Security lectures back in the States, Ed proceeded to break several cardinal rules during this stage of his evasion attempt.

For a start, he walked down the middle of a small town's main street as the populace was emerging from the church, but fortunately they were not accompanied by any Germans and proceeded to ignore the odd-looking stranger. An even graver error that could have cost him his life was committed later in the day. For a civilian to venture anywhere near a railroad track, let alone commence to walk its length, was an act that invited a bullet from any member of the German armed forces whom he might encounter. Rail systems were regarded as prime targets for sabotage and the *Wehrmacht* and SS personnel were naturally issued with "shoot to kill" orders. Thankfully, the spell of track-side wandering passed uneventfully.

His sense of isolation momentarily persisted after he clambered back onto a road and trudged onward. Initial salvation occurred shortly after, when he was overtaken by a cyclist who stopped and indicated he would help—presumably Ed's wearing of his coveralls made him stand out and had persuaded the Frenchman that here was an Allied airman; this was despite the possibility that he might equally have been encountering an enemy infiltrator. For Ed, the meeting was the start of a protracted journey extending between two and three weeks that would see him being transferred between several locations, one of which was in Paris.

A German patrol "swoop" upon one house saw him whisked outside to a hollow in the ground that he occupied for several very uncomfortable but detection-free hours. In contrast, his spell in Paris was uneventful, and while there he witnessed the bombing of what would have been the Renault and Hispano-Suiza plants by the now-retitled 3BD. By now, his clothing was more suited to that of a Gallic gentleman. His profession as stated on false ID papers was that of an umbrella maker, but he was described as being both deaf and dumb—an eccentric factor, but necessary in view of his total lack of aural and verbal understanding of the national language.

From Paris he was moved to the NW coast of France and the port of Brest, one of the most heavily fortified locations in that region. The upstairs room in which he was housed was part of a bakery that already contained forty evaders, mainly airmen. The apparently suicidal act of collecting a group of such individuals within the heart of a German military concentration such as Brest could be justified by the "Scarlet Pimpernel" principle—namely, placing oneself where your adversary would least expect you to be.

The intention to literally "ship" the evaders out of the country was the reason for the action and the house was positioned in close relation to the dock side where the vessels were moored. The men's minds were on more basic matters when, on a Sunday morning, the critical transfer from the premises to the selected fishing boat commenced. In groups of two or three, the evaders were led to the quayside and down into the hold, but for whatever reason, only seventeen had made the move when the operation was cancelled.

The prospects for a speedy release from the naturally unhygienic conditions inside the boat were totally dashed. This was due to the fact that a prolonged spell of bad weather ensured the boats remained at their moorings for nearly a week. It was the following Saturday before conditions moderated to a degree where the fleet stood out to sea again. As ever, the Germans had ordered the two-man crew to open the hatches for internal check. However, what was a cursory examination by the soldiers was surely due to the malodorous state of the surroundings—not only from the smell of the previous fish content, but also the unwashed bodies of the evaders!

A course for the fishing grounds was maintained in the company of the fleet until the coastline had disappeared, whereupon a northerly course was assumed. For whatever reason, there were no guards around on the surrounding vessels, nor were there any German ships acting as "escort"; otherwise, the attempt could not have succeeded. This was a surprising but very welcome lapse on the enemy's part. It was almost certain that severe restrictions would have been applied in retrospect, especially since the operation was surely precipitate, but rather well thought out beforehand. The safe return of the seventeen valuable Allied servicemen must have been set against the inevitable penalties the occupying authorities would bring to bear upon the Breton fishermen whose loyalty to the Allied cause was unquestioned during WWII.

It was during Monday that a very welcome landfall in SW England was made. After disembarkation and initial official handling, Ed was transferred to London, where a two-week spell of intensive debriefing occurred. During that time, his identity was fully confirmed by his regular pilot, Lt. Frank Chapman. The Continental odyssey had been undertaken over an amazingly brief period, added to which Ed was the group's first evader, a fact with which he could regale his family in the future. (Tragically, his only child was destined to die in Vietnam while serving as a paratrooper—truly a shocking contrast with his father's good fortune in WWII.)

Equipment "Beefs"

Lt. Gleichauf's 533BS crew, as with any other team, regularly discussed the quality—good or otherwise—of their flight equipment, which was expected to provide the best guarantee of both security and comfort. During one "bull" session in their hut, several specific items were mulled over regarding their limitations. One among the number opined as to why the USAAF parachute harness' main attachment was a horizontally-aligned fitting, compared to the RAF circular disc into which the main straps were fastened and which could be released by simply turning the front and banging the center. The danger with the USAAF fitting was particularly highlighted if landing in water; if the canopy remained billowing out, the effect was for the harness to tighten up under the strain and make its release highly problematical, with all that it inferred for being dragged along and under the surface. ("Harry Houdini could not get out in one of our chutes—he'd drown like a rat in a fish net" was one expressed opinion.)

Another complaint related to the current oxygen mask, which often induced a blocking of the nasal passages to the extent that speech soon became almost incoherent—none too good when a gunner might be calling in fighter attacks or even in less stressful circumstances; as one man stated: "Hell, when the pilot tells me to speak clearly, how can I with a mouthful of snot!" A third "beef" concerned the heated suits, or rather, the illogical application of heat to the extremities; for example, the electric gloves on hand provided more than adequate comfort for the palm of the hand, from where the heat emanated, but nothing for the fingers! The situation regarding the harness attachments would never change, but it was likely that appropriate measures could improve the oxygen mask's and heated suit's levels of efficiency.

There appears to be some form of altercation going on between Lt. John A. Moeller and Sgt. Bob S. Elroy, but it seems friendly, to judge by the smile on the officer's face. The latter is grasping the receiver offered to him, but his colleague has occupation of the telephone box. Both men are 91BG members, but the location is unconfirmed.

The crews led by Lts. Schaper and Cox "ditched" their B-17s off the 6 September Stuttgart mission. These five among the sixteen crewmembers surviving the experience in all are posed at a B-17's waist window and most are wearing the standard polo neck sweaters issued by the ASR Service of the RAF or Royal Navy.

Lightning Strikes (42-3073/LL: A) bears artwork depicting Hitler scurrying from his 'stricken" outhouse. This B-17F survived ten months in combat until 21 February 1944, when it was fatally crippled by fighters and crashed, albeit without any of Lt. Bill Gibbons's POW-bound crew still on board.

Bacta-th"-Sac was the wistful title applied to this 535BS B-17G, an early Douglas airframe lacking "cheek" gun windows. Assigned on 16 September, she finally took Lt. Warren C. Hess's crew on their fifth mission (1 December 1943), but suffered mechanical failure that culminated in the crew bailing out into captivity.

An officer looks on as a group of armorers attend to the mounting of a 1,000-lb bomb under the inner wing of a 91BG bomber. The air resistance created by such externally-mounted weapons was a prime factor in ensuring that the missions flown with this configuration would be limited in range.

Lightning Strikes is seen with three other group bombers, all four exuding a steady banner of condensed air from the engines' heat effect. These high-altitude 'screens' could become a dangerous hindrance to good visibility that in turn was vital when flying tight formation.

This Handley-Page Mk. V 'special" Halifax from an RAF Bomber Command squadron is under repair at Bassingbourn. The No. 3 engine propeller is dangling from the heavy rescue truck's crane with the cowling sections and spinner lying under the wing. The photo was taken during September 1943.

Annie Freeze, although assigned to the 381BG on 15 June 1943, never flew operationally with the group; the B-17F was then transferred to the Combat Crew Replacement Center (CCRC) at Bovingdon. The full view of her "bellied in" at Langford lodge in Northern Ireland shows her with armament fitted. The close-up of the nose area picks out the artwork that provides her name.

Hells Belle (42-5060/LL:G) describes a very low pass over a 324BS contemporary. The bomber transferred from the 385BG in mid-September and lasted until 1 December, when it was declared MIA, along with Lt. Guinn and crew; all ten survived as POWs.

This is Rebels Revenge, which arrived at Bassingbourn via the 96BG on 24 August 1943, but whose operational career was short-lived compared to her predecessor, Delta Rebel No. 2. On 27 September, during what was only her fourth mission, she was downed, along with all but two on Lt. John Perrett's crew.

This practice flight was flown just 48 hours prior to Rebels Revenge's demise. She is seen on the left with 42-29591/LL: Z The Shamrock Special in the left background. The single B-17 in the center is Skoal (42-5795/LL: B); received from the 95BG in September, it was successfully "ditched" by Lt. Bob Tibbetts on 26 November, with all ten airmen rescued.

Capt. Hawkins (center) was the 381BG Photo Section officer who survived a bail out from a group bomber in July 1944 during the Assembly stage of a mission. Capt. George Porter (right) served in group HQ (S2 Section) and his massive postwar photo album provided many of the pictures in this book.

The 91BG was no exception in creating a good-sized band, with five trumpeters and four saxophonists forming the main core.

This briefing session picture is dated 19 September 1943, but no mission was flown on this date. However, the names of Lt. Sample at lower middle of the formation chart alongside the white screen and Capt. Winters as Sample's No.2 in his element confirms the location as Ridgewell. Sample was KIA on 8 October, while Winters became 532BS CO and completed his combat tour.

Sgt Percy Casey (second from left) is one of a clutch of ground crew NCOs serving with the 534BS at Ridgewell; to his right are Sgts Stayzak, Chase and Bakke. The officers are Lts. Delchamp (left) and Stull; the latter would die on 31 March 1944 when 42-29751/ GD: N Miss Abortion/Stuff crashed on landing approach off a local flight.

Clark Gable is seen with Col. Robert W. Burns (351BG Deputy CO) on return from the actor's fifth and final mission to Nantes, France. The strain of high-altitude combat is clearly etched on the 43-year-old 'supernumerary's' face, who would return to the states in November to complete the gunnery training documentary Combat America.

Chapter Seven
"Black October"

Into the Abyss

The fortunes of the VIIIBC bomber crews over the past several months had traced a steady and sometimes volatile downward path, with the first venture to Bremen on 17 April firing a warning shot across the bows of the "self defending bomber" theorists. Subsequent events during either specific missions (Schweinfurt and Stuttgart) or the sustained operational spell in late July known as *Blitz Week*—with its toll of 88 MIA crews—had left little or no margin for belief in the continued efficacy of the aforementioned theory as October 1943 was entered.

As it was, the current lack of truly long-range escorts with which to ward off the *Jagdwaffe's* savage thrusts on the B-17s and B-24s promised a hard time for the combat crews should the authorities push for more deep penetration missions into the heart of the Third Reich—and this basically desperate scenario was about to erupt and reach its savage conclusion before the month had reached its mid-point.

The overall strength of the three BDs in terms of bombers and crews was by now fully recovered from the depredations borne upon their ranks during late July and mid-August, culminating with the double-strike upon Schweinfurt and Regensburg. Up at VIIIBC HQ, the fixation with "bottleneck" target categories was still apparently concentrated on ball bearings, however. Added to this specific aim was the natural desire to get in effective strikes against several more general target categories—such as aircraft and U-boat production centers, as outlined in the Combined Bombing Policy—before the looming autumn and winter weather patterns allied to ever-shorter daylight hours inhibited operations over central Europe.

The 1BW and 4BW crews rousted out of their beds on 2 October found themselves briefed for the latest assault upon the port of Emden. The late September run to that thoroughly blasted target had cost the Command seven crews, but this time round just two out of 339 going over the Primary remained behind. Two days later, the Primary was deeper into Germany, in the form of Frankfurt, which was allotted the 1BW. The bulk of the 155 crews got through to the target area, with the 1CBW reportedly releasing upon the city center. As occurred five days before, overcast conditions ensured that *H2X* assistance was again called upon for bombing.

Lt. Lloyd S. Schaper had already survived an English Channel "ditching" off the costly Stuttgart mission exactly four weeks previous, in which three of his crew drowned. Now his luck was about to run out, at least in terms of completing his combat tour. OR: U (42-3274) was damaged during the inward leg, but managed to gain the bomb line before fading out of sight. The subsequent crash at Limburg, NW of the target, ended with all but one of the crew surviving.

Maj. Blaylock had led nineteen B-17s up from Polebrook, but only seventeen regained the airfield circuit. One of the casualties featured the latest "ball boys" B-17 in 42-5807/DS: T **Minor Ball**, which completed the bomb run; however, a flak barrage over the Schelde estuary, near the port of Flushing, brought the bomber down, along with all on Lt. Daniel D. Nauman's team, with only two of the ten bodies being subsequently washing up. Already down east of Frankfurt was 42-30785/YB: R, in which Lt. Theo W. Reed (P) and two of his colleagues had forfeited their lives.

Torrid Combat Debut

Flying his second mission on 4 October was a 91BG bombardier who would not only rise to Group status in his "trade," but would experience a series of personal incidents all garnered within a space of six days. On the above-mentioned date, he received a frantic call from the ROG, who said both waist gunners were stretched out and motionless. Lt. Charles Hudson immediately vacated his compartment and, on the way back, collected three walk-around oxygen bottles.

On reaching one gunner, who was clearly unconscious and bore a blue, frost-fringed face, he wiped his face clean before applying the mask; he then turned to the other gunner, who was actually propped up against the fuselage, and carried out the same action. Finally, having established that both waist guns were inoperable, Hudson replaced the waist hatches. The bomb run was imminent, so he returned to operate the Norden bombsight; once completed, he returned to administer whatever treatment was still deemed necessary, but this amounted to restoring one gunner's circulation, the other having by then almost regained his senses.

Four days later, following the ball turret door giving way and partially casting its occupant out into the freezing airflow, the incident was noted on an adjacent B-17 and reported to the crew. Hudson again grabbed walk-around oxygen bottles. On reaching the turret, he discovered that the gunner had somehow pulled himself back inside and rotated the turret to clamber out, but had severely cut his head. Worse still was the frozen blood over his face that was choking him to death. Hudson immediately thrust fingers into the airman's mouth to permit air to enter his lungs, after which he attended to his wounds. Unknown to Hudson was a third looming incident that would have a direct effect upon himself.

Black Week's Advent

On 8 October, the twenty-one crews assembled in Ridgewell's Briefing room were informed: "Men, your target is Bremen," an operational fact that was accepted with the same degree of latent fatality as any other mission. Capt. Ed Manchester's 535BS veteran team was within a handful of runs before completing their combat tour; their copilot, Lt. Bob Weniger, had been detached to fly with Lt. Cormany's (535BS) Lead crew as tail gunner and Observer for the formation. In contrast, Lt. Ed Miller's team was embarking on its first mission, but had also surrendered Lt. Carlton Long (CP) to fly with another veteran crew led by Capt. Dexter Lishon (534BS); Long's place was taken by Lt. Joe Doerfler, whose apparent temporary assignment would ironically become permanent thanks to what was soon to transpire.

The 101PCBW had bled fully to the tune of sixteen B-17s over the city back in April, and there was no reason to believe that access to this Primary would prove to be less costly, as events were to establish. The 1CBW, along with the 41CBW, had been assigned the city's shipyards, probably at Vegesack, on the western fringe, and progress as far as the target approach was surprisingly little disturbed by fighter opposition. A mix of scattered cloud and smoke pot emissions was encountered that seemingly resulted in several formations seeking Targets of Opportunity.

The 381BG was the Wing's Low group, the same location when it had bled freely over Schweinfurt, and its luck was again out; but this time it would be flak that would deal the initial blow. A storm of bursts enveloped the formation, and within bare seconds the tight-knit Elements were being scattered across the sky. The Lead B-17 (42-30864/MS: R) had one engine disabled and suffered an engine fire in a second. Lt. Cormany and Maj. Bill Ingenhutt (535BS CO) eased the stricken B-17 into a dive that evolved as a vain attempt to extinguish the flames.

Having failed in this desperate endeavor, they called for a bail out, to which all on board appeared to have responded before the bomber erupted into the ground near Bassum, roughly 25 miles due south of the briefed Primary. Lt. Bob Black (B) usually flew with Capt. Manchester, but today he was fated to be the sole fatality from Cormany's crew; his body remained missing for many years before being discovered and interred at Margraten, Holland.

A second B-17 in immediate serious difficulty was Manchester's **Tarfu** (42-29941 /MS: R). The initials followed on from his first and now salvaged steed **TS** and stood for "things are really fouled up," although a more crude variation was inserted for the penultimate word, the term referring to the airmen's view of higher command miscalculations. The No. 4 engine had been knocked out by flak, and as Lt. Keith D. Moore (B) recalled: "We then lost No. 3 to a fighter attack, after which we had drifted out of formation. I heard our pilot mumble to Capt. Eldon D. Dukes if he would take over and assumed he had been hit. Sgt. Matthew Berk (WG) was wounded and Sgt. Wade McCook (TG) asked permission to get him back into the rear fuselage for First Aid [a request that was granted and would be the salvation for both within minutes]. The fighter attacks were now persistent, and soon I heard another barely audible statement, this time from Jukes, that seemed to suggest we bail out. The latest fighter pass really messed up the bomber, with most of the nose Plexiglas shot out and 'Smitty' [Lt. Marvin D. Smith (N)] and me showered with fragments. The aircraft canted to one side and we landed up over the now-open nose hatch. We were without our masks and liable to pass out, so

I kicked him out; just as I prepared to go I noted Capt. Elton D. Jukes (CP) motioning me out."

Moore momentarily passed out, but recovered to note metal fragments and one large section of a B-17 hurtling down, but with no sight of **Tarfu**. The remnants probably belonged to his aircraft, which did come apart, with both pilots being among the six crewmembers killed; the wreckage tumbled down at Talge, several miles W. of Diepholz. The vagaries inherent in combat operations worked very favorably for Berk and McCook; the rear fuselage section, having separated under the violent plunging gyrations after the B-17 went out of control, drooped into an angular or vertical descending motion, akin to a leaf from a sycamore tree. The two airmen huddled inside managed to retain their position as well as survive the final contact with the ground following a descent from approximately 20,000ft.

A similar but even more violent disintegration occurred to Lt. Arthur M. Sample's mount, 42-29854/VE: B **Old Flak Shack**. The "original" B-17 managed to hold course as the turn for home was made south of the target. Then, according to reports, a rocket struck home, blowing the aircraft apart. Sample, Capt. Norman C. Mackay (532BS Lead Navigator), and six other airmen forfeited their lives, but Lt. Edward A. Cytarzymski (N) and Sgt. James R. Forbes (WG) arguably enjoyed even better luck than Manchester's two gunners in being blasted clear and able to pull their ripcords.

Piling on the Pressure

The carnage among the Ridgewell contingent continued apace with the loss of another 535BS bomber (42-3123/MS: Z **Ron Chee** flown by Lt. Leslie A. Kemp, Jr.). The crash site at Fladderlohhausen was very close to where **Tarfu** had descended, but this time round none of the ten crewmembers emerged alive. The fifth loss during the immediate withdrawal stage involved the 533BS' 42-30765/VP: R **Nip and Tuck**, which was on fire after both inboard engines were ignited. This time round all but three on Lt. James W. Hartje's crew made a safe exit, with the B-17 crashing at an undisclosed location south of Bremen.

Another 532BS aircraft to be downed was in the hands of Lt. Jack S. Pry; 42-30009/VE: S **Feather Merchant** was flying as Lead in the squadron's second Element. Flak severed the oil lines in No. 2 engine during the bomb run, and by the time the bombers were turning for home, the propeller was violently "windmilling"; the result was that the aircraft steadily lost pace with the others, but appears to have caught up momentarily with Lt. Sample's equally isolated machine before it blew up. By then, the constant fighter attacks had riddled the airframe, excising a sizeable portion of the port outer wing. It was then that Pry issued the bail out command, but only eight members reached the ground alive, Sgts. Alfred A. Johnson (LWG) and Irwin W. Smith (BT) being the unlucky exceptions. This bomber also came down in the area round Diepholz.

The circumstances in which the final group loss was incurred are somewhat obscure. One crewmember recalled that Capt. Dexter Lishon's 42-30722/GD: G **Bobby T** was actually a "spare" for which there was still no slot when Assembly was complete. The bomber still headed eastward and presumably hung onto the formation. It was last seen west of Bremen, by which time it had attracted fighter attention, whose single pass ignited both inboard engines; the subsequent bail out was successfully managed by the ten airmen, but the exact crash site was undisclosed.

Individual Horror

The 381BG's second martyrdom was complete in terms of aircraft loss, but the most shocking incident involved a pilot on a returning B-17. Lt. Hal Minerich was piloting the 381BG's 42-5846/MS: X **Tinkertoy**, which had barely made it back across the English Channel on 6 September. A fighter landed several strikes up front, including two 20mm shells that slammed into and penetrated the metal forming the left side cockpit frame. Lt. Minerich could have known nothing, as they impacted inside and tore off his head. The resultant blood spray covered the cockpit walls and floor, as well as badly obscuring forward visibility via the windshield.

Lt. Duncan A. Sellars (CP) was wounded, but still remained capable of flying the B-17, although the psychological effect of what had happened right beside him must have been dreadful and indeed, was certainly a factor in his remaining off combat status for a prolonged period. T/Sgt. Earl F. Miller (Eng.) found it almost impossible to remain at his post due to the slippery nature of the turret plinth caused by frozen blood, but in any case was now tasked with assisting Sellars. Meanwhile, the gruesome effort to remove the pilot's corpse from his seat was practically solved by Sgt. John Wood (BT); he utilized the parachute pack clips on his harness, attaching these to Minerich's harness and dragging the latter out of his seat, which was then taken over by Miller—a clearly unpleasant but necessary measure.

The nose Plexiglas had been almost totally blown off, but the compartment's occupants were still alive. The bomber held course for home, although the blood-streaked windshield was a major hindrance. Again, Sgt. Wood came up with a practical if basic partial solution; he urinated on a cloth and attempted to wipe the Plexiglas. The application of the hot body fluid in sub-zero temperatures would have probably been counter-effective, but the desperate overall situation merited action of any kind, however beneficial. The battered bomber came through its ordeal and was brought back by the Copilot and Engineer to Ridgewell. Lt. Sellars's act was later deemed worthy of America's second-highest military decoration (Distinguished Service Cross), one of only two to go to a 381BG combat crewmember.

Only one other 1CBW crew was culled today, becoming the latest 91BG casualty, as a flak and fighter combination was the reason for its demise. The crew concerned was led by Lt. John J. Karp and the B-17 was the non-titled 42-2952-/OR: S, a March transfer from Molesworth. Three of the gunners were killed during the action, but the remaining seven got out and down in the vicinity of Diepholz, a town that was now the epicenter for a spate of 1CBW crashes, with this example going down at Neustadt-Wagenfeld. In the event, any sense of relief among the Bassingbourn crews regarding their easy "treatment" over Bremen would be brutally expunged within 24 hours, while the other two Wing units would also increase the loss factor to the tune of thirteen overall.

Extended Gamble

The Cyclone engines were barely cooled down and superficial damage corrected on the aircraft concerned before the next Field Order came down the line. To date, the VIIIBC had flown but a handful of deep penetration missions that involved a round trip run from East Anglia. The plan on 9 October seemed particularly fraught with danger, in that all three Divisions would follow a single route, with the 1BD heading for Anklam and Gydnia and the 3BD assaulting Marienburg, while the 2BD took on facilities at Danzig. In addition, all four Primaries were located up the Baltic coast and, furthermore, were upwards of three hundred miles inside the Third Reich. "Pinetree"'s assumption that the *Jagdwaffe's* units would be slow to react to this geographic variation in target selection was surely regarded as a flawed gamble in the eyes of the combat crews.

Lucky, Lucky, Lucky!

Lt. Paul Gleichauf's crew had shared the "near thing" aspect of **Tinkertoy**'s run to Stuttgart when they attained English shores shortly, prior to total fuel starvation. Now, even greater fortune came the team's way, as the pilots attempted to lift their heavily-laden B-17G—one of the first chin-turreted bombers to be assigned to the 381BG—off the runway.

Sgt. John Comer (Eng.) later recounted:

"I knew that with such an extended time over enemy soil we could easily run out of ammunition, so I arranged with Sgt. Chamberlain [a 533BS armorer who regularly obliged Comer whenever he raised the issue] for extra rounds that increased our total capacity to over 11,000. The extra cases were carefully stacked by me in the radio room. Our progress down the runway was extremely labored and we barely scraped off the runway.

"We wallowed bare feet above the ground before commencing an inexorable descent that almost certainly would end in a fatal impact. Gleichauf's call to Lt. John Kels (CP) for a swift lowering of the gear resulted in the aircraft being literally 'bounced' into the air, followed by an equally swift retraction as we shot upwards; sufficient airspeed was by then on hand and the B-17 headed upward, leaving all ten airmen to bless their luck."

The cause of the incident was not due alone to the extra ammunition loaded in anticipation of a protracted air battle—it was the gunner's error in moving the excess back to the waist and tail gun positions, along with the tail gunner taking up his post instead of remaining in the radio room that exacerbated the situation to the point of near disaster. John later surmised: "Lucky, Lucky, Lucky!" as well as expressing his immediate desire to choke the tail gunner to death for his crass stupidity that was a definite factor in creating the potential disaster for bomber and crew.

So Far, So Good

Fifty-four 1CBW bombers were mustered for the mission to form part of an armada nearly 400 strong. The radar "signatures" would have appeared on the enemy screens long before even the North Sea was traversed, but the hopes of the mission planners for a relatively free run from fighter attention seemed to be justified even as the Danish landscape was reached. Sadly, the immunity from aerial attack ended at this point; the initial encounters were sporadic in nature, but proved all too real for the individual crews feeling their lethal sting.

The first of five Polebrook losses was incurred at this stage and involved **Cue Ball** (42-30790/DS: Q). Fighter gunfire set the port wing on fire, leaving Capt. Harry B. Morse, Jr., with little option but to bail out the eleven-man crew, who drifted down to face the uncertain existence of the "Kriegy." This was to prove the sole group loss on the inward route.

The natural routing of the stream out over the Baltic Sea before cutting SE to the IP at Neubrandenburg, in the case of the Anklam-bound portion, brought with it the heightened danger of death from drowning or exposure for crews brought down. This was to be the fate of all but four crewmembers out of the four 1CBW teams whose bombers ended up in its waters.

The first of two Bassingbourn crews so affected was led by Lt. Charles B. Pinning in 42-29711/LG: V, none of whom came through their aircraft's descent into the sea off a Danish island. The second such loss probably occurred around the same time and involved the 323BS' 42-30772/OR: V, which was another victim of the fighters; this time round two of Lt. Thomas H. Walsh's (MIA) crew ended up being plucked from the sea by the enemy in undisclosed circumstances.

The air battle steadily intensified, and the fact that the bombers were destined to spend at least four hours within effective fighter range brought with it the distinct risk of ammunition running short or even out for the gunners. This was a constant worry for John Comer, as he later recalled. Luck was to be on the side of most of the crew both today and in the future in a manner that would desert three teams during this mission. The most fortunate in terms of human loss was Lt. James I. Loftin's charge. His B-17 was another group "original" (42-29958/GD: J **Battlin' Bombsprayer**) whose operational career was brutally closed off by fighter strikes that brought it down at Schonberg, in Holstein Province, a terminal fate shared by just two crewmembers out of ten.

The *Jagdwaffe's* intervention against the attacking force was in retrospect concentrated against the Anklam-bound duo of CBWs, judging by the final MIA figure of 28, since nearly two-thirds came from their formations. In the case of the

1CBW, the punishment extended on either leg, with what was probably the final loss within the target area affecting the 91BG in this instance. As the IP was at hand, Lt. Alexander W. Stewart's 42-29778/LG: M had its No. 3 engine fired up by cannon shells and when last observed, was straggling with fire spreading from at least one other engine. Whereas the pilot was the sole officer fatality, only T/Sgt. Leo R. Severson (Eng.) survived from among the six Enlisted men.

Over 90% of the original force of 115 crews unloaded on the target, but at least one had the frustration of being unable to do so. This was Lt. James D. Judy's team flying in 42-5178/LG: L **The Old Standby**, a nine-month group veteran. The Lieutenant had brought his bomber back from Schweinfurt in total isolation with just two crewmembers still on board, but ill fortune struck even earlier today. The first fighter pass on the 91BG killed one gunner and disabled the bomb door operating gear, ensuring that the load could not be released. The target was traversed and a course for home commenced. Then further strikes were borne that wounded another gunner, but still left the B-17 basically intact. Fortune was still favoring the surviving crew, but only for the ensuing hour or so.

The ever-frigid Baltic and North Sea waters became the final resting place for three more crews: two from the 351BG and one from the 381BG. In the former instance, 80% of Lt. Joseph H. Turley's crew, including himself, were fated to be recovered for burial or become names on Madingley's "Wall of the Missing" after 42-29868/YB: K **Flap Raiser** was taken out by fighters off the Danish coast. (A group history asserts the crash occurred off Denmark's eastern fringe, but either way the result was terminal.)

Ridgewell's second casualty involved 42-3180/VP: Y **Forget Me Not II**, a title that was reportedly abandoned after one more similarly-titled B-17 went MIA. The circumstances of its exact fate would remain unknown, since none on Lt. Herbert Carqueville's crew came through the experience; in this case all ten names exist on Madingley's "Wall of the Missing."

More Attrition

Tondaleyo (42-29740/OR: P) was on just her fifth mission at Bassingbourn, having been a September reassignment from the 95BG. Lt. Morris M. Gutta and crew had charge and were part of the homebound formation as it overflew the region around Flensburg. It was then that strikes landed on the airframe sent the B-17 out and downward to crash near Leck, along with half of the ten men concerned. The assaults were displaying little sign of even slackening, and two Polebrook crews were downed around this same time period. Lt. Howard G. Maser's 42-29603/DS: R **Spit Ball** also came down SW of Flensburg at Vollstedt, having previously suffered an engine fire and structural damage to one wing; nine of the ten on board survived to become POWs.

F/O William H. Warring had experienced similar problems with his bomb doors to that of Lt. Judy until after the bomb run was completed, but then managed jettison action. The end for 42-3152 / YB: A **Sleepy Lagoon** finally came over Schleswig Province, near the town of Kappeln, but fatalities were again confined to one airman. This was the culmination of a chain of misfortune affecting aircraft and its crew that had included a fire during the outward leg; then, on reaching the target, the bomb doors were jammed and only released sufficiently for the load to be jettisoned on the way back.

The North Sea's outline was beckoning to the hard-pressed force when the first out of the final trio of 1CBW losses occurred. Lt. Judy's B-17 was still on hand, but now a fresh bout of fighter-inflicted punishment was swiftly added to by a flak burst that induced a diving turn. The motion was corrected, but the now isolated bomber was strafed and set ablaze, leaving no practical option for the pilot but to press the bail out bell; the last sight the parachuting airmen had of their mount was of the flames consuming the entire fuselage thanks to the load of retained incendiaries having been ignited. One of the small group of German islands in the North Sea level with the German/Danish border was to prove the last resting place for Lt. Lloyd A. Christman's 42-30867/TU: N after it became yet another *Jagdwaffe* victim, whose gunfire killed two gunners but left the other eight able to jump clear into enemy hands.

Maj. Landon C. Hendricks (533BS CO) was squadron Lead in 42-30012/VP: K, according to T/Sgt. Comer. The bomber had not shown any sign of difficulty even as the enemy coastline formed by the Frisian Island chain was being bypassed. It was then he was seen to lower the landing gear, which was the signal for the deputy Lead B-17 to take over before VP: K fell behind. With the fighters still pecking at the formations, there was little chance of the crew attaining friendly shores; although debriefing reports indicated he had been seen to "ditch" his charge, the tragic outcome was ten more names for Madingley's "Wall of the Missing." The Major was a particularly close acquaintance of Comer's pilot, Lt. Gleichauf, and John was to indicate in his superbly-pitched book *Combat Crew* that he could sense the pain in the Lieutenant's voice as he reacted to Hendricks's act of virtual sacrifice by saying that the latter had done so in order not to hinder the group's progress for home.

Hudson's Luck

The protracted battle for survival that had failed in the case of Lt. Judy's B-17 was similarly faced by Lt. Hilary "Bud" Evers and crew manning 42-3073/LL: A **Lightning Strikes**. The loss of one engine on the way over saw the damage added to by a flak burst during the bomb run that wrecked the hydraulic system and meant that the bomb bay doors could not be closed mechanically.

The drag thus induced on the B-17's airframe, coupled with the reduction in power, temporarily left the aircraft straggling and the fighters duly closed in. Lts. Hudson and Bruce Moore (N) were frantically adding to the defensive firepower when the nose Plexiglas was penetrated by fragments, one of which broke the bombardier's left wrist as it knocked him down. He refused Moore's offer of First Aid, tucked the arm into his life preserver, and returned to his gun. Though he suffered further wounds to both of his arms, he continued to man his weapon.

It was a miracle that the bomber, unlike Lt. Judy's B-17, resisted the enemy's malign efforts to effect its destruction. Once out over the North Sea, the shot up bomber eased out of formation and all surplus equipment was ejected; in addition, Evers went back to the bomb bay and hand-cranked the bomb bay doors shut as the aircraft slipped steadily downwards. By the time the English coast appeared, the wave tops were dangerously close, apart from which a second engine that had long been faltering finally failed.

Thankfully, enough height was retained to clear the coastline and make a safe landing on an unnamed airfield. Lt. Hudson was subsequently awarded the DSC for his persistent gallantry and went on to resume operations. He would also win through to VE-Day while still at Bassingbourn. Lt. Evers's crew would complete their combat tour in early 1944.

Comment

Several postwar accounts of the 9 October mission have asserted that the Anklam sub-force's routing was expected to act as a diversion for the other elements of the bomber stream, whose targets were located further to the east. If so, then the effect was only partially successful, since ten of the overall 28 MIA casualties were borne by the latter formations. This mission also cast up a more specific limitation affecting the earlier B-17F airframes still on hand that lacked the "Tokyo tanks" introduced on recent production line aircraft.

The distance flown this day required the installation of supplementary fuel tanks in the bomb bays of the older bombers, whose standard capacity of 1,700 U.S. gallons compared badly with the 2,780 U.S. gallon capacity enjoyed by the newer production airframes. The "knock-on" effect of this necessary measure was to reduce the already limited bomb load capacity by at least 50%; the sparse incendiary content on Lt. Judy's B-17 was a prime example of this restriction.

The rubberized bomb bay tanks with their 400-gallon capacity were bulky by nature, and once emptied the crews faced two choices: first (naturally favored by the authorities on economic grounds) was for the tank interior to be flooded with CO_2 in order to cut down, or better still, cut out the risk of a fuel vapor explosion should the exterior be punctured by gunfire or shell fragments. The problem with this action was that there was no guarantee that an element of vapor content was not still remaining, with all that this implied for a possible disaster.

The second course of action generally favored by the airmen was to jettison the tank. However, the bulk of the equipment, coupled with the various metal excrescences existing within the bomb bay frame, sometimes hindered a clean release. On such occasions where a "hang up" occurred, the tank's exposure below the lower fuselage line inevitably prevented full closure of the bomb bay doors; the resultant drag was a hindrance to forward motion that could result in the B-17 in question falling behind and being hung out to dry as fodder for the *Jagdwaffe*.

The Grim Reaper Eases off

The first two missions out of the quartet due to make up the second week of October had cost the VIIIBC fifty-eight crews confirmed MIA, along with a number of shot up bombers and dead or wounded crewmembers brought back to their airfields. Even worse lay ahead within the ensuing five days, albeit not for the 1CBW. Its three groups had been stripped of twenty-one crews during the Bremen and Anklam missions, so the prospect of escaping a similar degree of punishment on pending deep penetration runs seemed poor.

The third daily run into the German hinterland was of far shorter duration than Anklam, and equally important was virtually within the (admittedly extreme) range of P-47 cover. The city of Muenster lies within 50 miles of the Dutch/German border and was targeted by over 300 B-17s. As it was, the *Jagdwaffe* reserved the vast bulk of its effort for the inaptly-titled 13CBW from the 3BD, culling twenty-nine crews, including all but two from the 100BG's formation.

The sole loss from the 1BD's sub-force of 139 bombers came from Bassingbourn in the form of Lt. Earl Verrill's 42-37737/LL: K, a B-17G received just fifteen days previous. The bomber attained the Primary, but a flak strike on No. 2 engine set up an uncontrollable "windmilling" condition of the propeller. The drag effect inevitably led to the other group aircraft forging ahead and the pilots' attempt to retain position within the CBW, at least by diving into a lower group, came to naught, especially with the loss of a second engine.

The call to jump over Dutch soil near Appeldoorn was acted on by most of the crew, but Lt. John A. Lilley (B) pulled his ripcord immediately on exiting; the tragic result was the canopy snagged the stabilizer. Even more ironic was the fact that he would have survived had he remained on board, instead of which he was dragged to his death, either through suffocation by the airflow while the B-17 remained aloft or by impacting with the ground following Verrill's decision to successfully "belly in" his charge. The cruel vagaries of combat flying had again been demonstrated here.

Self Defense's Death Throes

The Command had now lost eighty-eight crews in direct combat—the same figure as for *Blitz Week*—and had achieved this tally in half the time taken for that Campaign to be completed. Ninety-six hours later, that sorry figure was to be raised to 148 in the course of the second Schweinfurt mission, destined to be recorded as *Black Thursday*. The 1BD absorbed fully 75% of the final figure, which was largely incurred during the outward leg to the Primary; the Lead 40CBW surrendered no less than twenty-nine B-17s, including a near-total wipe out of the 305BG, paralleling that of the 100BG at Muenster.

Lt. Bernard Yorba and crew were relative newcomers to the 381BG and were reportedly down to fly as a "spare," ready to fill in should an assigned crew "abort." In an ironic twist, their B-17 was

42-29803/GD: P, which had transferred from the 305BG. The group Assembly was in progress when another 534BS bomber pulled out and reversed course for Ridgewell, whereupon its slot was taken up by Yorba; the fate of both aircraft and crew was thus unknowingly sealed. Even more ironic was that its predecessor had "aborted" in questionable circumstances. The copilot had sharply disagreed with his fellow pilot as to the justification for the action, but felt compelled to hold back during the subsequent harsh grilling of both pilots by Col. Nazarro.

This specific crew, with one exception, successfully completed their combat tour in early 1944, but the copilot in effect was regarded by the other members as the *de facto* aircraft commander, even though he never actually attained that status officially. After WWII, the pilot died at a relatively early age and alcohol was suspected as playing a large part in sealing his untimely fate. The invidious pressures of combat operations affected individuals in greatly varying manners, and this may well have played a part in what ultimately transpired in postwar years for this hapless soul.

The group reached the Primary with a still-intact formation that provided very sharp contrast to the horrendous events two months previous en route to the same target. As it was, Yorba's B-17 would prove to be the sole Ridgewell loss after being shot up by fighters and finally exploding close to the target, the fragments distributing themselves at Hausen. All four officers and two Enlisted men apparently bailed out before their aircraft's violent end.

The same loss pattern affected the other two 1CBW groups. A frighteningly exotic weapon not long introduced into regular *Jagdwaffe* service was the 21cm spin-stabilized rocket; the accuracy factor of this particularly explosive variation was questionable to say the least, but any strike on an airframe was likely to prove fatal. The 351BG was in the target area when 42-6096/DS: W **Onda Ball** was a reported victim, although the immediate effect was to set the bomber on fire; it subsequently blew up, but not before being safely abandoned by all on Lt. Oliver W. Crismon's crew.

The final 1CBW casualty was Bassingbourn's 42-5714/OR: N, which suffered an engine loss and serious depletion of the oxygen system over Schweinfurt, but still retained its slot until approaching French territory; then a fighter pass resulted in both inboard engines going "out." Sgt. Claud J. Smith (TG) was already dead at his post and one airman bailed out prior to Lt. Robert M. Stone directing his charge downward for what proved to be a successful crash landing near Metz that all eight survived. The parachutist, named Lt. Arthur G. Foster (N), also managed to evade capture, but only regained Allied lines nearly one year later.

Compulsory Retrenchment—a Misnomer?

The shocking loss scale borne by the VIIIBC over the previous seven days probably induced USAAF authorities to draw in their operational claws in a manner similar to that occurring largely during September. However, the extended build up to full bomber and crew strength following Schweinfurt/Regensburg was not repeated in October. A mere six days after *Black Thursday*, nearly 300 crews were sent out to bomb Dueren, west of Köln. However, the intended first use of the RAF blind marking equipment *Oboe* by the 1BD failed on technical grounds, although one group did release over the target area. This mission proved to be the final one for the month.

Oboe was normally a very accurate method of target marking, having first been used with deadly effect on 5/6 March 1943 by RAF bombers over the normally smoke-shrouded Ruehr, with Essen and its massive Krupps armament complex the specific target. Two radio signal stations were utilized: the first tracked the marker aircraft along a north/south arc, with the second sending out an intersecting beam signal directed onto the target. When the two signals were finally received by the aircraft, the marker flares were released. The one limitation on the equipment's use was that the signals' receipt and re-radiation from the marker aircraft were limited by the earth's curvature; in practice, this meant that *Oboe* was currently only effective as far as the general area of the Ruehr as an example, although following D-Day, the dispatch of mobile stations onto the Continent permitted its use ever-deeper into enemy territory.

A regularly touted overview of the Daylight Offensive at this point in its conduct avers that the Schweinfurt mission sounded the death knell for missions directed at targets well within Germany until such time as effective escort cover could be provided. It cannot be denied that the pace of operations was to prove somewhat staccato during the ensuing two to three months, but then the same pattern had been largely experienced during the Campaign's conduct to date. Bremen, Köln, Muenster, Frankfurt, and similar key industrial targets could hardly be counted as "short" in terms of range, while the escort provision was only really beginning to be realized in terms of effectiveness—and that on a partial scale—as 1944 was entered. The ever-shortening daylight hours were no real inhibitor to winter operations, since the bombers were often dispatched as daylight was just seeping in and could attain their targets and return prior to dusk conditions returning. The prime difference compared to the previous winter was that the advent of electronic aids now ensured missions could be launched and generally executed regardless of weather conditions over the Continent.

Evasion against high Odds

For any USAAF airman landing in enemy-Occupied Europe, the odds against evading capture varied from impossible to good; the latter situation usually arose when the individual or individuals concerned gained access to various Resistance cells. The equivalent degree of good fortune for anyone coming down inside Germany would appear to be nil, and indeed, capture and incarceration in a *Stalag* was almost always the result. Even then, there were (admittedly) very rare incidents where the seemingly vast odds against successful evasion were bucked, as the following account reveals for two Ridgewell aviators.

Capt. Bob Nelson (532BS Operations Officer) and S/Sgt. Raymond Genz (TG) were on board Lt. Painter's B-17 on the way to Schweinfurt when their protracted bid for freedom commenced; in Bob's words:

"The fighter attacks commenced soon after our escorts departed and we were rapidly in deep trouble, with both port engines of **King Malfunction II** displaying flames. Lt. Painter dived the bomber in a desperate but vain bid to extinguish the fires, during which time the RPM governor control failed. Once back in level flight a bail out was initiated, and after all but the pilot and I were confirmed as exiting I was told to jump; Painter said he would follow, but never did. [He actually went in with the aircraft, which impacted south of Bad Muenstereifel.]

"Genz and I floated down within close sight of each other and reached the ground unscathed, although I observed someone firing at us. We both maneuvered our parachutes away from the clearing that was our original intended target and landed in a small wood; fortunately, the branches caught the canopies, but I was lucky not to suffer injury when I badly misjudged the height before releasing the harness and smacked hard into the ground.

"We were standing together, discussing what to do, when Sgt. Kellogg (BT) came limping onto the scene. One of his legs had incurred a bad injury and he said for us to go on without him. After providing basic First Aid to his wound, we all scrambled up a nearby slope; Kellogg was covered with leaves and there we stayed overnight, hoping [successfully, as it transpired] that we would avoid detection by any search party. By the following morning, Kellogg's condition had become critical enough for him to take up the option of surrender; we carried him down and concealed him by a roadside, from where he could give himself up to the first available soldier or civilian.

"Having done so, we began our attempt to get back to England. The countryside possessed numerous small villages, so it was absolutely essential that we skirted our way around them; our flight gear, in particular Genz's electric blue suit, stood out like sore thumbs. We had adopted a southwesterly course with the help of our escape compasses. A major problem was the lack of proper food, and the blackberries, sugar beets, and green apples we managed to forage were no more than an adequate substitute. Our liquid needs were met by drinking water from available streams. [It was fortunate that the duo were making their evasion effort at this stage of the year; the lack in winter of much of what was currently available to them would surely have fatally impinged upon their physical endurance.]

"We had been on the move for a number of days when we were enticed towards a village by the distinct smell of cooking, where we spotted a couple of pies sitting on the window of what I took to be a restaurant. Ray's natural instinct as we walked by was to reach for one, but I stopped him, fearing the discovery of its loss might result in pursuit and apprehension. Ray's physical condition was already frail, since he was suffering from pyorrhea, so although he did not challenge my action, next morning, after we emerged from a barn that provided overnight rest, he declared that he was all for giving up. I made a pact with him—if we managed to walk through a small town up ahead without being apprehended he would desist from ever raising the subject again. Fortune was still on our side, because nobody took any attention of us, even though our first attempt to clear the scene found us going down a dead end and we had to hastily walk back into the center before finding a proper exit.

"Our first contact with 'friendly' soil was in Luxembourg, where we had our first contact with the Resistance Movement. We had initially convinced the individuals concerned we were airmen by displaying our dog tags, but this in itself was no guarantee of our authenticity, since we could be German collaborators deliberately sent to infiltrate our Allies' ranks. A more detailed interrogation of our American background probably won the day for us and we were then given food and drink, which we promptly threw up thanks to our shrunken stomachs being unable to cope.

"Civilian clothes and false ID papers were given to us and we began the next stage of our bid, initially still on foot before reaching a town where we entrained for Paris; a short stay there was followed by a move to Clermont, in Vichy France. While there, it was suggested we head for Switzerland, but we held out for Spain and were duly taken by train, first to Toulouse, then to Lourdes. A potential crisis arose during the latter stage to Lourdes, when we saw our guide arguing with either the conductor or a gendarme and appearing to call on their loyalty to allow us to progress—an argument that she very thankfully won.

"The initial bid to get us out over the Pyrenees was thwarted by deep snow, but after a few days we were on our way as part of a fifteen-strong party of evaders with our guides. The journey lasted anything up to a week and was physically rugged; our Spanish guide's insistence on saying 'Mañana, Mañana!" when we asked how close we were to freedom was very frustrating, but finally we crossed over into Andorra and then Barcelona, where we reached final sanctuary in the British Embassy.

"The final stage of our journey was to Gibraltar via Madrid; we were sworn in as Canadians for the journey, since the U.S. had no diplomatic relations with Spain. Our stay in Gibraltar was very pleasant, but after several days we were alerted to stand by for an aircraft heading back for Britain. And so it was on 22 October we landed back, barely two months after facing the distinct likelihood of a berth in a *Stalag* for an indefinite time period!" (Bob informed the author of his and Ray's visit to Ridgewell on 4 November. Among the tips provided to the personnel was Bob's suggestion of maintaining oral hygiene by cleaning one's teeth using a twig or similar pointed object; he was convinced that his companion's pyorrhea condition had arisen due to this lapse, something avoided by Bob adopting the foregoing procedure.)

This is the Lead crew of Capt. Robert O. Fricks (second right, standing), with whom Darrell flew his later missions. On 11 January 1944, he took over for his 91BG contemporary, whose bombsight had been disabled, and accurately sighted on the FW production plant at Oschersleben to ensure a solid bombing pattern both for the 381BG and following groups. This action earned him a second DFC.

An Element of 534BS B-17Fs demonstrates the difficult-to-achieve ability of flying a tight formation. This was a necessary requirement in combat to ensure a sound defensive formation against attacking fighters, as well as providing the best opportunity for a tight bomb pattern.

Lt. (later Capt.) Darrell C. DeBoLt.was a group "original" bombardier assigned to Lt. Dexter Lishon's 534BS crew. After his crew was MIA on 8 October 1943, he became the squadron Lead Bombardier and completed his combat tour around March 1944.

Lt. Martin Downey, a 534BS copilot, demonstrates some aspect of the recently-flown mission to three of his colleagues. Martin was badly injured during one mission in November 1943, but recovered from the experience to resume operations and survive his combat tour.

The cost of combat. The truncated remains of a B-17 are seen here: the tail section at top left and a severed and flame-shrouded wing in the center above the inverted rump of the fuselage. Ten airmen are either already dead or fighting to escape the grip of centrifugal forces. The date is 8 October 1943, when Lt. Arthur Sample's 532BS bomber exploded in this manner, leaving just two survivors.

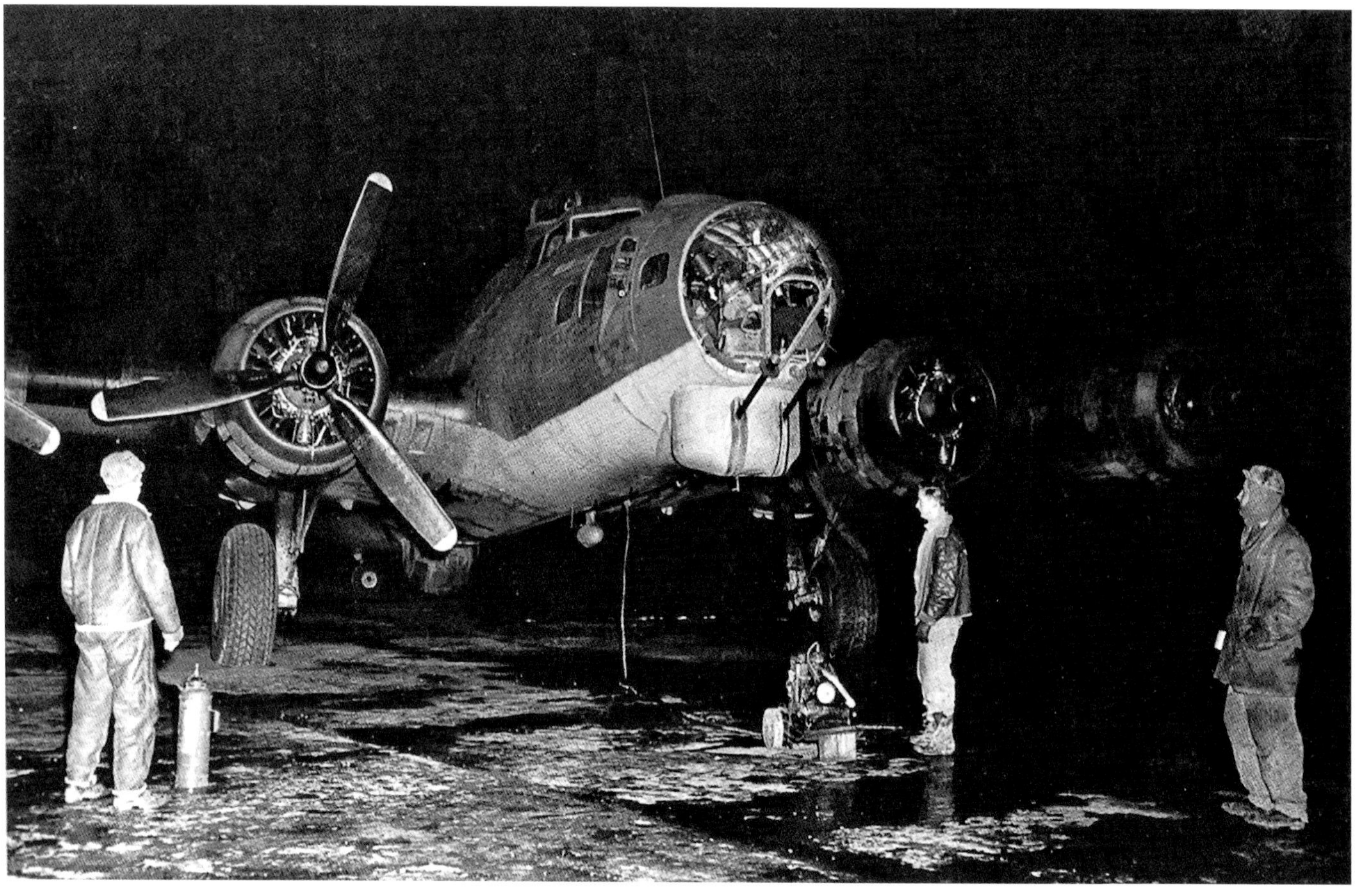

The Stygian atmosphere of an East Anglian airfield provides a dreary backcloth to this B-17G as the engines are being brought to life. Nos. 1 and 2 have already been started; No. 3 is ready to be activated as a mechanic on the left stands by with a fire extinguisher. The auxiliary power unit is plugged into the aircraft in order to save the internal battery system.

A 323BS B-17 displays the Dark Green blotching applied to many bombers up to mid-1943. Transferred from the 306BG in mid-September, its combat career with the 91BG was cut short during the Black Thursday run to Schweinfurt, when it was abandoned over France on the way back by Lt. Robert M. Slane and eight of the ten-man crew.

Lt. H. M. Jowett examines the damage to 42-29679/LL: A1/M Ramblin" Wreck on return from the 9 October Anklam mission. The B-17F was a transfer from the 95BG that completed 28 missions in all prior to transferring to AFSC on 5 April 1944.

This stripped-down B-17 bears a number of mission "bombs" on the nose, but is otherwise anonymous in terms of the group with which it served. It is functioning here as a transport for B/Gen. Williams (CG, 1BD) while he was visiting Bassingbourn. The tail of an RAF Short Stirling is seen in the background.

Joe Giambrone, Crew Chief for Memphis Belle, is snapped at a later stage of his time at Bassingbourn, when he has now advanced to the rank of M/Sgt. The B-17E behind is the former 97BG bomber that led the first ever VIIIBC mission (17 August 1942). After relegation from operations it became a "hack" aircraft with the 322BS (LG: X) during March 1943.

The Lucky Strike (42-29923/VE:K) sports fifteen mission marks on its nose. Assigned to the 381BG on 11 September 1943, she would put in another eleven missions before being finally "written off" in a crash landing at Cawston, in Norfolk, on return from Kiel (4 January 1944); Lt. Kraut (B) and Sgt. Rivera (BT) were killed from among Lt. Evans's team.

The often protracted distances between the ground crew billets and Mess halls and the aircraft dispersals was a physical chore in negotiation, even on a bicycle. At Ridgewell, the situation has been eased for this party of 534BS mechanics, with a flat-load trailer bearing the men being hitched to a Jeep.

This picture of an airman being removed from a 351BG bomber may well be a demonstration of the "corset" equipment surrounding the "casualty's'" body. Fitting of the equipment to an individual by the Medics enabled a smoother and faster transfer from aircraft to the waiting stretcher.

T/Sgt. Gilbert Staats (left) and S/Sgt. Ray Ater (Engineering Section) are engaged in conversation with several children while sitting inside a local church near their airfield at Ridgewell. Many of the USAAF airmen were not many years advanced in age compared to the older British children.

T/Sgt Dean Carrier a 535BS crew chief holds a ruler to the left windshield frame on 42-5846/MX: X Tinkertoy. The gaping hole in the frame was where a Fw190-delivered cannon shell penetrated before exploding and decapitating Lt. Hal Minerich (P). Lt. Thomas Sellars (CP) was faced with this horrendous evidence as he brought the B-17F back from Bremen on 8 October 1943. His endeavour was later rewarded with a Distinguished Service Cross.

The calm after the storm is encapsulated in this pacific scene at Bassingbourn on 15 October—the day after the Black Thursday debacle for VIIIBC over Schweinfurt. Lightning Strikes at left with 42-5729/ LL: E Piccadilly Commando/Buccaneer behind are non-Tokyo Tank B-17Fs, as confirmed by the auxiliary tanks lying under their port wings.

Chapter Eight

Winter Doldrums (November 1943/January 1944)

VIII BC Structural Changes

The establishment of groups within all three Divisions was increased during November 1943. In the case of the 1BD, this figure was raised from nine to ten with the arrival on the 3rd of the 401BG, which took up residence at Deenethorpe and was assigned to the newly-created 92CBW. However, the existence of three full CBWs within the Division created a temporary problem, in that each CBW structure merited three groups, which left no slot for the new unit. Gen. Eaker's senior staff had anticipated this situation and accordingly made the decision to transfer the 351BG from the 1CBW and link it up with the 401BG. Both airfields were geographically adjacent to each other, compared to the greater distance between Polebrook and either Bassingbourn or Ridgewell, so this may well have been an added factor in reaching the decision.

The reverse reduction from three to two groups within the 1CBW was short-lived, although it would be six months before the last group (398BG) would arrive to join the 1BD and effectively restore the situation to standard CBW requirement for three independently based and operating units. In the interim, a Composite sub-force shared between Bassingbourn and Ridgewell would replace the 351BG; this was an arrangement that reportedly did not sit well with the latter unit's combat personnel and may well have evinced a similar if muted reaction from their colleagues stationed further to the west.

November's final figure of eleven launched missions, of which most were completed, albeit with notable variations in force strength, also witnessed virtually all being directed against targets in Germany. The naval port of Wilhelmshaven was targeted on the 3rd by all three Divisions, and in the van of each were several PFF-equipped aircraft of the 482BG. Some or all bore the American variation of *H2S* code-named *H2X*; this was an adaptation created by the Massachusetts Institute of Technology (MIT) whose wavelength was refined from the original 10cm signal to one of 3cm. The vast majority of the 566 crews sent out duly released their loads through the undercast.

All but one of the twenty-four 91BG crews achieved their primary function, but only twenty-one were subsequently on hand over their airfield's circuit. **Bomb Boogie's Revenge** (42-30805/LL: H) fell into the same category as **Rebel's Revenge**: 1) from a point of view of being a replacement for an MIA veteran predecessor, and 2) for sharing the same fate within a short time of being assigned. Whereas **Bomb Boogie** had lasted almost six months before its demise, its successor was only completing its second mission today. The presence of P-47s, along with the first P-38 group within the VIIIFC (55FG), did not prevent the *Jagdwaffe* from tangling with the bomber formations. One wing was set on fire and a section became detached, undoubtedly throwing the B-17 out of control; Lt. Robert A. Pitts's (P) death was mirrored by a further six on his crew.

Two further crews were taken down, although both managed to drop their loads beforehand. **Vagabond Lady** (42-37742/LL: J) was another B-17G assigned in late September, but was not being flown by her regular crew; instead, Lt. Bill McAdams had charge of the bomber that had recently returned to combat status following major repairs off the 4 October run to Frankfurt. Fighter-inflicted damage culminated with the aircraft easing out of formation as the bombers skirted the eastern end of the Frisian Island chain; whether or not the B-17 was unsuccessfully "ditched" or went out of control would never be known, since nobody on board lived through the incident, nor were their bodies recovered.

The other casualty was another B-17G (42-39802/LL: D) that suffered an engine fire and did not even progress as far as its companion in distress. Instead, it descended into the North Sea close to Spiekerooge Island, its fate shared by seven airmen, including Lt. Kenneth B. Rutledge (P). The three survivors were hauled out of the water by personnel on two boats, but whether they had previously bailed out or managed to emerge following their B-17's "ditching" remains unclear.

"Happy Valley"

The Ruehr industrial complex in Western Germany was rightly feared by the Allied bomber crews for its concentrated flak defenses. The region possessed a plethora of heavy industrial targets and was accordingly a key factor in the Nazis' current ability to sustain the conflict, even if their ill-gotten empire showed signs of fraying at the geographical fringes in Russia and Italy. The VIIIBC had not made too many ventures into this smoke-shrouded manufacturing hinterland to date, but the latest thrust occurred on 5 November, with Gelsenkirchen, on the northern edge, selected as the target.

The advent of electronic aids for the Command's bombers was a timely measure, since the persistent haze created by the factory chimneys had hitherto been a hindrance to visual target sighting, even in daylight. The city's marshalling yards were the joint Primary for the 1BD and the 3BD and absorbed the loads of 323 of the 374 B-17s involved at a statistically acceptable cost of eight crews.

Lt. Donald K. Hopp was piloting the 381BG's 42-30852/MS: Y **Blowin' Bessie**, which attained the target, but suffered flak damage to both port engines before a fighter pass added to the crew's problems. The steadily straggling B-17 got as far as Holland's Diep, south of Rotterdam, above which it was abandoned by some or all personnel, the latter assertion being based on debriefing reports claiming "ten parachutes were seen." Even if true, the tragic fact was that only Hopp, Lt. Marshall E. Tyler (N), and T/Sgt. Alexander M. Girvan (Eng.) ended up alive. The estuarial waters of the region later surrendered the body of Lt. William J. Johnson (B), but his other six unfortunate colleagues remain MIA to this day.

By all rights, Lt. Hayden Brown should have also expired after attempting to bail out of Lt. William Butler's shot-up 532BS B-17. He lost consciousness at the nose hatch and the accidental deployment of his parachute, which wrapped its lines around the ball turret, also pulled one leg outside, ripping off his flying boot. Although the formation remained at its 28,000ft altitude for a prolonged period before descending to normal breathing heights, Brown not only survived the normally terminal effect of anoxia, but also suffered no material effect from frostbite, despite the calculated -40 degree temperature! Once again, Luck had played its part in this instance.

Fortune also favored Lt. Gleichauf's crew to a lesser degree at the mission's conclusion. They were manning 42-37719/VP: X **Hellcat**, one of the first B-17Gs to reach the 381BG. Flak had knocked out the hydraulic system, leaving the pilots with no mechanical means of braking, but chances were that the bomber's momentum could be partially reduced by directing it off the runway onto the grass when well down its length. To their horror, Lts. Gleichauf and Kels were confronted with the sight of personnel lining the runway fringes, waving and cheering them on.

The inevitable result was that the aircraft careened off the runway end and finally slammed into a ditch after crossing a narrow road. Two women sitting on a fence directly in the B-17's path managed to scramble clear, but Sgt. Comer's concern was directed towards the seemingly fatal outcome for a British soldier on a bicycle who was blithely traversing the bomber's headlong plunge and whom he was sure had failed to avoid contact with No. 4's propeller. After evacuating their seemingly "written off" charge, John was tapped on the shoulder—to find the soldier very much alive but mud-encrusted and now minus his bicycle that one of the main landing gear wheels had shattered. **Hellcat**'s condition was in fact repairable and she returned to operations, only to go MIA on 11 January with Lt. Nason's acolyte crew.

The next four missions involving the 1CBW up to the 16th passed off without any combat losses, although the single mission that involved just the Wing itself proved a relative failure when the *Oboe* PFF sets failed to pick up the signals from the two UK Stations and bomb loads were widely scattered. The crews then "enjoyed" a further nine days free of operations before being briefed on the 26th for the latest attack on the industrial content of Bremen. The full ten-unit strength of the 1BD was employed, with the 1CBW dispatching 58 crews, a total suggesting the deployment of three group formations for the first time. Nearly one-third from both groups did not bomb and a single 91BG crew returned minus their B-17.

Skoal (42-5795/LL: B) had arrived in September and was flying its seventh mission, this time in the hands of Lt. Robert Tibbets. The combination of *Jagdwaffe* fighters and the flak handed out a sharp rebuff to the bomber formations, with no less than twenty-nine being culled in one form or another, even if this represented just less than 5% of the 633 crews dispatched. The Tibbets-piloted B-17 was damaged sufficiently either before or after the bomb run for its return to Bassingbourn to finally become untenable when out over the North Sea. However, the decision to make the unavoidable and ever-unpredictable action of "ditching" ended positively for all ten airmen at least, after they took to their dinghies and were later picked up by an ASR Launch.

Winter Doldrums?

The onset of European winter weather conditions probably induced an added sense of lassitude among the personnel—now known as Seasonal Affective Disorder—adding to the natural stress arising from combat operations. The Daylight Offensive's seemingly stalled advance towards regular and decisive strikes across the full breadth of the Third Reich following the events of October had cast up the prospect of a wholesale switch to nocturnal bombing alongside the RAF. The practical difficulties in doing so probably sounded the death knell of this action, but what still hung in the balance was control of the air over central Europe, without which a successful outcome for the Offensive was clearly in jeopardy.

A corollary arising from control of the air was the wholesale demise of *Jagdwaffe* operations, which would not only benefit the Allied Bomber Commands, but also the Allied Navies transporting and guarding the Anglo-American Armies for the planned Invasion of Western Europe in mid-1944. The absence of escorts for any *Luftwaffe* bomber counterattacks against the cross-Channel operation would almost certainly result in a wholesale slaughter administered by the RAF and USAAF fighter strength, thereby guaranteeing a secure passage for the Invasion Fleet.

The twists and turns of strategic policy never settled on many minds down at the airfields, as the personnel got on with the tasks at hand, survival being the all consuming "aim of the game." The remainder of the month saw two more missions, of which only one was completed to any degree. It was back to Bremen on the 29th, and this time round only the 41CBW out of full Division strength released either on the Primary or Targets of Opportunity; the 1CBW was among the absentees after extremely high cloud cover thwarted their advance. Twenty-four hours later, another "Happy Valley" run was briefed, this time to Solingen, but on this occasion Mother Nature's cloud blanket resulted in a total mission abortion. The town's industrial facilities' reprieve from dislocation was only to be another twenty-four hours, but any sense of achievement in striking the target would be diminished both at Bassingbourn and Ridgewell.

December Blues

Leverkusen as a target evinced nothing more than the normal range of reactions from the crews at Briefing, but within hours, three 1BD groups would count the cost in MIA teams, with nine shared between the two 1CBW units. The Ruehr-based Primary was due to be hit by all three Divisions, but the 3BD's participation was cancelled by weather. The target was located in between Köln and Solingen, all three being situated within the southern edge of the Ruehr. Consequently, the target approach was further south and east before angling back on a western track. Of the eight fighter groups on hand, only the 55FG's P-38s could provide a guarantee of constant cover, and that spread dangerously thin among the 300 bombers penetrating enemy airspace. Thus, the *Jagdwaffe* was provided with the latest opportunity to strike hard at the *'Viermots'* (four-engine aircraft).

The weather conditions doubtless added to by the industrial haze was destined to defeat even the PFF sub-force's effort to locate the Primary and recourse was had to taking on the Secondary that had been spared the day before—Solingen. The flak gunners were adding to their aerial contemporaries' unimpeded attacks on the bombers and the first of five MIA B-17s for the 91BG occurred even before the IP was reached. The operational career of 41-24511/LG: W **Wheel N' Deal** went back to August 1942 as a 306BG "original" B-17 prior to a January arrival at Bassingbourn.

Now it was positioned in the Low squadron with Lt. John Wennerberg's relatively new crew on board. The combined damage inflicted by ground and aerial gunfire resulted in the bomber separating from the group and making a run for home in a northwest direction. The prior absence of fighter escorts during the target approach was rectified by the arrival of two P-47s; sadly, they could provide no immunity from the flak barrage that enveloped its lumbering victim and resulted in an engine oil tank being set ablaze. The resultant bail out left nine survivors before the aircraft crashed into the Rhine.

The return course commenced with a clockwise sweep that seemingly took the formations in between Bonn and Koblenz, judging by the second group loss crash site NW of the latter city. This was 42-6086/OR: P, which came down near Leutesdorf on the Rhine, with its demise sadly matched by all ten on Lt. Jens T. Weiby's crew. **Hell's Belle** (42-3060 /LL: G) had been present since mid-September, but had only flown several missions. Its progress back today was finally halted south of Dueren; by then it was on half power, leaving Lt. Charles Guinn with little option but to "belly in" at Boich.

The stretch between the Rhine and the region around Dueren witnessed the main carnage inflicted on the 91BG and continued with a second bomber that consumed its crew. This was 42-29794/LG: O flown by Lt. Leonard F. Anderson, which descended into the ground at Vossenack. Further back at Zuelpich, NW of Euskirchen, the shredded remains of 42-39836/LG: M littered the ground after its mid-air disintegration caused by flak; in spite of this, Lt. Charles L. Early and seven of his fellow airmen got to the ground alive.

Ridgewell's Share

The 381BG's sufferings during *Black Week* were now well behind the individual and collective memory, but the ever-unpredictable nature of combat operations took a similar unpleasant turn over

Solingen, with four B-17s destined to be shorn from the 25-strong formation. Adding to the general depressed mood on return was the commonly expressed view that the circumstances of each crew's loss were basically unobserved; the 535BS contingent was particularly affected, since three of the four MIA crews came from its ranks.

Lt. Warren O. Hess was in trouble with 42-3540/MS: N **Bacta Th' Sac** on the way in, with engine power fluctuation the source; the turn towards Solingen ended with the B-17 lagging permanently behind. The straggler was picked on by a Bf110 whose fire added to the power problem and the bombs were jettisoned, followed by a course for home. The bomber made progress sufficient to gain Nazi-occupied territory before a further attack reduced power to "nil," whereupon the crew bailed out and two of whom evaded capture; sadly, Sgt. Edgar Delp (TG) subsequently died from injuries received while at his post.

Whereas Hess's crew were on their fifth mission, F/O Donald E. Noxon's team were sixteen-mission veterans just returned from a rest home. Their aircraft was 42-31111/MS: R, appropriately titled **Four Aces-Pat Hand** (related to the last four numbers of its serial). Target flak had inflicted enough damage for the bomber to become detached from the group. It simply failed to return, nor was any subsequent trace of it or its unfortunate occupants ever confirmed—the cruelly anonymous sea was almost certainly their last resting place.

The third squadron B-17 taken down also owed the start of its demise to the flak encountered around the IP: 42-31097/ MS:, reputedly named **Mission Belle** and being flown by F/O Harlan V. Sunde. Once again, damage was sufficient for the pilots not to maintain contact with the formation. A solo homeward run was commenced, this time at low level. All the effort came to naught over Holland when a "ditching" in a river close to Nieuw-Lekkerland was only partially successful; the fuselage was split at the center section by the impact and added to the deaths of two gunners was the life of Sunde.

The last crew to be lost was that of the 532BS' Lt. Jason H. Duncan, flying 42-39506/VE: A **Full Boost**. A fire in No. 2 engine after the bomb run was completed was subsequently doused, but the same sorry pattern of position loss within the formation then occurred. The pilots managed their solo run to within roughly 40 miles of the Channel coast; then, fighters caught up with their B-17 and the result was a mid-air explosion east of Cassel, near the Franco/Belgian border. Only Duncan and three Enlisted men emerged alive from the incident.

The group's aircraft loss was raised by one when Lt. Harold H. Hytinen carried out a forced landing with 42-39808/GD: F at Allhallows, Kent; three crewmembers were hospitalized, but whereas they seemingly recovered, the same could not be said for the 534BS bomber, which was declared fit only for "salvage." (The debriefing comments on the MIA crews' "disappearance" has to be put in the context of when they occurred, namely when the fighter attacks were coming in and probably distracting the gunners' attention in particular from doing other than concentrating upon their adversaries' assaults.)

December's inaugural mission that had cost both 1CBW groups dearly was the sole monthly sortie that the 91BG would have cause to recall, whereas another relatively expensive mission awaited the 381BG. Four days elapsed after Solingen before the 1BD again rose to battle—all in vain, since the projected assaults upon several French targets were totally disrupted by weather. Better fortune awaited the entire Division following a five-day period on the ground, when well over 200 bombardiers released on Emden's port facilities at a cost of one B-17. Then it was back to Bremen (13th) for the 1st and 41st CBWs; amazingly, this particularly "hot" defensive source failed to score among the 171 making bomb runs. Such good fortune could not be expected to sustain itself, but did so just three days later, when a single Divisional loss was again incurred over the same Primary.

Partners in Fate

A WWII Hollywood musical "Hers to Hold" contains a B-17 production line sequence at the Lockheed-Vega plant. The fuselages are being run forward on overhead wires and one of these bears the serial 42-5845. This currently anonymous airframe would evolve into the 381BG's GD: A **Whaletail II**, while its production-line successor (42-5846) would join her at Ridgewell as MS: X **Tinkertoy**, becoming the group's reputed "jinx ship." Both had enjoyed notable combat careers over the past nearly six months and were making their latest foray on the 20th, with yet another mission to Bremen outlined.

Escort cover, in addition to featuring P-47s and P-38s, also included the P-51Bs of the 354FG, the latter design being a still-unknown harbinger of better times to come for the hard-pressed B-17 and B-24 crews. The sleek North American fighter had recently entered the combat lists on the 5th, and today would witness its fourth full engagement with the *Jagdwaffe*. Unlike the two previous missions to Bremen, the bombers were to face the usual fierce measure of counter-assault that would take out twenty-seven crews, of which twelve were culled from within the 1BD's ranks.

The 1CBW was rapidly closing on the target when one of the fighters closing in on a pass from eleven o'clock was either disabled or alternately featured its pilot making an error of judgment in maintaining a clean break through the 381BG formation. At any rate, his aircraft collided with the rear fuselage of **Tinkertoy,** which was positioned in the Low squadron's second element. The outcome was not immediately fatal for the veteran B-17, since she was reported as completing the bomb run before developing a spinning action.

The latter maneuver was later confirmed by Lt. John Anderson (N), who had scrambled to the nose hatch and jumped bare seconds prior to the B-17's explosive disintegration in between Delmenhorst and Oldenburg; he was one of only four survivors, including Lt. Dorman Lane (P). **Tinkertoy** had been No. 3 to **The Rebel** (42-31075/MS: S), flown by Lt. Waldo Crossan. Fighter-inflicted punishment during or immediately following the bomb run caused his charge to slip down and out of formation, where it was further shot up before being abandoned to crash north of the target at Wesermuende, along with three crewmembers.

It would appear that Lt. Bernard F. Hollenkamp was still on hand with 42-3563/VE: after "bombs away," according to the MACR, but the B-17 then began to lag, a fatal move that invited the attention of a fighter *Schwarm* as the formation was NW of Oldenburg. Fire erupted in the rear fuselage and was the likely cause for the five personnel stationed there losing their lives; the other five jumped into captivity, while the bomber went down into *das Stapelermoor*, a marshy area.

The surviving crews headed for the North Sea and Ridgewell, but one B-17 was wallowing around with its port elevator almost removed by flak, among other damage. In spite of this critical situation, Lt. Leo I. Canelake managed to keep **Whaletail II** in position until within less than 20 minutes flight time from the East Anglian coast. Then, Lt. Richard Niederitter, who had flown behind the crippled aircraft within the High squadron, happened to glance back and downwards. What he observed was Canelake's mount, whose absence he had not picked out due to other distractions, now low down above the heavy-running seas in an apparent "ditching" approach.

A call to his tail gunner to make a sighting report was hindered by the latter's Plexiglas being badly frosted over. Even if the attempt had been successful, the water temperature would probably have proved fatal, while discovery by the ASR Service would equally have proven either too late or even impossible. The sole recognition of their sacrifice was their names inscribed upon Madingley's "Wall of the Missing." And so **Tinkertoy** and **Whaletail II**, having been created alongside each other on the production line, had finally gone to their operational Fate side-by-side.

Osnabrueck lay NE of the Ruehr, and therefore any mission to the city could not be construed as short-ranged in nature. The 1st and 2nd BDs were dispatched there on the 22nd, while the 3BD attacked Muenster to the SW. The Primary target was Osnabrueck's communications network, but only seven of the Division's ten groups actually bombed, the remaining trio being thwarted by a combination of technical failure and in one case being under-flown on the bomb run by another unit.

Five groups suffered single MIA casualties; one of these was from Bassingbourn's 28-strong formation. The group was on the homeward leg and crossing out over the western end of the Frisian Islands when the already flak-afflicted 42-37738/LG: T fell out and assumed a southerly course parallel to the Dutch coast. The seeming intention of Lt. Edward M. Steel, Jr. to head down to the narrowest possible distance between the Continent and SE England came to naught roughly 40 to 50 miles onward, around the port of Ijmuiden. It was then that the B-17 was abandoned to its fate. Unfortunately, the parachute of Sgt. Gerald D. Glaze (BT) was blown out over the North Sea, whose chilled waters claimed his life; a cruel variation compared to his nine colleagues, who drifted down onto solid ground.

"Hands across the Sea"

Stone, in Staffordshire, was the 8AF reception center for combat personnel, and it was there on Christmas Day that the recently-arrived crew of Lt. Jim Tyson found themselves a long, isolated way from home and accordingly somewhat deflated in spirit. Jim and his navigator, "Giant" John Howland (The nickname applied to the vertically-challenged 5ft 3in airman.) decided to walk into the adjacent town; Frank Palenik (B) also made a solo visit and both parties were to have their spirits lifted. In the former case, a Mrs. Doris Redman approached the aimlessly wandering duo and invited them back to her parents' house. There, in John's words:

"We wondered what had transpired, given our prior impression of the English as 'cold' and 'aloof'—it was surely a world distant from the reception we received, as the conversation was warm and personal in a manner that we had last experienced in our own homes; the food was a further flip to our morale, as it was delicious. These folks had put themselves out in this respect, considering the rationing constraints they regularly faced compared to our almost sumptuous availability of food and drink."

Three days later, the Tyler crew received their posting to the 381BG, based within the dank surroundings of Ridgewell, but the reception accorded the three officers—Frank having received a similar invitation and fine treatment from a separate family—sent them on their travels in a little better frame of mind as they entered the lists of aerial combat with all its hazards.

The next seven days that encompassed the Christmas Festival passed off without any call on the Command's services, but the 30th resulted in another thrust well into Germany when Ludwighafen's oil refining and industrial sources were targeted. The 91BG dispatched twenty-eight crews, but only twenty-seven made Assembly, the exception already a wreck on Steeple Morden. The No. 3 engine on 42-39863/LL: caught fire during take-off and No. 1 also ignited at this critical stage.

The 355FG's airfield was close by, so Lt. Frank C. Ammann headed there for what was a very risky crash landing, bearing in mind his volatile fuel and bomb load. Luck was on both the B-17 and her crew's side, although the extensive damage suffered in carrying off the action ensured "salvage" treatment for the airframe. The crew's luck would extend to tour completion, although not involving an immediate stateside return; instead, their operational career culminated with a diversion into Sweden on 11 April, along with their battle-damaged B17G.

A second group bomber was "written off" during the return leg. Lt. Wayne D. Hedglin had become separated in the poor visibility conditions and his wanderings over southern England in search of an airfield as dusk was settling in culminated in another successful crash landing near Old Windsor, west of London. As with the Ammann incident, so was 42-31178/DF: rendered "salvage," although her crew survived the incident. These two "operational" losses increased the group's

December casualties falling into this category to three. On return from Bremen (20th), Lt. Howard F. Weber had "bellied in" 42-37767/LL: D at Cambridge airfield after suffering progressive fuel starvation to the engines, but the nine airmen emerged alive.

Year-end Target Switch

The French Atlantic port of Bordeaux is located close to the border with Spain and had been targeted several times in the past. Now Old Year's Day 1943 was the occasion for the VIIIBC to send a huge force of nearly 600 B-17s and B-24s to attack several airfields at or in the vicinity of the city, with one CBW directed against a merchant "blockade runner" moored in the Gironde. The protracted run to and from the Primaries ensured the *Jagdwaffe* would be aloft and present for a lengthy period, while the bulk of the escorts would not be on hand for a similar period of time, leaving defensive measures to the bomber gunners. By the day's end, twelve groups would be short by an average of two crews, but with the 351BG mourning no less than seven casualties.

Bordeaux/Merignac had long been a base for the long-range Fw200 *Kondors*, which had acted as "eyes" for the U-boats, as well as indulging in attacks upon the Allied merchantmen themselves. An arcing approach route out over the Atlantic was adopted, but this action did not throw the German fighters off the trail and they were closing on the formations well before the target area. The 91BG's formation included the six-month combat veteran **Oklahoma Okie** (42-29921/DF: Z), in Lt. Bayard Dudley's hands.

A fierce pass out of the sun that was not intercepted ended with cannon shells riddling **Okie**'s airframe and setting the radio room and the port inner wing on fire. Sgt. James Ross (WG) had his flight suit alight as he was donning his parachute pack and was fortunate enough to break open the rear door that had jammed, as well as having the airflow extinguish the flames when he exited. Scarcely had he done so when the B-17 exploded, expunging the lives of half the crew, including both pilots. Ross by contrast not only survived, but gained access to the local Resistance, who subsequently spirited him across the Pyrenees into neutral Spain.

The Primary was obscured by cloud, so a switch to the Secondary (Cognac / Chateaubernard) became necessary. However, the 381BG had surrendered one B-17 as the coast was crossed and the turn north towards the target was on hand. Lt. Earl B. Duarte and Glen A. McCabe—handling 42-39910/MS:—had their aircraft so badly shot up that it fell back, whereupon the bomb load was jettisoned, but course was still held as far as approach to the Secondary. The bomb doors were jammed open, so the chances of overcoming the drag and holding position for the several-hundred mile return leg were minimal.

The pilots, probably realizing this, then banked to starboard and headed south with the perceived aim of gaining Spanish airspace. No. 2's propeller began to "windmill," adding further drag to the bomber's progress, and when problems arose with No. 3 the decision to abandon the B-17 was taken. All ten made safe exit, but the pilots gained the tremendous bonus of not only evading capture, but following Sgt. Ross into Spain; Sgt. Russell Jevons (Eng.) initially evaded capture, but was apprehended two months later. The bomber came to earth north of Toulouse.

The flak gunners in the area did their best to add to the punishment, and although the strike or strikes on 42-29895/LG: T did not bring her down, they unknowingly sentenced the B-17 to ultimate destruction. One engine and the supercharger on a second were knocked out and the inevitable result was the B-17 falling back, followed by the decision to adopt a noticeably lower altitude.

The aircraft lumbered on northwards until approaching the Brest Peninsula's southern tip. It was now that their immunity from fighter attack ended, although it was only the FW190s' third pass that sealed their prey's fate. Lt. Stuart B. Mendelsohn (normally the pilot, but flying right seat to "spell" Lt. Laverne B. Wood) was killed instantly and the B-17 began to describe a shallow dive to starboard that steepened dramatically when halfway towards the ground.

The surviving seven crewmembers still on hand prepared to jump, but T/Sgt. Richard Hansley (Eng.) hesitated too long, despite the urging of T/Sgt. James M. Guinn (ROG), who cleared the rear hatch scant seconds before the bomber impacted at Bannalec, east of Quimper. Guinn's good luck was added to by his becoming one of three immediate evaders. However, he and Lt. James A. Schneider (B) returned to England, whereas Lt. Woods later ended up being betrayed, as well as receiving rough treatment from his SS interrogators.

January 1944

The coming months would witness the European conflict either heading firmly towards an ultimate successful conclusion or being faced with the prospect of a protracted struggle to achieve this aim. The latter scenario would arise should the Anglo/American forces be thwarted in their bid to invade the Continent and so present the Axis with a two-front battle on the ground.

Control of the air had long been perceived as an absolute priority in easing the path for this highly desirable scenario, but with the *Overlord* invasion plans focusing on a landing no later than June, the current aerial situation over the Continent was not showing any real signs of swinging in favor of either the USAAF or the RAF. Indeed, the German night-fighter force (*Nachtjagd*) were in clear ascendancy against the Lancaster and Halifax crews determinedly wending their nocturnal paths over central Europe, but suffering ever-swingeing losses in the process, while their USAAF contemporaries were being equally challenged by the *Jagdwaffe*. The primary means with which to break the latter enemy force logistically, if not also spiritually, was steadily coming on hand in the form of the P-51 Mustang, but only time could tell if its burgeoning presence would yield this critical result.

Last Lap Tragedy

In the meantime, the American bomber crews bent to their duties in the best possible mood and style. The year was four days old before the inaugural mission was launched, but on the previous evening, Lts. Dave McCarthy (534BS navigator) and a 532BS contemporary Lt. Ralph Waldman—friends over several months—met in Ridgewell's Officers Club. Both were veteran airmen, but the latter was about to fly his 25th mission on the morrow with Lt. Cecil Clore. Before retiring to their billets, Ralph persuaded Dave to accept his good luck charm received from his wife (a toy donkey); he reasoned that the item would see Dave equally delivered from injury or death and free to return stateside after completing his combat tour.

The aforementioned mission was directed towards Kiel and Lt. Clore, Ralph, and several other members of the crew were doubtless looked upon with degrees of envy from their contemporaries. Not flying today was Lt. John Donovan, who had already experienced two strokes of combat fortune, one of which was being absent from Lt. Sample's crew on 8 October after being sent to a rest home. Now, he had recently flown his 25th and was about to depart for the Combat Crew Replacement Center (CCRC) at Stone; here, he anticipated again meeting up with Clore, with whom he had flown his final run of missions.

Dave McCarthy's B-17 was part of the formation and due to take off after 42-31278/VE: A, bearing Clore and crew. **Our Mom** duly followed, but as it was coursing down the runway, a massive flash occurred some distance ahead. Shortly after becoming airborne and banking to starboard over the airfield, Lt. Ed Klein (B) called to say the B-17 was passing over a scene of devastation and fire that tragically and still unknowingly to Dave signalled the demise of all ten airmen on Lt. Clore's bomber. The wooded area at Bloom's Farm, on whose fringe he apparently attempted an emergency crash landing, claimed the bomber.

It seems that the pilots put her down in good order, but a wing tip snagged a tree before her momentum was halted, the resultant impact detonating part of the bomb load and the entire fuel load. Instead of a passage home for Clore and all others on their 25th, what now awaited them was a headstone at Madingley, while the ghastly incident further presaged long term if not permanent grief for their kin. Ralph's parting "gift" to Dave, who later completed his tour, had ironically not provided the same salvation for its original owner. (In a postwar conversation with the author, John Donovan recalled his utter shock after telephoning the base and being informed of Lt. Clore's tragic loss, along with his crew.)

The 381BG contingent was among the 263 Division B-17s that attained the target and headed homeward. On board 42-29923/VE: K **Lucky Strike**, Lt. Rowland H. Evans experienced problems with his fuel reserves, with flak damage to one or more tanks the probable cause. At any rate, by the time the group crossed over Norfolk with no airfield in sight, the pilots felt impelled to attempt a forced landing near Cawston. Unfortunately, the B-17 ran across a ditch that shattered the fuselage behind the wing roots and left only eight crewmembers alive, with Lt. Irving Kraut (B) and Sgt. Julius E. Rivera (BT) losing their lives. Lt. Evans was on borrowed time that would run out fatally on 22 February. Two aircraft and twelve airmen had been surrendered without any direct enemy intervention. As it was, January was to bring another bout of hard times to the combat crews at Ridgewell, with the latest cataclysmic event just seven days distant from the Kiel run.

The 5 January mission provided an unusual variation in tactics, with four geographically spread out targets outlined. While the 2BD and part of the 1BD headed NE to Kiel and the 13CBW went towards the Ruehr, six further 3BD groups went even further to the SW to attack Bordeaux/Merignac airfield. The final sub-force, consisting of the 1CBW and 401BG, was dispatched towards Paraday/Meslay airfield at Tours, roughly 100 miles due south of Le Havre. All four Forces were provided with P-38 and P-47 escorts, but still lost 24 crews in all. The least affected statistically were the Tours-bound formations, which came back just one short out of 78 carrying out bomb runs; the mission also saw the 91BG completing its "century" mission, the first bomb group to reach this milestone.

No flak was encountered during the bomb run, but a rocket-bearing fighter landed a strike around the bomb bay section of 42-30676/VE: A **Baby Dumpling**. Lt. Jack R. Zeman's aircraft described a slow turn to starboard that was briefly reversed before it dropped into a spin; reports at debriefing stated a wing detached on the way down to the crash site at Les Hunes. The B-17 actually came violently apart and Sgt. Raymond F. Chevaux (LWG) was particularly lucky to escape unscathed, as he was only halfway out of a hatch at the time. As it was, only Lt. William C. Walker (B) lost his life, while Chevaux was one of four evaders.

The VIIIBC title for the overall Force of British-based heavy bombers was switched to that of "8th Air Force" on 6 January, while the Command HQ moved to High Wycombe. The bombers remained on the ground this day, but the respite was brief, as an "Alert" was called that evening affecting no less than 502 crews. The city of Ludwigshafen possessed major chemical production plants and was now lined up for its latest battering on the morrow.

Lt. Arden D. Wilson had been fortunate to divert into an RAF airfield on return from Tours, having suffered a disabled engine and with Sgt. Richard H. Nisbet (ROG) seriously wounded. As it so happens, this airman's current misfortune was to be temporarily reversed 48 hours later, although his luck did finally run out on 6 March over Berlin. Wilson had been assigned 42-3078/GD: M **Winsome Winn/Hilda**, a group "original." The outward route witnessed the propeller on a newly-installed engine "windmilling," followed at some stage by a second engine on the same wing beginning to malfunction and setting up an asymmetric flying attitude. The pilots nevertheless managed to hold formation position as the homeward leg approached the Franco/German border.

It was now that several fighters made a pass that resulted in the ailing

B-17 losing contact with the group. Once isolated her fate was sealed, although the gunners fought back valiantly; Sgts. Peter Kucher (ROG)—an unlucky replacement for Sgt. Nisbet—and Anthony F. Greco (TG) lost their lives either during the one-sided air battle, or in the latter's case thanks to a failed parachute. Their eight fellow airmen made their exit and drifted to earth near Schiffweiler, where **Winsome Winn/Hilda** found her final violent resting place. The 381BG had now lost four aircraft and 32 combat crew in four days, but exactly double this figure in MIA bombers would be incurred before the same time span was completed.

Oschersleben Martyrdom

T/Sgt. John Comer (533BS) had completed his combat tour over Tours (5th) and was the latest member of Lt. Paul Gleichauf's crew to reach this magic status. Six days later, he prepared to depart Ridgewell, but was awakened by the Charge of Quarters (CQ) arousing two of his regular crew still with a handful of missions to go: Sgts. Jim Counce (WG) and George Balmore (ROG). He made his farewells as the two airmen departed the Nissen hut, having said he would meet up with them stateside in the near future, and later set off for the Embarkation Camp at Chorley, in Lancashire.

The Fw190 production plant at Oschersleben, SW of Berlin, had already been targeted in July 1943 and was again up for assault by the 1BD, along with a second aircraft production plant at nearby Halberstadt. Once again, the B-17s and B-24s were being dispatched on a deep penetration mission that would ensure some considerable time spent beyond escort cover, other than for the mere handful of P-38s and P-51s currently on hand. In addition, events involving this specific location would be woven into the darker pages of the 381BG chronicles both today and exactly six weeks hence.

A general weather pattern of cloud and rain showers met the formations as they droned upwards and out towards the Continent. Far from improving, the weather then began to deteriorate to an extent that persuaded the new "Boss" of the 8AF, Lt/Gen. Jimmy Doolittle, to issue a "recall" for all but the 1BD and one CBW from the 3BD; in either case, these sub-forces were adjudged to be close enough to their Primaries to complete their bomb runs. The wisdom of this decision would undoubtedly be called in question by the crews—that is, those who survived the punishment handed out principally by the *Jagdwaffe* that equalled the scale of *Black Thursday*.

The 1CBW was in the van of the 177-strong Oschersleben sub-force of seven groups. The formations were not only largely bereft of escort cover, but encountered the *Jagdwaffe* when still between 150 and 200 miles short of the Primary. The 91BG was Lead for the CBW and soon began to feel the full weight of the German pilots' thrusts. The formations were across the Dutch/German border and in between the *Duemmersee* (Duemmer Lake) and Hannover when the first gaps were rent in the CBW ranks; however, these reportedly affected the 381BG alone, although the punishment handed out was not to spare the 91BG, either.

The operational career of 42-29487/DF: K **Ritzy Blitz** spanned ten months, during which she had accumulated upwards of 50 missions, compared to Lt. Wayne Hegdlin's crew with an average between two and three. The group was SW of Hannover when yet another fighter pass saw the B-17, which was thoroughly riddled and had one engine on fire, fall into a spin. The centrifugal forces exerted probably held at least three of the nine airmen still alive inside what was an aerial tomb, while a fifth suffered a failed parachute. Hegdlin was more fortunate, as he was one of the five who did get clear before the bomber slammed into the soil at Wennigsen/ Deister.

Lt. Edwin Reid's 42-31372/OR: P **Malayan Lady** was shot up very early in the overall battle and began to fall behind. Fire erupted in the forward area and further damage included part of the starboard stabilizer's excision that further impeded a normal flight pattern. There were even eyewitness accounts of a marginal collision with an Fw190, but whether or not true, the outcome of the unequal combat was that the bomber pitched into a steep dive SW of Hannover and crashed at Bad Muender; the pilot was among the seven fatalities. (A separate report indicates the crash occurred on the return leg.)

Blonde Bomber (42-3057/LG: N) was another veteran with nearly 30 missions under her belt, but now Lt. Wayne Murdock's B-17 was also steadily absorbing strikes. The pilot had brought home his bomber on 31 December with the bomb bay fuel tank jammed halfway out after being jettisoned; he and the crew's luck had held then, but not so today. By the time the bomb run was in progress, the B-17 was on fire with one crewmember already dead. The bail out just west of the target was effected by the other nine airmen, but the pilot's parachute apparently failed.

Ridgewell's Woes

The 91BG made it through to the target with just one previous loss, but not so its companion unit, which was now short of at least four crews, one of which had reversed course over the Dutch/German border after suffering serious damage to its engines. 42-37719/VP: L **Hellca**t bore the acolyte crew of Lt. Donald E. Nason that included Sgt. John R. Lantz (WG). The ground was barely visible when the overall state of the ailing bomber impelled the pilot to ring the bail out bell; unfortunately, instead of solid ground the crew were exiting over the waters of the Ijsselmeer, immersion in which spelled imminent doom for the heavily-clad airmen. Sgt. Lantz proved to be the extremely lucky exception to being drowned or killed by exposure, and even then, he was on the point of losing his battle with the elements when a Dutch fishing boat crew dragged him out.

The air battle's intensity cast up several more losses between the Osnabrueck/Hannover stretch of the inward route, the first of which was **Betty Lou** (42-37962/VE:L), which was originally assigned as a "spare" but duly filled in for an "aborting" bomber. Gallenbeck, several miles SW of Osnabrueck, was where the stricken bomber came down following the severing of its fuselage that ironically was caused by parts of a disintegrating Bf109. Once again, the fierce centrifugal forces almost certainly pinned all but two of those on Lt. Robert V. Saur's team who were still alive firmly in position, with both waist gunners being the ones to whom continued life was granted; they may well have been thrown clear, since the airframe's breaking point was in the vicinity of where they stood. The group's progress was not much further advanced when another B-17 was culled: 42-29999/VP: Z **Fertile Myrtle**, piloted by Lt. Matthew J. McEvoy. This time round, the spiralling descent entered into by the shot up bomber happily did not impede the exit of all ten on board before it crashed near Melle.

A third loss at this stage had tragic consequences for nine airmen led by Lt. Wilfred R. Perot on board what was also the third of six MIA casualties destined to come the way of the 533BS. The tight formation flying, along with the head-on passes indulged in by the fighters, always held potential for what the bomber crews feared—mid-air collision. In this case, an Fw190 failed to avoid impacting with 42-5878/VP: Q **Yankee Eagle**'s starboard inner wing. Just prior to this cataclysmic incident, Sgt. Edwin B. Bosley had made what he later described as an illogical act of donning his parachute pack; had he not done so, he may well have shared the tragic fate of his nine colleagues, who failed to survive the subsequent violent gyrations of the B-17 now bereft of its starboard wing. It was still his good fortune to scramble clear of the B-17 as it tumbled downwards in order to deploy his parachute.

Saving the Day

Capt. Darrell DeBolt, an original member of Lt. Lishon's 534BS crew, was now a squadron Lead bombardier who was noted for his consistently good performance in carrying out what was always a difficult task. The 381BG/91BG composite High group was following the 91BG, which would now open the attack for the Force; the irony in this situation lay in the fact that the 1CBW's original slot as the last in the 1BD stream had altered to this position thanks to operational complications within the overall Task Force en route to the target. However, the Lead B-17's bombsight was damaged during one fighter attack and the resultant bomb pattern was well scattered and clear of the Primary.

Capt. DeBolt duly "zeroed in" his Norden and his release was so accurate that the group's overall bomb pattern smothered the plant; successive groups also focused accurately upon the Primary. A consequence of this resurrection from potential failure to success for the overall bombing effort was a second DFC for the Lead bombardier. The formations now turned for home with the knowledge that the fight against the defenses would continue unabated for upwards of two hours before crossing over the North Sea, with more attrition among their ranks anticipated. That grim scenario awaited no less than seven crews from the 1CBW.

Comrades in Death

Lt. Gordon W. Crozier's 42-37720/VY: W was bearing Sgt. George Balmore as a "stand in" ROG. This B-17 progressed as far as the bomb run before Nemesis struck in the familiar form of a Fw190 or Bf109's gunfire that ignited No. 3 engine. It then seems from the reported time of the final crash in between Hannover and Hildesheim that course was held for home until approaching Paderborn, around 80 miles away from Oschersleben. The situation had clearly deteriorated, since Crozier signalled for the crew to jump. One man out of the ten would never obey the order, since he was already slumped over his table with a hole in his head; Sgt. Balmore was the individual concerned and his terminal condition was confirmed by the pilot before he exited the B-17, which then piled in near Schlangen.

Sgt. Jim Counce had flown the waist gun position for his former pilot, Lt. Gleichauf—now back in the States—but was today available as a "spare" and was assigned as a nose gunner on Lt. Ernest M. Klein's team operating 42-31417/VP: R **Patches**. The nose compartment was particularly vulnerable to battle damage when fighters attacked from the 12 o'clock angle, as was the regular case today. Sure enough, a burst of accurately delivered fire shredded the nose, as well as disabling both in-board engines.

The now-laboring B-17 was abandoned between Hildesheim and Hannover by the eight surviving crewmembers, a figure that tragically did not include Counce among its number. (The other fatality was recorded as the navigator, but Lt. Louis H. Gill (B) also appears on the crew list; this is a seeming anomaly, since he and Counce could not have jointly functioned in the already confined compartment.) Whatever the aforementioned circumstances, the fact remained that Counce and Balmore's bonding as combat crewmembers had not been denied, even in death.

Three days following this mission, John Comer was joined at Chorley by Lt. Ferrin (533BS), who was also homeward bound but who had still been at Ridgewell on the 11th. After making several evasive responses to his colleague's questions on how the mission had progressed, Ferrin's belated revelation that Lts. Klein and Crozier had both gone down had a stunning effect on John. When his first son was born, he incorporated both of the deceased names within the boy's own title, so all embracing was his continuing sense of identity with his deceased fellow airmen.

Even More Attrition

It was the 381BG that had bled more freely during the inward route, whereas the return leg displayed a more grimly even share in the losses between the two groups. **Little Jean** (42-31230/DF: A1), in the hands of Lt. Allan A. Uskela (KIA), was in that arguably most vulnerable location, namely No. 6 in the Low squadron, but still held gamely for the target. This was despite suffering severe damage that included part of the vertical fin being chopped off, the wing surface behind the port engines being badly buckled upwards, and a largely shot out cockpit instrument panel.

The pilots managed to make the target and even assumed a homeward course for several minutes before beginning an inexorable bank down to port. The surviving crewmembers commenced bail out, but only four among the ten ended up alive; the bomber came to earth west of Helmstedt, a town that would become a potential "flash point" in the Cold War, since it was a major entry/exit point between Democratic and Communist Germany.

Lt. Austin G. Larsen's 42-3118/GD: Q **The Green Hornet** was another B-17 that failed to last for many minutes of the return route. It was down to half power by the time the bail out order was given, to which all but one crewmember responded, Sgt. Ross N. Defenbaugh (RWG) having been killed at his post. The gunner's ill luck was compounded by the fact that he had "stood in" for the regular occupant. The undisclosed crash site was believed to be somewhere SW of the Primary.

Lt. Billy F. Chason had charge of 42-3514/VP: V **Doll Baby**, but the Fates had decided against the bomber and its crew. First an engine caught fire, and although this was extinguished, it failed totally. Then a second engine caught fire as the formation was approaching the *Duemmersee* and soon after fell out of formation. This time round, all ten airmen bailed out successfully, with the bomber coming down due east of this distinctive geographic feature.

Once again, a 91BG crew seems to have been culled almost simultaneously with a 381BG contemporary, because 42-31076/LG: X **Chief Sly's Son** descended to its destruction near Steinfeld, mere miles NW of the *Duemmersee*. Problems for Lt. J. C. Page began during target approach, when fuel tanks in the port wing were set on fire. Nevertheless, the bomber went over the target and made it back to this region. Then, the latest fighter attacks killed Sgt. Arthur G. Ginder (Eng.) and the fire intensified to a degree that impelled the bail out order to be given. Page and two other officers were still on board when the B-17 went into a spin and disintegrated soon after; only the pilot survived the explosion to join the other six airmen as a *Kriegie*.

The Fight Avails

Thirteen 1CBW crews had failed to run the defensive gauntlet, but at least one if not two more should have added to the tally. Both belonged to the 91BG, one of which was the group and 1BD Lead, 42-5804/OR: R **Hells Halo** bearing L/Col. Theodore Milton as Air Commander, along with Capt. Leroy Everett and crew. The loss of one engine well before the target was bad enough, but a second was disabled during the bomb run; compounding these difficulties was a fire in the cockpit caused by cannon-punctured oxygen tanks and flares set off by the flames.

The fire was thankfully extinguished, but the fact that the B-17 was now effectively on half power should have ended in its isolation and almost sure culling by fighters. Formation position was in fact retained, but when the B-24 airfield of Hethel appeared the propellers on the shot up engines that had been allowed to "windmill" were now "feathered." The brake system was inoperable, so the landing was fast and could have culminated in a collision with a 389BG bomber, had not the pilots swerved sharply off the runway; so ended the 13th mission for Milton, as well as Lt. Larry O'Neill (B).

Whereas **Hells Halo** enjoyed a five-month operational spell with the 91BG, 42-37940 /LG: **Spirit of '44** was barely four weeks on group establishment when it made its "final bow." It is not clear at what exact stage of the mission Lt. Eldridge V. Greer's crew commenced their solo run for home, but it could not have been long after the bomb run, because the pursuit of the isolated B-17 that had by now lost both outboard engines was destined to extend for an estimated 200 miles. The pilots had dropped down to as low an altitude as possible while the gunners exchanged fire with a pair of twin-engine fighters who held on relentlessly to their likely prey.

The bomber was maneuvered in a switchback pattern consistent with both the available engine power and bomb bay doors being jammed open, but the heavier firepower of what were probably Bf110Gs inevitably perforated the fuselage in particular. It was a simple miracle that not only did the bomber regain friendly shores and divert into another B-24 airfield at Shipdham (44BG); furthermore, none of the crewmembers received any notable injuries. The same positive outcome did not apply either to **Spirit of '44** or **Hells Halo**, both of whom received "salvage" treatment.

Ironic Humor?

The day following the Oschersleben disaster, Lt. Theodore Homdrom, a 535BS Lead navigator, was in the squadron washrooms, as he and other officers were attending to their ablutions. During the session, he heard one of his contemporaries shouting out: "Oh, shucks, seven years of bad luck!" after dropping his shaving mirror that duly smashed on the floor. Theo's instant response was to say: "That's not bad luck—you will have to live seven years!" He later recollected that his retort could be regarded as a bit questionable in terms of humor. On the other hand, the remark has to be put in the grim context of what the airmen were facing all the time. Any measure, however short-lived, to reduce the dreadful pressure placed upon their minds was no bad thing. Whether the individual in question came through his combat tour remains unclear.

Summary

The Oschersleben mission had again demonstrated, if the fact needed to be so highlighted, that the cost of unescorted thrusts into the Nazi hinterland was continuing to be too great in sustaining the Daylight Offensive. Of course, the fact that a sizeable proportion of the bomber stream had not been on hand in order to dilute the overall effect of the *Jagdwaffe* assault should be taken into account. This factor could not be regarded as totally irrelevant, given, for example, that the Oschersleben sub-force's 159 effective sorties were gained at a cost of 34 crews—a loss ratio of nearly 25%—compared to the Halberstadt comparative statistics of 107, or 8%.

The ultimate perceived savior of the bomber crews in the form of the P-51 was not yet available in any numbers, in addition to which the pilots were currently confronted with several operational problems that included guns jamming during tight maneuvers. In the meantime, the trusty P-47, whose overall performance was advancing thanks to improved engine and propeller performance, as well as more efficient drop tanks, would, along with the P-38, continue to at least thwart the worst effects of the *Jagdwaffe's* counteroffensive.

One of the operational misnomers regarding the Daylight Offensive is that the P-51 was the "savior" of the bombers. In fact, even during the critical months of March and April, the North American design would only be on hand in triple-figure numbers halfway through March, compared to its Republic contemporary; it would continue to be outnumbered by between two- and three-to-one until well into the latter-mentioned month!

Reduced Operational pattern

The steady pattern of monthly missions up to Oschersleben (four) now displayed a noticeable lapse in progress over the ensuing thirteen days, as well as target selection. Three days later (14th), the Divisions dispatched over 500 crews between them, but these only ventured as far as the Pas de Calais for the latest assault on V-1 sites. A full week then elapsed before an even larger 8AF force split its bombing effort between the Pas de Calais and the Cherbourg Peninsula, with V-1 sites again being the focus; this time round, adverse weather resulted in only 50% of the sorties being completed. However, the MIA losses on both occasions were marginal, with the 1CBW unaffected.

A switch back to German targets occurred three days later, but the intended assault on Frankfurt's aviation-based industry was totally thwarted by weather. The bombers landing back at Bassingbourn were short one among their dispatched number, but the bomber in question was not a crumpled wreck on the Continent; rather, it was bare miles distant from the airfield, along with four of its crew. Shortly after take-off, 42-40009 /DF: K developed a fire in the top turret that proved incapable of being extinguished, leaving Lt. Marco DeMara with little choice but to order a bail out.

Those in the rear had no problem exiting, but a jammed nose hatch threatened the survival prospects for the five occupants "up front." Sgt. John W. Webb (Eng.) got out though the forward exit thanks to Lt. Everett S. Offman (CP) holding it open and pushing him out. What then transpired was three of the officers were still on board when the B-17 came down in a field at Ickleton and burned up following an attempt at a crash landing. Lt. James B. Baine (B) somehow got clear beforehand, but died thanks to partial or total parachute failure. Webb's descent ended sharply but safely on the back of a horse! DeMara's action was recognized by the later award of a DSC. (The nose hatch door opens outwards, so how it could be held open seems a contradiction.)

Month End Operational Surge

A daily sequence of missions on the final four days in the month was flown by the 8AF. However, those dispatched on the 28th and 29th featured small B-24 forces making PFF assaults againstV-1 sites, and in the former instance inaugurated the use of the RAF's G-H electronic system. These contrasted with full-scale attacks against German targets the other two days, beginning with a PFF-led run to Frankfurt. The briefed 863-strong force ended up with 95% making bomb runs, of which 345 were from the 1BD; the Division in turn surrendered eleven B-17s out of the overall total of 29, of which two were from Ridgewell.

The *Jagdwaffe* was in its usual hostile and effective mood and the group experienced one pass just as the stream skirted round Koblenz. Lt. Robert J. Mohnacky's 42038045/GD: C absorbed heavy punishment that set the bomb bay on fire. The bail out signal was given as the stricken bomber was held level for the other crewmembers to exit, but only the five airmen from the radio room back got clear before the machine went out of control. Reichenberg, SE of Koblenz, was where the B-17 came down, along with the other five hapless occupants.

Worms is some 40 miles SSW of Frankfurt, so it seems that the other 381BG loss was incurred in its vicinity as the return course was being taken up. This was 42-37844/GD: J, flown by Lt. Lawrence H. Mickow, also a fighter victim. The lottery aspect of operations arose here after the bomber exploded, because the pilot was still donning his parachute pack at the time, he was blown clear and able to pull his ripcord. One officer and three Enlisted men were not so fortunate, however.

The 91BG suffered one "operational" loss in the form of 42-37987/LG: **Man O War-Horsepower Ltd**. This bomber had lost touch with the group over the English coast and tacked onto another unit. The bomb run was completed, but then the fighters struck, knocking their target downwards with two engines disabled. Two Bf110s made a particularly damaging pass that injured two crewmembers, one fatally. The heavy cloud layers proved to be the straggler's immediate salvation, but the extended flight back was fraught with difficulty, with the English SE coast being reached at minimum altitude. The subsequent crash landing in Kent was successful, but the B-17 was adjudged a "write-off" from what was its first and final mission following a mere seven-day sojourn at Bassingbourn.

Expensive Month End

Lt. Robert P. Deering was by now a reasonably experienced combat flier, but he was fortunate to still be present at Ridgewell. On 13 November, he had missed group Assembly and the "recall" signal to head out blissfully for the Continent, only to find himself in splendid but lethal isolation over Holland when the cloud cover broke. He got back safely on that occasion and now was in the formation heading for Brunswick. The luck that had carried he and his crew back home two months previous sadly ran out today; fighter gunfire exploded 42-31407/MS: T **Wolverine** before any of the ten occupants could get out, with the wreckage littering the soil near Hildesheim, SW of the Primary.

Two more group crews were destined to go down, bringing the loss tally to five within 24 hours. **Martha the II** (42-

30761/VP: W) was still on hand as Dutch territory was being overflown, but then a fighter landed strikes that set a wing on fire. Further flak-inflicted damage saw the B-17 falling out and heading down for an ultimate crash landing bear Duerne. Lt. Henry D. Steele (P) was one of six survivors, with two of the four fatalities tragically incurred other than in direct combat.

Lt. Wilbur E. Eason bailed out too near the ground; Sgt. Peter Hlynski (WG) was arguably even more unfortunate, since his parachute deployed properly, only for him to drift backwards into a fence, contact with which broke his neck. He was reportedly given the Last Rites by a priest summoned to join those Dutchmen already gathered round the dying airman. Five of his colleagues evaded capture for some two months, but were then caught in Brussels, presumably while in transit to Spain.

The saddest loss for the 381BG was arguably the one involving Lt. Carl O. Baer and crew on an "original" B-17F 42-30029/MS: P **Chaps Flying Circus**. The bomber had been regularly flown by Capt. Frank Chapman, who had since completed his combat tour, and the aircraft's title was a reference to he and his crew. The formation was well out over the North Sea when the pilot called to say he would be forced to "ditch," since he was nearly out of fuel. Before switching off he remarked to Lt. Bill Ridley (group Lead pilot): "Be sure there's a hot meal waiting for me tonight."

Contact with the ASR Service was made and the B-17 was lined up for emergency action. The other crews duly landed and their general mood was one of optimism that the ten absent airmen would soon be reported safe. The hours passed without any positive information and next day, the crew were posted MIA. The ever-cruel sea had seemingly claimed its latest aerial victim, but it was the washing ashore of Lt. Baer's body near Great Yarmouth several days later that confirmed this grim and ever-sickening fact, and so the pilot's wish for "a hot meal" proved tragically unfulfilled.

Transferred from the 95BG in June 1943, The Shamrock Special (42-29591/LL: Z) was involved in a ground collision during November that smashed the rear fuselage. In this picture, a replacement section is now fitted with the original about to be towed away. The following April, the rejuvenated B-17F was reassigned to AFSC with 26 completed missions.

The date is 26 November 1943, and this combat-expired B-17E with a heavy-framed nose Plexiglas and a "ripple" camouflage separation line has arrived at Ridgewell to serve as a group "hack." In fact, the bomber was an "original" with the 97BG; named Peggy D, 41-9043 participated in the inaugural VIIIBC mission on 17 August 1942.

Col. Joe Nazarro (381BG CO on left) is photographed on 15 November 1943 at Ridgewell with Maj. David E. Kunkel (534BS CO). Both have been awarded the Silver Star by Col. William Gross (CG 1CBW, center). Within seven weeks, Nazarro would be reassigned to HQ, VIIIBC.

This trio of 535BS gunners serving with the 381BG have just returned from the mission to Bremen. They are happy because they have bucked the trend for the number 13—today's December date—to demonstrate its malign nature. They are (R-L): Sgts. Carson, Bennett, and John T. Mills, the latter of Native American stock.

16 November 1943. Sgt. Frank Kucher (ROG) points to the bomb symbols on Sgt. Fred Rumberger's A2 jacket, which also bears the 535BS' "Lucifer Jr." title. Fred completed his combat tour, whereas Frank was killed the following 7 January, one of two fatalities on 42-3078/GD: M Winsome Winn/Hilda when she was MIA during the Ludwigshafen mission.

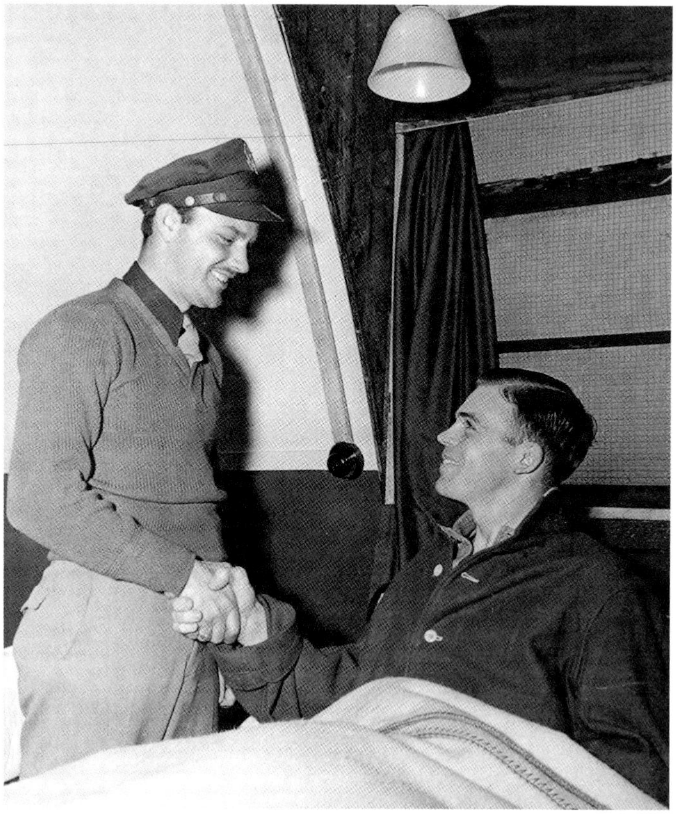

Lt. Hayden T. Brown shakes hands with Lt. William Butler (P). On attempting to bail out of the shot-up B-17, he had become trapped without his oxygen mask at the nose hatch; despite being stuck in this normally terminal situation, he not only survived anoxia, but also frostbite to one foot after its boot became detached. Mission date was 5 November 1943.

Bad Egg came off the production line one ahead of Memphis Belle, but had a prolonged combat career compared to her famous contemporary. She flew over 40 missions before being declared 'salvage" on 1 January 1944, during which time the bulk of her airframe had been replaced thanks to regular battle damage. She is seen with the original dappled camouflage scheme applied to B-17s during 1942-43.

Lt. Bill Ridley (third from right) and his 535BS crew in post-mission discussion. The pilot would complete his tour, as would gunner Sgt. Joe Long (third from left). Bombardier Lt. Carl Dittus (right) would become a POW, while navigator Lt. Malcolm Van Hise (left) would be deaLt.the cruellest blow; on 30 January 1944, he was MIA with Lt. Baer's crew following a failed "ditching."

The Type C hangars at Bassingbourn are evident in this picture, but the line-up of aircraft are not the normal "occupants' of the base. Instead, the twin-engine B-26s of the 386BG have seemingly taken over. Picture date is 9 November, but "medium" operations around this time were reportedly nil; the reason for the group's presence here is also obscure.

This huge hole in Skunkface/Terrible Ten's rudder is likely an element of the severe overall damage inflicted on 22 December 1943 that rendered the B-17F inoperable for three weeks. The 322BS bomber was finally lost on 20 February, along with two of Lt. Kidd's crew.

Lt. Thomas A. Sellars shakes hands with Lt/Gen. Eaker at VIIIBC HQ. The occasion was the presentation of the DSC to the 381BG copilot, who on 8 October brought Tinkertoy back to Ridgewell after Lt. Minerich (P) was decapitated by a cannon shell.

Lt. Harold Henslin (left foreground, carrying his parachute pack) leads his crew away from Tinkertoy (42-5846/MS: X) on 13 December. Seven days later, the group "jinx" ship would fall over Bremen; Henslin would sadly share her fate the following 28 April when on a supposed "milk run" mission to St. Avord airfield in France.

This is Duke of Paducah's partner in misfortune seen heading out on one of the December missions to Bremen. Unlike the Duke, 42-29895 was fated to be MIA off the long-range run to Chateaubernard next day (31 December). Lt. Stuart Mendelsohn (P) and one other airman perished after flak took out the straggling bomber over France.

The general and frustrating anonymity of ground crew photographs is happily breached here (L-R): Sgt. Mike Sabagh (381HQ); Pvt. Larry James and Cpl. Goldmer E. Elkins (both 2021 Fire Platoon); and Sgt. Tom Halligan (381HQ) decorate a Christmas tree in preparation for the group's party to which local children will be invited. The date is 12 December 1943.

Just nine days before Black Swan's demise, one of her regular crew, T/Sgt. Edward Fee (Eng.), completed his combat tour. He is surrounded by fellow airmen whose faces reflect both lightheartedness and wistful thinking. Note the box at bottom left whose truncated title unwittingly matches the very fortunate airman's surname.

The smashed Plexiglas nose canopy and slash in the starboard fuselage were caused by a collision with 42-29895/DF: H (the) Black Swan on December 30, 1943. The drama of the incident was diminished, however, as it occurred on the ground. What was 42-37736/DF: G ended its days as a radio relay ship.

Black Magic (42-5428/LG: T) will need all the power offered by her title. She is in serious difficulty, returning from the 12-31-43 mission. Attempts to jettison the bomb bay tanks resulted in its jamming halfway out to cause a dramatic loss in speed. Lt. Wayne Murdock nevertheless held on course and reached friendly shores. The bomber survived further missions prior to retirement from combat, but Murdock was KIA eleven days later.

Chug-A-Lug (42-30765/MS: U) lies sprawled on a hillside west of London on 29 December 1943. Lt. Bill Ridley was conducting a 'slow-time' engine test when power was lost and contact with a copse of trees brought the B-17F down to this fortunately intact state. The bomber's three-month spell with the 381BG was now effectively over since she was declared 'Salvage' three days later.

Lt. Eldridge Y. Greer and Maj. Don Sheeler (322BS CO) pose by 42-37940/LG:, with Greer being presented a toy bomb. The occasion was a "christening" ceremony centered on the B-17's name. On 11 January, Greer brought the B-17G back from Oschersleben in an epic solo flight under constant fighter assault. After landing at Shipdham (44BG), the battered aircraft was declared "salvage" on 13 January.

EA10983.

REVIEWED AND PASSED
U.S. ARMY
31 DEC 1943
PRESS CENSOR
E.T.O. U.S.A.

OFFICIAL U. S. ARMY AIR FORCES PHOTO DISTRIBUTED THRU OWI.
PRO-HQ-43-498
AN 8TH AIR FORCE BOMBER COMMAND STATION, ENGLAND --- At the close of 1943, Flying Fortress Squadron Commander Major Donald E. Sheeler, [illegible]), South Bend, Indiana, hands toy bomb, the key to Hitler's Festung Europa, to Pilot 1st Lt. Eldridge Y. Greer, Houston, Texas, after christening Greer's bomber the "Spirit of '44". On the ship, the infant 1944 handles a much bigger bomb, symbolical of what Hitler can expect during the New Year

Lt. William Johnson, a 533BS bombardier, stands by the nose of 42-29761/VP: W Martha the II with 28 mission "bombs" on its fuselage. Bill survived his combat tour and was awarded the DFC for extinguishing a fire that threatened to destroy the B-17 during a mission. Martha the II by contrast was lost on 31 January '44.

The stocky 5 ft. 5 inch figure of Col. Conway S. Hall emerges from a staff car. This officer served throughout the entire existence of the 381BG between January '43 and May 1945, finally finishing as the group's third and final CO; his previous functions had been as group Operations Officer and group Air Executive.

Lt. Robert Zadnick (532BS pilot) is holding a projectile-like piece of metal that is the probable cause for the tear at the top right of his parachute pack. He is probably reflecting on his fortune at not having to use the parachute, because the likelihood of shroud lines having been severed could have had a fatal effect had he bailed out. The date is 30 January 1944.

Chief Sly's Son (42-31076/LG: X), flown by Lt. J. C. Page, was one of the 91BG casualties on the Oschersleben mission. The B-17G was more fortunate eleven days previous, as seen here when she lost No. 3 engine during the long-haul run to Bordeaux but still managed to regain her Bassingbourn dispersal.

Wee Willie (42-31333/LG: W) commenced operations on 24 December 1943. The miniscule total of four mission "bombs" would grow to 127 by 8 April 1945, but no further. On that day, the veteran B-17G would be torn apart by flak and go down, along with Lt. Robert E. Fuller's nine-man crew.

Lt. Greer (back, left) and crew are home from Oschersleben. Next to Greer is Lt. W. Word (CP), who would gain his own crew, along with Lts. Dobbs (B) and Anders (N), respectively, on his left; all would become POWs on 22-2-44. Sgts. G. Walton (ROG, directly below Anders) and W. Wade (WG, second from right front) would be killed that day. Greer survived his combat tour.

This picture of Lt. James Tyson's 535BS crew was taken when still serving directly with the 381BG in early 1944. Front row (L-R): Lts. Frank Palenik (B), John Howland (N), William Doherty (CP), and Tyson (P). The crew, minus Lt. Palenik, would transfer to Bassingbourn during March for PFF operations with the 324BS.

A 534BS B-17G in the foreground is flanked in the far background by what is probably another 381BG sub-unit. What was GD: J barely lasted one month with the group; assigned on 20 December, she was lost along with half of Lt. Mickow's (POW) crew the following 29 January during the mission to Frankfurt.

This dramatically struck photograph of a Bf110 skirting the flank of a Bassingbourn formation is not taken on a mission. The fighter is part of a group of captured aircraft operated by the RAF. Known as the RAFWaffe, the intention was to provide orientation lessons for the USAAF combat crews, as well as a recognition guide for the gunners, not all of whom were versed in this very necessary art.

Practice flights were a regular feature of 8USAAF operations but this picture of a 91BG formation appears to flout the requirement for a tight pattern. The Element in the high background is well distant from the photographer's section. However, the overall group formation may still be at the point of forming up. Scattered formations were .meat on the table' for Jagdwaffe pilots.

This is a close-up of the Bf110 after it landed back at Bassingbourn. This aircraft is a C variant, operational during the early stages of WWII. The same concentration of armament in the nose of the F and G variants provided a lethal threat to the USAAF "Heavies" up to the point where the "Little Friends" began to dominate the skies over central Europe.

Chaps Flying Circus (42-30029/MS: P) is a group "original" bomber that now bears an impressive mission log on its upper nose. Lt. Chapman's charge will soldier on until 30 January, when she will lose out in a "ditching" action that will also claim the lives of Lt. Carl O. Baer's team; she will be the penultimate aircraft from the "original" cadre to be MIA.

Chapter Nine

Blow for Blow (February/March 1944)

Comment

The balance of aerial power over central Europe was still finely pitched as February 1944 commenced. The blows dealt out to the Nazi industrial capacity were arguably still proving costly to both Allied Bomber Commands in terms of casualty rates inflicted primarily by their *Jagdwaffe* and *Nachtjagd* adversaries. The withdrawal of material and human resources from the Russian and Italian Fronts in order to bolster the Home Defense network (*Reichsverteidigung*) was of clear benefit to the Allies, albeit only in the longer term. The immediate requirement was for the permanent dismantling of *Luftwaffe* strength within the ensuing two to three months at most if the planned Normandy Invasion strike was to enjoy freedom from that entity's counter-blows. The strategic knock-on effect from this desired situation would be almost unfettered access to the enemy's hinterland and subsequent destruction of its manufacturing industry by the bombers.

The recent appointment of Lt/Gen. J. H. "Jimmy" Doolittle to command the 8AF was to bring a basic change not so much in bomber tactics, as in those applicable to fighters. The new incumbent in effect declared war on the *Jagdwaffe* by requiring Gen. Kepner's (CG, 8FC) pilots to seek out Bf190s, Fw190s, and their twin-engine contemporaries as opposed to settling themselves as a screen around the bomber stream. The losses borne by unescorted groups or even CBWs being set upon by those enemy units gaining access was expected to be more than exceeded by the scale of disruption and/or destruction meted out by the USAAF fighters before the enemy was anywhere near the bomber formations. In truth, the aggressively-minded Doolittle had little option but to initiate what was a critical operational gamble if the aforementioned conditions both for *Overlord* and the Bombing Offensive were to be brought to fruition.

By now, the use of PFF equipment was a regular factor in operations, although there were occasions when even its presence was thwarted by the weather conditions, strange as this might seem. The sets were capable of providing at least a sound opportunity of striking at hitherto cloud-enclosed targets, but the degree of accuracy was inevitably scaled down. The first week of February brought a flurry of five missions, four of which were major in terms of aircraft number and target type. On the 2nd, Wilhelmshaven felt the weight of over 600 bomb loads, and next day, the marshalling yards at much-tormented Frankfurt were hammered by roughly the same number. Overall bombers losses were 24, the majority incurred on the 3rd and involving a duo from Bassingbourn.

Neither crew got through to the target and were finally brought down during attempts at solo homeward runs. Flak at the IP crippled 42-39803/DF: Y **The Wolf** and the crippled B-17 was eased into a descending turn. Lt. Fewer R. McGee got his charge as far as the region around Krefeld before more flak strikes impelled the crew to bail out, of which one (Sgt. Clifford K. Kirkpatrick, WG) died from his wounds. Lt. James P. Lutz had previously fallen out due to flak damage incurred by 42-39771/LL: H. He too dropped down to ground level and progressed as far as Eindhoven, Holland, but by then one engine was on fire and two others were malfunctioning thanks to further hits. His forced landing on an airfield there not only left all ten airmen alive, but commenced a successful evasion from capture by two among their number.

The latest combat casualty borne by the 381BG off this mission was 42-30834/GD: E **Micky Finn**. Both starboard engines were knocked out by flak that also totally disabled the hydraulic system for the wing's landing gear. The resultant forced landing at Ridgewell when even the port landing gear only partially deployed was carried off perfectly by Lts. John J. Kuhl and Ashley L. Hamory. This was the second such incident involving the pilot, because on 20 December, he had "bellied in" 42-37754/GD: I **Whodat Dingbat**. However, he suffered a (happily short-lived) psychological relapse following this latest occurrence, during which his mind was swept clean of events over the ensuing three or four days.

"Nell's" Last Gallant Act

The next 48 hours involved missions to French airfields, with the 1BD heading for four airfields (5th) and Nancy/Essay on the 6th. In the latter instance, cloud cover forced a switch to a Target of Opportunity, but in both cases the 1CBW returned without any MIA casualties. However, another 381BG bomber was resting at Dunkeswell (a U.S. Navy airfield in Devon), her combat days over. **Touch the Button Nell** (42-40025/MS:), in Lt. Henry Putek's hands, had suffered an explosion behind the top turret while heading for the Primary.

The force had blown out the cockpit side windows, cracked the windshield, sprung the bottom framing ahead of the pilot, and disabled the turret. The B-17 was pulled out of formation and the bail out bell rung as smoke and flames surged through the compartment. The three other officers jumped, but Putek was literally stuck with his charge, since his parachute pack had been destroyed. T/Sgt. Lifford French (Eng.) grabbed a fire extinguisher and proceeded to extinguish the flames, despite incurring severe facial burns in doing so. The other five airmen were still on board when the bail out order was revoked, but the overall situation was now very fraught,

Out of formation and wallowing along at medium altitude with jammed bomb bay doors, the B-17 was soon picked up by fighters, one of whose strikes wounded Sgt. Herb Burgasser in one eye. The attacks were concentrated from behind, allowing a better return fire concentration from the gunners. Even so, the airframe was soon well riddled and more damage incurred by flak around Paris, where the undercast partially broke up. Putek and French, the latter now in the right seat, had to keep their oxygen masks on in order to ward off the worst effects of the boreal gale jetting through the perforated windshield.

The good fortune that sustained them for between one and two hours prior to crossing the Channel and making landfall, despite the absence of a navigator, then appeared to be deserting them as they approached the coast. The AA batteries located near or at Torbay or Exeter—judging by their relationship to Dunkeswell—on seeing a bomber looming up with open bomb bay doors not unnaturally interpreted this as a hostile action and opened up, causing Putek to bank away seaward; his immediate thought on receiving such a greeting was that he was on the wrong side of the Channel! His doubts soon quelled by identifying the region, he made a second approach that elicited no similar reaction from the guns, the personnel having presumably confirmed the bomber's "friendly" status, and a safe landing was then carried out.

French and Burgasser were rushed to hospital, but the latter's eye condition had deteriorated to the extent that it had to be removed. When later visited by his colleagues, he joked that his limited vision was "Not too bad—just like being in a London blackout!" French was later awarded what would be only the second DSC to go to a group member, while Putek received the Silver Star; **Nell's** condition fully merited "salvage" action. (Lts. Alfred T. Coffman (CP), Conrad M. Blalock (N), and Harvey L. Christiensen (B) all beat the odds on captivity and subsequently returned to England.)

"Big Events Looming"

A mixed pattern of missions and relative formation strength occurred over the next nine days. Frankfurt's marshalling yards were visited on the 8th and 11th, although only two 1BD CBWs went on the first run and nine groups on the second. Meanwhile, the other two Divisions struck mainly at V-1 sites, with the 3BD alone going to Brunswick (10th). The combat crews were then granted a four-day period free from operations, a pause that was unknowingly leading up to the most sustained period of operations since *Black Week*.

However, the outcome of what was to be recorded as *Big Week* would contrast noticeably with the clear tactical and strategic defeat borne on the former occasion. What had been some time in the planning stage was about to be launched thanks to an equally sustained spell of basically sound weather patterns. The USAAF authorities were naturally bent on not only destroying the *Luftwaffe*'s strength in the air; equally important was the denial of these resources to the Front line forces by fatally disrupting the aircraft production facilities.

The Big Gamble

Sunday, 20 February, held no particular significance for the 1,000-plus bomber crews assigned to the day's mission, other than another mission that would hopefully end in success. What they were unknowingly embarking on was the first of five major strikes at Germany's aviation industry, all conducted within just six days. The majority of the targets lay either in a clutch within the Brunswick/Magdeburg/Leipzig triangle or up on the Baltic coast, and in either case were well beyond range of full escort cover. The Baltic-bound formations were perceived to be particularly vulnerable to sustained and unhindered *Jagdwaffe* attention. The possibility of Schweinfurt-scale losses had been factored into the overall operational equation by Gen. Doolittle.

Four Primaries were allotted the 1BD, with the 1CBW assigned locations around Leipzig. The city's Heiterblick plant was the main Primary, with the nearby airfield at Mockau reportedly the other. The weather conditions of cloud-flecked skies with light snow squalls held little promise for successful penetration to the various Primaries. In fact, a good proportion of the formations either got through to their assigned targets or bombed Targets of Opportunity.

The 381BG dispatched two separate formations totalling 41 crews in all. The formation led by Lt. Bill Ridley reached the IP at Halle intact, as did the other Division groups, the escorts having done a sterling job thwarting their *Jagdwaffe* opponents. It was now that one Element momentarily swung out of position just as nine Bf110s made a lunging attack. Lt. Kirch J. Cogswell's crew were on their third mission, but the heavy punishment administered to 42-3562/VE:, including the loss of No. 1 and 2 engines and a fire below the cockpit, spelled an arbitrary conclusion to their combat tour.

Lt. Bill Borrego (CP) recalled how his attempts to extinguish the flames failed, while a second blaze that started in the bomb bay now licked the auxiliary fuel tank mounted there. The bomb load was hastily salvoed and the nine crewmembers still alive began to depart their doomed bomber, with Sgt. Wilfred L. Miller (TG) particularly fortunate to both bail out and survive his wounds, including one knee cap blown off by a 20mm shell.

Both pilots exited the B-17 as it descended in a shallow spiral, with Bill Borrego taking two attempts to hook up his pack, having nearly lost it out of the gaping bomb bay as it dropped from his harness during the first bid! Once in mid-air, his reaction as he initially free fell was not one of apprehension, but rather virtual hysterical elation coupled with a nervous, uncontrollable burst of laughter.

His subsequent descent under the canopy was prolonged and naturally chilly in the frigid winter sky, but he landed in a snowdrift. An armed civilian and a *Wehrmacht* guard rushed up to him, the former administering a blow with his gun to Bill's face that split his lip; fortunately, that was the extent of the "summary justice" handed out and he was marched away to face the first stage of his passage to *Stalag Luft* 1.

The 91BG had similarly sent out two formations that also surrendered just one B-17, in this case 42-29656/LG: S **Skunkface**, another veteran bomber transferred from Molesworth the previous September. Lt. Ernest B. Kidd had attained the target with the formation, which was well on the way home over western Belgium when an Fw190 struck. One engine was damaged and Sgt. Rex Wertmen (BT) was killed. The crew abandoned the aircraft, which came down near Mons; Lt. William H. Huish slipped his captors next day, but although he gained Resistance cover, he was murdered with other evaders after their hide-out was raided by an SS or *Gestapo* squad.

Hard Times Again

The first *Big Week* mission had progressed amazingly well, both in terms of effectiveness, but even more so in terms of loss, the duo from the 1CBW being among the 21 crews declared MIA with seven more bombers declared "salvage." The ever-variable fortunes of combat would turn this cosy situation on its head for the Wing over the next 48 hours, however, beginning with a projected assault on airfields (21st). For some reason, only the 3BD had PFF-equipped B-17s on hand, the result being that the other two Divisions, on also finding their targets "socked in," had no recourse but Targets of Opportunity.

Two 323BS veteran B-17s were part of one 91BG element with both fated to join the MIA list: 42-30712/OR: R **Miss Minookie** and 42-3040/OR: Q **Miss Ouachita**. The sub-formation was particularly exposed to assault after losing position when the CBW altered course while seeking a Target of Opportunity. The trio of bombers was set upon by fighters from II/JG1, whose number included Maj. Heinz Baer, an *Experte* (Ace) with 200 victories to his credit. Lt. Neal P. Ward's OR: R did not last long after it was shot up, with two crewmembers killed and two further individuals subsequently lost after the others jumped clear near Luechtringen.

Miss Ouachita's agony was more extended, although Lt. Spencer K. Osterberg did regain contact with the group following punishment that killed one crewmember and left an engine and the center fuselage on fire. Further damage to the oxygen system then impelled the pilots to pull out and head downward in a run for home. The fighters in pursuit kept up the pressure, and when the B-17 overflew a fighter airfield their number was added to. Lt. John Beran was killed and all too soon the pilot, realizing the odds on survival were insuperable, "bellied in" the bomber north of Lingen, where the survivors were apprehended.

The duo of 323BS losses was mirrored by the 401BS, beginning with 42-3073/LL: A **Lightning Strikes**, yet another group veteran with over 20 missions. Fw190s directed their fire onto the starboard wing, knocking out both engines in quick succession. A heading for home was made as the B-17 dropped steadily downwards, but a steady outbreak of fire around No. 3 engine soon became all-enveloping, whereupon Lt. William Simmons's crew took to their parachutes. Lt. Irwin Piacentini's 42-31572/LL: Y **My Beloved** was also barely one month on group strength and sustained fighter-inflicted damage that impelled the pilots to also make a solo run home. The bid ended with a crash landing south of Muenster, from which only seven crewmembers emerged alive, their pilot being one of three fatalities.

T/Sgt. John Parsons (Eng.) later provided a more detailed account regarding **Lightning Strikes**'s demise to Lt. Simmons as follows:

"We were No. 3 in the Lead element within the Composite group's High squadron. The target approach was too far south and east of the briefed route, so the CBW banked left but too quickly, leaving our group and especially our squadron out on its own—a situation that was ready-made for the fighters to exploit. In our case, the bomber took a devastating strike around the No. 3 engine that tore it up; the fuselage was shot up, but miraculously nobody was injured. The No. 3 fuel tank was punctured and fire had taken a firm hold as the aircraft swung in a wayward manner.

"The communications system was "out" and the parlous state of affairs impelled the crew to begin bailing out. In one of those madly illogical acts, Lt. Clyde P. McCallum (CP) picked up a parachute pack and snapped it on—but because it bore the marking D1, indicating allocation to Lt. Simmons, he detached it and sought out his D2-marked pack instead, after which he calmly stepped down into the nose and exited. This was done in spite of the looming demise of the B-17.

"I indicated to Lt. Simmons that it was high time we both made our escape, to which he acknowledged before calmly waving me forward to the nose hatch. Once there, I waited for him to follow, but after several seconds I turned back to see what he was doing; it was then that I saw him lever himself out of his seat and come down into the compartment, upon which act I was satisfied he was OK and I jumped out. As I looked up after opening my parachute I saw the blazing B-17 disintegrate."

Oschersleben's Recurring Curse

The 91BG's punishment on the 21st was to be repeated next day, in addition to which the same target was involved as when it and the 381BG had been set upon on 11 January—Oschersleben. As on the previous occasion, the weather conditions intervened to prevent the 3BD from assembling and for a recall signal to go out to the 2BD when well into enemy airspace. So it was that the 1BD again became the principal focus for *Jagdwaffe* activity and the stage was duly set for another severe beating for the bombers.

As far as the 1CBW was concerned, the cloud cover that had hindered the B-24 formations ironically began to break up as German airspace was looming, and with it came the initial fighter onslaught. The intention to strike this specific Primary out of several allocated to the 1BD came to naught and the crews sought out Targets of Opportunity that in the Wing's case transpired as Buende, SW of Minden. The price paid for this reduced strike effort was sharp at eleven B-17s overall.

More Bassingbourn Misery

Four crews had gone down twenty-four hours earlier, and now that figure would be extended by one, although only in respect of aircraft. The Wing was enveloped in a succession of fighter passes and all too soon the effect began to tell. The region between Minden and Hameln to the SE accommodated three of the MIA bombers. Flak appears to have been the initial catalyst in determining the fate of 42-39815/OR: N **Emeigh**. The loss of an engine by a shell saw the ever-lagging B-17 soon turned for home with Lt. Ken Sutherland having the bombs salvoed, but the odds against success were to prove too great.

Latched onto by two fighters whose fire rendered at least three crewmembers lifeless, the order to abandon the aircraft was swiftly given; the vicious spin that then developed saw only Lts. Fred McBride (N) and Leslie A. Price (B), along with Sgt. Fred A. Tabor (WG), separating themselves from its fatal embrace and jump. **Emeigh**'s crash site at Luedge was none too distant from where its squadron companion **Paper Dolly** (42-37746/OR: T) ended its combat career at Boesingfeld, S of Minden. The B-17 was bearing Lt. Frank Kolts's crew on their 14th mission, but the incessant fighter thrusts culminated in the aircraft swinging out of formation; Lt. Ehud Merkel (CP) and the six Enlisted men got out and down alive.

There were few "original" B-17s now on hand with the group and today's cull included 41-24490/DF: C **Jack the Ripper**. No. 3 engine was set on fire as the bomb run commenced, whereupon Lt. James R. Considine dropped out to port and headed west. The cloud layers that provided a form of cover sadly opened up long enough for the shadowing fighters to home in and disable two further engines, as well as cause the landing gear to droop, further retarding the B-17's already laboring progress. The end was imminent and all ten crewmembers took to their parachutes several miles east of Muenster, with only Lt. Henry S. Schaub failing to survive, reportedly due to his parachute's failure to deploy.

The 322BS' 42-39898/LG: L **Boston Bombshell** appears to have been on the return leg when matters went sour for Lt. William D. Wood and crew. Fighter strikes killed one crewmember and gravely wounded a second, as well as setting an engine ablaze. The steady altitude loss culminated in a crash landing of the B-17 some miles east of Muenster, near Warendorf. The impact was heavy enough to fracture the central fuselage and smash up the nose compartment; the nine survivors exited, but T/Sgt. Woodrow Wade's severe injured state later ended with him dying in hospital.

Four crews were down on enemy soil, but a fifth—also from the 323BS—enjoyed much better fortune compared to their bomber. **Sugar Blues** (42-37939/OR :) was two months on group establishment, but absorbed heavy punishment during the bomb run to Buende and fell back out of position. Once again, the pilot, Lt. Roman V. Maziarz, opted to drop down "on the deck" and make a solo run home, this being an action that unlike **Jack the Ripper** and **Boston Bombshell** culminated in human success, at least.

The enemy coast was successfully cleared, but the scale of damage, probably further exacerbated by dwindling fuel reserves, decided the pilots to prepare the crew for a "ditching." The impact with the North Sea not only left the bomber intact and afloat long enough for the life rafts to be deployed; the subsequent spell of nearly five hours exposed to the chill winter conditions found all ten in good spirits when reached by the ASR Service.

Ridgewell's Second Penance

Lt. Lee W. Smith's 381BG crew were manning 42-39895/MS: S **Bermondsay Battler**, one of four B-17s named in connection with badly-blitzed London boroughs. Lt. T. Paxton Sherwood had flown the previous day's mission as copilot, but Lt. Rowland H. Evans had displaced him today—a very fortunate break for his predecessor. One of the first fighter passes hammered Smith's B-17 so comprehensively that it immediately slipped out and down to finally crash at Hiddesen, none of the ten airmen surviving in the process. This was but the start of another bad day for the Wing as the attacks rained in upon the 1BD.

The 535BS was destined to lose two more crews soon after, with nine of the twenty airmen sharing the Smith crew's fate. Worse affected was Lt. Charles H. Downey's team in 42-31533/MS: U, which came down SSE of Hameln with the pilot and six others losing their lives. Sandebeck, SE of Bielefeld, collected the remains of 42-31696/MS:, along with two members of Lt. Henry's Hustedt's crew who were killed as the bail out procedure was being enacted. The same area was where the 532BS' 42-31443/VE: M **Friday the 13th** tragically lived up to her omen-laden title. Fire had erupted within the oxygen system on Lt. Francis J. Flaherty's bomber and he became one of the six crewmembers who failed to come through the B-17's detachment and final impact near Brake-Senne.

The remaining pair of MIA casualties came from the 533BS, adding to the six lost on the previous occasion. Lt. Hal E. Roling's 42-39946/VP: was taken out by a precise flak strike that excised the entire forward fuselage ahead of the top turret and all four officers, along with Sgt. Asbury N. Thompson (Eng.), were lost. The latter airman might have survived, had he not been up attending to the Bendix chin turret guns at the time. The beheaded airframe fell out of the sky to impact at Evenhausen, east of Bielefeld, but not before the other five crewmembers succeeded in jumping clear.

The carnage among the group ranks was completed by the loss of Lt. Francis N. Fridgen's 42-97474/VP: Z **Homing Pigeon**, also known as "Fridgen's Pigeons" among the crew. The badly battered B-17 made it through to complete the bomb run, but was ultimately impelled to be force landed near Unna, on Dortmund's NE boundary. By then, several crewmembers were either dead on board or had died through bailing out as the B-17 was about to come down. Only Fridgen and three others survived the experience.

In 1986, Sgt. Lowell Slayton (TG) visited the crash site, where he met with several eyewitnesses of the incident. One was a then-young woman who told Slayton how she had cradled one of his buddies in her arms shortly before he expired—so exposing one of the basic contradictions of war, namely how impersonal hostility can turn to compassion when confronted by a stricken human being, even in the midst of a comprehensive conflict.

Piling on the Pressure

The scale of punishment specifically inflicted upon the 1BD (34 bombers MIA) would have been a severe logistical blow several months back. Now, the availability of both aircraft and crews was more than sufficient to continue operations right away—although it was to be 48 hours before the next step in *Big Week*'s progress was taken. Consecutive daily runs to Schweinfurt (of dreaded import for both 1CBW groups) on the 24th and a twin thrust at aviation industrial plants in Stuttgart and Augsburg next day was made by the 1BD. The loss of fifteen MIA B-17s out of 506 dispatched over the two days was a surprisingly marginal one, given the distances flown; the escorts' kill/loss ratio of 64/13 was a likely factor in achieving this result, as well as growing proof of the steady if not yet constant inroads being made into the *Jagdwaffe's* aircraft and pilot strength.

A single 1CBW casualty was incurred during the latter occasion when Augsburg was the Primary. Lt. Donald G. Henderson (POW) had brought 42-37786/VE: B safely through to the target, but then, on the return leg, apparently suffered damage or mechanical problems that caused the B-17 to lag steadily behind and below. Eyewitnesses reported the bomber finally disappearing after a large wooded area was being overflown, but it appears that its fate was sealed by a single Bf109, the aircraft crashing at Willmandingen, near Reutlingen, along with six of the ten crewmembers.

Pivotal Month (March 1944)

Berlin had been the focus of attention for RAF Bomber Command since the previous August and now, as March commenced, the 8AF was equally bent upon raining further punishment on the metropolis, which contained a veritable plethora of industrial targets to add to its railroad, airfield, and administrative facilities. Four full missions would be completed by the 22nd, but the first month's strike against a German target involved the much-afflicted city of Frankfurt.

Over at Ridgewell, Capt. Woods was due to carry a special "supernumerary" in the shape of Capt. Brown (group Chaplain). He had long wished to fly a mission, otherwise feeling he could not administer spiritual comfort without having at least a peripheral knowledge of what the crews were facing. He fully recognized that he would take up valuable oxygen reserves and might get in the way, but permission had been granted by Col. Leber (group CO) and he was ready to board 42-31761/VP: O **Rotherhithe's Revenge**, a B-17G destined to survive WWII with some 121 missions flown.

The Division marshalling yard Primary was bombed by under one-third of the 327 dispatched bombers, but the *Jagdwaffe* and flak defenses only culled eight crews in all, with the escort Force now including two P-51 units—again playing their part in ensuring their adversaries were at least held at bay. The single 1CBW loss involved Lt. Eugene Shultz flying 42-39891/VP: V; flak damage in the target area resulted in steady height loss as the pilots tailed the formation homeward. Last seen over Belgium, all ten airmen finally abandoned the ailing B-17, which crashed north of Arlon.

Sgt. John T. Farr (RWG) evaded capture, whereas Sgt. Robert M. Trapnell (BT) was not only apprehended, but later died during the forced march of POWs from *Stalag-Luft IV* the following winter. Capt. Woods returned his crew and "supernumerary" safely to Ridgewell; this crew would complete their combat tour, while the Chaplain reportedly flew at least one more mission—and equally important—survived the experience.

Berlin was to appear on the Briefing maps for three of the next four days, but the initial two attempts to penetrate the enemy defenses were to be thwarted by the crews' natural enemy, Mother Nature. On the 3rd, a Force of over 700 B-17s and B-24s rose off their airfields and headed eastward, albeit in vain. A combination of expanding cloud layers whose opaqueness was added to by massive contrail patterns exuded by the bombers' engines saw the formations turning back, a small element of which deposited their loads on Targets of Opportunity.

The 1CBW's return route reportedly intermingled with that of a 3BD contemporary and the collision between two B-17s from the latter sub-force was originally regarded as fatally scattering its debris upon 42-37986/GD: K, bearing Lt. Robert H. Rogers's crew. All ten airmen bailed out safely, with their flak-damaged charge coming down in NE Holland near Groningen, but whether the abandonment was due to the foregoing circumstance has since been largely discredited.

The "ditching" of the 91BG's 42-37965/OR: U **My Desire** had an ultimately tragic outcome for half of Lt. Walter M. Pickard's team. Accumulated engine failure due to flak strikes saw the bid for a safe landing end scant miles from the English coast, but all ten crewmembers survived the impact. Unfortunately, only one dinghy could be partially inflated, to which the crew clung while a nearby fishing boat's draught was too deep for it to approach; instead, the crew launched a life boat, but only five airmen could be accommodated therein. The bid to save the remaining five by towing the dinghy back to the fishing boat as they held on tragically yielded no positive result, since exposure to the chilled waters saw all of them losing their grip and drifting away to their deaths.

Undaunted, the 8AF authorities directed their crews toward Berlin next morning. However, the weather conditions again largely thwarted the bid to either assemble or gain enemy airspace further than the Ruehr before turning back upon the "recall" signal. One CBW did get through, but on return claimed no knowledge of such a signal. Losses among the 1BD were again marginal, but this was of little comfort to the four crews concerned.

Lt. David D. Keyes had charge of a B-17 named **Spare Parts** (42-30151/VE: Q) that had been at Ridgewell since June 1943, when it had ironically lived up to its title. The crew had flown the B-17F twenty-four hours previous on their inaugural mission when bad oil leaks occurred in an engine. Swiftly attended to before being put back on combat status, this "clunker" now exhibited one total engine failure followed by a second running out of oil. The decision to turn back and salvo the bomb load was followed by the further problem of drag caused by the jammed bomb bay doors. The cocktail of mechanical disasters finally compelled the pilots to seek a suitable crash landing site near St. Omer, in NE France, rather than risk a failure over the sea; all ten emerged in sound order, but were promptly rounded up by personnel from a nearby military site.

"Tail of a goat"

Lt. John Wierman was copilot to Lt. Richard "Slick" Coyle (533BS). Their spell of operations with the 381BG was brief, since the crew was to go MIA off its third mission on 6 March. However, a whimsical incident as preparations for a mission were under way was later recounted by John. The engines had been switched on and the pilots were in the process of running them up when he noticed the crew chief appearing to laugh his head off. The source of his amusement was a tethered goat in the field directly behind the bomber. The powerful slipstream emanating from the combined 4,800hp output of the Wright Cyclones had struck home and lifted the hapless animal off the ground.

Power was eased off, but the animal's return to the soil was brief, because a second application of power cast it back into the air. It emerged intact from this second "flight," but it was still fortunate not to end up strangled to death or dying of fright. John's crew were made aware of the incident and joined in the laughter. To some people, their reaction might smack of heartlessness bordering on cruelty. On the other hand, any form of relief from the tension of a forthcoming mission, however marginal or basic in form that this might be, had to be considered relevant. However, the goat's attitude towards its "persecutors" would not have been so accommodating!

Big B at Last

"Don't send my boy to Berlin; the dying mother did cry;
Don't send my boy to Berlin; **I'd rather see him die**" - *anonymous*

For the crews alerted and heading for the Briefing rooms in the still night-shrouded skies on 6 March, the feeling that any mission to *Big B* would induce a particularly harsh response from the German defenses hung heavy in their minds. The psychological, let alone operational, kudos of striking at the heart of the Third Reich were conversely expected to have a deleterious effect upon the Nazi hierarchy's morale, not to say that of its citizenry. A more immediate benefit to the 8AF would be the burgeoning assaults by the 8FC "Little Friends" upon the *Jagdwaffe*, whose pilots were surely going to mount the stiffest and maximum opposition to this particular incursion.

The Divisions would fly in trail before splitting up for their specific targets, then return line abreast. Both B-17 sub-forces would assemble their CBWs, however, in parallel pairs, other than the Composite 40/41CBW, flying alone at the left rear of the1BD, which was to be in the overall Lead position. Finally, the 1CBW was "up front" and positioned to port of the 40CBW. Both Wings could accordingly expect to feel the initial counter-thrusts of the *Jagdwaffe*, but in fact, this dubious "honor" would go the way of the ironically-numbered 13CBW element of the 3BD. In addition, a hard day was in prospect for other units that included both 1CBW groups, although the vagaries of combat operations would, for example, see three of the eleven 1BD groups returning with no MIA losses.

The escort strength of 801 fighters outweighed the 730-strong bomber force, but naturally could not guarantee the "Big Friends" more than a relative freedom from uninterrupted access by the German fighters. That comprehensive situation was never to be realized, and it was only the promise of wearing down the *Jagdwaffe* strength in fighters and pilots to a point where it became ineffective that bolstered morale among the combat crews.

The 1BD's experience of fighter attacks commenced over the Dutch/German border, but the 1CBW seems to have been largely spared the growing storm of aerial-based assault until the bomber stream had banked marginally SE at Celle and was bypassing Magdeburg to the north. However, the 91BG was short of one B-17 at this point, with flak the initial cause. Lt. Ben J. Foumey, Jr.'s 42-38118/OR: N had two engines knocked out as Hannover was looming up, leaving him with little option but to release his bomb load and head back at minimum altitude.

His course unfortunately intersected with Quakenbrueck airfield, currently home for IV/NJG1's Bf110G-4 night fighters. Worse still was the fact that *Oblt.* Herman Greiner had just gotten airborne and immediately latched onto the lumbering B-17; his firing pass was conducted with flaps and landing gear still deployed and he nearly stalled out his mount in the process. As for OR: N, its homeward progress was halted bare miles west of the airfield at Nortrup, when a crash landing left all but two crewmembers alive.

A sizeable force of Bf110G-2s and Me410s from I and II/ZG26 with a Bf109 escort from JG3 were homing in on the 1BD; the overall figure of 113 was completed with Fw190s and Bf109s from two further *Gruppen*. The aircraft had formed up over Magdeburg and were directed to a position that aligned them head-on to the 1BD's reported course. However, the stream's SE change of direction threw this factor out, added to which the replacement escort cover had just arrived on the scene. The 4FG and 357FG P-51s were badly outnumbered almost two to one, but took on the Germans and disrupted their intention of swamping the bomber defenses, although they could not totally prevent passes being made.

The heavy armament of the Bf110G and Me410 "twins," including 21-cm rockets, made for a fearsome striking power and several bombers were fatally crippled within the two CBWs, including two further 91BG machines. The No. 3 engine on 42-31911/OR: Q was set on fire, with the flames rapidly enveloping the inner wing, whereupon Lt. Douglas C. Harding rang the bail out bell, to which all ten airmen responded positively and floated down near Ramstedt, where the aircraft impacted.

No such personal luck went the way of four members of Lt. Paris Coleman's (KIA) crew flying in 42-31079/LL: J after strikes set the central fuselage ablaze; one hapless individual was observed crawling out of the radio hatch with his parachute already flame-affected before impacting with the stabilizer and further ripping the canopy on its surface; either way, his fate was clearly sealed.

The first of three 381BG casualties appears to have been Lt. Milton Fastrup's 42-31448/VE: **Half Breed**, whose demise was prolonged in nature after an engine was set on fire. The pilots dropped out of formation and commenced a run for home that extended as far as the region between Köln and Aachen. There, the B-17 was intercepted by *Oblt.* Walter Matoni, a JG26 *Experte* who wasted no time bringing his prey down close to Eusweiler, happily without any of the ten occupants, who took to their parachutes.

This B-17's fate contrasted sharply with the one dealt out soon after to 42-3225/VP: T **Linda Mary**, Ridgewell's last "original" bomber to feel the enemy's lethal sting. Sgt. Raymond F. Legg (RWG), another veteran from Lt. Gleichauf's tour-expired crew, saw his luck finally run out; his was the sole fatality in Lt. Richard W. Coyle's team and probably accompanied the bomber to its destruction SE of Gardelegen. Also on board was the "Tail of a Goat" raconteur, Lt. J. Wierman.

A fourth 91BG crew went down almost simultaneously to Lt. Coyle, with the crash site very close by. The close-packed nature of the formation coupled with the fighter flow through its ranks was tailor made for collisions. **My Darling also** (42-31578/LL: L) had already suffered an engine fire from fighter strikes when an Fw190 failed to get out of its path. It was surprising in such circumstances that anybody survived the incident out of Lt. Bob Tibbets, Jr.'s crew, but two gunners escaped the lethal hand dealt out to their eight fellow airmen. The IP was approaching when another 91BG bomber was fatally set upon. **Hell and High Water** (42-31869/LL: Y), flown by Lt. Clyde V. Mason, had its port wing set on fire, while two gunners were either killed during the assaults or failed to bail out safely before the fire-stricken B-17 impacted near Trebbin.

A number of B-17s had incurred fighter damage that was not immediately fatal, one of which was Lt. Bryce S. Evertson's 42-97483/LG: L. The pilots held formation until the bomb run on a Target of Opportunity in Berlin was complete and the formation headed out over the city's NE suburbs. Then, the No. 1 engine damaged earlier erupted into flame and the bail out order was issued, which all ten occupants achieved safely before the aircraft fell away to its doom in the city district of Wilmersdorf-Bernau.

The 1CBW had lost nine as the Rally Point was attained, with a third Ridgewell B-17 involved. The bomb run was in progress, but the fighter attacks were still persisting, one of which ended with 42-31533/GD: B erupting in fire. Half the crew, including Lt. Edward E. Haushalter, lost their lives and the aircraft peeled out of formation to come down SE of the original but now cloud-shrouded Primary at Erkner. All three Divisions had achieved poor to moderate results in terms of bombing their Primaries, and to add to this relative failure, 69 crews were declared MIA. However, the "Little Friends" had really gone to town with "kill"/loss figures of 81/11—a continuing augury for the *Jagdwaffe* being permanently placed on their back foot in both material and human terms.

A further nine bombers were "write offs" on or adjacent to British soil, with both 1CBW groups contributing one. Bassingbourn's 42-37761/OR: L **Blue Dreams** suffered fuel tank leakage that impelled a diversion into nearby Steeple Morden; unfortunately, Lt. Walter E. Wilkinson forgot to lower the landing gear, but the crew were fortunate that the resultant impact did not detonate the bomb load. At the other end of the mission, Lt. Rodney T. Cahill "ditched" 42-37983/VE: N close to the shoreline of Kent, an act that was survived by all on board.

Berlin Besieged

The 8AF's first successful thrust at *Big B*, at least in terms of bomber numbers, if not material destruction, gave notice to the enemy that the capital could expect continued attention. Ironically, RAF Bomber Command's 1943/44 campaign centered on Berlin had virtually run its course, but now its American contemporary would take up the challenge with equal if not more effect. March would witness three further major missions to the city, two of which would occur within 24 hours of each other. On the 8th, the single Primary of Erkner's VFK ball bearing plant outside Berlin's SW fringe was focused on by the bulk of the 539 crews making their bomb runs. This time round, although the 37 loss total in B-17s and B-24s was barely half that on the 6th, it was the 3BD that again absorbed an even greater proportion of these MIA casualties.

The risk inherent in attempting a solo run for home was again demonstrated by Lt. Claude M. Williams and crew on 42-39892/LL: B. A combination of flak damage and engine problems when approaching Berlin was severe enough for the pilots to take this course of action. Fighters quickly picked up the B-17 and delivered a devastating strike that killed four gunners. The bomber was abandoned roughly halfway between Berlin and Hamburg, after which it exploded in mid-air SSW of Wittenberge. Lt. Thomas A. Pirtle reached the target in the 381BG's 42-38029/VE: M, but fighter-inflicted damage finally led to a bail out over Holland; all ten reached the ground safely, of which two evaded immediate capture and two succeeded wholly until September, when British forces liberated Antwerp, where the men were currently secreted.

The bombers' engines were barely cool and the crews back in their billets when a Mission Alert was called for the morrow, with Berlin again targeted. The force of 529 dispatched was fewer in number compared to the two previous missions, but was still enough to cause sizeable damage. However, the Primaries of aircraft production plants at Oranienburg and Brandenburg were spared thanks to cloud cover; instead, the B-17 Divisions unloaded on the center of the city. *Jagdwaffe* efforts were marginal, probably thanks to the weather, so bomber losses were minimal at eight MIA.

Five missions were flown over the next seven days and the 1BD was involved in three. The first was to Muenster (11th), when a single CBW from each B-17 Division was dispatched. Just one more group was involved in an abortive attempt to attack V-1 sites in the Pas de Calais (13th). Three days elapsed before the 1BD crews went out again, and this time around all eleven groups were committed to a "deep penetration" run into SE Germany.

Augsburg's industry was assaulted, along with the 3BD, who again bore more than half of the 23 bombers going MIA (13). **Mount N' Ride** 42-31585/OR: B had put in a handful of missions since her 1 March arrival, but flak damage to two engines incurred over a group target listed as Lechfeld caused Lt. Doyle P. Bradford's aircraft to soon begin lagging behind. The proximity of Switzerland initiated what was to be a successful bid to reach that neutral country's soil, where the crew became one of seven landing or crashing that day, with the survivors being interned.

A drip feed of losses beginning on the 16th now afflicted the 91BG for the remainder of March, with another crew MIA two days later. Lt. Harry L. Theophilus and crew had flown 42-39967/DF: **Mary Kay** on ten previous occasions, but flak over Oberpfaffenhofen so damaged the B-17 that it fell behind. Switzerland was none too far distant, so a heading was taken up. However, fighters caught the aircraft when almost there, and although the resultant spin that occurred was corrected, by then, the bomber was almost on the ground bordering the Bodensee at Bregenz. Theophilus and three others were killed and the other six taken prisoner, since the B-17 came down on Austrian soil, tantalizingly in sight of Switzerland.

Navigational SNAFU?

Frankfurt was laid on for its latest pasting by all three Divisions, but the majority of the 445 crews sent out turned back due to adverse weather, albeit not until well into Continental airspace. The failure to reach the Primary was then compounded by what could be described uncertain navigation, judging by the experience of the 381BG, if not the 1CBW at least. Lt. George B. Mackintosh, Jr., had returned from Sweden after he and Osce V. Jones diverted into there the previous 24 July, and was now back on combat status and piloting 42-31381 /MS: O **Jaynie B.**

Engine failure had resulted in the bomber lagging behind the group. The solid undercast prevented any chance of orientation and the formations broke out to find themselves close to an unfamiliar coastline—little wonder, since it was part of the Brittany peninsula in NW France! (In the author's 2000 Schiffer Publication *Ridgewell's Flying Fortresses*, covering the incident, this region was wrongly quoted as Normandy.) With dwindling fuel reserves, the decision to turn back and "ditch" off the enemy coast as opposed to risking the same action in the vaster expanse of the English Channel ended with success, at least regarding all on board emerging alive and intact; in addition, the B-17 remained afloat for upwards of twenty minutes.

Not so reassuring was the failure of one life raft to inflate; eight of the crew managed to wedge themselves within the restricted space afforded by the other intact dinghy, despite the bulk of their flight gear. Meanwhile, George and Sgt. Eugene F. Copp (WG) hung on the dinghy's securing lines as they floated in the none-too-warm Atlantic waters. It was as well that their time of immersion soon ended after a French vessel with German guards arrived on the scene to fish the crew out.

Sgt. Copp's presence was rather unusual, in that he was not regular combat crew, but was normally a stateside gunnery instructor. On 4 March, he and two contemporaries had arrived at Ridgewell, where they were expected to fly three missions before returning to their normal posts. The other two had failed to survive their first outing, while Eugene would have been heading back home had Fate not intervened to dispatch him to a *Stalag* instead. At least he would still be alive in May 1945, following some fourteen months of incarceration.

Buckeye Boomerang II had replaced its named predecessor in late January. Now, 42-31672/LL: was heading home on its own after becoming totally separated from the 91BG formation. Lt. Frank D. Turk's crew progressed as far as the region SW of Dieppe before two Bf109s caught the straggler and fatally damaged her. Most on board were already gone before the bomber exploded, depositing remains over Saint-Ouen-le-Mauget. The pilot was blown clear, but Lt. James D. Grube (N) became the sole fatality, while Sgt. Don C. Stairs (ROG) evaded capture to return to Britain—even though he landed in close proximity to a mixed French/German group gathered around one of his colleagues!

The 8AF was now regularly thrusting deep into enemy territory in a manner largely unthinkable just several months previous. Two days following the Frankfurt failure, it launched its latest foray against *Big B*, with aviation plants at Basdorf and Oranienburg the focus. However, both remained inviolate from assault thanks to cloud cover and the city center took the brunt of 657 bomb loads instead. Once again, the *Jagdwaffe* was conspicuous by its absence and ironically, the 8FC lost twelve pilots to a single German; on the other hand, just twelve bomber crews were MIA. A single 91BG crew was among this total after 42-97125/LL: was abandoned by Capt. Charles R. Phillips's crew west of Berlin after suffering heavy damage. Next day, Muenster remained largely free from 1BD attention with Targets of Opportunity the majority and mandatory choice.

Frankfurt Again

Lt. Kenneth T. Haynes, Jr. (532BS) had flown one mission as a "supernumerary" and was now back with his assigned crew, preparing for a mission to Frankfurt (24th). The previous evening, his tail gunner, Sgt. Arthur M. Plows, had sought advice from the veteran tail gunner Sgt. Tom LaMore as to how he should conduct himself—not so much regarding his function as a gunner, but rather, in a manner ensuring he would not let down his fellow airmen in any emergency situation. After the lengthy discussion was complete, he turned to Tom as he exited the latter's billet door and said: "The cold ones are on me tonight," a pledge that was tragically never to be fulfilled.

A gloomy early morning atmosphere pervaded the area as the 381BG took off, with Tom's crew, led by Lt. John A. Rickerson, lifting off in turn. The B-17 was barely two minutes clear of the airfield when, as Tom recalled, the darkness behind was briefly lit up by a huge flash. He could not have known that 42-38102/VE: A had faltered and gone in at Birdbrook, just two miles off the runway end, bearing all ten of Haynes's crew to their deaths. A further irony lay in the fact that Tom would never have savored the drinks proposed by Sgt. Plows, even if the tragic incident had not occurred, since he was unknowingly flying on a one-way mission.

The regular winter weather conditions of cloud-heaped skies casting up dangerously low visibility levels added to by ever-thickening engine exhaust trails provided the perfect scenario for close formation's top risk—mid-air collision. The formations were diverting from the original Primary at Schweinfurt in the direction of Frankfurt's Secondary choice when disaster struck. Lt. Rickerson, in 42-31490/VE: K, had 42-40008/VE: E off his starboard wing, but Lt. Thomas P. Tompson's mount was slow to turn to starboard.

The result was that its No. 1 propeller's blades knocked off the other B-17's nose Plexiglas, but far worse resulting from the contact was the destruction wrought upon VE: E by Rickerson's No. 4 propeller, which ripped into the companion bomber's cockpit area. A grotesque death dance evolved for several thousand feet, as the bombers' frames remained interlocked before separation occurred. The spinning mass that was VE: E then swiftly expanded into a massive explosion, expunging the lives of all but Sgt. Rinaldo Cavalieri (WG).

The other B-17, although eased back into level flight, was also in deep trouble with one engine on fire, a second disabled with a "feathered" propeller, and heavy starboard wing damage. The fire was extinguished and the crippled B-17 headed on its extended flight home, but one that became steadily less likely of fulfilment, as altitude was steadily lost. Finally, the region around Lille, France, was reached, and it was close to the village of Carvin, SW of that French city, where the bomber was eased down for a successful crash landing. The crew evacuated the aircraft and scattered, seeking as much cover as was feasible in what was a flat, barren stretch of countryside, but Sgt. LaMore, despite being badly injured during the collision, first ensured the airframe was set alight using incendiary sticks supplied for this purpose; only then did he manage to make his way to a ditch adjoining a small copse of trees, where he collapsed.

He was destined to be one of six among the crew to evade capture, Rickerson and Lt. Donald M. Wilson (CP) being included. However, Tom's and Sgt. Durward I.

Williams's (WG) tenure of freedom would only last some two months before apprehension through betrayal would occur. Tom would partake in Resistance activities during this period, thereby placing himself outside the Geneva Convention for POW treatment when captured; what transpired between then and VE-Day would test his physical and mental faculties to the limit, as well as forming the basis for an autobiography, *The Apples are Green*, published around 2002. (The title refers to a typical coded heading for radio messages from Britain aimed at specific groups within the Resistance Movement.) The atmosphere on return to Ridgewell among the 532BS personnel in particular was surely subdued, especially when given all three MIA crews had gone down without enemy intervention.

The Odyssey of "Whodat"

A flurry of daily missions between 26 and 29 March closed off the 1BD's operational account, during which time only three 1CBW bombers were placed in the MIA category. The single 381BG example would attest to the structural integrity of the Boeing design, as events on the run to Rheims/Champagne airfields (28th) confirmed. In the words of one survivor from Lt. Daniel C. Henry's crew on 42-37754/GD: I **Whodat—The Dingbat**: "when the explosion occurred it seemed the world had come to an end."

The flak barrage put up was sporadic, but one missile burst right alongside the B-17's rear fuselage, snuffing out the lives of S/Sgts. James F. Norcom and Richard Toler (WGs), along with Frank J. Kurtz (TG). The massive hole torn in the airframe around the waist windows also canted the tail section marginally to starboard; in such circumstances, it was amazing that the subsequent precipitate descent adding further pressure to the weakened air frame did not result in its total fracture.

Henry and Lt. Robert R. Crisler managed to regain control, whereupon the pilot cancelled the order to jump that had been promptly issued. Control was proving difficult, since the elevators were jammed in the "up" position, while the rudder cables were severed; however, Sgt. Sebastian Quaresma (Eng.) jury-rigged the latter unit's connections with spare wire. Meanwhile, Sgt. Kyle B. Wheatley's luck was diametrically opposite to his dead fellow airmen. His ball turret had been vertically aligned at the time and it had also jammed—had it been at any other angle, he would not have been able to regain the aircraft's interior, since the entrance hatch was at the turret rear and could only be accessed from its current vertical angle.

Quaresma's examination of the rear fuselage confirmed the extent of the damage and caused him to later state on seeing the waist gunners' bodies that he "never wanted to see anything like that again." The bomber's dangerous exposure to fighter attack was soon ended after an eight-strong group of 20FG P-38s led by Lt. Chet Halberg spotted its plight and closed in. The course for home was finally confirmed, but only after Halberg had made frantic hand signals to the pilots that far from going in that direction, they were heading away.

The wallowing B-17, along with its escort, finally won through to the English Channel, where the P-38s ended their cover and final course was taken up for Ridgewell. The personnel there could hardly believe what they observed as the B-17 slowly circled the airfield and the five other crewmembers prepared to bail out. S/Sgt. Carl A. Mongrue's (ROG) arm wound proved no barrier to his jumping, and in fact, all five descended safely, although Lt. Fred L. Beardsworth's free fall was breathtaking, as he only pulled the ripcord when almost on the ground.

Their obligation to the crew satisfactorily completed, Henry and Crisler then banked away to the east towards the Suffolk coastline. It was patently obvious **Whodat** could never be brought down safely and that it was necessary to abandon her to a watery fate, along with her posthumous trio of airmen. Both pilots jumped out near Bawdsey after directing their charge out to sea, where she obligingly descended to become a permanent tomb for other than Sgt. Kurtz, whose body was washed ashore two months later.

A second 381BG crew regained friendly soil in 42-37933/MS: R **Superstitious Aloysius** after an engine malfunctioned on the way over. Although power was "out," the fire that started became steadily more intense as altitude was lost. By the time Lt. James R. Liddle had the bomber back over SE England, the situation had deteriorated to the extent that a bail out was deemed mandatory for fear of the aircraft exploding prior to a safe landing.

Several crewmembers, including Sgt. Emory Y. Naha (TG), a full-blooded Native American of the Tewa tribe, spilled their parachutes inside the fuselage, but all ten airmen got out and down safely. Lt. Joe Scott (N) used his initiative when he and Sgt. Floyd C. Hanson (ROG) were temporarily "billeted out" at a hotel in Ashford—he sold the French Francs from his escapekit to a third party in order to settle the bill, the manager being so impressed at Joe's action that he loaned him ten pounds.

The final mission at month's end took the 1BD alone to another much-assaulted city (Brunswick), but the conditions forced a switch to the Secondary at Waggum, during the course of which nine out of 233 crews were MIA, a figure including two 91BG B-17s. It was barely a week since 42-97246/LL: had arrived at the base, and now she suffered so much punishment from fighter strikes that she finally succumbed NE of Bremen; Lt. Julius D. C. Anderson (P) was one of five fatalities. Lt. Edgar C. Downing's crew was more fortunate, in that all ten not only survived the "ditching" of 42-3506/DF; well out of sight of the Dutch coast to get into dinghies, but subsequently drifted eastward, right into the path of a *Kriegsmarine* force of patrol boats that picked up the undoubtedly chilled airmen late in the evening.

"Sold down the River?"

By the beginning of March, Lt. Jim Tyson's crew, which included John Howland's very precise navigational skills, were combat-hardened veterans. However, during the first Berlin mission they were firmly rebuffed by the group CO for breaking radio silence and calling the Lead aircraft, this despite the very pertinent fact that their navigation plot confirmed the formation was off course and likely to overfly Hannover if persisted with. A similar rebuff was handed out two days later for the same offense.

On the second occasion, the Colonel said they had nevertheless flown a good mission and put before them the prospect of becoming a PFF-trained crew, one that was duly taken up. However, on arrival at Chelveston for the perceived PFF School "course," they found out the very next mission would be "training on the job" status. Moreover, they were soon to become aware that Lead crews rarely if ever went out on other than "hard" missions of lengthy duration (no milk runs for them!). In addition, they would be expected to fly to the airfield providing Wing or Division Lead prior to the mission with a resultant lack of proper amenities on hand, given that they usually transferred late the previous evening. In all, it appeared as if Col. Leber had knowingly sold the crew a "dud" bill of goods—at least, this was John's natural interpretation of his superior's motive for relieving himself of a "problem" crew! A small consolation lay in the fact that the accommodations at Bassingbourn were away ahead of Ridgewell's utility equivalent.

By now, the original concentration of PFF-equipped bombers within one group (482BG) had evolved into the first stage of devolvement. A specific squadron within one group for each Division would now operate the Division's PFF cadre of aircraft—in this instance, the choice fell upon the 324BS at Bassingbourn, to which Lt. Tyson, along with Lt. Carl Clark's team (also 535BS), were duly detached during April.

Miss Ouachita (42-3040/OR: Q) is probably the centerpiece for a publicity photo, judging by the number of ground personnel on hand. The oval cut-out for the forward-firing weapon is an unusual variation. Originally with the 303rd and 306th BGs, it served with the 91BG until 21 February 1944, when it was MIA along with two of Lt. Spencer Osterberg's crew.

This christening ceremony for two 381BG bombers is actually taking place at Kimbolton on 15 February. Rotherhithes Revenge (42-31761/VP: O) was newly assigned on 31 January, whereas 42-39895/MS: S Bermondsay Battler in the background arrived on 22 December. Revenge was destined to put in around 120 missions, but Battler was MIA just seven days after the foregoing date.

Lt. John Silvernale (second from left, sitting) and his 534BS Lead crew are back from the final "Big Week" mission (25 February). Mildred Smith plays the accordion and Sue Coyle hands out sandwiches; Sgt. Ernie Neves (ROG) stands on the right. Sgt. Don Carr (Eng.), collecting a sandwich, will be the unlucky exception to the crew's tour completion, being killed on 31 March while participating in a local flight.

Maj. Marvin D. Lord receives either a Silver Star or DFC from Col. Gross (CG, 1CBW) following completion of his combat tour. This 532BS "original" pilot had commanded the squadron following the loss of Maj. Post on 30 July 1943. He would assume higher command status at Bassingbourn, only to meet a tragic fate on 3 February 1945.

A snow-covered field somewhere in Germany forms the last resting place for the 533BS' 42-97474. The mangled propeller blades indicate an attempt at a crash landing was made, but the tail section's absence equally confirms a very heavy impact with a full crew survival rate accordingly reduced—in this case only Lt. Francis Fridgen (P), along with Sgts. Abernathy (RW) and Lowell Slayton (TG), survived. Date is 22 February 1944, with six 381BG crews MIA.

The value of a flak vest is amply demonstrated by this slightly-bemused 91BG airman. He is holding the remnant of the bullet or shell round that tore a hole marked by the circle. The heavy 20-lb vest was a physical encumbrance, especially for the waist gunners, but was responsible for saving countless personnel from serious injury or death, as in this instance.

This photo purportedly shows a debriefing session at Ridgewell on 5 March 1944, but no mission was flown that day. Gen. Gross sits center left, facing the pullover-clad figure of L/Col. Hall. Standing third from left is Capt. Melvin Hecker (originally with the 535BS but now a 532BS pilot), who completed his combat tour three days after the photo's date.

Spare Parts (42-39151) from the 532BS lies forlornly in a field NE of St. Omer in the Pas de Calais with four German soldiers leaning against her port stabilizer. On 4 March, the oft-malfunctioning veteran B-17F had suffered progressive failure, with Lt. David Keyes finally having to force land her; all ten crew ended up POWs on what was only their second mission.

The planned mission has been "scrubbed" and the frustrated 91BG crews are taxiing back to their dispersals. The rough edge of the 50-foot wide perimeter track is evident here; it is all too easy for a bomber to slip off to one side and suffer miring of its landing gear in what was often soft soil, thus disrupting the further progression of any following aircraft.

This 532BS B-17G (42-37786/VE: B) was transferred from the 401BG during November 1943; it is an early Douglas-built example that lacks "cheek gun" windows in the nose compartment. On 25 February 1944, it was MIA along with Lt. Donald G. Henderson's crew. The pilot survived, but six of the other nine did not.

The tragic vagaries of combat are encapsulated in this picture of Lt. Lee W. Smith's 535BS crew taken on 14 February 1944. Lt. Pax Sherwood (kneeling next to Smith, who is on the left) was replaced by Lt. R. Evans on the 22nd, when the entire crew went down in Bermondsay Battler. Sherwood survived the conflict, although he ended up a POW the following 13 April.

Mary Kay (foreground) arrived at Bassingbourn in late January and flew fifteen missions before succumbing on 18 March 1944, when Lt. Theophilus and three other crewmembers were killed. The other B-17 is 42-29739 The Village Flirt, which was so badly damaged on 20 February it was retired from combat and later transferred to the AFSC.

The leafless trees and bleak 1943/44 winter atmosphere are evident around this 91BG dispersal. The truck's hose is about to channel fuel into the B-17G's tanks and the "doughnut" landing gear wheels will steadily bulge under the extra load. The original caption records the aircraft as 42-31513/LL: S, which arrived on 22 February but was declared "salvage" the following 6 April after catching fire on landing.

S/Sgt. David Gildin (535BS tail gunner) poses by the tail of his B-17 that appears to have been "bellied in"; the impact was severe enough to shatter the join between the main fuselage and the tail section. The incident reportedly occurred on 16 March 1944, when the 381BG went to Augsburg.

Blue Dreams (42-37761/OR: L) ended her operational career on 6 March 1944, albeit in an unfortunate manner. The six-month veteran with 29 completed missions "aborted" the Berlin-bound mission, but the landing at Steeple Morden (355FG) by Lt. Walter E. Wilkinson ended as seen due to an oversight in lowering the landing gear.

Lt. Bill Majors (second from left, kneeling) is posed with his crew in front of 42-31678/DF: L: Little Patches. T/Sgt. George Parks's (Eng.) tall frame is directly below the artwork. The crew flew this B-17G on eleven March missions, but battle damage saw the aircraft reassigned to the 401BG; it survived the conflict with a tally of over 100 missions.

On 20 March 1944, Male Call (42-97471/VE: N) suffered a collapsed landing gear on return. However, the problem was created by human, not mechanical circumstances. The copilot operated the controls for the landing gear instead of the flaps, whereupon the bomber settled down squarely at the runway end!

Big Mike's operational fate seemed sealed following an over-shoot into a deep ditch on 6 March 1944 that resulted in severe damage. M/Sgt. Charles Barbier (448 Sub Depot) successfully persuaded the authorities that his team could resurrect the airframe into operational condition; following weeks of effort, the B-17G came back on line and was dubbed Frenchy's Folly in respect of the M/Sgt.'s Franco/American roots!

Pist'l Packin' Mama was originally assigned to the 401BG, but was dispatched to a Modification Center on arrival, from where it was reassigned to the 91BG in November 1943. It received heavy damage during two successive February missions and was finally transferred to AFSC during May, having completed 25 missions.

In this picture, Lts. Bernard E. Beckman (P) and David H. Brophy (N) are kneeling in front of the errant B-17G, where they are presumably being granted "absolution" by Chaplain Collett; this despite the failure being attributed to Capt. Doug Winters on board as group Command pilot and occupying the copilot's seat.

This 91BG B-17F (42-29815/LG: P) was from a production batch lacking "Tokyo tanks." Original assignment to the 306BG was switched to the 91BG during September 1943. Here the aircraft bears over 20 mission "bombs," but the restricted fuel content finally forced its withdrawal from combat duties in April 1944, after which it returned stateside.

T/Sgt. Charles Ayers (right) stands next to Steve Drosdek while "Whitey" Strednak is on the left. The team saw The Joker (42-29888/VE: H) all the way through from 22 June 1943 to her retirement from combat and stateside return in May 1944. "Whitey" was subsequently Crew Chief for Flak Magnet (43-37675/VE: N), which also survived combat.

Sweet Patootie's time with the 381BG lasted from assignment on 19 February 1944 until the following 3 September. Then, Lt. Omar Fulton experienced progressive engine failure that finally resulted in a crash landing in France after he turned back from the mission to Ludwigshafen; all nine airmen later returned to Ridgewell.

This 91BG "original" B-17F, unlike its named contemporary in the 322BS (41-24479 /LG: R, also an "original" bomber), came through its combat career. It bears its final 41-mission figure and is ready to return stateside. Note the pair of .5 weapons in the nose, whose bulk precluded the carriage of a bombsight. The picture date is 20 March 1944.

My Baby was assigned to the 322BS (LG: D) on 24 March 1944 and is seen in pristine condition. It then transferred to the 324BS (DF: Z/: D), the sub-unit tasked with PFF duties. It was MIA on 5 September with Lt. Bob Kelley's crew, having failed to complete its 58th mission. The Olive Drab panel on the tail gunner's position is a point of note.

Capt. Jim Tyson (Front center) and crew are seen following transfer to PFF duties at Bassingbourn. Tyson is flanked by Lts. John Howland (N) on Tyler's right, with Lt. Bill Doherty (CP) to his left. Among the five Enlisted men is S/Sgt. Arnold Farmer (TG) second from left.

Sgts. Howard Wilson, Fred Floyd, and Bob Samuels (seen left to right) are posed with a 4,000-lb "Blockbuster"; all served with the 448 Sub-depot at Ridgewell. This calibre of USAAF bomb could not be accommodated within the B-17 or B-24 bomb bays, while there is no known photo evidence of its mounting on external racks, let alone use in combat.

Chapter Ten
Enter the 398BG

Operational Priority Switch

The steady advance in launching 8AF operations ever deeper into the Nazi heartland during March was never to materially slacken henceforward. A good deal of credit for this sea change in Allied fortunes had to go to the fighter escorts. The influx of P-51-equipped groups had reached five by month's end; although the P-47 groups were able to give a good account of themselves, it was to be the North American design with enhanced range capability compared to its single-engine contemporary that would leave no area in central Europe free from its attention, as many a *Jagdwaffe* pilot was to encounter to his cost.

This said, the needs of Gen. Eisenhower and his *Overlord* hierarchy were now granted priority. The Transportation Plan, entailing the bombing of all major rail, road, and even canal links leading to Normandy saw both Bomber Commands directed to support the 9USAAF and 2nd Tactical Air Force (RAF) in the key task of hindering enemy reinforcements intended to counter the D-Day landings. Strategic operations were not to be totally ignored, however, and in fact, the balance between these and the tactical aspect of the heavy bombers' use would indeed remain finely balanced over the ensuing five months regarding participation in the plan.

The 8AF crews remained largely ground-bound up to the 8th, apart from two 2BD forays against V-1 sites; even then, the Primaries for all three Divisions were aviation industrial locations and airfields in western Germany. For whatever reason, the 1BD's participation was limited to the 1CBW striking at Oldenburg with 59 crews, all of whom returned—a sharp contrast to the 2BD, which surrendered thirty crews assaulting Brunswick.

Six groups went out next day as part of an overall assault on aviation plants up around the Baltic Coast, and it was only on the 10th that the first mission that even partially reflected the pre-*Overlord* aspect of operations was launched. A series of French and Belgian airfields, along with aviation industry sources, were focused on, with locations in Brussels assigned the 1BD. To date in April, the Division had suffered appreciably lower MIA losses (7) compared to the 2BD (57) and 3BD (17), but this positive situation would deteriorate within 24 hours.

Aircraft production facilities were targeted on the 12th, with the 1BD going after locations at Sorau and Cottbus, S of Berlin and over 100 miles further east than the 2BD's targets around Magdeburg; the 3BD headed to locations on the Baltic. The presence of more than 800 escorts did not hinder the *Jagdwaffe* from inflicting heavy casualties, particularly among the latter sub-force's ranks, totalling thirty-three crews MIA, while a further thirty-one were culled from the other two Divisions. The operational stage when the "Big Friends" could venture over central Europe and enjoy virtual immunity from fighter assault still lay several months ahead.

Lt. Frank C. Ammann had regularly flown 42-39929/LL: K **Lackin' Shackin'** since its assignment to the 91BG in December, and the crew was now roughly halfway through their combat tour. During what appears to have been the homeward leg after bombing Stettin as a Target of Opportunity—one that was reportedly attacked by a third of the 341 crews sent out—the B-17 began to lag behind after suffering a 50% power loss thanks to flak. An undercast condition must have been present, since some time later, what the crew took as Danish territory below turned out to be Sweden's southern coastal strip.

The B-17 was under attack by a German fighter at this time, but it was downed by the return fire from anti-aircraft batteries based near Ystad. The bomber was hit by one AA shell, whereupon Ammann headed down for a landing after most of the crew bailed out, but the uneven terrain resulted in heavy contact. The ten duly joined the ranks of interned Americans, although all were repatriated to Britain before the year's end.

Ridgewell's blood debt for the month also commenced today with 42-31497/GD:, flown by Lt. Robert W. Hesse's crew. A combination of flak and fighter strikes disabled two engines and the bombs were salvoed as target approach appears to have been on hand; one of the affected engines then burst into flames and all nine on board jumped into captivity before the B-17 went in SW of Weisswasser; one crewmember was still at large two weeks later, although he was subsequently apprehended.

13 - Unlucky for Some

The name Schweinfurt was by now firmly woven into the darker aspects of the 8AF annuls; this target had proved costly for the 1BD in particular during the previous three missions—92 MIA crews in all, with additional Category E casualties adding to the toll. So when the Briefing map ribbons were seen to extend to the city, there would have been an immediate downturn in morale evinced by the 172 Division crews assigned to the mission—and on the 13th, as well!

Among the 381BG contingent was Lt. James F. Mullane and crew, with Lt. T. Paxton Sherwood filling in as copilot. This officer had flown with the group since arrival on 1 September, and was reportedly going on his final mission—something that would be achieved, albeit not in the hoped-for manner. Solid fighter opposition was encountered, and as Sherwood later recalled, the formation was in imminent threat of assault by a sizeable *Jagdwaffe* force; however, the threat was basically thwarted by the appearance of a number of P-47s or P-51s, who pursued their quarry with both groups of fighters shooting overhead and away. The copilot said the impression of an aerial wild West scenario, with the bombers forming a "covered wagon circle," the enemy fighters as the "Indians," and the escorts as the "cowboys" was so strong in his mind that he felt like standing up and cheering loudly. The 1CBW's fortune was not matched by its 41BW contemporary, which bore eleven of the fourteen Division losses that were mainly inflicted by an Fw190 formation.

Any sense of euphoria arising from this incident was pushed firmly into the background as the target was being traversed through a flak barrage. A shell disabled one engine and the copilot's controls in 42-31357/MS: N **My Desire,** and to this was added a second motor that began malfunctioning. The degree of power reduction inevitably led to the B-17 losing permanent contact with both the group and the bomber stream. Course for home was maintained, but by the time the ailing bomber was south of Koblenz, the situation had reached a critical point that impelled a bail out by its nine occupants. Sgt. Thaddeus J. Tarczynski (BT) broke a leg on landing, but there were no fatalities. And so, Lt. Sherwood's residence for the ensuing thirteen months was destined to be at *Stalag Luft I*, Barth, rather than back in the States.

On 9 April, Lt. Harlan D. Soeder ended up running off the runway end with 42-30613/MS: S. Although the B-17 tipped up onto its nose, which was caved in by the impact, all the crew emerged unscathed and undoubtedly blessing their good fortune that the volatile bomb and fuel content had remained inert. Nine days later (18th), all but one of the ten airmen was part of a 381BG formation heading for the aircraft production plant at Oranienburg, on Berlin's NW fringe. Targets of Opportunity within *Big B* had to be sought following the inability to sight upon the Primary, but MIA casualties were very light at three out of 275 B-17s dispatched.

Unfortunately for the Soeder team, their charge (42-37733/MS: N **Patches N' Prayers**) was one of the unlucky exceptions; shortly after "bombs away," previous flak strikes that had adversely affected two engines caused the pilots to order a bail out following one motor catching fire. The bomber's crash site SSW of Ludwingslust was minus all nine of the crew. The absence of Sgt. Robert L. Megee (WG) was probably due to the General Order issued around this time that reduced the waist gunner complement on B-17s from two to one.

Eschwege's Toll

The month's continuing emphasis on strategic missions was maintained next day, with the Division assigned production facilities and airfields around the Kassel region; in the 1CBW's case, it was allotted the airfield at Eschwege, SE of the city. The bulk of the 744 bombers dispatched bombed their assigned Primaries, while the escorts seemed to have largely held the ring against effective *Jagdwaffe* intrusions, since only five "Big Friends" failed to return. The meager loss tally was of small comfort to Bassingbourn and Ridgewell, since they shared this figure.

T/Sgt. George Parks was Engineer to the diminutive but determined-minded Lt. Tom Gunn, whose acid comment as they flew eastward in brilliant sunshine in 42-37938/OR: E was: "What a beautiful Sunday—and we have to go to war!" The blinding light allied to the monotonous dinning noise emitted by the engines had an almost barbiturate effect upon George as he manned his turret, while the harsh contrast between the Plexiglas-generated heat and the sub-zero surface of the glass was a further distraction—one that was brutally curtailed as the target was appearing.

The first shocking indication to the crew of enemy fighter presence was the grey wolf-like outlines of what George described as Bf109s as they shot through the formation, followed almost immediately by a B-17 erupting in flame and smoke. Within a matter of seconds, the forward compartment filled with smoke from a fire igniting in the bomb bay, while the vertical fin was shredded in the center as the B-17 dipped to port. George grabbed a fire extinguisher and put out the flames before returning forward to assist the injured copilot out of his seat and to take his place. By then, the B-17 was developing a flat spin attitude that increasingly inhibited movement, while the smoke residue from the fire was still obscuring forward vision. Somehow Gunn and his new "copilot" managed to bring the bomber back into level flight, an action made all the more difficult due to the instrument panel being largely shot out.

A form of bomb run was completed on their own, despite the need to hold course using the starboard aileron and asymmetric engine control, the rudder cables having been totally disabled, among other damage. Turning for home with the North Sea over 200 miles distant, the chances of running the defensive gauntlet on their own appeared poor to terminal, especially when a crewmember called out "fighters." Luck was very much on their side, since the "bogies" proved to be P-51s, who duly took up position. However, their leader called to say his formation would stay with the cripple "until it went down," his words clearly influenced by the B-17's parlous external state. Happily, the expected fatal outcome did not materialize and several torturous hours later, a safe if crabbing landing was made at Bassingbourn thanks to a binding starboard wheel brake. This mission was one of the worst experienced by George during his combat tour, which was to extend to 37 in total.

That evening, three group dispersals out of 27 holding mission-assigned B-17s were bereft of their normal occupants, one of which may well have been the flame and smoke-shrouded bomber seen by Sgt. Parks. This was 42-97605/LL: D , which had one engine and the bomb bay set alight with the bail out order acted upon by seven airmen on Lt. John E. LaFontin's crew; unfortunately, he and Lt. Lynn I. Bostick (CP) were still on board when their charge exploded and crashed to earth close to Roehrig, roughly ten miles due north of Eschwege.

The other two group crash sites were to the SW of the target, suggesting that both B-17s' death throes were more extended, judging by the 20-25 minute increase in time of loss. On the other hand, the attacks had reportedly commenced when the formations were circling for a second target approach, granting more credence to the sizeable geographic separation in crash locations. Lt. Sam L. Evans was one of four fatalities on board 42-97519/LL: A **Spirit of Billy Mitchell**, which had been damaged during the initial fighter pass but progressed as far as Herlesfeld, over which it finally disintegrated.

Hoosier Hot Shot (42-38006/DF: H) was on her 22nd mission, compared to Lt. Stan Swenumsen's crew making their fifth in this B-17. Luck was out for both after fighter strikes ignited three engines and the doomed bomber rolled over and descended for some distance before blowing apart near Waldkappel; the pilots and six of the other eight airmen miraculously survived the vicious disintegration to parachute into captivity.

On 8 April, Lt. Leslie A. Bond had brought battle-damaged **Carolina Queen** (42-97214/GD: B) back to Ridgewell, but was initially thwarted from crash landing due to an inability to jettison the ball turret. L/Col. Hall (Deputy group CO) had brilliantly solved the problem of the missing tools with which to release the turret on the circling bomber by putting replacements in a canvas bag, taking off in another B-17 to equalize the speeds, and "fishing" the bag in through **Queen**'s radio hatch, after which a safe turret-less "belly in" action was completed.

The vagaries of combat operations now dealt the pilot and all but two of his eight colleagues a cruel blow after fighter gunfire tore 42-3525/GD: C apart, the two survivors having jumped clear immediately beforehand. The crash site at Fretterode was scant miles distant from where Lt. LaFontin's 91BG B-17 descended. The initial damage to Lt. Robert W. Rayburn's 42-38004/GD: A **Ol' Man Tucker** was added to by a flak battery that seemingly administered the fatal blow; the shell or shells' impact caused a central fuselage fracture over Fretterode, with the pilot and two of his eight-man crew joining him in death.

Concentration by over 800 "Heavies" on targets in the Pas de Calais and Cherbourg Peninsula (20th) still did not confirm the B-17s and B-24s switching to tactical operations, since the locations attacked constituted V-1 sites. In fact, of the eight missions launched before the month end, only three could be said to fall into this category. The assault upon the key marshalling yard complex at Hamm 48 hours later was achieved with a 2% MIA rate, although the insertion of a handful of Me410s into the 2BD's ranks as darkness covered East Anglia resulted in further casualties within that Division.

The latest 91BG crew failing to return were on the aptly-named **Just Nothing**, a title based upon 42-40000/DF: F's serial. The B-17 had latterly become a regular Lead ship with Maj. Charles Lee (Group Operations officer) in the right seat, along with Capt. Harvey Hesse's crew. The ever-solid flak barrage over the Primary set No. 3 engine on fire and returning personnel reported how the crew soon began to evacuate the bomber, which exploded almost immediately after "bombs away"; ten airmen reached the ground alive, but the pilot was the sad exception.

The loss of **Just Nothing** commenced a drip feed of losses up to the 29th split between the CBW's groups and switched to the 381BG on the 25th. The extended run to the Munich region (24th) witnessed seven

Primaries well pounded, but although the 8FC pilots again hammered the *Jagdwaffe*, the defenders in turn inflicted a stinging rebuff to the 1BD in particular, with 27 out of 40 crews failing to return. The 1CBW remained intact today, but not so 24 hours later, when almost all of the Division crews failed to reach Mannheim's marshalling yards or even release their loads. Flak damage to two engines on 42-3511/MS:, flown by Lt. Andrew G. Claytor, had created such a strain on the return leg that the bail out order was given between Paris and Creil. The advantage of descending into Nazi-occupied territory was once again demonstrated by what befell seven of the nine-man team; they gained access to the local Resistance groups and remained permanently free from capture.

Operations on the 27th were notable, involving the dispatch of two separate missions, the first of which involved further attacks upon V-1 sites. La Glacerie, on the Cherbourg Peninsula, was targeted by the 1CBW, but the flak batteries were on the ball, even as the formation approached the French coast. **Mary** (42-32072/LL: L) was fatally struck and peeled away and down into a spin. Lt. Thomson G. Tilson managed to temporarily halt the lethal gyration through use of the autopilot and it was probably this action that enabled him and all but Sgt. Stanley E. Johnson (ROG) to get out before their aircraft again developed a spinning motion that culminated in its fiery destruction S of Breuville.

"No Easy Missions"

The foregoing heading has been quoted from the 535BS microfilm records for 28 April 1944, following the mission to St. Avord airfield in France. This was the Primary for a reduced-scale Divisional effort involving the 1CBW and two other groups. Little opposition was expected over the target, while the distance into enemy territory would not involve a very lengthy time span. But risk was inherent during any mission, regardless of distance or scale of opposition, and this fact would be brought to bear for two crews, one of which was a veteran team on board 42-38061/MS; P **Georgia Rebel II**. The pilot was Lt. Harold F. Henslin, with Maj. Osce V. Jones as CP and Lt. Arthur ..L Guertin (N); the latter two officers had been on 42-3217/MS: T **Georgia Rebel** when she diverted into Sweden on 24 July 1943.

The 117-strong Force gained the target area with no "aborts" and the light flak barrage thrown up was acting more as a deterrent as the bombers were on the bomb run—that is, until the run was being completed. Then, a shell impacted with the port inner engine on Henslin's B-17, tearing it completely free. S/Sgt. Bill Blackmon (WG) had just noted what was a tracking sequence of bursts, with the strike constituting the third or fourth within the pattern. What swiftly transpired was a progressive disintegration of the airframe as the B-17 began its inexorable descent to impact close to the airfield.

Bill Blackmon fought against the centrifugal forces that were alternately applied and slackened as the fuselage seemed to adopt a wayward downward path; he finally reached the rear door and pulled himself out into mid-air before descending onto the edge of the airfield, which was still under assault. Almost immediately, he was confronted by two weapon-brandishing Germans who hustled him into an adjacent shelter. His luck was in, as was that of Maj. Jones and S/Sgt. J. W. Padgett (ROG), but for Henslin and the remaining six airmen, today was the final act.

Back at Ridgewell, Lt. Theodore Homdrom would later bless his good fortune that had impelled Maj. Jim DeLano (Group Navigator) to have him substituted by Lt. Guertin, even as the crew were embarking, on the grounds that as Lead navigator the status merited his being used on longer-range runs. At the time, he was naturally disgruntled at missing out on what promised to be a "milk run," but which developed into diametrically opposite fates for he and his long-term friend Guertin. (In 1984, the 8AF-oriented documentary *All the Fine Young Men* was produced by Karen Rutledge, the pilot's niece, a central core of which was quotations from Harold's letters home. Bill Blackmon was one of several spokesmen appearing that also included Henry Putek (P) and Carl Mongrue (ROG), fellow-381BG combat crewmembers from the 535BS.)

Also lost during the bomb run was the 91BG's 42-97199/DF: in Lt. James C. Cater's hands. The flak gunners landed strikes that set No. 2 engine on fire and the B-17 staggered on for some distance as all ten crewmembers successfully bailed out, leaving their charge to come down not far from **Georgia Rebel II**. The pilot was one of four evaders, but one (Sgt. Herbert A. Campbell - WG) lost his life on 2 July, reportedly while being captured. F/O Bernard M. Swinburne (B) was also caught on the 29th while being transported in a French truck; he and the driver were arrested, but the latter's ultimate fate was undoubtedly terminal, compared to the airman, whose final destination was a *Stalag*.

April's penultimate mission was the latest to feature *Big B* and an extremely costly one it would be, with 10% of the 618 crews making bomb runs going down. The 1BD was least affected, with ten declared MIA out of 210. **Queenie** (42-31353/LG: Q) had survived four months on combat status, but the intense flak barrage over the city bit into the B-17's starboard inner wing and she flopped into a spin. The ever-increasing pressures induced upon the airframe in these circumstances led to its disintegration several thousand feet below, at which stage four parachutes were sighted. This figure nearly matched with the survivor equivalent (five), but Lt. James F. Purdy, Jr. (P) shared the terminal fate of the remaining five among his crew.

May 1944

The "ad hoc" arrangement for the third Composite group formation within the 1CBW that had existed since the 351BG's departure was almost at an end as May 1944 commenced. This was thanks to the recent arrival of the twelfth and final group assigned to the 1BD: the 398BG, commanded by Col. Frank P, Hunter, who had taken up residence at Nuthampstead, several miles SE of Bassingbourn. The unit was activated on 1 March 1943, but during July was reassigned the function of a Replacement Training Unit, so killing off any prospect of an early entry into a combat theater.

The reversal of this frustratingly static existence only occurred the following January, and now the personnel were on hand within the 8AF to add their weight to the Daylight Offensive—but one that would involve an unfortunate inaugural mission on 6 May. A further logistical complication was the non-retention by the group of all but five of the 72 B-17s brought over to England between late April and the beginning of May.

In the meantime, the month opened with a "double header" of missions, in which the 1CBW only participated in the second to marshalling yards at Troyes and Rheims, in France. The cost was minimal, albeit not for the 91BG crew concerned. The 323BS crew led by Lt. Albert McCardle had switched over to a 401BS B-17 (reportedly 42-102392/LL:) that had flown almost all of the group missions since its arrival on 22 April. Target flak proved to be the executioner, with the forward fuselage thoroughly devastated in a manner suggesting at least some of the eight fatalities were incurred at this point; two gunners were the lucky exceptions to this sad conclusion.

May would witness the 8AF operating at varying strengths for the majority of the remaining thirty days, although the 1BD was not called upon again until the 4th; the intended assault on Berlin and Brunswick was totally thwarted by weather conditions, however. A similar situation arose two days later, although the Division force was less than 100 in number. What was the first mission for the 398BG proved to be a shambles thanks to a series of administrative and technical lapses.

The cooks were not alerted in time, briefing was a hurried affair, trucks were not on hand to transport the crews to their aircraft, and bombing up was reportedly incomplete. Finally, the Assembly process by those crews not getting airborne in time ended with their linking up with either the 91BG or 381BG. Perhaps it was as well, since the mission to attack V-1 sites in the Pas de Calais was "aborted" thanks to weather conditions. A repeat of the situation to any degree would have to be avoided next time round; happily, this proved to be the case next day, which was just as well, since the target was *Big B*.

Back-to-back missions to Berlin were hardly stuff to raise individual morale, but the result of the first run at least must have surprised the crews in terms of enemy resistance. The *Jagdwaffe* was clearly conspicuous in its absence, since the 8FC pilots made no claims at all. Meanwhile, the "Big Friends" suffered a casualty rate of just over 1% (8) among the 553 B-17s and B-24s gaining mission credit, but among this figure was Bassingbourn's **Merry Widow** (42-31580/OR: A), bearing Lt. Nenad Kovachjevich's veteran team that included Lt. Edward Wallner (N) flying his 30th. One engine was disabled by flak and the B-17 steadily lost altitude while holding a homeward course. But as Hamburg was being bypassed, a further flak barrage added the fatal touch. Both pilots held their charge steady as the other seven jumped clear, but they appear to have failed to safely extract themselves prior to the final crash near Heidenau, SW of the city.

The ebb and flow of aerial combat in the ETO produced a relative downturn in 8AF fortunes 24 hours later, with a 5% MIA loss factor occurring among the bomber formations returning to Berlin. However tragic for the airmen concerned, this was an acceptable situation in cold statistical terms, since the Offensive could still be positively prosecuted with the numbers of replacements, both technical and human, now regularly on hand.

What appears to have been the first concerted switch to tactical bombing operations by the 8AF occurred between the 9th and 11th, when a plethora of marshalling yards and airfields ranging from Belgium to the southern Franco/German borders were struck. However, the 12th signalled the start of the American assault on Germany's synthetic oil production facilities, a several month long campaign whose creation and initiation has in postwar historical annuls been primarily credited to Gen. "Tooey" Spaatz (CG, USSTAF). A heavy toll of *Jagdwaffe* resources was incurred over Merseburg and three further Primaries (12th), but a similar bomber loss factor to that suffered on the 8th was realized in turn. While the 8FC enjoyed another good "kill" tally next day, the bomber crews heading for refineries up on the Baltic suffered minimal casualties, but had recourse to Targets of Opportunity due to adverse weather conditions at the Primaries.

The 1CBW had participated in all but one mission since the 7th, in the course of which just one B-17 had been declared MIA. There then ensued a period of five days during which a small-scale run involving the 41CBW alone was made to V-1 sites. Planned missions between the 15th and 17th were "scrubbed" according to 381BG records, for example, to add to the pressure upon the personnel. And then came the "Alert" on the evening of the 18th that early next morning saw nearly 600 crews filing into their Briefing rooms to be given the news that they would again face the challenge of *Big B*'s defenses, while the 2BD went to Brunswick.

The presence of solid cloud patterns all the way in, although inhibiting visual target sighting, was to prove no tangible barrier to bombing thanks to PFF-equipped bombers being on hand. The *H2X* sets were far from perfect in picking out precise targets, but on the other hand, the sheer size of Berlin, coupled with its manifold industrial locations, provided at least some chance of landing effective strikes. Although sixteen bombers were culled from the two Divisions' formations, the bulk of the destruction seemed to go the way of the flak gunners.

The shell bursts were peppering the sky as the bomb run was near completion with the Friederichstrasse railroad station zeroed-in on when the 91BG's 42-97455/LL: J **(The) Keystone Mama** received her death blow. The ex-457BG B-17 absorbed a strike on the starboard wing that caused the wing tip to fold up, according to Lt. Joseph J. Kozina (CP), followed by the bomber zooming upwards in an arc before going into a vertical dive.

The Lieutenant's attempts to bring her out into level flight proved fruitless, and he had naturally no knowledge that the slack controls were due to much of the tail section having been severed. His attempt to gain the nose hatch was seemingly denied, as he was cast about the cockpit by the centrifugal forces and quickly rendered unconscious; he would never establish how, on regaining consciousness, he was falling through the air, but it is likely the airframe's disintegration was the cause for his miraculous escape—one that was not shared by Lt. Robert S. Wylie (P) or the other seven on board.

The 381BG records state that a bomb run was made on railroad yards in the face of a flak barrage described variously as "meager" or "intense and accurate" at debriefing, with the latter assertion probably more accurate. The pedestrian pace of the bombers meant that the flak gunners had more than ample opportunity to zero-in their weapons for a solid barrage that would inevitably result in casualties that included a duo of group B-17s.

Lt. Earl Sharp was previously "grounded" due to a sinus condition, but had resumed operations, with today being his 17th mission and flying as 533BS Lead. The initial hemorrhage destined to prove fatal for 42-97454/VP: U was caused by a strike upon No. 2 engine, which lost oil pressure and worse still, resulted in its propeller resisting "feathering" action. Then, just after "bombs away," No. 3 and 4 engines suffered supercharge failure, whereupon the landing gear was lowered as an indication the B-17 was dropping out of formation.

Any thoughts of making a run for Sweden were soon scotched when the electrical system largely failed; in addition, the sense of hypoxia gaining strength in Earl's body was confirmed when he glanced at his oxygen hose to see a large gash emitting the precious air. With fire gaining in intensity on No. 2 engine, it was clear the B-17 was doomed and the bail out order was passed by word of mouth. All nine crewmembers got out, but Lt. Wayne T. Hardwick's parachute failed him. In addition, Earl suffered a dreadful fracture condition to the pelvic region that ensured a prolonged and very uncomfortable hospital incarceration before transfer to *Stalag-Luft* 3.

A further nine airmen would not grace their Ridgewell surroundings again, but at least their lives were spared. Lt. Harold C. Blog was assigned the group deputy Lead function in 42-32088/VE: M **Dry Gulcher**, but the bomber suffered heavy flak damage during the bomb run; it too dropped out of formation and staggered on for some distance before finally being abandoned NE of Berlin, near the now-Polish town of Moryn. In contrast to the swift rounding up of the others, the pilot and F/O George W. Dennis (N) remained at liberty for some 48 hours before being apprehended.

The CBW loss pattern finally extended to its still-acolyte group from Nuthampstead, and in a rather cruel manner. Although flak had struck home on 42-97339/N8: Y, the bomber's fate was sealed when it drifted off to one side and directly under the newly-released fragmentation bomb load of another B-17. Lts. Ira C. O'Neal (P) and Roger D. Comer were killed either through the bombs' impact on the cockpit area, or more likely because they were trapped along with all but two of their crew after the aircraft snapped into a vicious spinning motion.

The crash site was recorded as Alt-Rudnitz, around 40 miles outside Berlin's NE fringe, suggesting that some form of aerodynamic recovery, albeit not more than temporary in nature, was experienced by the B-17. However, Ruednitz is several miles outside Berlin's NE boundary, and may well be the correct crash location. And so, the group's blood debt in MIA aircraft and crews that would reach sixty-one, along with several "operational" losses prior to VE-Day, had now commenced.

The run to Berlin initiated an almost daily pattern of missions up to month end only broken on the 26th. Assaults on two French airfields (20th) and V-1 sites (21st) by the Division resulted in no MIA casualties; the following day's attack on Kiel yielded just two B-17s lost in action, while a single 305BG crew went down during the 23rd mission to bomb airfields and marshalling yards in France. This quartet of loss-free missions for the 1CBW was gratifying, but nobody was under any illusion that the pattern would continue indefinitely, especially when a return was made on the 24th to Berlin.

"Concentrate, Will Ya!"

A paramount requirement of the pilots manning a B-17 or B-24 was to pay precise attention to all aspects of control, from start up to switching off on return. Failure to do so at any stage could and probably did lead to accidents or fatal incidents while aloft. Lt. Bill Doherty (CP), of Lt. Tyson's PFF crew, was felt by his navigator, Lt. John Howland, to be a pilot who had never really shed a desire to be a fighter jockey, although he was basically to prove a sound partner for his fellow pilot.

A day after flying a mission, John and Lt. Doherty were carrying out their ablutions when John noticed a huge bruise on his colleague's upper left arm. When enquiring as to the cause, he was told the following. He and Lt. Tyson had been going through the start up procedure, with the latter reading off the necessary details from a board. Suddenly, the board was firmly rammed into Doherty's arm with the verbal imprecation to "Pay attention!" It appears that the copilot's attention had wandered and the physical act was an added way of reminding him to keep his mind on the ever-critical task at hand. The Lieutenant would come through his combat tour and then fulfill his original wish to transfer to an 8FC group—only to be killed during November while flying with the 364FG.

Hard Knocks Again

Berlin's tenth bout of punishment was due to be administered by the 1st and 3rd BDs, who between them sent out over 600 crews. The weather conditions were sound enough to reach the target, but also patchy enough for PFF assisted bomb runs in some instances. Despite a strong escort presence, a three-figure number of enemy fighters penetrated the screen to cause heavy casualties to two groups, who between them lost fifteen crews out of 33 MIA overall.

The Berlin defenses had indirectly contributed to the first 398BG loss on the 19th, and now a further two crews would feel either the flak gunners' or fighters' sting, with just six survivors out of the twenty-one airmen concerned. Capt. Unite L. Brodin was piloting 42-107231/N7: A, which was Lead for one of the two group sub-formations and also bore Maj. Judson F. Gray (603BS CO) as Air Commander.

The bombers were bare seconds away from dropping their loads when a shell impacted in between the starboard wing's engines, creating a blaze; within seconds the B-17 blew up, with the affected wing breaking free and the fuselage splitting in two. The normal copilot, Lt. Jerome T. Hans, was riding as tail gunner/ observer and became one of only three crewmembers to get out alive prior to the wreckage tumbling to earth within the city's NE boundary.

The other group loss was probably incurred when a large *Jagdwaffe* force engaged the 1CBW, inflicting particularly heavy punishment on the 381BG. The gunfire that struck home left Lt. John W. Ingram's (KIA) 42-107132/3O: V floundering behind and below the formation with one engine "out" before the tail section broke off. The resultant aerodynamic imbalance saw the machine descending out of control and smashing into the ground between Tempelwalde and Gratze. This time round, only three of the ten airmen managed to parachute to safety.

Ridgewell's Torment

The area around Tempelfelde and Gratze where Lt. Ingram's B-17 came down was to prove the epicenter for several more crash sites that involved the 381BG. Whether or not the group was in the process of making a second bomb run when the assault occurred, as some accounts indicate, the result was a largely brief but bloody experience for six crews and a miraculous recovery from disaster for a seventh. S/Sgt. Richard Schneider (TG) recalled that he was trying to attract the attention of a fellow tail gunner in a nearby B-17 by moving his guns up and down when that bomber (42-31698/VP: N, flown by Lt. Clarence D. Wainwright Jr.) was shockingly enveloped in smoke and flame as the first fighter pass was initiated. The starboard wing was sawn off by the fusillade of shells and it plunged downward to impact adjacent to the road linking Tempelfelde and Gratze. Only two of the nine crew survived, one of which was Schneider's friend he had been signalling to, Sgt. Floyd M. Nalley, Jr.

Lts. Carl A. Gardon (flying 42-31291/ GD: F) and Lt. John A. Wardencki's 42-97214/GD: B **Carolina Queen**—which the now-deceased Lt. Leslie Bond had "bellied in" at Ridgewell on 8 April— were both within the Lead group's Lead squadron. Gardon's B-17, in No. 6 position, had fire catch hold around No. 3 engine and almost immediately blew up, according to an eyewitness in the Element's other wingman B-17. However, the bomber's agony must have been more prolonged, since Sgt. John S. O'Neal (TG) recorded that the B-17 dived and levelled off several times prior to his bailing out. Only the pilot and Lt. William C. Mosley (B) failed to survive, with their B-17 crashing in between Bernau and Werneuchen. As for the other squadron B-17, it suffered a violent disintegration in mid-air, either from fighter-inflicted punishment and/or being involved in a collision. Whatever the reason, all nine crewmembers had their lives brutally expunged as the wreckage descended in between Tempelfelde and Gratze.

The 532BS' sole casualty was 42-38919/VE: J, flown by Lt. Clarence W. Ezzell, which was seen to falter and lose height and position after suffering problems with No. 1 and 3 engines, according to different eyewitnesses. The B-17's fate was reportedly quickly sealed by fighter assaults that saw its despatch between Melchow and Biesenthal, with two gunners out of the nine on board failing to get clear before the bomber disintegrated in mid-air. Lt. Carl H. Dasso had charge of the 535BS' 42-39890/MS: Y **Return Ticket**, a veteran aircraft that now would belie her optimistic title. The savage battering administered by the fighters resulted in the airframe breaking into several sections and scattering themselves close to where its Wardencki- and Wainwright-piloted contemporaries had crashed.

The confused nature of debriefing reports often emanating from a mission seems to have been highlighted in the case of 42-31878/MS: Z, containing Lt. Walter K. Higgins's crew. One officer said he saw the bomber explode shortly after leaving the target, while a second claimed the bomber descended some twenty miles north of the city. On the other hand, Lt. Herbert W. Burns, Jr. (CP) stated that the pilot had ordered him to bail out and that the B-17 was badly damaged; in addition, all four survivors exited via the rear hatch, an act that was less likely to have succeeded had the aircraft swiftly disintegrated.

All four were recorded as captured in the region where the other group losses occurred, whereas the burial sites for their deceased fellow airmen were up around Rostock, some 100 miles NNW of Berlin. If the foregoing details are all correct, then it appears the bomber's violent demise was much more prolonged than stated at debriefing. Regardless of what actually transpired, five more Americans had paid the ultimate price and four others were heading for a shadowy POW existence.

The loss tally could have easily climbed to seven in the case of 42-97174/GD: P **Joanne**. The bomber was second element Lead within the 534BS formation, but was totally enveloped in the smoke and flame from an exploding B-17. When it emerged , Lts. Williams and Paul D. Lear (CP) were presented with an almost totally blanked-out windshield caused by soot, added to which every inch of fabric had been stripped off the stabilizers and rudder surfaces.

Furthermore, only eight crewmembers still remained on board, Sgt. Jack R. Ross (TG) having bailed out on the not-unnatural assumption his aircraft was doomed. In spite of this fraught situation, the pilots managed to hold formation and get their charge back down at Ridgewell. After debriefing, each crewmember was separately questioned regarding the justification for Sgt. Ross's action; as it was, an examination of the fire-blackened tail section with its skeletal control surface frames should have rendered any such "grilling" unnecessary.

The 91BG returned home one crew light, the B-17 concerned now lying submerged close to the Swedish coast, along with Lt. Frederick T. Neel (N). Fighter-inflicted damage that included setting fire to the fuselage of 42-107178/ LL: K was severe enough for several of the crew, including Lt. William F. Nee, to jump clear. The navigator put out the flames before taking over the controls assisted by Sgt. Donald F. Spaulding (TG) and heading out over the Baltic. Just as neutral territory was reached, the bomber became steadily uncontrollable and five of the six still on board parachuted; unfortunately, Sgts. Spaulding and Robert Heimbach (WG) came down in the sea and joined Lt. Neel in a watery fate.

The punishment handed out to the 381BG over Berlin was to prove the last severe example occurring at Ridgewell prior to VE-Day, although the overall MIA total was very far from complete. The 91BG by comparison and the 398BG to a lesser degree had several very painful experiences ahead of them. The bombers went out on all but one day of the final week of May (26th) to attack what was still a majority of strategic category targets (four to two). No Division losses were experienced over French airfields and gun batteries (25th), but twelve crews were MIA two days later when Ludwigshafen and Mannheim were attacked.

Among this figure was 42-107042/ LL: Z **The Liberty Run**, whose pilot, Lt. Richard T. Pressey, was on his 18th mission. Flak prior to reaching Ludwigshafen had disabled one or two engines and the bomber became a straggler soon after turning for home. The imminent assault by enemy fighters was repulsed by the P-51s arriving to Pressey's emergency call, but he finally realized the chances of returning home were fast diminishing. Consequently, a southward course for Switzerland was adopted and a happily unintercepted passage culminated in a safe landing at Payerne under "friendly" Swiss fighter escort.

A second 1CBW loss involved the 381BG's 42-107023/VE:, flown by Lt. Andrew H. Stuart's crew. The pilots had experienced power loss on one engine early in the mission, but had pressed onward until well inside the Continent before reversing course for home, descending almost to ground level in so doing. The B-17 was bypassing Romilly-sur-Seine, SE of Paris, when it was intercepted by fighters; the damage inflicted around the rear fuselage probably adversely affected the flight controls and the resultant heavy crash landing surprisingly left all eight crewmembers—who had scrambled clear and gathered together—intact, other than for a broken leg suffered by Lt. Charles K. Eisen (B), who was assisted out of the burning airframe. The ninth airman (Lt. Donald H. Blyth - N) was assumed to have already departed the scene, but unknown to his colleagues, his body was lying under the port wing, having been pitched out through a large fuselage fracture incurred by the heavy impact. Three of the crew were fortunate enough to evade capture.

The next three missions were all deep penetration affairs, with oil and aircraft production sources picked out. The 1CBW's involvement on the 28th left it loss free, but next day, a run to oil plants at Poelitz, on the Baltic, cost it one crew, although the nine airmen and the B-17 concerned did not end up in enemy hands. Instead, Lt. Robert J. Guenther guided 42-32076/LL: E **Shoo Shoo Shoo Baby** all the way across the Baltic to Sweden's Bulltofta airfield and internment.

Engine problems and subsequent detachment from the formation had impelled the pilots to adopt the course of action. Unlike most if not all of her contemporaries that diverted into Sweden or Switzerland, this B-17 would not only return stateside; after extended service with the French Section of the National Geographic Society, she would be painstakingly re-built to her WWII operational condition during the 1980s and end up on permanent display at the USAF Museum, Dayton, Ohio.

Rebuff over Dessau

Dessau, SE of Magdeburg, possessed aircraft production facilities and had already been targeted on the 28th, albeit mainly as a Target of Opportunity. Two days later, it was one of three targets in the Magdeburg region allotted to the 1CBW, which was one of three Wings dispatched. All these Primaries were struck squarely by 241 B-17s, of which only nine were MIA. However, two-thirds of the latter were culled from the 1CBW, with fighters the principal cause.

Lt. Bob van Buskirk's 532BS crew, headed by Leonard Zapinski, had commenced operations on 9 April, and were now flying their 21st mission; a progress rate that would have taken up to three or four months to achieve scant months before. Bob, as bombardier, had control of the Bendix chin turret on 44-6025/VE:, but had not hitherto had the opportunity to operate it. The Wing, with the 381BG as Lead, was closing in on the Primary when, according to Bob, he was momentarily stunned by the looming presence of enemy fighters. About ten Bf109s out of a large force hovering in the background and later estimated by Gen. Gross (CG, 1CBW and Air Commander) as between 30 and 40 swept in from ahead. Bob engaged them, but his postwar acid comment to the author was: "I didn't get them but they sure as Hell got us!"

One or more of the fuel tanks were ignited and the bail out order was given and acted upon by all nine crewmembers, only one of whom was even injured; Lt. Othmer C. Widosh (CP) suffered a broken ankle on landing. However, the B-17's agony must have extended for some minutes if the fatal damage was incurred during the bomb run; target approach had been from the SW, while the bomber's final descent was at Karow, some 40 miles NW of Dessau. Bob was the first out, and having landed used his compass to direct him westward; he walked and hid until the following dawn, only to discover he had virtually progressed in a circle and soon after joined his colleagues in capture.

The complete survival of Zapinski and crew was not mirrored on board the two other group losses. Shells ignited the starboard inner fuel tank on Lt. Merrill O. Burton's 42-102672 /VP; flying No. 5

within the Lead squadron, and it swung out and down to the right; after being seen to complete a half circle, it disintegrated, with the wreckage falling due south of Koethen. In these brief seconds, the pilot had yelled for all to "get the Hell out" as flames penetrated the central fuselage, but he was fated to become one of four fatalities. Another was T/Sgt. John T. Eylens (Eng.), who was last seen fighting the fires; on 16 March, he had saved his B-17 in somewhat similar circumstances, but there was no reprieve for he or his bomber today. This was a very experienced crew with between 25 and 27 missions completed, so proving that the Grim Reaper was not discriminatory in selecting his victims.

A second 533BS crew led by Lt. John Monohan in 42-38188/VP: K was culled at the same stage, coming down close to the airfield on Koethen's southern fringe. The bombardier and engineer were believed killed by gunfire that crippled the bomber to the extent that it fell out of formation. Monohan and one other crewmember also succumbed at some stage, the pilot being observed by Lt. Kenneth C. Nea (CP) to have "spilled" his pack by the forward escape hatch. Once again, an experienced crew with a mission tally similar to the Burton team had failed to run the enemy gauntlet.

Single B-17s were taken out of the other two groups' ranks. **Just Plain Lonesome** (42-39975/DF: Z) completed its bomb run, but Lt. Zack C. Collier called to say he had lost two engines and had no aileron control. The crippled B-17 disappeared following yet another fighter pass and that was the last ever seen of her or her nine hapless occupants, the clear inference being that the waters of the North Sea claimed both. Nuthampstead surrendered 42-102498/N8: W prior to bombing. Lt. Thomas L. Thompson (P) was fatally injured and his aircraft fell steadily down and back as the surviving crewmembers evacuated before the B-17 tore apart, scattering its remnants at Aken.

Ironic Prediction

S/Sgt. Bob Hittel (TG) had recently returned from Ridgewell's base hospital after suffering a frozen foot and was now flying as a "spare" with Lt. Burton. He was fortunate to survive the B-17's explosive end, but having done so floated down to a potentially hostile reception from a group of implement wielding farm workers that thankfully never reached fruition. Escorted to a village, he was reunited with Sgt. Robert J. Hammond (WG), both being ordered to sit under a tree. As they pondered their immediate fate, from the surrounding throng a young woman approached and handed each an apple from her basket.

Both were subsequently driven to a nearby *Luftwaffe* base (probably Koethen), and on arrival at the guardhouse were each allocated a cell upon whose doors they were ordered to chalk their surnames. Bob was as far as "Hit" when the guard swung his rifle butt, which Bob managed to evade. The clear inference of this act was the guard's misapprehension that Bob was going to chalk "Hitler" on the door! It was only when Bob's dog tag was proffered to the guard that the situation stabilized.

Bob's grandparents had emigrated from Germany, and at a later stage of his interrogation, when he was experiencing real hunger pangs while lying on a bed of straw, he recalled his grandfather's reaction whenever his then young grandchild would express distaste with certain food items during mealtimes. He would growl: "Du isst noch Stroh, Junge!" (You'll be glad to eat straw, my boy!") This expression now came back to haunt Bob with a vengeance, given his current rather parlous circumstances.

Adversarial Conundrum

Doctor Goebbels's inflammatory utterances for the population to regard Allied fliers as *Terrorfliegers* fit only for "summary treatment" was apparently being put into practice by a group of *Sturmabteilung* (SA) personnel who were close to one of the crash sites involving the Burton/Monohan-piloted B-17s and who were firing their rifles at several descending parachutists. A postwar witness whose father was on leave from the Eastern Front accompanied him to the scene. Without further ado, the soldier drew his pistol, placing it against the neck of the one he regarded as the main instigator and addressing the others, he yelled out: "One more shot and I will kill this man."

The incident highlights another basic contradiction arising from any conflict, namely how those at the sharp end of the military struggle generally have an unconscious sense of "fair play" towards one another, since they all face the same risks to life and limb. To a lesser extent, the gesture of the apple-bearing woman falls into this category; her probable attitude was that the American airmen were no longer imbued with a lethal intent toward her and her fellow Germans, but were now disarmed and reduced to being young, vulnerable human beings.

This 323BS bomber (42-31513/S) caught fire after it landed on 5 April 1944. The prompt attention of the Fire Section personnel could not prevent the shapely airframe from being swiftly reduced to the burnt-out state seen in this duo of pictures. There were no casualties among the crew, however.

Egg-Haid (42-97511/MS: K) joined the 381BG on 22 February 1944. In this shot, the ravages of weather and combat are evident upon her now-veteran airframe. The ever-present "bogy" of mid-air collision would claim her in the airfield circuit on 21 January 1945, along with 42-40011/GD: O Schnozzle and all eighteen airmen losing their lives.

A group of mechanics are carefully positioning the port elevator into its slot on 62-31542/OR: T Bunky. This B-17G arrived from the 457BG in mid-March 1944 and served until its unfortunate demise on 19 July; a mid-air collision with another group bomber resulted in the tail snapping off and Lt. Norman Burwick's entire crew going down in the separated sections.

This group of 381BG officers is part of the engineering staff. Second from left is Capt. Mitchell Hall, in charge of the 858 Air Engineering Squadron by VE-Day; L/Col. Jolicoeur, next to Hall at the front, was group Executive officer within the renamed 432 Air Service Group.

On 11 April 1944 Gen Eisenhower arrived at Bassingbourn to 'christen' 42-97061/LL: B. Col. Putnam (Group CO) watches as 'Ike' shakes hands with one of the parka-hooded airmen lined up alongside the B-17G.

Tony Starcer's fine artwork for Hi-Ho Silver is clearly evident in this picture of a crewmember's A2 jacket. The B-17G in question arrived simultaneously with Bunky; unlike its unfortunate "companion," it went on to complete a recorded 130 missions before returning stateside.

Gen. Eisenhower has mounted the platform aligned alongside his namesake General Ike and is in the process of smashing a bottle of Mississippi water on the B-17G's NMF skin. The aircraft would repay "Ike"'s trust by flying a mass of missions up to the cessation of the Daylight Offensive.

Lt. Welch, a 91BG bombardier, is making a point to his father, a U.S. Merchant Naval officer. The tail gunner's position bears an Olive Drab anti-dazzle panel and anti-flash covers on the guns. The picture date is 6 April; on the 29th, a Lt. John R. Welch (B) ended up a POW following the loss of 42-31353/ LG: Q Queenie over Berlin.

Lt. Len Zapinski's crew was assigned to the 532BS and flew 21 missions up to their becoming POWs on 30 May. The line-up is (Rear) Zapinski and Lts. Othmer Widosh (CP), Bob Fuller (N), and Bob Van Buskirk (B). In front are Sgts. Hamilton Harper (WG), George Pastre (ROG), Don Harness (TG), Bill Webb (Eng.), James Wilson (BT), and Kurdevitz (WG).

This party of Air Training Corps (ATC) cadets is being escorted around a hangar-based B-17G. Several among their number wear white "flashes" in their forage caps; this indicates they are senior members ready for induction into the RAF as "aircrew under training."

Two officers pose after receiving medal awards at Ridgewell. The individual on the right wears the DFC, while the other officer, who is believed to be Lt. Robert Van Buskirk (bombardier on Lt. Zapinski's 532BS crew), wears the Purple Heart—the award most airmen feared earning by suffering injury in combat but were arguably most proud of when granted.

The actor Laurence Olivier (left) speaks prior to 42-31990/MS: R's "baptism." Behind him are (L-R) Alfred Lunt; Mary Churchill, who will perform the christening; and actress Vivien Leigh. M/Gen. Fred Anderson (Deputy CG 8AF) is next to Ms. Leigh, while Maj. Halsey (535BS CO) is glancing down at the photographer. Date is 23 April 1944.

The rapt attention etched on the faces of all the airmen present in this picture suggests the photo was taken during a briefing session. On the other hand, the absence of heavy flight clothing might well indicate the activity was for a practice flight or a non-mission event.

Col. Claude E. Putnam is congratulated by Gen. Gross after completing his combat tour on 28 April 1944. He was the 91BG's fifth group CO, having assumed command from Col. Clemens Wurzbach the previous 12 December.

Lt. Tom Gunn (P), T/Sgt.George W. Parks (Eng.), and Sgt. Robert T. Smith (TG) survey the structural damage to their B-17G's (42-37938/OR: E) fin after the 19 April 1944 run to Eschwege. All three are glad to have survived the battering handed out to their bomber, none more so than Smith.

The heavy puncturing of the nose compartment skin on 42-37958/LL: G Old Faithful has still left both occupants free from serious injury. The occasion was a mission by the 91BG to Metz/Frescaty airfield. Fate was to be distinctly unkind to Lt. Mikonis and crew exactly two calendar months later, however.

"Gentlemen, your target for today is – Berlin" was a statement that concentrated the minds of all combat crew more than nearly every other briefed target. The solemn expressions seen here are recorded at Bassingbourn prior to the bombers heading for "Big B" on 29 April; the men are right to be concerned, since the defenses would cull 63 B-17s and B-24s from 8AF ranks. The officer in the middle of the second row bears a resemblance to Lt. Bert Stiles.

Col. Frank P. Hunter was appointed CO of the 398BG in March 1943, and after a protracted 10-month period for the group as a Replacement Training Unit it was switched to combat training duties. Hunter finally led his personnel overseas to their assignment within the 1CBW in April 1944. He is standing in the middle of this crew photograph.

Lts. Williams (left) and Paul Lear (2nd from right) were responsible for bringing 42-97174/GD: P Joanne back from Berlin to Ridgewell on 24 May. The other two officers are Lt. Parke Tamplin (B, next to Lt. Lear) and Lt. Piatt (N).

One of a number of famous American personalities wending a path to Ridgewell was Bing Crosby. The degree of interest in his visit is clear from the number of individuals having recourse to climbing up on the hangar support girders, given that the floor space is totally occupied. Bing's laid-out style of singing undoubtedly went down well with the audience.

B-17G 42-97562/DF: F/D's name Evenin Folks – How's Y'All? is based on U.S. band leader Kay Kyser's opening expression. The PFF-equipped bomber is seen with Maj. Weitzenfeld (left) and a Ground Complement officer named Hare. The picture date of 6 June is incorrect, since the aircraft suffered severe damage on take-off three days previous.

Chapter Eleven
"D-Day has Come. . .."

Comment

June 1944 would witness the greatest percentage of daily missions launched by the 8AF to date: 24 out of 30, with the 1CBW involved in the vast majority. In addition, the switch to tactical missions would be effected on all but three days thanks to the long-anticipated launch of Operation *Overlord* and the attendant need to thwart the German bid to feed particularly Panzer reinforcements with which to cast the Anglo/American troops back onto the English Channel. Almost as important was the parallel bid to fool the German high command that the Normandy landings were a diversion, shielding the Allied intention to direct their primary invasion effort against the beaches along the Pas de Calais coastline by hammering coastal defenses and the surrounding communications network located in that region.

Luck

Lt. Tyson's PFF crew at Bassingbourn were not called upon for the projected mission on 3 June, that duty going to Lt. Carl Clark's team, their fellow transferee from the 381BG. Clark's navigator, Lt. Clem Obler, was none too pleased at being rousted out of bed, nor would he have taken too kindly with John Howland, his room-mate and contemporary on Tyson's crew, acidly advising him to win the war for them both. Little did John know that his proposed extended slumber had but 60 minutes to run its course.

The B-17 prepared for the mission was 42-97562/DF: F/D **Evenin' Folks, How Y'All?**, on hand at the base since late February, but which also served very briefly at Glatton (457BG) during March. Nuthampstead was the intended destination, but it was one that was never reached. Unknown to the pilots as the throttles were cracked open was the unfortunate presence far down the runway of a stalled-out bomb carrier vehicle whose driver had deserted his post in panic as he heard the oncoming bomber. There was a great degree of luck for the Clark team, in that their B-17 gained enough distance to be airborne when reaching the vehicle; not so fortunate was the fact that the starboard landing gear impacted with its top frame. However, although the wheel structure was mangled and the No. 3 engine also badly damaged, the bomber was maintained in flight.

There was no question of attempting even a forced landing with the full fuel load being borne, so the pilots radioed in their intention to circle the airfield until the all-up-weight (AUW) of the B-17 was satisfactorily reduced before making the attempt. The landing approach was eased into, and once down, the wings were retained in level flight for as long as possible before gravity impelled the starboard wing tip to slide along the grass bordering the runway; even then, the bomber ground looped after the starboard landing gear gave way.

Despite this damage scale, the aircraft was restored to operational condition within five weeks. Long before then, the Tyler crew had been wakened and briefed for the task of leading the 398BG to assault gun batteries along the Pas de Calais coast. Lt. Howland's frustration at having his "beauty sleep" so disrupted was initially tempered by knowing that his roommate, along with the crew, had at least survived the immediate effect of the accident. However, he would have had to wait until landing back at Bassingbourn in order to confirm their safe emergence from the ensuing forced landing.

Now's the Time and Now's the Hour

Between the 2nd and the eve of D-Day, the B-17s and B-24s were directed against railroad facilities and airfields on the first day and the 4th, but the remaining three days' assaults were largely against coastal defenses in the Pas de Calais, with locations at Le Havre, on the eastern fringe of the *Overlord* beachhead, included on the 5th. Even as the bombers were settling down on their airfields on this date, the invasion fleets were casting off and beginning to assemble for the nocturnal crossing to Normandy. Having been postponed for 24 hours due to adverse weather, the die was firmly cast for the tens of thousands of soldiers under Gen. Eisenhower's Supreme Command.

The combat crews aroused at the usual ungodly hour in the night were doubtless shaken out of any lingering degree of lethargy by the momentous announcement that the invasion was on. As the 381BG records baldly state on 6 June: "This is what we were dispatched over here for thirteen months ago." The 8AF's immediate task was to neutralize the beach defensive chain in concert with the 9AF and RAF Bomber Command, but the solid cloud formations over the area were an unwelcome hindrance to accurate bombing. Added to this visual limitation was the unfortunate tendency for bomb loads to be released well clear of the actual beaches for fear of causing "friendly fire" casualties thereon; the consequence was most of the fortifications remained marginally damaged at best and intact at worst, although the aural effect of the thunderous cannonade probably unsettled the gunners in some instances even if death or injury was avoided. (The resultant heavy- and machine-gun duel with the Allied troops would proceed cruelly if short-term in the Germans' favor, particularly against the American forces striving to gain ground at *Omaha* and to a lesser extent at *Juno*, allotted to the Canadians.)

The few MIA losses suffered to date in the lead up to the landings had not involved the 1CBW, and this welcome break extended to the second D-Day mission later in the afternoon. This good fortune would extend to the seven ensuing missions launched from Bassingbourn, but not so over at Ridgewell, as evidenced the very next day, when the airfield at Kerlin/Bastard, near Lorient, was specifically allocated to the 1CBW, along with the 305BG. The target was one of a number regarded as platforms from which *Luftwaffe* bombers would be sent against the landing beaches, hence its selection.

The PFF Lead B-17 was from Bassingbourn and in the veteran Lt. Jim Tyson's (381BG) hands, with Lt. John Howland as navigator. The afternoon mission had left little time for this crew to transit to Ridgewell and prepare, but all went well as far as the bomb run, when cloud intervened to prevent the still-mandatory visual release. The formations wheeled round, but when John, having beforehand been informed of the presence of a sizeable flak battery site positioned in a way that permitted the gunners to engage the bombers throughout the entire 360-degree maneuver attempted to suggest to the Air Commander on board that a suitable course alteration be made in order to avoid its fire, he was sharply overruled.

During the subsequent circuit prior to the second bomb run, the formations were duly intruded upon by the flak gunners. All but one B-17 escaped their lethal intentions, the exception being Lt. John A. Martyniak's 42-97138/GD: I **Our Captain**. The damage incurred to No. 4 engine was not immediately terminal, but the bomber did drop out of formation, although still heading homeward following bombs away.

Further engine problems saw the B-17 steadily descending, but the pilot was still confident that he could attain SW English shores if all available surplus equipment was jettisoned. The ASR Service had been contacted, however, and a No. 267 Squadron Vickers Warwick bomber from RAF Coastal Command stationed at Portreath was put on Alert. This status was soon justified after a final call by S/Sgt. Paul Stewart (ROG) confirmed the sad fact that a "ditching" was inevitable as the Channel Islands were being bypassed to the west.

The bomber was successfully eased into the mercifully-calm sea and all nine airmen emerged, with but two suffering minor injuries during the abrupt transition from forward motion to a standstill. The dinghies were released and clambered into—none too soon, since barely two minutes elapsed between the impact and the bomber's complete submersion. Two Spitfires appeared overhead as the airmen scanned the horizon for Allied shipping, clearly unaware they were separated from such D-Day traffic by the Channel Islands and the Cherbourg Peninsula.

Little more than an hour had passed by before the Warwick, along with a fighter escort, loomed up. However, nearly 30 more minutes were taken up by its crew calculating the necessary wind and drift angle that would bring the released motorized lifeboat slung under its belly close enough for the American airmen to gain quick access, but not too close that it might descend directly upon them. Finally, the run at 300ft was made and the lifeboat drifted down under two parachutes that were duly released by small explosive charges once their cargo was in the water.

Although the crew soon paddled over to and clambered aboard their new "vessel," a degree of difficulty was experienced with one of the two motors due to a dinghy securing rope having wrapped itself around the propeller. It was fortunate that the other motor functioned and a course homeward was commenced. The vessel was not long under way when an ASR Launch came into sight, but the crew's problems were not completely ended.

Once aboard the Launch, its crew made to secure the lifeboat preparatory to towing it back, only for the rope to snag the Launch's propeller and permanently disable it! Fortunately, the Launch was similarly twin-motored and able to limp home to its base in SW England. Next day, the Martyniak crew were picked up at a nearby airfield by a group B-17 and flown back to Ridgewell. This incident was probably the most notable experience for the crew, who subsequently completed their combat tour.

Strategic Concentration

As far as the 1BD was concerned, the daily succession of tactical missions, with one exception on the 9th, extended through to the 17th; all 1CBW crews involved during this operational spell brought their B-17s back, although individual cases of injury or death were incurred. In fact, the 36 crews of the 8AF recorded as MIA in that period represented well below .5% of the number of individual sorties. But as ever, this cosy situation could not be guaranteed to be sustained, although the first full strategic mission dispatched on the 18th to attack oil production plants proved remarkably inexpensive at eleven out of 1,378 bombers sent out. Resources at Hamburg and adjacent Harburg were targeted by the 1BD, but deteriorating visibility in the region culminated with PFF-assisted drops on Secondary locations mainly within the city.

The 1CBW Command Pilot was Maj. John C. Weibel (Deputy CO, 398BG), while his crew, led by Lt. Ralph L. Halter, was also from Nuthampstead; however, their B-17 was 42-97626/LG: M, a PFF aircraft belonging to the 91BG. The bomb run had just been completed and a heading for the Rally Point was being adopted when flak struck home directly behind No. 1 engine. Shortly after, as attempts to "feather" the propeller were in progress, the weakened structure gave way; deprived of its lift, the aircraft went into an uncontrollable spin that ended SE of Harburg, along with most of the seven crew killed; only three officers somehow bailed out safely.

A companion crew from the group also failed to return to their base, although the Fates were kinder to the nine airmen concerned. The flak barrage caused sufficient damage to 42-102391/3O: B for Lt. Willard Hadges's charge to begin losing position following the bomb run. Lueneburg is some 20 miles SE of Hamburg, and it was to the east of the town that the pilots finally guided their B-17 down for a successful crash landing. Not only were injuries limited to one gunner wounded by flak, but two crewmembers were reportedly at large for more than a week, and when finally apprehended had travelled over fifty miles SW of the crash site!

The 8AF's Primaries the next day were located in SW France and comprised the by-now familiar location around Bordeaux, with Merignac and five other airfields targeted. This extended run involved 464 crews split between seven groups from the 1st and three from the 3rd BDs, of which barely half struck their Primaries at a cost of seven bombers; heavy cloud formations resulted in a good proportion of the force abandoning the mission.

The 381BG records indicate that the original intention was to attack Hamburg, but the switch to the present target was then made. One of the crews participating was Lt. John B. Doyle's in 42-107088/VE: E. This B-17 had previously brought the nine airmen through rough experiences on the late-May runs to Posen and Dessau, while today's mission was the thirteenth for the pilot and some or all of the others. The 51 bombers were split into two formations, with Col. Hall (Deputy CO) up front with the main one. The Primary was effectively struck by roughly two-thirds of the bombers and the remainder diverted to the (unstated) Secondary, where they too unloaded.

The first run having been a failure, the same altitude and heading was rather unwisely adopted, so providing the flak gunners with an enhanced prospect of landing accurate strikes. This bomb run was successful and returning crews were to report the mission as a long-winded "milk run"—with the stark exception of the Doyle-led team. A flak strike on the starboard wing root excised it completely from the airframe, as well as blowing Sgt. Charles E. Harker (ROG) out into space, the explosive concussion almost certainly bringing about his instant death.

The bomb load tumbled out of the bomber as the surviving crew fought against the increasing centrifugal forces. Lt. Bernard S. Leavitt (B) and Sgt. Robert T. Matthews (TG) won this physical battle to parachute into captivity. F/O Richard H. Richards, Jr. (N) was variously reported as also getting out but failing to survive for unknown reasons; alternately, his body was the sole identifiable one among the number discovered in or around the wreckage close to the SW fringe of Bordeaux. The fortunes of aerial combat were never predictable, even if the "unlucky 13" factor is added in.

The temporary concentration on strategic category targets during the month saw a return to Hamburg for the 1BD, with the city's industrial capacity successfully targeted by over 90% of the overall dispatched Force at a surprisingly small cost of seven MIA crews, one of which continued a "drip feed" MIA factor for Ridgewell. Lt. Mark R. Dunkel and crew were manning 43-37612/VP: **Old Iron Gut** when the B-17 received a devastating flak strike as the bomb run was nearly completed; the resultant disintegration following the aircraft going into a spin would have left eyewitnesses with the feeling that nobody had survived. In fact, one officer and two Enlisted men avoided the fate of Lt. Dunkel and five of his crew.

Bassingbourn's formation returned short of one B-17 in the shape of 42-97892/DF:, whose demise was equally vicious. The flak barrage during the course of the bomb run included one shell that caught Capt. Richard W. Burch's bomber squarely around the radio room shortly after "bombs away," thereby causing a structural bisection of the fuselage, with the halves forming a V-pattern; the forward element zoomed upwards and the tail section dipped into a dive. Only Pvt. Joseph A. Evers, manning his tail guns, reached the ground alive from among the nine-man crew.

Mid-Summer Mayhem

Berlin had to date received ten comprehensive bombardments involving varying degrees of punishment to its manifold industrial fabric. The previous four missions had only involved the 1st and 3rd BDs, but the projected run on 21 June called for the 2nd BD to join in as part of a thousand-plus bomber Force escorted by a similar number of fighters. The massive area covered by *Big B* ensured that any target entailed a lengthy exposure to the city's flak concentrations for the bomber stream. The *Jagdwaffe*, although now inhibited in its ability to strike *en masse* against the bombers in a prolonged unimpeded fashion compared to the previous winter, could still bring punishment to any element of the bomber stream currently lacking escort cover. This was to be the case for the 1CBW today, with all three groups providing 50% of the Division's MIA losses totalling sixteen.

Each Division was allotted targets spread between Basdorf (3BD) and Genshagen (2BD), on the northern and southwestern city outskirts, respectively; the 1BD was allocated targets within the city center, and therefore arguably faced the most severe attention from flak. In the event, its losses were more severe than the 3BD's figure of seventeen, while the 2BD surrendered nine crews.

The outward leg appears to have been adjoining the Baltic as far as the region around Poelitz before turning south. The Me410 *Hornissen* (Hornets) of II/ZG76 were based at Koenigsberg and accordingly available to tackle the incoming bomber stream; these twin-engine fighters were hopelessly outclassed by the P-51 and P-47, but proved lethal adversaries with their heavy armament, including a nose-mounted 50mm cannon, as well as externally-mounted WGr21 rocket launcher tubes, as would occur today.

The first sign of fighter trouble for the 1CBW occurred as the stream was about to turn towards Berlin. Prior to this, Lt. Sam Newton, whose position within the 91BG's Low squadron section of the 91BG's "A" Group—that in turn was flying Low position within the second of the two sub-forces dispatched by the 1CBW—became uncomfortably tight due to increased propeller wash as the Elements closed up and decided to move up to occupy a vacant slot in the High squadron.

While in the middle of this maneuver and consequently dangerously isolated, a crewmember called what he took to be a bunch of Mosquitoes flying off to the left at 180 degrees to the bombers. It quickly dawned on the crew that the Mosquitoes were turning to port as they were positioned at a five o'clock angle, and the illusion was firmly quashed when the aircraft evolved as Me410s. (To be fair, the Me410 outline was at first glance basically similar to its RAF contemporary.)

The encounter appears to have occurred in between Stettin and Anklam, judging by the subsequent loss pattern borne by the 91BG, in particular. Newton's B-17 had barely slipped into its revised position before the initial pass was made and all too soon several B-17s began to display variable degrees of battle damage. The first of five group losses basically occurred as Anklam was bypassed, although the bomber's death throes reportedly extended over a further 20 miles. Friedland lies SW of Anklam, and it was around there that all nine crew led by Lt. John R. Follett, Jr. drifted to earth. However, it is believed that their aircraft (42-97891/LL: M) remained aloft until the vicinity of Prenzlau before it finally impacted.

The next three casualties were probably incurred at roughly the same time based on where the B-17s came down. Lt. Robert E. O'Bannon was in charge of 44-6117/LG: Q, which developed a fire in one outer wing section; the overall damage was sufficient for the bomb load to be jettisoned, after which the aircraft slipped out of formation towards the east. A lake at Stolzenburg, almost halfway between Stettin and Neubrandenburg, received the wreckage; Sgt. Amos F. Estrada (TG) was the only fatality out of the nine airmen on board.

Lt. George A. Abbott's 42-102527/LG: A **Sleepytime Gal** was the other victim, as well as the third squadron bomber to be culled. (A surviving squadron pilot noted that three B-17s from his sub-formation were set on fire during the initial stage of the air battle to leave his and one other B-17 intact; this would appear to refer to the Low squadron that Lt. Newton had recently departed in order to join the High squadron.) Abbott's bomber was fired up on the port wing and the starboard inner engine and fell to its destruction several miles due east of Neubrandenburg. All but one of the Enlisted men, along with one officer, forfeited their lives, the likelihood for some or all of the gunners' fate being their greater exposure to the fusillade of shells emanating from the six o'clock attack angle.

Lt. Joseph P. Paskvan was piloting 43-37626/LG: M, and this B-17 was similarly fire-stricken around the inner port wing before descending inexorably; the crash site at Klein-Daberkow was in between and almost in a latitudinal line with the crash locations for the other two squadron aircraft. Whether or not the degree of injury reportedly incurred by the pilot and Sgt. James A. Bettis (BT) prevented their evacuating the falling B-17 is uncertain, but both were discovered within the wreckage; Sgt. Joe W. Bradford (TG) had also been injured and although he did bail out to be captured, he was destined to die during July, after being shot by a guard at his POW camp.

The 381BG formation was reduced by two during the fighter assaults, although only one involved a terminal result regarding the aircraft and two crewmembers. Lt. Roger L. Dassault's 42-31980/VE: J was fatally crippled by a rocket strike around the center of the fuselage and the bail out order was issued. Parachute packs were extremely vulnerable to destruction, either by being shredded or consumed by fire. The latter fate probably applied to Sgt. Howard L. Corum's (BT) pack; although Dassault made a quick check of the rear fuselage a spare was not found.

He temporarily lost consciousness as he reached the rear hatch and upon recovering found himself in mid-air, with the Sergeant clutching his legs in a desperate bid at survival. The inevitable happened when the ripcord was pulled because the shock effect of deceleration, estimated at anything up to a ton in strength, once again proved too great for human limbs to resist and the hapless gunner lost his grip and fell to his death. Dassault and seven colleagues drifted down safely, while the B-17 piled in at Schoenhauser, NW of Prenzlauk, a scant two miles distant from where Bassingbourn's 43-37626/LG: M ended up. The other fatality was Sgt. Elmer C. Meier (Eng.), although the circumstances are unclear.

The belated appearance of a good proportion of the assigned escort cover for the 1BD that had mistakenly linked up with one of the other two divisional forces up ahead before responding to the urgent requests for assistance resulted in *Jagdwaffe* pressure falling off. The 91BG had borne the brunt of the punishment; one crew each from the 41st and 94th CBWs had also disappeared, but their luck was in, since both successfully diverted into Sweden. What now lay ahead was the ever-daunting joust with *Big B's* flak battalions now barely fifty miles distant.

Ridgewell's added Tithe

A further Wing loss to fighters at this stage had a similar happy ending for the duo of Sweden-bound cripples and involved the 381BG's 42-38194/VP:V **Baboon McGoon**, flown by Lt. Arthur J. Bailey. Fighter strikes had crippled the bomber to an extent that the bail out order was issued, but was soon after cancelled—with unfortunate, albeit not fatal results for two crewmembers. Although now out on its own and wide open to individual dispatch, the bomber remained free of such lethal attention and had its nose pointed northward. The subsequent passage to Ringoby airfield passed off in order and the seven occupants still on board were processed for internment.

Meanwhile, Lts. Lloyd A. Peterson (N) and Erwin M. Brown (B) were down on enemy soil and clearly unaware of their ill- and fellow-airmen's good fortune. Lloyd recalled that he had lost his escape kit during his descent, but he then utilized the sun as a rough guide as he also headed towards the Baltic coast with the possibility of reaching a seaport and stowing away on a neutral vessel. His initial progress was rightly conducted well away from roads or paths, but towards evening, he made the fatal mistake of breaking this rule. Soon after doing so he encountered a cyclist going in the opposite direction; any lingering hope that he would be ignored disappeared when the man stopped, turned round, and produced a pistol before motioning Lloyd towards him. And so the first step towards *Stalag-Luft* 3 was unwillingly undertaken by the would-be evader.

Lt. Jim Tyson's veteran PFF crew was carrying the 381BG's Maj. Halsey (535BS CO) as Air Commander. Also on board as Pilotage Navigator was Lt. Theodore Homdrom, an equally skilled exponent of his art. The mission was also the final one of this team's combat tour and surely not regarded as the best manner in which to do so. As the city boundaries were being traversed, the flak barrage commenced and indeed, was regarded by John Howland (Tyson's regular navigator) as one of the roughest ever encountered. The Pilotage duty in a B-17 was poorly provisioned compared to the B-24; the Consolidated design's nose turret provided a separate, seated space from the bombardier, whereas the function had to be conducted standing or squatting behind the bombardier in the Boeing bomber.

Two of the Lead bomber's engines were playing up, but progress up to the bomb release was otherwise unimpeded. Then, a flak fragment shattered the starboard front Plexiglas frame in the nose and one of the glass splinters impacted Homdrom's right eye. John displaced the bombardier to take over the Pilotage function after Theo was moved aft for treatment. More flak fragments added to the airframe's prior punishment from fighter strikes, but several minutes later, the formation departed the city and its flak gunners' attention.

Damage to the B-17's standard control cable system meant that a switch back from autopilot during the bomb run could not be made. It was as well the bomber was flying Lead, because it would have been impossible for the pilots to maneuver the bomber in response to the other aircrafts' movements. Even when the protracted return leg had been negotiated and Bassingbourn's circuit joined, Maj. Halsey offered the crew the opportunity to bail out, since there was no guarantee of a safe landing approach; nobody took up the offer and all went well following a trial "landing" using a cloud layer as a guide.

Lt. Homdrom insisted on attending debriefing before being taken to the base hospital, where he spent several days before release, his eye condition thankfully clearing up. While there, he was visited by Col. Leber (381BG CO) and Gen. Gross (CG, 1CBW); a citation for the award of a DFC was read out and the medal pinned onto his pajama jacket signalled the completion of his 30-mission tour that extended back to 24 December, a near six-month period that virtually mirrored the Tyson crew's operational time span.

The 91BG's final MIA casualty had progressed as far as the target area when disaster struck. Although 42-97686/DF: was a group B-17, the bulk of the eleven-man crew led by Lt. Richard L. Rohrer were seconded from the 398BG, the exception being Lt. Theodore Cantrell (Radar Navigator). No. 3 engine was struck squarely just before "bombs away" and the B-17 swung to starboard as it dipped down. Further strikes set the bomber on fire and the eleven-man crew jumped out. Although their descent was into the city and subsequent capture was primarily effected in the neighborhood of Tempelhof airfield, the recorded crash site near Lychen was some 50 miles due north of Berlin, indicating that the abandoned B-17 had clearly taken its time in dying during its errant path.

On the 24 May Berlin mission, **Joanne** (42-97174/GD: P) had brought Lt. Williams's crew back to Ridgewell following the loss of most of her fabric-covered control surfaces thanks to flying through a fireball created by a disintegrating fellow bomber. Now she was unknowingly on her final run with Lt. Roy H. Pendergist in charge. The bomb run was completed and the Rally Point being headed for when the starboard wing absorbed a flak strike that set the bulk of the structure on fire. The bomber progressed to a point some fifteen miles outside the NW fringe of Berlin, where it smashed into the ground and was totally destroyed. Roy and six of his eight fellow airmen parachuted safely, the other two being found dead at the crash site. (In 1984, Roy informed the author that he had probably brought about both the B-17's and crew's downfall by maneuvering it in the wrong direction; the bald truth was that any evasive action held no guarantee of security from the flak gunners' insidious efforts.)

There could have easily been a fourth Ridgewell loss as the formation was clearing the city. A flak burst ignited the hydraulic fluid lines up front on 43-37704/MS: J **Button Nose** and the flaming spray descended fully upon the general area of the cockpit and Lt. Sam Myerscough (P) in particular. The potentially fatal outcome for both the bomber and its pilot was prevented by the prompt action of Sgt. Clarence Rolla (Eng.), who wrestled Myerscough to the cockpit floor as he exited his seat before smothering the flames with his hands and body; he then grabbed a fire extinguisher and successfully tackled the blaze.

The inability to utilize the brakes on making the landing run at Ridgewell was countered by the attachment of two parachute packs to one waist window and the tail, whose deployment maintained the B-17 on a straight if eventful course along the runway. The Lieutenant's condition following proper treatment was fortunately soon restored to normal and he went on to complete his combat tour. In contrast, **Button Nose** would not see August out before succumbing in battle.

Closing off June

The ensuing six missions following the latest *Big B* venture returned the B-17s and B-24s to the tactical theme, during which period the MIA loss factor was reduced to 1%, a total that included a quartet of 1CBW crews. A Ridgewell aircraft was culled on the 22nd. Tingry-Abbeville was the target for one of the three twelve-strong group formations, but the flak gunners were pumping their shells as the bomb run was progressing, a run that ironically did not result in bomb release. Lt. Samuel L. Peak's 42-97084/GD: H had both inboard engines disabled, followed shortly after by part or all of one wing detaching; the bomber zoomed upwards before commencing a descent that was cut short by its mid-air disintegration, from which only Sgt. Richard D. Oberlin (WG) somehow emerged alive.

Forty-eight hours later, the 381BG was approaching Tours/La Riche airfield. Lt. Bill Skogland, piloting 4232049/GD: D **Yankee Rebel**, later reported that the formation was making a 360 degree turn before commencing the bomb run when Lt. Victor R. Romasco's 42-102585/GD: A **The Betty L**, positioned in an element above, was struck by a shell; Lt. Harry S. Smith (CP) was in another B-17 and witnessed the B-17's radio room exterior panels and the hatch being blown away, followed seconds later by the stricken bomber slowly easing down to starboard with the No. 3 engine smoking.

Up to five crewmembers were reported bailing out, and in fact that figure from among the nine on board did survive; Lt. Ray L. Stewart (N) was even more fortunate in evading capture, but it was not surprising that Sgt. Paul G. Cosandier did not survive the damage to his radio room. Sgt. Grover L. Scroggins (BT) was found in the wreck. Prior to the fatal blow he had called up to say his turret was stuck, whereupon Romasco ordered Sgt. Harry E. Owens (WG) to get him out; whatever transpired, Owens also ended up dead.

The 381BG's blood debt in MIA crews for the month was now complete but the Reaper was not finished with its fellow units in the Wing. On the 25th, the 1BD dispatched 263 crews to attack two airfields at Toulouse and an oil depot at Montbartier. This extended run to France's Mediterranean coast was difficult enough to complete with a functioning aircraft, let alone one developing engine problems early on. Lt. Ferrall K. Goodrich had to feather No. 1 engine on 42-97292/LG: C/N **Batchelors Bride** and relinquish the squadron Lead, as well as salvo the bombs after dropping out in order to maintain touch with the formation.

By the stage of the bomb run's completion, the B-17 was down to half power and unable to maintain altitude with the stream, whereupon the decision was taken to head westward with an initial view to "ditching" the aircraft. The inability to climb over the intervening high ground finally saw a desperate bid to crash land in what was geographically hostile territory by utilizing a treeless slope. It was a miracle that although the bomber ground to a halt in less than 100 yards and liberally spread itself around, none of the nine airmen was seriously injured, although Sgt. William A. Fann (BT) was rendered unconscious for several days. The crash site was on Spanish soil, so the crew now faced internment.

The vagaries of combat operations dealt harshly with a second group crew by comparison. **Old Faithful** (42-37958/LL: G) had survived a six-month period and today bore Lt. Peter Mikonis's crew. Flak had set No. 3 engine on fire and what was probably a "strike" photo at the Primary captured the bomber trailing a thick rope of smoke. The fire was extinguished, but now the B-17 was hopelessly isolated. In spite of this, the bomber was headed north for what was the multi-hundred mile run for home. Upwards of six hours elapsed before the Continent's northern fringe was finally negotiated and a cross over into SW England effected.

The bomber's course now took it over Wincanton, some 20 miles inland, but tragedy then intervened; the fire effect allied to the air pressure exerted on the wing must have weakened the structure enough for it to finally fail, whereupon the B-17 flipped over and smashed into the ground, bearing all nine crew to their deaths—a truly unmerited fate in view of their heroic and hitherto successful bid to survive. The memorial erected nearby after WWII was a fully deserved, albeit posthumous recognition of their gallantry.

The flak over Toulouse/Blagnac airfield directly claimed another 1CBW bomber in the form of Nuthampstead's 42-102463/K8: Z barely seconds after the bomb run was completed. The strike caused No. 4 engine to catch fire, and all too soon Lt. John C. Godwin's afflicted charge pulled up steeply before plunging to its fiery destruction several miles NW of Toulouse; all nine crew bailed out, but one officer died after reportedly suffering a failure of his parachute harness.

July 1944

Although the Allies were well established in Normandy, by 1 July, the land battle was still very much undecided, as the German 7th Army cleverly utilized the rolling landscape in frustratingly effective defensive measures even in the face of the daunting numerical superiority in men and equipment enjoyed by their adversaries. The 8AF was accordingly to operate a mix of tactical and strategic missions, although the emphasis was swinging back in favor of the latter target type. As for the 1CBW, its crews would be out for between seventeen and nineteen days within the month commencing on the 4th. However, the intention to attack a bridge at Tours proved largely "abortive" thanks to adverse weather, although 381BG records state the group released upon Tours/La Riche airfield as a Target of Opportunity.

One crew was missing from debriefing at Ridgewell; Lt. Robert Bobrow's team in 42-38117/MS: **Touch the Button Nell II** was a loss due to mechanical failure. On the way over, the pilot reported the loss of No. 2 engine and a consequent inability to hold formation. He turned for home under escort, but an inexorable descent occurred despite jettisoning all spare equipment. The bomber finally developed a spinning action and only four crewmembers successfully cleared the plunging airframe. One of this number watched the pilots correct their charge's errant spiral and begin to pull it out of the dive, but sadly, it was not fully levelled off before it impacted and broke up, killing all still on board. A fifth airman had bailed out, only to get "hung up" on the "feathered" propeller and be dragged to his death.

Another tactical mission was flown two days later without loss, but the month's first strategic thrust at Leipzig/Mockau's oil production plant provided a rebuff for the 398BG, with two crews culled from the 36 dispatched. Lt. Boyd A. Nieswonger's 42-102508/N7: J suffered a strike around No. 3 engine as the group was heading out of the target area, whereupon the outer wing section detached. In these circumstances, it was surprising that all but Sgt. William H. Englehardt (WG) managed to take to their parachutes. All nine occupants of 42-102718/N8: T, led by Lt. Roger A. Folger, cleared their doomed B-17, which was abandoned around the same time. However, the fortunes that allowed Lt. Raymond C. Hopp (CP) to reach the ground alive were cruelly reversed when he was reportedly killed while trying to evade capture.

The July aircraft loss count for the 398BG had by now been doubled, although the nineteen airmen involved in the two other incidents survived. First, on the 4th 42-107114/N8: L, piloted by Capt. C. L. Douglas, suffered an irreversible engine fire over Sussex and had to be abandoned, crashing at Edburton. Two days later, Lt. H. J. Sleaman crash landed 43-37527/N7: C **Bad Penny** at an RAF airfield at Kent with salvage action confirmed days later.

Whereas Ridgewell's overall suffering for the month would be small regarding losses, fortune would deal more harshly with the 398BG, which bore seven more MIA crews, and even more so for the 91BG, which was fated to lose double Nuthampstead's casualty figure. On the 8th, the latest pair of Nuthampstead teams to feel the enemy's sting was that of Lt. George E. Wilson's in 42-102445/3O: R and Capt. Kearie L. Berry piloting 42-107096/3O: K, both 601BS B-17s. The flak strike on the former B-17 impacted between the port side engines and probably killed or injured the pilot to an extent he was unable to vacate his seat; he became the sole fatality among the nine crewmembers, the bomber descending SE of Rouen.

The other B-17 was similarly afflicted on its starboard wing with both engines disabled. The pilots turned back, but the bail out order was given as the coastline was crossed; although all nine airmen jumped, leaving the aircraft to crash into the Channel, only Berry and Sgt. Manuel C. Ray (TG) were fortunate enough to be picked up by the ASR Service; six of the other seven were destined to become names on "Walls of the Missing." (The rescue effort would have been risky to undertake, since the area was still under enemy control, so demonstrating the ASR Service's motto: "The Sea shall not have them.") Two further B-17s were absent, one of which (42-97380/N8: R) was abandoned by Lt. Lovelace's crew on return; the other was 42-97855/3O: A, which was crash landed by Capt. Tracey J. Peterson at Sandwich, in SE England.

The 91BG opened its MIA account for July with 42-97173/OR: **Take it Easy**. The 323BS aircraft was in group strength two months, and today it bore a mix of veteran and first-mission personnel, the former status involving F/O James W. Fore flying his 25th. The hazy weather conditions over the Pas de Calais forced the group to seek Targets of Opportunity, during which time this B-17 simply disappeared, its vague fate reported as "B-17 seen to explode in mid-air" with no other confirming details. In fact, only one of the nine-man crew was killed during the incident.

Nearly—But Not Quite

After flying a tactical mission (9th), beginning on the 11th, the 8AF bombers directed their attention for three successive days to assaulting facilities in Munich. Division casualties were amazingly restricted to one on the first sortie, but five crews (still a low percentage of the attacking force) were culled next day. The 1CBW's ranks had remained inviolate during these two runs, but not so on the 13th, with the 398BG again being the affected unit. In addition, Lt. Thomas K. Foster's crew did not even progress further than western Belgium. When bypassing Brussels a flak shell severed the fuselage and 42-97348/

N7: R's truncated airframe fell some distance before exploding. Only Sgt. Loren C. Brown (TG) out of Lt. Foster's crew not only survived, but also evaded.

Back at Ridgewell, the fire and salvage crews were attending to the smoking remains of a 534BS bomber lying in a railroad cutting near the base. Lts. John Houston (P) and William Scruggs (CP), both 27-mission veterans, had earlier lifted off in their bomber (44-6148/GD: M **Smashin' Thru**) for the mission, but soon had to turn back with mounting engine problems. The heavy mist and cloud conditions shrouding the airfield resulted in several overshoots as they sought out a runway. Finally, with power swiftly ebbing away the desperate pilots directed the B-17 towards a field for a crash landing. This venture initially succeeded, despite the bomber still bearing its bomb load. Tragically, its momentum was not fully spent before the field gave way to the railroad cutting into which the now-burning aircraft had slid.

The flaming airframe was hastily vacated by the pilots, who exited via their side windows, but a broken leg suffered by Scruggs prevented him from crawling further than the rim of the cutting before part of the bomb load erupted, expunging the lives of the other seven crewmembers. In addition, the copilot suffered extremely bad burns accrued either during the crash landing or by being sprayed by the fuel tank contents. He would in time make a full recovery after hospitalization, but this fortunate situation lay weeks and months ahead of him now. Lt. Houston was unscathed by comparison, but nevertheless equally lucky to survive.

The 8AF's mini-campaign against Munich was resumed on the 18th, with Stuttgart and Augsburg also targeted by the 1BD. The existence of cloud layers extending up to 30,000ft had a limiting effect on the number of crews attaining the Primaries; on the other hand, *Jagdwaffe* opposition was virtually nil, although the flak batteries were disturbing as ever. For the third time in July, the 398BG lost two crews, both claimed after bombing. The first down was 42-102599/N8; Z **Zoomeriago** bearing Lt. Curtiss D. Lovelace's crew. For whatever reason, the B-17 was seen to detach itself from the group ranks as the formation was swinging to the south of Munich, with all nine airmen recorded as jumping prior to the bomber going into a spin. Unfortunately, the pilot and Sgt. Gerard C. Antaillia (BT) did not survive.

The other aircraft (42-102476/N7: B) was still in formation as the group was SE of Strasbourg, but it was then that a sharp fighter pass resulted in a badly shot up fuselage with the ball turret particularly affected, its occupant (Sgt. Robert C. Warkentin) dying, along with Sgt. Charles B. McLean (TG). The other seven crew under Lt. Raymond J. Gallagher fared better, parachuting into enemy hands around Wolfach, in the vicinity of which their aircraft plummeted to earth.

Bad Week at Bassingbourn

Today's mission unknowingly commenced a stark five-day spell of heavy losses for the 91BG. On the way to the Secondary at Augsburg, flak punctured the port wing fuel tanks, and although the bombs were salvoed, an inability to close the bay doors added to the problem. Worse still, Lt. Donald DeLisle's copilot, Lt. Norman Kimmel, having revived a crewmember, suddenly collapsed over his controls on return, whereupon 42-31610/DF: M **The Liberty Belle**—christened in February by her assigned pilot Lt. John Klotz, who was by now back stateside—plunged out of formation. Although pulled out of its dive, steadily faltering engine power ended with the pilots having to "ditch" in the North Sea. The ever-dangerous process went off in sound order and within thirty minutes the nine crewmembers had transferred out of their dinghies into a rescue vessel.

On 5 July, actor Edward G. Robinson visited Ridgewell, during the course of which he christened 42-102664/VE: F **Happy Bottom**. Eleven days later, the relatively new B-17 was now in the hands of Lt. Jack McGregor, but whereas her crew were ultimately heading for a positive conclusion to their combat tour, the aircraft was heading for her last round up. Flak damage saw the pilots unsuccessfully striving to reach friendly shores, only to be forced into a "ditching" in the North Sea. All went well and a nearby Royal Naval vessel collected all nine airmen off the still-floating airframe. However, Jack had to be firmly dissuaded from going back to the cockpit in order to rescue his "50-mission crush" officer's hat!

Peenemuende, up on the Baltic coast, was home for key rocket research facilities, and along with facilities at Zinnowitz was targeted by the Division on the 18th. The strength of the 8FC escorts was probably one factor in the low figure of three MIA bombers out of 434 attacking crews during what was an extended period over hostile soil. However, two-thirds of this figure was credited to the 1CBW, although both crews came through unscathed.

As the IP was looming, 42-97457/LL: F, piloted by Lt. Donald K. Bare, began to straggle, having lost an engine. The decision was then taken to bank to port and head for Sweden, where a safe landing was made at Bulltofta. Joining the nine 91BG airmen in internment was Lt. Frank R. O'Black and his eight-man team manning 42-102663/VP: L **Yardbird**, which had also sustained flak damage deemed too severe for the bomber to regain British shores; the bomber was also the last of three group B-17s to divert into Sweden.

It was back to SE Germany next day, when the research base at Lechfeld was briefed for the Wing. Scheuring was several miles SE of the Primary and currently housed six 88mm flak guns that duly poured their fire towards the bombers. An unfortunate recipient of their attention was 42-102511/K8: P, which was literally ripped apart. A dreadfully graphic set of pictures shows the main fuselage with part of the wing structure still attached descending in a sheet of flame and impacting with the ground; another shows the separated tail section, within which Sgt. Gregory G. Gromicki had a bare lease on life of thirty minutes compared to all but one of Lt. Dallas A. Hawkins's team. The extremely fortunate exception was Sgt. Doyle C. Borchers (WG), who was literally blown out into space and able to deploy his parachute.

Mid-air collision was ever the principle bane of formation flying and today's incident involved 42-107075/OR: Q **Champagne Girl** and 42-31542/OR: T. **Bunky**, a transfer from the 457BG during March when its fellow squadron B-17 in fate also arrived. The invisible, wayward effect of prop wash here experienced during the bomb run was the likely reason why OR: Q was suddenly cast off to the left and into **Bunky**'s path. Its wing tip impacted with the other B-17's stabilizer, but as Lt. Norman Burwick desperately attempted to haul OR: T out of the way, the No. 1 propeller on Lt. Cyril Braund's bomber literally sawed the rear fuselage off into space. The main portion swooped upwards momentarily before assuming a diving spiral motion that probably held all crewmembers still alive firmly in place until the end; among those killed from this veteran team was Lt. Albert E. Steelhammer (B), flying what was his final scheduled mission—a goal achieved in a most cruel manner.

Meanwhile, OR: Q was being held aloft with great difficulty as it was headed towards Swiss territory. The roughly seventy-mile distance to that neutral country's border remained free of any fighter or flak interference, but the critical state of the airframe dictated that a landing was too fraught with risk. The nine airmen accordingly took to their parachutes, leaving their mount to impact harmlessly on a mountainside near Obersaxon. Four group losses inside 72 hours was bad enough, but the morrow's mission was to bring about a doubling of this casualty figure, with a general lowering of morale accordingly circulating among Bassingbourn's personnel.

Discipline's Ironic Overtones

The disciplining of combat crew members to react promptly to an emergency situation could and did sometimes result in a serious or even tragic outcome. On the morning of 19 July 1944, the 381BG was taking off in the early morning gloom. S/Sgt. Paul Stewart (ROG) was on board his 532BS aircraft as it cleared the runway end and commenced its climb. For whatever reason, the airman was already wearing his parachute pack. (A seemingly contradictory act, since working at his desk would have been none too easy with the pack's bulk—unless he had donned a backpack.) Whatever the facts, the pack's presence was the unconscious catalyst for what transpired.

The bomber gained barely several hundred feet in altitude when a malfunction caused the bail out bell to sound. Being in a better position to take the requisite action, Stewart headed for the nearest exit point, probably the rear main door; in spite of his colleagues' attempts at dissuasion he cleared the aircraft. Even then, he might have made a heavy but clean landing had he immediately pulled the ripcord, but probably delayed in order to avoid the canopy and/or its rigging lines becoming entangled with the airframe. By the time he deployed the parachute, the remaining height was too little to prevent extremely brutal contact with the ground that left him alive but critically injured.

The fact of the S/Sgt.'s action was radioed to the control tower and the teams of searchers duly set out to find him. However, the postage stamp nature of the surrounding countryside now cast up a frustrating barrier to Stewart's prompt retrieval—this despite the fact of the aircraft's take-off path and the short time—lapse between lifting off and the Sergeant's bail out. Frustration and concern beset the men's minds as time dragged relentlessly on before the search aircraft managed to find the site. Even then, the pilot experienced difficulty in leading the searchers to the spot thanks to the convoluted and narrow road pattern. It was upwards of eight hours before the Jeep staff in communication with the aircraft was finally able to pinpoint the location.

When found, Stewart said he had been conscious for practically the entire period; if so, he was clearly fortunate not to have succumbed to shock, given the time involved. Delivery to the base hospital confirmed his injuries as a fractured spine and both legs so comprehensively damaged that the bone structures would virtually have to be kneaded back into some form of shape. Further transfer to the General Hospital at Braintree saw him placed in a cast, but whether he ultimately regained a partial, let alone complete, ability to walk following his shipment home is unclear.

Sturmggruppe "Treatment" on Mission No. 200

The enemy defenses' effect upon the 8AF to date in the course of the six deep penetration missions during the month had been gratifyingly restricted; of the more than 7,000 individual crew sorties, barely 1.3% (89) had resulted in loss over the Continent. In addition, the figure was almost equally spread between the Divisions, although one or two groups had suffered more than the remainder. These circumstances conversely hid a burgeoning risk of complacency in general and especially among the gunners, whose expertise was not being regularly tested. Lt. Bert Stiles, a college classmate of John Howland, recalled that the pre-mission chatter prior to setting off for Leipzig included individuals referring to "catching up on sack time" and "sleeping most of the way in to Augsburg"—whether the remarks were exceptional or not, the temptation to relax one's guard must have been more prevalent with the *Jagdwaffe*'s presence much diminished in recent weeks.

The 1CBW's Primaries at Leipzig covered Mockau airfield and a ball bearing plant, and all progressed in order for most of the inward route. Stiles's literary gifts had him recalling in his posthumously-published book *Serenade to the Big Bird*: "There was Death all over the sky—the quiet threat of Death, who masqueraded as a seeming lady but whose conduct switched unpredictably to that of a whore," claiming individuals without regard to combat experience. For whatever reason, the group's 37 aircraft flying in the Low slot had become dangerously separated from the other two Wing elements and this ever-fraught situation promised harsh measures should enemy fighters intervene. A warning was now received about "bandits in the target area," one that was about to have horrendous consequences for the Bassingbourn airmen.

Stiles, flying as copilot to Lt. John Green, recalled that his initial indication of trouble as the formation split up for the bomb run—so creating a further sub-division of isolation within the already detached group—was hearing a gun open up, followed by glimpses of several black smoke puffs and bright flashes. His feeling that they were under flak assault was swiftly dispelled when the bomber's gunners frantically opened up on what was the lead element of a *Sturmgruppe* formation, and he saw a Fw190 shoot by before doing a half-roll maneuver. What was an intense air battle of relatively short duration had commenced, one that would decimate the group ranks in the process.

The leader for the Green/Stiles B-17 element was **The Peacemaker** (43-37552/LL: E), with Lt. Walter Langford (P) and Jim Fletcher (CP). Jim later recalled that he only saw one fighter during the frenzied action and watched one B-17 literally dissolve, with surfaces seeming to peel off. **Peacemaker**'s airframe was badly shot up, with the transmitter and oxygen systems disabled and No. 3 engine knocked out. In spite of this, the crew were destined to survive the onslaught and regain their airfield. The Stiles account of this B-17's situation was that it swung down to starboard with several Fw190s in hot pursuit. Jim Fletcher acknowledges that altitude was down to 17,000ft by the end of the air battle, which lasted fifteen minutes in his estimation. Lt. Marion Havelaar (N) provided a more detailed account of what transpired that is recorded further on in this section.

The B-17 whose loss was witnessed by Lt. Fletcher was 42-97954/LL: Z **Winnie, Frank, Joe**—an allusion to the leaders of the three major Allied countries—being flown by Lt. Donald Knapp. The rear of the airframe appears to have been most affected by the fusillade of gunfire that likely adversely affected the flight controls, sending the B-17 out of control. One officer and two gunners out of the nine on board failed to survive the air battle.

The most embattled squadron today would be the 401BS, although its four MIA loss figure was to be only one ahead of the 322BS. T/Sgt. Jack Gaffney had been Crew Chief for 42-31812/LL: H **Destiny's Child** ever since its arrival around late February, since when it had flown over fifty missions. Once again, the initial fighter pass landed fatal strikes that included heavy damage to the fuselage and No. 4 engine set on fire. Lt. Charles Van Ausdell managed to haul his charge out of its diving descent long enough for all but one crewmember to be reported as deploying his parachute; despite this positive report, the pilot did not survive, his death being mirrored by three among his eight fellow airmen.

The operational career of 43-37624/LL: P **Victory Queen** was by contrast short but concentrated, the aircraft having put in sixteen missions to date since her 24 June assignment. Lt. Frank Fusco's bomber was yet another victim arising from the first *Sturmgruppe* strike. No. 3 engine's eruption in flames impelled the pilot to maneuver his bomber first laterally, then in a shallow dive in an attempt to extinguish the fire. The crippled aircraft was then levelled off several thousand feet down, followed shortly after by its disappearance; in that spell, a total of six parachutes was observed. As it was, only the pilot out of the nine-man crew failed to survive.

Spreading the Cost

Superstitious Aloysius (42-31982/LG: S) was another veteran B-17 belonging to the 322BS, now almost five months on group establishment. It had survived heavy battering on an April mission and had been brought back to operational status, but today's run would not grant her a second reprieve. During the second fighter pass, the No. 2 engine caught fire and the fire rapidly spread to the wing. Lt. Allen G. Deshaw eased the B-17 out to one side, after which it commenced a rapid descent, with the crew beginning to bail out before the airframe tore apart. It was surprising that fatalities were restricted to one among the nine airmen; however, the dead man was reportedly killed by civilians in apparent revenge for the damage to property, if not human loss caused by the shattered remains of the bomber.

The second squadron crew to go down was on board 42-38027/LG: A **Heavenly Body**, piloted by Lt. Lucian E. Strong. This B-17 was over six months into her operational function and was regularly utilized as a group Lead ship before being regularly assigned to this crew. The exact circumstances of its loss seem unclear, although it may well have been picked off by a fighter after falling away from the formation. Whatever transpired, only five out of the nine ended up in a *Stalag*, with the pilot one of the fatalities. An unnamed B-17 closed off the squadron loss total, being 43-37819/LG: with Lt. Charles T. Walby and crew. Strikes on the starboard wing set it on fire and it pulled out of formation to finally disappear; Walby was one of two fatalities out of nine.

The least affected squadron was the 324BS, with a single loss. This was Capt. Francis S. Holmes's 42-97999/DF:, which absorbed heavy punishment to its starboard wing and subsequently fell away to disappear out of sight. This time around all nine crewmembers reached the ground alive to face the shadow world of *Kriegydom*.

The Liberty Run (42-102509/LL: A) was reportedly Lead ship for the sub-force containing Lt. Stiles's bomber and had amassed twenty missions in less than one month, a clear indication of the intensity of operations on either side of D-Day. She was fated to become the 401BS' final casualty, but her ultimate demise was initiated by flak, rather than fighters. Lt. Stiles stated that the bomb run was completed when Capt. William R. Martin (CP) called to say the pilot (Lt. Arthur Hultin) and one other crewmember were wounded, followed shortly after by a claim that a wing was on fire. Stiles states in his book that he responded to the plea to carry out a visual check by telling the caller all seemed in order. Almost immediately, and despite this reassurance, the bomber was eased out of formation and parachutes began to blossom, as all ten of the crew jumped clear to face upwards of ten months captivity.

Lt. Havelaar's report on **The Peacemaker**'s experience was somewhat more graphic than Jim Fletcher's. He had been checking his bombsight when he suddenly noticed a line of white smoke puffs ahead that instantly came to mind as "self-exploding cannon shells" before the intercom was destroyed just after a single word "fighters" was shouted by a gunner. The Fw190s shot by, followed almost immediately by what he recalled was the formation leader sliding across his vision shrouded in flame.

The ensuing several minutes entailed a confused set of images as the bombardier wielded his gun with indeterminate effect. Then, "where there had been smoke and flames, Forts, and Fw190s now was just sky." The damaged B-17 appeared to have slipped back from the formation and the navigator confirmed its overall critical state after returning from the cockpit. The order was given to jettison all excess equipment, but when the navigator pointed to the bombsight, the Lieutenant demurred and only reacted when presumably ordered to by his pilot. Even then, the sight was carefully detached and equally carefully eased out through the nose hatch—ingrained habit in handling such delicate gear clearly died hard, although he later freely acknowledged the ridiculous reaction when given the emergency.

Lts. Langford and Green had brought their battered bombers back, but eight B-17s and seventy-three crewmembers were not so fortunate. The sense of torment among the personnel at Bassingbourn was probably further increased by the fact that the Leipzig mission was the 200th occasion the group had been dispatched, but any immediate prospect of celebrating the occasion had been nailed firmly on the head.

The punishment handed out by the pilots from a *Sturmgruppe* was but the first of three such examples to afflict the 91BG during 1944, with August and November casting up a total of nineteen MIA crews spread between the two future catastrophes. The immediate aftermath of the Leipzig debacle was that the 91BG would not go operational again until the 24th, even if the Division was to launch but a single large-scale effort during this time.

The eleven remaining July days witnessed the 8AF operating on eight, in which the Divisional effort was equally split between tactical and strategic targets. The second mission within the latter category was to a major synthetic oil production complex whose name would be ranked alongside Schweinfurt in terms of notoriety—Merseburg, whose massive defensive ring of flak guns was rightly regarded with dread by the bomber crews. On this occasion, the seven crews culled from among 652 crews from both B-17 Divisions making the bomb line was surprisingly marginal.

However, the single 1CBW casualty appears to have been incurred despite the flak barrage encountered. The disabling of one engine on 42-102579/N7: C **Stinker** on the way over saw Lt. Wilbur S. Dwyer's charge experiencing difficulty in maintaining position, even when the errant motor was restarted. The straggling B-17 finally banked away to ultimately crash NE of Charleroi, Belgium, by which stage its nine occupants had taken to their parachutes; the descent onto Allied soil also enabled two gunners to evade capture.

The high July casualty rate at Bassingbourn, and to a lesser extent at Nuthampstead, was to be ratcheted up one more notch in the case of the former unit. On the 31st, Munich received its latest bombardment from a force that included the full 1CBW strength. The Primary of Schleissheim airfield being "socked in" by cloud, recourse was had by the group to a PFF-assisted bombing of the main city marshalling yards. **Priority Girl** (42-97304/OR: C), originally the mount for Lt. Pryor, had then been taken over by Lt. Harry W. Supchak following his predecessor's combat tour completion. Target flak disabled both port engines and the inevitable loss of formation position finally impelled the pilots to head south for Switzerland; this desirable goal was never reached, but the bomber's loss over enemy soil was not equalled by any of its nine occupants.

The 381BG's relative immunity from loss during July also received a jolt when its 36-strong formation headed for the BMW plant at Allach. Lt. Jack B. Pearson was guiding 42-102423/VP: Q along the flak-intruded bomb run when it appears strikes reduced engine power by 50%. At any rate, eyewitnesses reported the last sight of the ailing B-17 was one of it taking up a similar southerly heading to its 91BG fellow straggler. This bid for neutral salvation also failed, but although the pilots were finally forced into a crash landing near Biberach/Kies, the nine crewmembers emerged intact, albeit as more candidates for a *Stalag*.

The crumpled lower surface of the detached nose compartment on a Bassingbourn-based B-17 suggests that the aircraft "nosed up" during landing or take-off as opposed to "bellying in"; the intact main fuselage skin and D/F loop (the latter indicating a G variant) tends to support that theory.

"The sun is rising out of the red of battle" (A quote from the Clark Gable commentary for "Combat America.") seems an apt choice for this shot of a 381BG bomber. The relatively clear skyline towards the east promises a successful launch for the group's latest mission into the heavily-contested skies over the Third Reich.

The five Ridgewell-based pilots seen here are (L-R) Lts. Joe Hainzer, Victor Romasco, Don Soale, Harry A. Smith, and Robert A. Douglas; all are with the 534BS apart from Hainzer, and all will survive the conflict. However, Romasco will become a POW on 19 June 1944 following the loss of his 42-102585/GD: A The Betty L.

"D-Day has come!"—or rather, it will commence within hours of this briefing shot at Bassingbourn. The reactions range from the hand-clasping individual on the right to bright smiles in general and one or two more phlegmatic expressions; the latter airmen doubtless pondering the hard road still ahead and whether they and/or all on hand will win through to savor the fruits of victory.

Two airmen are posed with a weapon-bearing Jeep that is intended to provide a mobile form of airfield defense. The 534BS B-17G in the background is Our Captain; on 7 June 1944, it was "ditched" off the Channel Islands by Lt. John Martyniak with all nine crewmembers surviving to be rescued by the ASR Service of the RAF.

Maj. George G. Shackley is seen receiving the DFC from the 381BG CO, Col. Leber. George was a Group "original" pilot who commanded at least two of the Group's squadrons at some point and finished up as the Air Executive; even more pertinent was the fact that he survived combat operations.

These three anonymous ground personnel stand alongside 42-31575/VE: P. This B-17G arrived on 22 February and has now (4 July) amassed upwards of 60 missions; she would also go on to return stateside in May 1945. The mechanic stripped to his trunks is taking full advantage of the warm weather—a relatively rare occurrence even in an English summer.

L/Gen. Doolittle and another senior officer are observing Lt. Lloyd Peterson (N) at work during this "Big Brass" visit to Ridgewell. Lloyd was on Lt. Arthur J. Bailey's 533BS crew but failed to join the others in Sweden on 21 June; he and the bombardier bailed out from the seemingly doomed B-17, only for the pilots to regain control and head for the neutral haven.

This picture was originally utilized in the author's First in the Field title, but with the wounded officer not named. In fact, this is Lt. Theo Homdrom, a 535BS navigator whose eye wound was incurred on his final mission (21 June 1944) but which proved not to be serious. He is being awarded an Oak leaf Cluster to his DFC by B/Gen. Gross (CG, 1CBW).

Lt. John Howland, navigator to Lt. Jim Tyson's PFF crew, is awarded the DFC by Col. Leber (381BG CO) after completing his combat tour in late June 1944. His short but sturdy frame earned him the title "John the Giant." Maj. Karl Greenlee (Ground Executive officer) stands at left.

Old Faithful (42-37958/LL: G) heads several aircraft on the perimeter track; the line has halted and is angled so that engine run-up airflow does not strike each successive B-17. The picture was taken during the bomber's early December/January operational spell. She was finally lost on 25 June 1944, when she crashed near Wincanton, killing all of Lt. Peter Mikonis's crew.

A farm laborer standing on top of a hay cart provides a pacific and piquant contrast with the reality of war as exemplified by the taxiing 398BG bomber. The apparent absence of the distinctive 1CBW color markings indicate the photograph was taken prior to their July introduction.

Col. Henry W. Terry arrived on 17 May 1944 to assume command of the 91BG from Col. Putnam. His tenure of office as the group's sixth CO would span the remaining period of 8AF operations and into May 1945. He is seen with Charles Hudson (group Bombardier) after the latter has been awarded the DFC medal adorning his tunic.

Kneeling down are are 534BS pilots Lts. John Houston (2nd from right) and Bill Scruggs (2nd from left), along with their crew. On 13 July, a failed emergency landing that saw the B-17G end up on a local railroad track prior to exploding left only these two named individuals alive. Note the gash in the B-17 fuselage behind caused by a "runaway" propeller detaching itself.

All USAAF airfields experienced visits by celebrities, and in this case it is actor Edward G. Robinson. This intellectually gifted actor arrived at Ridgewell on 5 July 1944, when he "christened" the 532BS' Happy Bottom. Here he stands by the No. 2 engine propeller with Col. Leber (left center) while surrounded by a throng of ground personnel.

Lts. Manion (N, left) and Sam Whitehead (P, right) prepare for a mission. Their 534BS colleague in the middle is Lt. Samuel L. Peak (P), who alone out of the trio will never return home. On 22 June 1944, 42-97084/GD: H Spare Charlie was downed on a short-range run to the Pas de Calais with just one of the nine-man crew surviving.

Col. Harry P. Leber took over command of Ridgewell from Col. Joseph J. Nazarro at the beginning of 1944. He held the post for one calendar year, when he relinquished charge to Col. Conway S. Hall (Group Air Executive). He was a more flamboyant character than his fellow commanders, with the majority of B-17 "christening" events occurring during his time in charge.

Two of the crew manning 43-37552/LL: E The Peacemaker are examining part of the heavy fighter-inflicted damage to their bomber. The occasion was the 20 July 1944 run to Leipzig, when eight crews were culled from group ranks over enemy territory. The airman on the right is Lt. Marion Havelaar (B).

What seems to be a B-17F airframe judging by the serial number and Medium Green paint on the fin center section is in fact B-17G 42-97267/MS: X Tomahawk Warrior, as confirmed by the NMF airframe surrounds. Note the crude application of the triangle paint, as well as its off-line base angle. This bomber caught fire and exploded at Ridgewell on 26 April 1945.

Phoney Express arrived in mid-July and was assigned to the 600BS. The bomber is raised up in this picture; the airman working on the tail seems precariously poised with a large counter-weight on the plank-end balancing out its unsupported front end! The aircraft was crash landed in Holland on 26 November, with all nine on Lt. Kermit R. Pope's crew surviving as POWs.

Combat and ground crew personnel are milling around the 535BS' Los Angles City Limits (42-107018/MS: U). The officer peering down at the stretcher bearing Lt. Joe Scott (N) is probably the pilot. Joe collected flak in one arm but recovered to complete his tour of duty.

B/Gen. Gross shakes the hand of L/Col. Conway S. Hall after awarding the 381BG's Air Executive the DFC. The stocky-built officer served throughout the group's entire existence from creation at Pyote, Texas, until VE-Day. He assumed command of the group from Col. Leber during January 1945. The picture was taken in June 1944.

A brilliantly sun-shot cloud formation provides a sharp background for this anonymous mechanic as he walks with his toolbox along the wing of an equally anonymous B-17. Whatever effort he and his colleagues have put in on the aircraft will leave the combat crew at ease, knowing that their charge will be on the "top line" for the forthcoming mission.

This clutch of 91BG aircraft includes 42-97851/LL: K Qualified Quail (right) and 42-102504/LL: O Times A-Wastin' (directly ahead); the former was abandoned on the Continent after the 14 January mission, while the other was MIA on 8 April 1945. LG: Q in the center is 44-6117, with 43-37626/LG: M to its left; both were claimed over Berlin on 21 June 1944.

Chapter Twelve

Oil and Transportation Strangulation

Comment

The final week in July 1944 had initiated a critical advance in the battle for Normandy, in which the 8AF had played a salient part. On two successive days (24/25th), the "Heavies" had carpet bombed the enemy defenses directly fronting the U.S. Army around St. Lo. The subsequent push by the armored and infantry support units had gathered ever-greater momentum for the breakout into the French hinterland, with a view to sweeping eastward and ultimately linking up with a parallel push south of Caen by the Anglo/Canadian forces to encircle the German Seventh Army.

That conclusion was several weeks away from at least majority fruition, while a German counterassault at Mortain would cause a temporary hitch in the American advance. However, Hitler's (thankfully) insane order for Gen. Von Kluge's hard-pressed forces to counterattack, or alternatively to stand and fight regardless of the situation, would hand a continuing advantage to the Allied armies in the field, given the burgeoning material and human resources within their ranks.

The utilization of the B-17s and B-24s in tactical operations was destined to continue during August, albeit with a reverse frequency compared to July's reduced operational pattern. As it was, the assault upon Germany's synthetic oil resources begun in mid-May would continue to be indulged, although another key potential strategic "choke point," namely the enemy transportation system throughout Western Europe, would now come evermore into the equation.

Driving Home the Point

Tactical missions dominated the first three days of the month, with "double header" runs launched on the 2nd and 3rd. On the 1st, the Wing went after airfields at Melun/Villaroche and Chartres, the latter allotted to the 91BG with 36 B-17s dispatched. The Primary was thoroughly plastered, but the flak, although assessed as "meager," still culled one B-17 from the group. This was 42-97879/DF: E, which took a strike in the forward fuselage; it went into a flat spin and only the tail gunner out of Lt. Arthur L. Stevens's crew was able to escape the clutches of the centrifugal forces and bail out. Col. Hunter (398BG CO) was Air Commander on Capt. G. L. Douglas's 43-37892/N8: L, which sustained serious engine damage from the flak and was barely able to bring its ten occupants back for a crash landing at RAF Merston; three days later, the scale of damage deemed it fit only for salvage. The CO's luck at surviving this mission would sadly not extend beyond mid-January 1945.

The assaults made during the first sortie (3rd) were further extended from the immediate battle zone to encompass marshalling yards in Western Germany, along with an oil refinery. The 1CBW was one of three Division Wings dispatched, with the 91st and 381st BGs going to Mulhouse and the 398BG directed to Saarbruecken. The 91BG and 398BG returned intact, whereas one B-17 was missing from the Ridgewell circuit on return. Lt. John C. Wilcock, in 42-32049/GD: G **Yankee Rebel**, had called his element Lead, Lt. Donald Soale, to report loss of an engine, followed soon after by his peeling away and back. The pilot's body was later recovered from the sea 24 hours later by an ASR Launch, but the other eight on board ended up permanently MIA; Terneuzen, on the Scheldt estuary, was the reported crash site, with flak the executioner.

The incident set off a niggling series of Wing losses over the intervening few days that continued on the 4th. The 381BG's deputy Lead (B-17 42-97594/VE: B **Dry Gulcher**) had to be abandoned during Assembly and crashed near Wethersfield, with Sgt. Harold Norris (TG) still on board. The 1BD was tasked with bombing Peenemuende's research center and aircraft plants at Anklam, the 1CBW forming part of the former sub-force.

The bomb run was barely over when the first of two 398BG bombers became casualties. The flak barrage caught 42-107186/N7: L and blew her apart, leaving no survivors among Lt. John S. McArthur's team. Then, with the return leg under way, Lt. Nigel B. Carter's 42-107098/ 3O: Y fell out and down before temporarily levelling off and recommencing a downward path that ended at Koltenhagen. All nine crewmembers enjoyed a diametrically opposite fate to the McArthur nine, since they survived, albeit as POWs.

Although 426 Division crews went out to Nienburg, SSE of Bremen, next day, only two crews failed to return, one of which added to Ridgewell's monthly figure. Sgt. Richard Schneider (TG) had flown regularly on Lt. Salvatore J. Melomo's crew, but he was not on flight status this day—a fortunate situation, but one that would ever haunt him. The crew were manning 42-97771/VP: within the Lead squadron, but flak as the formation crossed between Cuxhaven and Wilhelmshaven killed Lt. Charles S. Freeman (N) and forced the pilots to initially drop down into the Low squadron; even then, position proved evermore difficult to maintain, so the bombs were salvoed and course reversed.

The enemy coastline was not long out of sight when one or both of the starboard engines caught fire. The surviving crew all took to their parachutes, even though the chances of survival in the sea were minimal in these circumstances. It was very fortunate for five among the nine that German patrol boats in the vicinity—whose presence probably acted as a further spur in making the bail out decision—arrived on the scene to pick them up. Even then, they were very fortunate to escape death by exposure, since some two hours elapsed before rescue was achieved. The pilot was among those claimed by the North Sea.

For the third day in succession, the 381BG returned one short from a mission, this time to Brandenburg. The bomb run was just completed when flak struck home against 44-6020/VE: X **Underground FarmerB**, flown by Lt. Allan Webb. The loss of both starboard engines induced an asymmetric flight path that the pilots found hard to control; Lt. George Gomez, along with his colleague up in the nose, was blown out into mid-air when the Plexiglas frame was blown off, but he at least survived as a POW. Meanwhile, the errant B-17 was brought back as far as Luebeck, on the Baltic coast, before the situation became critical enough for bail out to become mandatory.

Webb and the other six airmen vacated the bomber, with all but Sgt. Jack S. Patrick drifting down into the city's suburbs; the hapless gunner landed in the sea, from where his body was later recovered by a German vessel. Also claimed off the mission was 42-102467/N8: J **Agony Waggon III**. Flak as the 398BG headed in over the Weser estuary hit home, forcing Lt. Issac N. Alhadeff to "feather" an engine; almost immediately, the B-17 swung off to port and assumed a descending angle. The final crash site for the aircraft was at Stade, but this terminal fate was not mirrored by the nine airmen who ended up POWs.

The 398BG was not included next day when the Wing went to attack oil storage facilities in France, but all three groups went out (8th) on a ground support run to Caen to prepare the way for the Anglo/ Canadian breakout to link up with the U.S. Army in the bid to trap their adversaries within a gigantic pocket centered upon Falaise. An unfortunate degree of "short" bombing killed some Canadian soldiers, but the assault appeared to have been generally effective; the flak gunners in turn took out seven crews, of which three were from the 1CBW.

Capt. Thomas Barnicle was group deputy Lead, along with Lt. Beackley (P), in 43-37704/MS: I **Button Nose**. During the bomb run, a shell impacted around the bomb bay, but amazingly, the concussion did not set off the bomb load, although a fierce fire developed. The clearly doomed B-17 was quickly turned towards nearby Allied lines and once satisfied this had been attained the crew all jumped clear; the blazing B-17 crashed into a schoolhouse within the Canadian sector that was fortunately unoccupied at the time. All crewmembers landed safely and later reassembled at a C-47 base, from which they were flown back to Ridgewell next day. (Capt. Barnicle's involvement in an evening Crap game, during which he won a sizeable amount of money, would not have endeared him to his temporary hosts.)

The number two in terms of loss afflicted the 398BG for the fourth time within one month. Capt. John M. Baker was in charge of 42-97399/N8: H, but the flak shell that hit home between the port side engines excised the structure at that point, inducing a roll over and spinning motion; only two crewmembers out of the nine escaped death, the pilot being one of the fatalities. Also fatally crippled during the bomb run was 42-107223/N7: A, flying group Lead with Capts. Robert L. Hopkins and Meyer C. Wagner at the controls. The B-17 suffered strikes to both inboard engines and finally crashed SW of Caen, with Hopkins and two others killed in the process. By contrast, Wagner not only survived, but also avoided being captured, as transpired with the remaining five on board.

Lead-up to Disaster

Over the ensuing week, the 1CBW was called upon six times, with the 398BG excluded on the 15th. In addition, the Wing remained grounded on the 10th; Ridgewell records at least indicate this respite was necessary in order to bring the operational aircraft establishment back to a normal level—relaxing for the combat crews, but conversely throwing more pressure on the ground crews. During this period only two crews failed to return, with both claimed on the 13th, when a railroad bridge near Rouen was targeted. The 398BG surrendered 42-102516/3O: H **Bronx Bomber**, flown by Lt. Harold D. Weekley, but not only did all nine crewmembers survive, no less than seven evaded capture, although the pilot was one of the unlucky exceptions as a POW.

Bassingbourn bore the latest deletion from its ranks, 42-107030/LG: T **Fifinella** being the victim on what was its 55th mission, with Lt. Thomas Smith's crew making their 16th run in this B-17. A flak strike ignited hydraulic fluid and exploded oxygen bottles up front, but the bomb run was completed before the bomber began to go through a series of shallow dives interspersed with the pilots levelling off in between. It finally went into a steep dive, but although only two parachutes were seen in this time, only the pilot out of the nine on board failed to survive.

The Nuthampstead loss was actually the second incurred within 24 hours; Lt. Charles J. Searl's crew were all killed when their 42-107191/N8: K **Tomahawk Warrior** crashed NW of London during the Assembly stage of the mission. This B-17 had already survived a mid-air collision during a 4 May practice flight. The 13th had proven unlucky for the Smith crew, but events about to unfold 72 hours hence would push their loss, however sadly acknowledged, firmly into the background.

Another Sturmgruppe Debacle

Aircraft production facilities at Halle and Delitzsch airfield, west and north of Leipzig, respectively, were on the cards for 1CBW attention on the 16th. The outward route bypassed Kassel and Eisenach—two names that would be darkly woven into the 445BG's history in late September and would impact to a lesser, although still painful degree, upon the 91BG on today's mission, as it headed for the former listed Primary. The 324BS was High squadron within the group, which in turn was High unit for the Wing and accordingly more exposed to fighter assault. Eisenach was just being left behind when a group of fighters that was almost certainly a *Sturmgruppe* formation launched a slashing attack on the squadron. The enemy's approach was barely picked up before the rain of fire descended on the bombers with shocking effect.

Flying No. 2 in the Lead element, Lt. L. C. Marpil's tail gunner had very recently called in a gaggle of fighters engaged in a frenetic melee. Even so, this airman appears to have been just as much taken by surprise at the sudden pace of the *Jagdwaffe* pilots' appearance and effect, although the presence of cloud banks may well have concealed their approach. Just the one pass was made by the enemy force, compared to the protracted series of assaults occurring on 20 July, but the result was almost as severe for the crews; in addition, and unlike the Leipzig mission, the losses were to be concentrated within one squadron in terms of crews if not aircraft.

Within a matter of less than one minute, no less than six B-17s were fatally affected, several of whom met particularly violent ends. One among this number was **Lassie Come Home** (42-31673/LG: B), a seven-month veteran at Bassingbourn now making her 76th mission. Lt. Leonard Figie's charge was set on fire in the central fuselage and almost immediately disintegrated, probably thanks to the bomb load erupting; the pilot and three crewmembers somehow emerged alive from the incident.

Lt. Reese W. Lindsey's 42-38000 / DF: E flared majestically upwards, with fire streaming from the starboard fuel tanks before blowing apart, killing all but the tail gunner. A third B-17 (43-38012/DF: L) went out of control in a dive with fire streaming from No. 4 engine; shortly after it rolled onto its back and exploded. This time round, the fatality/ survival rate on Lt. Vincent A. Fonke's crew was reversed, with only one out of the nine airmen losing his life.

Texas Chubby—J'ville Jolter (42-31634/LG: O) had enjoyed almost the same operational longevity as its aforementioned 322BS stablemate, but now joined her in death. Lt. Halsted Sherrill and four of his crew had amassed more than 110 missions between them, but their expertise was to avail them nought, as the torrent of gunfire sent their B-17 into a spin that all too soon resulted in an explosive result upon the airframe; this time Sherrill shared the terminal fate of half among his eight-man crew.

Two further crews were culled from the squadron, beginning with the one led by Lt. John L. Leslie. His B-17 (44-6126/DF: P) was set on fire and fell away to her doom, leaving four out of nine crewmembers to survive her fiery fate. The other crew were on board yet a third seven-month veteran B-17, this time 42-39996/LG: N **Boston Bombshell**, the second group aircraft to reportedly bear this title and equally destined to fail in combat. By now, Lt. John V. Dunlap's bomber was nearly up to a half-century of missions, but no more—fire caught hold at once, and when last seen she was wreathed in flames. Only the pilot and one other officer ended up alive.

Two more crews were fortunate to survive: one arising from the *Sturmgruppe* incident and one on the return leg. Lt. L. C. Marpil's 324BS B-17 lost Sgt. Clayton O. Tyson (WG) during the assault and had another gunner bail out, during which time the bomber fell down to around 14,000ft. The oxygen system was disabled and No. 2 engine had to be switched off. The solo course homeward resulted in an inadvertent "visit" to Bremen that saw more holes added to the airframe before crossing over Belgium and finally regaining English soil. By now down to 2,000ft, all power was suddenly lost, but the convenient availability of Halesworth airfield allowed the pilots to execute a swift circuit and "dead stick" landing; even then, a collision with a hangar was only marginally avoided.

The other crew were arguably even luckier in 42-97938/OR: E **Betty Lou's Buggy**. The recent introduction into *Jagdwaffe* service of the rocket-propelled Me163 *Komet* saw one from 1/JG400 that had reportedly already disposed of another B-17 from the 40CBW now commencing a pass upon Lt. Reese E. Mullin's aircraft. Since the B-17 was out on its own after losing two superchargers to fighter gunfire, the odds on its surviving this encounter appeared very slim. As it was, the German pilot did not open fire, but just pulled up level with its lumbering adversary. Almost immediately two P-51s arrived on the scene and proceeded to pursue the now-fleeing fighter to its destruction.

The latest heavy rebuff handed out to the 91BG was to be its penultimate example up to VE-Day, although the final occasion would see the loss scale doubled, as the *Sturmgruppe* assault method again came to its ever-lethal fruition. The thirty-two missions flown in that interim spell would result in just three crews being downed, while the other two groups would suffer around ten MIA losses between them flying a similar number of missions.

After flying two tactical missions (17/18th) with the 1BD only involved on the latter date, the 8AF "heavies" remained ground-bound until the 24th. In addition, the return to carrying out their strategic brief on a regular basis was initiated this day with a range of target types struck, with the 1CBW involved in bombing an armament plant at Weimar and Kolleda airfield. Four more missions were flown up to the month end with no losses to enemy defenses.

September 1944

The 1CBW would operate an average of fourteen missions between the three groups during September, with Germany's synthetic oil industry featuring in almost half that figure (six). Ludwigshafen's resources came in for concerted attention from the 1BD on the 3rd, 5th, and 8th, but the 91BG was excluded from the first mission. The full Wing went out on the other two occasions, but returned three light spread between these missions. The first of what would be single losses in successive sorties by the 91BG involved 42-107033/LG: D **My Baby**, an original 324BS B-17 transferred to the 322BS during May. Successive power loss to two engines due to a mechanical/flak mix forced Lt. Ernest B. Kelley to turn for home following the failure to follow on as the group climbed to clear the cloud barrier.

No sooner was this action taken than fighters appeared whose gunfire caused a scale of damage that impelled the pilot to ring the bail out bell. All nine airmen evacuated in order, but a failed ripcord on Kelley's pack had him frantically pulling at its surface to access the pilot chute; this managed, the airflow did the rest in deploying the canopy. Even then, he was fortunate to survive a strafing run by a fighter. Having landed near Bazailles, France, just scant miles from the Franco/German border, it was still amazing that just one of the nine-man team failed to avoid being captured.

The third monthly run to Ludwigshafen added just five further MIA crews to the three lost by the 1BD on the two other missions; a statistically marginal figure out of 950 crews gaining mission "credit," but not so for the personnel involved. Bassingbourn's contribution concerned 43-38348/LG: O **Roxy's Special**, whose tenure of service with the group was to last exactly three weeks. A flak strike in between the IP and Primary tore off the starboard wing and Lts. Donald Brazdons (N) and Frank Bohlen (B) reached the ground alive from Lt. David McCarty's crew—the latter officer being blown out through the nose and drifting down into the target zone that was still under attack! He further managed to evade capture for a week.

The 398BG suffered its latest casualty with the demise of 42-97385/3O: X **Shady Lady**, flown by Lt. Warren J. Wade and one short of a mission half-century. A steady loss of position and height on the way over thanks to power loss finally forced the pilots to turn back, by which stage the bomber was functioning on just two engines. Although two crewmembers did bail out and evade capture, the others remained on board when a wheels-down forced landing was successfully effected on French soil. So far all had gone well for the pilot and his six colleagues still on hand, even if they were soon apprehended.

Matters turned tragically sour, however, when Wade and Sgts. Wilbert Y. Burns (BT) and Eugene Gamba (TG) were summarily shot by their SS escort after attempting to overcome the latter as they were being transported by truck from their original place of incarceration to Haguenau. A fourth crewmember believed to be Lt. Burt D. Bream (N), who had been shot in one hip during the attempt, was told that if he could not pick himself up and start moving he too would be executed; the subsequent bid to obey was reportedly extremely unpleasant in achievement, but the grim alternative looming up within seconds surely acted as a spur.

The Ruptured Duck (42-107205/DF:) had come from the 398BG in early August, but today signalled her combat exit. A flak shell's impact killed Lt. Gilbert Willis (CP) and seriously injured Lt. Elbert Weeks (P) in one arm and one thigh. However, he only consented to being given medical aid after his fellow pilot's body was removed from his seat, the crew only then becoming aware of their "Old Man's" condition. He then continued at the controls until a newly-occupied airfield in France appeared ahead; the subsequent landing was fraught with difficulty that included the presence on the runway of bomb craters, as well as a bulldozer.

By now, he was weak from the loss of blood caused by severed arteries in his arm that had only been temporarily stemmed through prior application of a tourniquet and he had to be lifted out and into an ambulance. It was some time before the B-17's fate, along with the gallantry of its pilots, filtered back to Bassingbourn; Weeks subsequently recovered to be awarded the DSC, while **Duck**'s overall condition saw her finally added to the list for scrapping; however, this status was only recorded during the following April.

Mannheim's industry was the assigned target next day, according to 381BG and 398BG records, whereas Bassingbourn detailed an oil plant at Ludwigshafen. In fact, 8AF records indicate the 1BD force had to have recourse to striking the Secondary (Ulm) or six Targets of Opportunity thanks to adverse cloud formations. For the third successive mission, a 91BG crew paid the ultimate forfeit on board 43-37594/OR: O **Strictly G I**.

On board, Lt. Niel C. Jensen was heading the crew normally in Lt. Dale Burkhead's care. The bomb run was just over when a flak shell fired up No. 4 engine, with the B-17 being eased out of formation. Its isolated run for home barely lasted several minutes before it was seen to develop a flat spinning motion, followed by a violent explosion close to Karlsruhe, S of Ludwigshafen. that took the lives of five gunners, but not the other five crewmembers up front.

A military vehicle plant at Gaggenau (10th) was struck by the 91BG and 381BG, while the 398BG went to Stuttgart, roughly 30 miles further east. Lt. Ernest Germano's 44-6095 /VP: N **Fort Worth Gal** was the sole Wing bomber to fall to the flak gunners over the formerly named Primary; after suffering engine damage, it peeled off to starboard before turning for home. Six parachutes were reported, but in fact, only Sgt. Harry Siders (TG) failed to survive. His death was variously ascribed to a broken neck on landing, civilian "summary justice," or failing to clear the exploding aircraft. Either way, he was another tragic blood sacrifice on the Allies' protracted road to freedom.

The 398BG was also one crew short on return, with 42-107105/K8: A **Marie Notre Dame** being the absentee, along with Lt. Parke Wright III and crew. A flak shell striking the central fuselage cast the bomber into a steep dive that culminated in its disintegration, doubtless thanks to the overwhelming air pressure exerted upon the airframe; only the pilot, two other officers, and one gunner avoided a fatal outcome from among the nine personnel.

A mini-pattern of single losses every 48 hours was practiced upon the Nuthampstead airmen, culminating on the 12th, when the 1BD executed one of the longest-ever missions to the Czechoslovakian industrial city of Brux, which possessed a synthetic oil refinery. The group's Lt. James B. Field, flying in 42-102597/3O: V **Stinker**, had been steadily falling behind over northern Germany thanks to supercharger failure and finally swung to port in a clear bid to reach Sweden. The neutral soil was almost on hand when a fighter swept in to land fatal strikes on the B-17. The bomber descended into the Baltic and exploded with only Lt. Lyman N. Cranston, Jr. (CP) ending up alive in Swedish hands from among the crew.

As far as the 1CBW was concerned, the remainder of September would now be almost free from any aircraft losses sustained in combat, although personal cases of injury or even death would occur. Nine missions in all were flown up to the month end, and it was only on the penultimate one to assault Magdeburg's oil manufacturing resources (28th) that the Grim Reaper struck out to again cull one 398BG B-17.

For once, there was an extra man compared to the normal nine airman complement, with Capt. William Hendrickson, Jr. listed as a waist gunner. Fire caused by a flak strike shortly after "bombs away" soon gained in intensity, but the doomed bomber (42-102607/3O: F **Lodian**) still managed to stagger nearly 50 miles to a point NW of Stendal before succumbing; by this stage none of the crew led by Lt. Russell C. Conrow was still on board.

"Tail" of a Pig

Lt. Art Bailey—a 532BS pilot at Ridgewell during 1944—provided a fund of anecdotes both serious and whimsical regarding his and his crew's time at the base. The following account falls squarely into the latter category, but is furthermore a fine example of how combat crewmembers coped with the stress of operations when off duty.

The ubiquitous bicycle was the primary choice for the majority of U.S. airmen, which in this case was utilized by Art's crew, as well as several other 534BS officers in order to visit a fair that was being held in the near vicinity of the airfield. Art never did establish the exact location, but recalled it was some ten miles distant. Then, in his words:

"The ride was mainly downhill on narrow roads that threaded the beautiful English countryside and proved to be a refreshing change from our normal routine which we now found really exhilarating. The fair was in full session by the time we arrived and we noted one particularly large gathering of people surrounding a platform on which one gentleman from among the local dignitaries was pleasantly haranguing his fellow citizens to bid for the prize he was holding in one hand—a single orange. Our initial impulse to enter the bidding race was held firmly in place, however. As Americans, we regarded it as good citizenship to join in and thereby express our gratitude towards our Allies; on the other side of the emotional scales was the feeling that by so doing we could easily run the risk of offending by seeming to flaunt our comparative wealth.

"Later in the day Ed, the other crew's bombardier, rushed up to say he had entered and won first prize in a skittles competition that he proudly announced was 'a live, grunting, squealing pig.' Our curiosity aroused, we then accompanied him to the pen, where we anticipated looking upon a nice little piglet—instead of which we were simply shocked to take in the daunting sight of a beast with an estimated weight of around 60lbs!

"Our immediate reaction was that Ed's venture had been fun and the details would form a good story for our grandchildren—but Hell, it was getting late, so let's forget the pig and get back to base before darkness fell! However, Ed was adamant that he was not going to abandon his prize and after a discussion and with some natural misgivings, the challenge of gaining the prize back to Ridgewell was accepted.

"Now, it was one thing to have gained the prize, but quite another to take unfettered possession. We had drawn quite a crowd of spectators as a burlap bag was acquired with which we entered the pen. On one side were five officers in full Class A uniforms and on the other one a grimy and naturally agitated pig. The subsequent sounds of battle now consisted of encouraging yells from the five, the mad squealing of the bemused porker, and jeers from the spectators.

"The pig was finally encased within the sack, by which stage the victors were gritty and agitated individuals. As it was, this was but the beginning of the event, and the real challenge lay in transporting our prize the distance to our base, which was moreover primarily uphill—and had to be made on bicycles!

"What was probably the largest crowd assembled for any event this day, as we realized that none of us were really capable of pedalling away with the sack on our own. The resulting discussion resulted in an outcome of pure Yankee ingenuity (at least that was my opinion!). We got a pole of some six or seven feet length to which the sack was tied and which we considered two cyclists could grasp the ends.

"The two crew bombardiers volunteered for the task that evolved as a total failure; this was due to Ed and Bob proving unable to coordinate a standing-start launch. Stan and I then took over, but we also failed. By this point, we noticed that Hal [the other crew's navigator] had melted into the throng as though disavowing he ever knew us. The crowd was by now several deep and gathered around in an arc just like a marathon event.

"What we needed was a flying start, so with Ed and Bob again mounted up and Stan and I holding the pole at some twenty feet distance, our two cyclists attempted a flying start. Ed unfortunately arrived ahead of Bob as they charged towards us and the pig got bounced. The second attempt was a humiliating failure because Stan held his pole end too low, with the result that it jammed Bob's wheel and pitched him off; he duly picked himself up and got dusted off as the crowd howled with delight at the spectacle. [So far, the effort suggested that the Americans had been imbibing some of the local Ale! Ed.]

"However, the third attempt ended with a beautifully executed launch, so we were shakily on our way. The pole's greater than anticipated flexibility when coupled with the cyclists erratic behavior caused the burlap bag to make contact with the ground on more than one occasion; this naturally upset our future roast pork!

"The trip back to Ridgewell was a long and gruelling nightmare, since by this stage darkness had fully occurred and the totality of the 'blackout' had to be experienced to be truly believed. On two occasions we were literally forced off the road by on-coming trucks that we could neither hear nor see until they were almost on top of us. A warning would be yelled and the two unfortunate pig 'escorts' had little choice but to veer off into an invisible ditch. How we managed to start up again in the stygian darkness I will never know.

"We finally arrived back physically and mentally numbed, but soon recovered. Hell—after all, we had performed our most challenging mission of WWII! By now, the pig was well subdued and this was a factor that led to another inspiration. The other crew's copilot had a well-deserved reputation for a less than discriminating taste in female company and furthermore, would often return from the Officer's Club absolutely blotto.

"His bunk was over in one corner by the billet door, so we tied the pig under his bed blankets prior to turning off the lights. Then we waited while all the time attempting to stifle our giggles. Sure enough, around midnight the door burst open and a body ricocheted off a wall and staggered over to the bunk. We were quickly rewarded by the pig's squealing and a cursing copilot threshing away in the dark. This was a moment to be savored forever!

"Next day, we scavenged two bedsprings and constructed a pen outside our billet. We fed the pig for several days until the odor resulted in an order for him to go. A local farmer with whom we regularly traded cigarettes for eggs agreed to take him upon the understanding that when we completed our tour's final mission, it would be on hand for a roast feast. However, on completion of our missions our single obsessive thought was to get home. As a result, the pig was simply forgotten, so his posthumous presence at our celebrations never occurred!"

October 1944

Luck of the Draw (1)

The thirteen missions involving the 1CBW during October were to disprove the negative aspect of this figure, at least in terms of MIA losses among two of the three groups, since none were incurred for the 91st and 381st BG; a similar clean record was sharply marred during the 398BG's penultimate mission to the tune of three. On the other hand, there were several incidents where B-17s were badly shot up but successfully came back, with Köln's defenses featuring in two. On the 5th, Lt. W. J. Evans (P) and W. Ritter managed to stagger back as far as the Emergency airfield at Manston, in Kent, where they crash landed 42-107094/K8: M; none of the nine crew were badly injured, but the damage inflicted was sufficient for salvage action to be taken.

A return to the city's marshalling yard complex at Gereon on the 15th—the second of three missions conducted within its boundaries between the 14th and 17th—was in progress when a shell exploded close to the starboard cockpit side of **Pella Tulip** (42-102703/VE: M). The copilot's Plexiglas was shattered and the roof above his head shredded, while the top turret glass was also partially blown out. With the ever-perverse manner of explosive blast, Lt. David R. Rautio (CP) was only marginally affected physically, whereas Lt. Charles W. Reseigh (P) was more seriously injured.

Fire around the top turret was successfully put out by S/Sgt. John M. Nushy (Eng.), after which he assisted his pilot down into the nose for medical attention by the bombardier. With an almost total instrument failure in the cockpit and the oxygen system also disabled, Lt. Rautio had little option but to descend to breathable altitude, especially since his helmet, mask, and goggles had all been blown off his face. The landing gear had also descended thanks to hydraulic failure and it took the efforts of three gunners—one of whom was Sgt. Erling Anderson—over a protracted spell to hand-crank it back into the nacelles.

The boreal gale whipping through the windshield brought with it the constant danger of frostbite to the copilot's face and hands, the worst effects of which were partially countered by Sgt. Nushy massaging his face regularly. Jammed landing flaps, engine problems consisting of No. 4 "running away" and No. 3 finally fading out, and a knocked-out radio all added to the difficulties of regaining British shores—a decision that was nevertheless made, despite the closer availability of Continental airfields.

The navigator's maps had also disappeared, but F/O. Maryan J. Winicki managed to steer a course using a flak map and a magnetic compass. The North Sea was finally traversed and the first available airfield (Debach, home of the 493BG) headed for. The landing was bound to be made without brakes, so parachute packs were attached to the waist windows and radio hatch. However, after deployment their ability to hold the bomber on course was compromised by the asymmetric pull of the port engines, which inexorably pulled the aircraft left, straight towards a dispersal containing a B-17.

Just when collision seemed inevitable, the wheels engaged a patch of soft soil that "dug in" the landing gear and checked its momentum scant feet short of the static companion bomber. Lt. Reseigh was able to walk to the ambulance despite serious leg and arm injuries and eventually made a full recovery, as did Lt. Rautio from what was a mild case of facial frostbite.

At least two other crewmembers were very fortunate to avoid serious injury or even death. F/O Winicki had been standing up in the astrodome, bereft of his flak helmet, and had barely responded to his pilot's order to don the vital headgear when the explosion occurred. As for Sgt. Nushy, he had been bending down within the top turret to correct a fault in his oxygen system at this point, and although his face was peppered by Plexiglas fragments, that was the extent, however awkward, of his discomfort.

Luck of the Draw (2)

The influence of the enemy was not necessary to cause aircraft losses, as was instanced on 15 October at Nuthampstead. The throttles on 42-97746/K8: T were cracked open and the PFF bomber moved smoothly down the runway and lifted off for Köln. Within bare seconds of raising their B-17 into the air, Lts. Charles E. Kourie and William L. Meyran encountered insuperable problems that resulted in the aircraft barely avoiding impacting with houses in Anstey village before plunging into a pond and disintegrating, killing all ten of its hapless occupants.

The projected mission that had already claimed one 398BG B-17 and crew was to result in a further incident affecting Lt. Laurence Delancey's crew on board 43-38172/3O: P **Lovely Julie**. The bomb run was in progress when a flak shell struck the bomber's nose compartment, extinguishing the life of Sgt. George E. Abbott (Togglier) and blowing off most of the upper panels, as well as casting the sections directly ahead of the windshield upwards to badly obscure forward visibility; amazingly, Lt. Raymond LeDoux (N) survived the blast.

Delancey and Lt. Phil Stahlman managed to hold course for home in spite of the horrendous scale of damage. Several hours later, to the ground personnel at the airfield their return to the airfield was aurally evident minutes prior to entering the circuit thanks to the slipstream around the battered forward airframe emitting a high screeching tone. The B-17 was landed safely, but the scale of damage resulted in subsequent salvage action.

The veteran 91BG was to "enjoy" the month as the first one in exactly two years of combat operations where there were no aircraft or crews joining the MIA list. However, individual airmen were still caught up in the maelstrom of battle, as instanced on the 15th. Capt. Ivor O. Tufty's B-17 lost two engines shortly after bombing and the order was given to stand by for a possible bail out, but was never confirmed. As occurred in a good number of such emergencies on 8AF multi-crewed aircraft during WWII, the gunners complement in this case acted precipitately, if understandably in the circumstances, and promptly jumped, leaving the other four members to return to Bassingbourn—a far more comfortable option than that of a pending bunk at a *Stalag*. The flak barrage also claimed the life of one crewmember and wounded four others on a second group B-17.

Luck of the Draw (3)

To the personnel watching on as 42-97880/DF: F **Little Miss Mischief** taxied along and into her dispersal, there seemed no doubt that the occupant of the ball turret was dead. Most of the circular Plexiglas panel, along with the surrounding frame edges, had been blasted away, while one gun barrel was bent upwards almost at a right angle to its normal position. The ambulance that rolled up to the dispersal disgorged the two attendants and within minutes Sgt. Ed Abdo (BT) was brought out—but the anticipated blanket-shrouded corpse amazingly materialized into a living individual, albeit one bearing injuries.

During the bomb run, Lt. Paul McDowall (P) had felt the rudder pedals slacken, and soon after he was made aware of the severe damage to the area around the ball turret. The state of the fuselage interior, which was liberally shredded by the effects of a flak burst, gave little hope for the ball turret's occupant, but when access to it was made his colleagues were astounded to find that the gunner was far from being a shattered corpse. He could not be extracted due to the loss of power, but at least blankets could be fed to him with which to ameliorate the intense cold; he was also given a morphine injection. Finally, walk-around oxygen bottles were provided since the oxygen system had been knocked out.

However, since the return flight at altitude would extend over at least one to two hours before the B-17 could lower itself to a less severe temperature, the survival prospects for Abdo still appeared to be problematic. He somehow summoned up the necessary physical and mental strength to do so, and having been extracted from his turret was transported to hospital. Once there, it was established that two toes would have to be amputated—thanks to frostbite!

Odds for Survival....Poor?

Lt. John Rice and crew's introduction to combat was to prove a very rough one as they headed out for the fourth monthly run to Köln (17th). Turbo-supercharger problems left 42-31550/GD: G **Green Hornet 2nd** trailing well behind the 381BG formation, then No. 1 engine "blew" during the bomb run, followed by No. 3 being crippled by flak, whereupon the B-17 plummeted downwards and was only levelled off around 8,000ft.

A call for escort cover resulted in a single P-51 appearing, but at least the enemy defenses were successfully negotiated. However, No. 3 failed totally over Belgium and the bomber began to sink inexorably until at 1,800ft, the pilot signalled for a bail out. All but Lt. Rice jumped, he being compelled to undertake a crash landing after "spilling" his parachute pack; this was an act that was safely brought off, leaving him thankfully intact, but which signalled a "salvage" status for his mount.

Eleven days elapsed before the crew assumed their places for a mission to Muenster, but the situation again went sour, albeit not quite to the same extent. A "runaway" propeller on No. 3 caused so much vibration during the return leg that the possibility of abandoning the B-17 was actively considered. Fortunately, when disintegration finally occurred the shaft broke cleanly and the errant propulsion unit sailed clear of the airframe, leaving the pilots to make a safe if eventful landing at Ridgewell. The return had to be made alone, since the aircraft could not respond to the order for the formation to climb above an intruding weather front. This crew would eventually complete its combat tour, but to the nine airmen, the odds of that happening must have seemed poor on the evening of 28 October.

The Rice crew's good fortune was not matched by a trio from among the Nuthampstead force of 36 B-17s. All three bombers were fatally affected during the bomb run and turn off the target. Lt. Harry J. Connolly's 44-6519/K8: F, with less than a month's service at the base, suffered the malign effects of a near miss alongside its rear fuselage that blew off the tail section; only Sgt. William M. Hamor, Jr. (ROG) from among the nine-man complement managed to fight his way out of the abbreviated airframe to deploy his parachute before the final impact at Nienberge.

The sole discernible damage to 44-8199/3O: R—a PFF aircraft—as it dropped out just after bombs away was a "feathered" propeller, but Lt. Roy M. Sheely, Jr. subsequently called to say he was bailing out the crew, all nine of whom successfully evacuated the B-17, leaving it to pile in near Arnhem, Holland. The final loss involved 42-102543/K8: B, flown by Lt. John M. Farmer, that was observed with a smoking engine and a thick stream of fuel emanating from the port wing; this B-17 also staggered as far as the Dutch/German border before coming down to leave the pilot and six of his eight colleagues still alive.

The physical misery suffered by B-17 gunners thanks to the original open waist hatches on B17Fs and early B-17Gs was greatly diminished by the fitting of permanent fixed frames during 1944. The flexible attachment extending through the lower-central gap allowed for free movement of the machine-gun. Note the slipstream deflector (left) that suggests the revised cover was an in-the-field modification rather than one applied at the Boeing plant.

An impressive tally of 43 mission bombs adorns the nose on this by-now veteran B-17G. It arrived during April 1944 and joined the 323BS (OR: M). The exact number of missions it flew before its loss, along with Lt. Liekhus (P) and crew on 2 November, is not confirmed, but this picture was probably taken towards the sad conclusion to its operational career.

A Nuthampstead "original" bomber from the Douglas plant, this 603BS aircraft is settling down for a neat three-point landing, as opposed to the normal "tail high" approach. It would complete 27 missions before being blown apart by flak over Peenemuende on 4 August; none of Lt. John S. MacArthur's crew survived the incident.

The contrast between the brick-buit C-Type hangars typical of an RAF Permanent Station as seen at Bassingbourn and the utility T2 structures over at Ridgewell is evident in this photograph. The latter was of simple metal outline with no office rooms on the outside. WWII aircraft usually only saw a hangar's interior for major repairs or inspections.

Happy Valley Express—a sardonic reference to the flak-filled Ruehr industrial complex—is seen just after "bombs away." The aircraft served between assignment on 11 August 1944 and the following 22 January; it was declared "salvage" after suffering heavy damage on the mission to Aschaffenberg, but no casualties were incurred among Lt. Van Blarcom's team.

Old Battle Axe was originally assigned to the 323BS, as seen in this photograph, but subsequently moved to the 401BS (LL: J). It was a specialist B-17G that initially served in a PFF role, but then switched to an RCM function with jamming of the Luftwaffe's Wuerzburg radar equipment in mind. It survived the Conflict.

Jezebel (42-38144/LL: O) bears an impressive tally of over 50 mission "bombs," having survived the late winter air battles after assignment to the 91BG in late February 1944. Her service with the group would extend to 14 February 1945, when she would be abandoned on the Continent due to heavy battle damage.

Sweet Patootie (42-31569/GD: E) has ended her six-month presence with the 381BG after being "bellied in" on the Continent (3 September). The crash site at St. March, France, left all of Lt. Fulton's crew alive, despite the apparent impossibility for the pilots to do so given the excised nose section. The reason for the shredded rudder surface in the right hand trio of pictures is not known.

The Ruptured Duck was destined to live up to her physically debilitating title after arriving from the 398BG and commencing operations on 6 August. On 8 September, she was badly damaged, with the pilots forced to divert into a Continental airfield; she never returned to Bassingbourn, although salvage action was strangely delayed until the following April.

This 532BS B-17G (42-97422/VE: Q) came through the critical period of operations for the 8AF following its assignment on 21 February1944. Now its combat days are over as it lies astride a solid hedge after over-shooting off a practice mission. The date is 1 October, and within 48 hours it will be adjudged "salvage."

Mary Lou's final mission on 7 October culminated in this crash landing by Lt. Spawinski on return from the mission to Freiburg. The top of the ball turret support frame has been forced up through the fuselage skin, but this in itself should not have been the full reason for "salvage" action a week later; the overall damage scale must have been the cause.

A 398BG "original" bomber has made its final and rather undignified flight. Lt. K. S. Hastings was coming in off a weather sortie on 26 October, but landed too far along the runway and over-shot. The resultant damage was severe enough for "salvage" action to be taken on 42-102586/N7: N.

One of a number of marital unions between 381BG personnel and British women is being celebrated here. The bridegroom is Maj. Gaillard (right), while the couple are accompanied by a beaming Maj. Bill Fullick, an "original" Group member and its current Lead bombardier. The date of the event is unclear.

Mary Lou (42-97504/OR: P) is seen making a landing approach during the early autumn of 1944. She was by then a combat veteran who would attain a 70-mission tally from her original assignment to the 91BG in late January 1944, having survived a still-hard and sometimes costly period of operations for the 8AF.

The Köln flak barrage on 15 October inflicted this scale of heavy damage to the cockpit area on 42-102703.VE: M Pella Tulip. Ironically, Lt. Reseigh (P) was seriously wounded, whereas Lt. Rautio (CP) and Sgt.Nushy (Eng.) were relatively unaffected, demonstrating the extremely wayward pattern of blast effect. The picture was taken at Debach (493BG), where salvage action was declared next day.

The interior around the main blast zone on Little Miss Mischief further accentuates the structural damage caused by the flak gunners. The bomber was not salvaged; instead, the rear section was replaced and she flew further operations until early April, when a heavy crash landing saw her reduced to salvage status.

Lt. Paul McDowall (P) and a fellow crewmember inspect the horrendous flak damage, particularly to the ball turret, borne by their B-17G 42-97880/DF: F Little Miss Mischief following the Koln mission on 15 October 1944. Incredibly, the gunner, Sgt. Ed Abdo, not only survived, but his serious injuries were limited to two amputated toes—due to frostbite!

The weather conditions in England were often extremely harsh for the mechanics, but the rolled-up sleeves of this trio involved in detaching No. 2 engine on 42-40017/MS: W Me and My Gal indicates a welcome improvement, however temporary in duration. This veteran B-17G was finally "written off" after Lt. Elmer Wulf brought off an amazing crash landing in Belgium on 14 February 1945.

This picture of the DeLancey crew recorded on 16 November holds a very poignant memory for the eight survivors from the Koln incident. The head-and-shoulders image in the center of the back row is that of Sgt.Abbott; the Officer on the left is Lt. Phil Stahlman (CP).

The tangled remnants of Lt. Laurence DeLancey's 398BG B-17G's nose section bears gruesome witness to the blast effect of a flak burst that expunged the life of Sgt. Abbott (Togglier) over Köln on 15 October 1944. The pilot's task of successfully getting back was made more difficult by the metal panel draped across most of the windshield.

A 602BS aircraft is pictured after an apparent over-shoot that culminated in a collapsed starboard main landing gear; the aircraft seems otherwise intact. The 398BG bomber arrived on 18 October, and was reassigned twice following incidents that led to initial "MIA" categorization. Note how the aircraft letter is raised in order to avoid contact with the wing fairing strip.

Three Elements of the 381BG present a firm but loose formation over Ridgewell as the first trio commence breaking-off into the landing pattern. What appears to be the crew of the B-17 on the right watches the action. Date is 5 October 1944 when Targets of opportunity within Koln displaced the intended Primary strike also located within that city's boundaries.

Chapter Thirteen

Air Supremacy in Place

Comment

The almost relentless hammering administered by the 8AF—with a degree of assist from RAF Bomber Command—handed out to the Nazis' synthetic oil production sources was by November having a potentially terminal effect. Production levels compared to the previous May, when the bombing campaign was inaugurated, were drastically reduced in spite of the enemy's best efforts at repair and regeneration of the various plants. The subsequent effect on *Luftwaffe* operations in particular was not only curbing its ability to challenge the bombers' incursions, but further down the line, the parallel restrictions in training schedules meant that the *Nachwuchs* (new pilots) arriving at front line units were dangerously short of even flying experience, and accordingly easy meat for the rampaging Allied fighter pilots; their ranks were being shredded, with ever more among them failing to survive more than one or two combat flights. Nor were the *Experten* (Aces) around in numbers to pass on their expertise, their ranks having also been seriously thinned out since early 1944.

The few shots left in the *Jagdwaffe* locker as exemplified by the Me163 and Me262 backed by the latest and effective versions of the Fw190 were simply inadequate for the primary task of home defense duties. However, one "sting in the tail" measure for the B-17s and B-24s was the *Sturmgruppe* tactic, which had regularly reaped a bloody harvest of bombers and their crews over the past several months, and events during the second November mission would enhance this frightening reputation.

Aerial Holocaust

Oil was still a primary source for assault, with the bulk of the month's effort directed at this commodity. Although overall production totals had already been badly eroded, the ability of the Germans to reinstate the manifold plants' ability to function following their latest pounding was to see the oil campaign extending over several more months before reaching an absolute conclusion in the Allies' favor. However, the 1BD's venture to Gelsenkirchen (1st) involved a single Wing.

The following day, the 91st and 398BG were part of a seven-group thrust heading out for one of the most assaulted as well as feared locations: Merseburg/Leuna. This massive complex was ringed by an equally massive flak system that had brought down a sizeable number of bombers in the past. However, this mission was to witness the bulk of the 26 Division losses being credited to fighters, with the *Sturmgruppe* pilots to the fore.

The 91BG's clean sheet in October was about to be bloodily smeared today in an even greater manner than had been handed out either during the first Schweinfurt mission or the two previous brushes with the *Sturmgruppe* units during July and August. Thirty-seven crews were mustered for the mission, and with Assembly completed, the formations headed out on a straight course.

The absence of any variation in direction that was usually introduced to keep the Germans guessing the bombers' intended target or targets was a clear indication that the authorities back in England regarded the *Jagdwaffe* as a spent force; such confidence was probably bolstered by the events in October, when enemy fighter activity was sporadic in general. If the foregoing assumption is correct, then the action taken here was justified, at least up to the target; from thereon, matters were to turn somewhat sour for both B-17 Divisions.

The steadily solid cloud formations indicated that PFF assistance would be necessary on the bomb run. As events transpired, a major malfunction with the *H2X* set on the Lead bomber resulted in what was operationally termed a "Gross Error," but which was known to the combat crews as "Agricultural Bombing"; the bomb pattern had descended upon open country well away from the Primary. As if this was not bad enough, the flak defenses had struck home terminally against one B-17, indicating that the formation had inaccurately traversed the target area.

Just after "bombs away," **Jub Jub Bird** (42-31883/LL: Y), which had amassed 68 missions since its late-March assignment, ran into a flak burst that exploded below the forward fuselage and blew most of the panelling outwards, as well as detaching the nose compartment. Fire caught hold of the truncated airframe and Lt. Ray L. Nickola (CP) recalled that Lt. Herbert Chouinard (P) made no effort to assist him in pulling the aircraft out of its dive, clearly having been seriously injured or killed by the blast; he along with Sgt. Arnold E. Kramer (WG) were the sole crew members managing to bail out and survive.

At this stage, the group was already one B-17 short. Soon after crossing into Germany, **USA the Hard Way**'s crew were extremely fortunate to avoid any fatalities when one flak shell out of a four-burst pattern that landed the ultimately fatal blow passed through the starboard side of the pilot's compartment without exploding. However, the resultant severing of control cables, along with hydraulic lines, initiated a fire fed by the cocktail of fluids and added to by exploding oxygen bottles that could not be extinguished, so sealing the fate of 44-6093/LL: J. All nine crewmembers led by Lt. John J. Askins (P) jumped clear near Cloppenberg, where the bomber descended, but Lt. Randall Archer (CP), who ironically had been at most risk by being closest to the shell's impact point, did not survive. Two crews were now down, but the main event was still to unfold.

"The Sky Falls In"

The 91BG was stationed at the rear of the 1BD stream and not far ahead was the Glatton-based 457BG. Now, as the turn off the target was initiated, both groups managed to become separately isolated from the Division's ranks, providing the ever-lurking *Sturmgruppe* units with the perfect opportunity for a strike; the absence of immediate escort cover was the extra necessary ingredient for this scenario to evolve. The ensuing 20 to 25 minutes would see the Bassingbourn formation further reduced by the same factor of eleven as occurred on 17 August 1943; unlike the Schweinfurt experience, today's martyrdom would extend over minutes rather than hours.

The punishment handed out by *IV (Sturm)*/JG3 during the imbalanced air battle was to affect the 322BS and 323BS in almost equal measure, with the 401BS adding a third to its final MIA figure of three. An early casualty seems to have been 44-8208/LG:, an *H2X*-equipped bomber that was in the hands of Capt. Roy Hammer's Lead crew. It was seen to peel out of formation with fire streaming from the inner starboard wing and radio room; however, its torment was extended, with reports of two groups of parachutes emerging prior to its final demise around the end of the battle. (The process of reforming from the bomb run was still underway according to Hammer's copilot, so raising the level of vulnerability of the overall formation, which was so fragmented in terms of "Group integrity." Lt. Oron Harper also stated that the B-17 was abandoned after the fourth fighter pass with only one of the crew being killed.)

As it was, the squadron's Low position made it particularly susceptible to enemy attention and four further crews would be consumed. The initial fighter pass added to the flak damage suffered immediately prior to this assault by 43-38202/LG: T **Miss Slipstream**. This B-17 became separated from the squadron when prop wash cast it to one side and strikes on the port wing set it ablaze. Lt. Charles R. Hackstock, copilot to Lt. Dale E. Brant, recalled that the tail section broke off as the B-17 was taking evasive action, but in spite of this the nine airmen bailed out over Koethen, although Lt. John Gustafson suffered a failed parachute; the pilot also did not survive, although he was believed to have reached the ground alive.

The individual passes mounted by between four and eight fighters in successive parallel formation waves cast out a weight of firepower while the heavily-armored Fw190s were virtually resistant to any return fire, even if the gunners were fortunate enough to bring their guns to accurately bear upon their adversaries in the fleeting seconds generally available to them. In addition, the high escort of Bf109s, having been similarly free from 8FC attention, now joined in the conflict.

Lt. John Hamilton's 42-98012/LG: U **Cannon Ball Too** was another immediate victim, according to one crewmember, but was recorded as still being on hand for several minutes, despite fire having caught hold on both wings, as well as around the radio room; when last seen, she was going down but under apparent control. In fact, the B-17 disintegrated several thousand feet above the ground, blowing Sgt. Joseph A. Cress (ROG) sideways just as he pulled his ripcord while in its immediate vicinity; he was lucky to both escape being struck by the welter of scattered debris as well as avoiding his canopy being collapsed by the blast. Half the ten-man Lead team survived, but the pilot was among the other unlucky element.

One veteran squadron B-17G closed out its combat account: 42-38083/LG: V **Man O' War II**, flying its 78th mission since arrival in January. The starboard wing and tail section were shot up and the bomber peeled off to port, where it then became a virtual "shooting gallery" for several pursuing fighters. This one-sided combat proceeded for several minutes before the fuselage broke in half. Despite the aerodynamic imbalance caused by the fracture, all four officers on Lt. Leroy B. Hare's crew managed to jump clear; the five gunners, in grim contrast, were either killed during the battle or failed to escape the centrifugal forces and follow suit.

Only one-third of Lt. Russell H. Brown's team in 44-6298/LG: A **White Cargo** was similarly blessed after the ailing bomber that had been lagging behind was finally finished off. The squadron loss figure was completed by 42-38212/LG: P **Gal O' My Dreams**, which held position for some considerable time before drifting away and down in an apparently controlled manner. As it was, fire was raging in the bomb bay and one gunner was already dead with a second badly wounded and finally assisted to bail out, an action he did not survive. A steep dive entered was finally arrested at a bare 1,000ft, but when the aircraft finally impacted at Gross Oesingen, Lt. Thomas P. Burne was still on board, while two of the other three officers also died from out of this veteran nine-man crew.

Spreading the Cost

A quartet of 323BS B-17s failed to return, one of which was another veteran machine. **Winged Victory** (42-97563/OR: U) was a March arrival with almost seventy missions under its belt. Its current crew, led by Lt. Oscar Snow, had taken this B-17 on double-figure missions. Its final demise near Koethen, where the crew all jumped, indicates that it progressed roughly as far as the 322BS' **Miss Slipstream**; Lt. Alfred Zwicky (CP) was the sole fatality, being the one seen with a burning canopy according to one of his colleagues. A second long-term squadron veteran (42-97234/OR: M **Bomber Dear**) now completed her 66th mission by succumbing to gunfire as fire enveloped its airframe; Lt. John H. Liekhus (P) was united in death with four of the crew.

43-37625/OR: W/Q **Cheri** was the regular B-17 flown by Lt. Arvin Basnight's crew and named for his wife. It was fortunate for them that they were at a Rest Home, with their place taken by Lt. Robert Harris's team, because their bomber was knocked out of formation during the first wave of assaults and was then relentlessly pursued by a single Fw190 as it fell away on fire. Seven of the nine on board, including Harris, managed to bail out of the doomed aircraft, whose crash site was reported as Ottersleben, a SW suburb of Magdeburg.

The final squadron casualty was 42-97956/OR: L **Pard**, which had arrived almost simultaneously with **Cheri** and now also faced its "last round-up." The battle was in full swing when Lt. Hanford Rustand appeared to maneuver his B-17 over towards 42-32116/OR: B **Hi-Ho Silver**. Whether this was a voluntary action with a view to providing fire support for his fellow airmen in the adjoining bomber as was later asserted would never be established.

The tragic outcome of the move only resulted in **Pard** absorbing fatal punishment that dispatched it to crash at Libehna, due south of Dessau, along with its pilot and all but two of his eight-man team. Ironically, **Hi-Ho Silver** would not only survive the onslaught, but progress to a figure of 130 missions, after which she was ignominiously scrapped at Kingman, AZ, along with thousands of her kind.

The trio of 401BS losses was completed by 42-97984/LL: G **Sherrys Cherries**, another July assignment to the group. It is unclear at what stage of the roughly 23-minute battle Lt. James E. Faris's charge was taken down, although the reported crash site near Koethen, where **Winged Victory** and **Miss Slipstream's** crews bailed out, indicates it occurred during the initial series of attacks. Three of the nine crewmembers, who were actually from the 323BS, lost their lives, being the waist and tail gunners, who likely bore the brunt of the rear-mounted punishment.

The frenetic nature of today's one-sided air battle was aptly described by Lt. Wayne B. Frye (N) on Lt. John W. O'Neill's crew flying in 42-97061/LL: B **General Ike**:

"As we neared the target, the flak really started coming up. It sure was big.... we could see enemy fighters ahead of us on the other side of the target and were afraid we were going to get it from them. After we turned off the bomb run we saw them preparing for the attack. S/Sgt. Robinson (TG) kept us informed of their activities—no words can describe how terrible this was.

"T/Sgt. Hollenbaugh (Eng.) and S/Sgt. McCarter (BT) were calling out fighters all around the clock. I sure admired Robinson, who was shooting like mad and calling out every plane close to us. I heard him call out that he had blown one up. Then an Fw190 came in and Hollenbaugh really poured lead into him. The pilot was either hurt or out of control, but he tried to ram into our right wing, just missing it as he went down.

"A Bf109 slow-rolled over our B-17 and I called Hollenbaugh to get him....the top turret was small on this ship and he could not sight him straight up in order to fire. Just then, an Fw190 stalled out right in front of where the left cheek gun normally was but we had none. I could see the pilot's face as if I were in the cockpit with him. Hollenbaugh called and said he had knocked down another fighter.

"An Fw190 came diving in front of us and I started to open up with the right cheek gun. I could see my bullets going from his right wing tip on into the cowling; pieces started to fly off, the engine caught fire, and he started to spiral. Them my gun jammed and I had to try to fix it while also writing down observations in my log book.

"I kept wondering where the dammed P-51s were. The two ships in our Element were shot up and fell out. Our pilots were doing some wonderful evasive action as the fighters kept incessantly attacking, some coming in throttled back with flaps down, just sitting at six o'clock. B-17s were going down all around us. We logged sixteen separate attacks on our ship. After eight minutes, the fighter attacks finally ceased.

"I had seen one B-17 going down apparently under control followed by two fighters who chopped him right in half. Our fighters finally showed up and I saw one down a fighter on a sweep. It was a pretty sight, but why in hell were they not there all the time? Robinson called up to say we had six planes left out of twelve in our original squadron.

"When we landed, we saw bullet holes all over the bomber and one in the tail big enough to put a wash tub through, this thanks to a 20mm burst. Everybody waiting for us asked questions, but I was so sick at heart I sat on my equipment bag and could not respond. There were lots of empty bunks in my room that night. We lost thirteen B-17s. Mullins our Element Lead got back on two engines after we had counted him as number fourteen."

Nuthampstead's Share

Although the 398BG escaped the *Sturmgruppe's* attention, it still crossed three B-17s off its establishment. One was a victim of flak defenses when 42-107053/N7: M **Esquire** caught fire around the No. 2 engine thanks to a strike just after completing the bomb run. The fire-stricken bomber pulled out and down under the formation and all too soon the situation impelled Lt. Russell E. Reed to initiate a bail out that all nine crew carried out in sound order. Krumpa lies about ten miles SW of the Primary, and it was here that 43-38670/3O: W ended her two-month career with the group.

Fire in the bomb bay as the group turned off the target initiated the B-17's loss, but all other than the pilot, Lt. Robert G. Campbell, ended up POWs. The sole loss ascribed to fighters involved Lt. Herbert H. Newman's 42-102562/N7; G **Knock Out**. The B-17 progressed roughly sixty miles from the target until near Polleben, SSE of Aschersleben, where it came to earth; by then, the pilot and four gunners were dead, with some or all the victims of fighter gunfire. These losses spelled the onset of a bad month for the group, with nine more crews destined to be culled from its ranks.

Comment

The Merseburg mission's overall MIA tally of forty bombers demonstrated that the *Luftwaffe* was still capable of striking hard, but only under favorable circumstances—a scenario that was becoming more and more the exception to the rule with the Allied escorts generally emerging on top. Even today's "victory" was gained at an inordinate cost to the *Jagdwaffe*. The claims for 56 "kills" submitted by the 1BD's escort element was supplemented by 71 similar claims by the remaining 8FC cover for the other two Bomb Divisions.

This was a stunning reversal in terms of *Jagdwaffe* pilots and aircraft, even when allowing for a proportion of the 8FC claims ending up disallowed for lack of confirmation. The Allied control of the air spaces over Europe was by and large confirmed at this stage of the conflict. In contrast, the *Jagdwaffe*'s human and material resources were not only permanently over-stretched but were fast diminishing, the occasional *Sturmgruppe* "feast of attrition" notwithstanding.

The 381BG flew three successive daily missions (4th-6th) and returned unscathed from the first two, but not the third, during which it incurred two-thirds of the month's MIA losses. The 534BS crew led by Lt. Dudley K. Brummett was flying their sixth mission in 43-38114/GD: N **No Comment Needed**. His bombardier, Lt. William Barker, had already reached a stage of perfection at his lethal art that had Maj. Bill Fullick (group Bombardier) grooming him as a Lead bombardier. Sadly, any prospect of this occurring was harshly terminated by a flak burst or bursts during the bomb run to strike the oil refinery at Hamburg/Harburg. The fatally crippled B-17 was safely vacated by all nine airmen before it finally came down.

Lt. Barker had sustained an ankle injury that prevented him from walking properly after being apprehended. In an act of unconscious irony, when it came to moving Bill, his guard casually slung him on his shoulder along with his rifle—presumably unloaded—and "piggy-backed" him along. While there, several soldiers appeared and started to physically goad Bill. After one particularly sharp lunge, Bill reacted by striking his tormentor. Immediately, the rifles borne by each man were cocked and pointed at him. It was as well that an officer appeared on the scene who after ordering them to "shoulder arms" proceeded to roundly berate the men—seemingly not for the intended act of execution, but rather because the men had been striking an officer!

Lt. Boyd C Fox (CP) recalled the circumstances of his B-17's loss:

"We encountered heavy target flak, but cleared the area still intact. I noticed No. 3 was leaking oil, but the instruments registered fine—that is, until we were approaching the coast. Then Sgt. Frank Horsch (TG) asked what was causing the smoke puffs effect, but a request for external check by Sgt. Watson (BT) revealed nothing. Finally, I spotted a small flame emerging adjacent to No. 1 and when this was pointed out to Lt. Brummett, he peeled out of formation and dived in what was a vain attempt to extinguish the fire. The order to bail out was made, but by now we were out over the North Sea and had to make sure we reversed course sufficiently to be back over land before executing the order.

"When my turn came to jump from the rear hatch I hesitated because the ball turret now pointed down. I sat down and eased out into the air with the intention of warding off contact with the gun barrels with my feet; my grasp on the door frame was surprisingly firm even against the slipstream; when my body was almost horizontal I let go and was whisked clear, but then spun around thanks to the propeller wash. I then did a potentially fatal thing in promptly pulling my ripcord, since I was scared I would black out due to the spin. Luckily, the parachute shroud lines, although winding round, did not prevent the canopy from opening, as they were unwinding following the cessation of my spinning motion.

"I landed in a field of rhubarb and was approached by a farmer and his wife; the man told me to leave my parachute as I was gathering it in and I was escorted to their house. After a short spell, when a group of the farmer's neighbors looked in on me, two soldiers arrived on bicycle and marched me to their unit. From there I was taken by car to a fighter base and held for several days prior to transfer to *Dulag-Luft*, at Oberursal, for interrogation. My ultimate destination was *Stalag-Luft* 3."

The other B-17 taken down by flak was 42-97330/MS: S **Chug-A-Lug IV**, which now had the doubtful distinction of becoming the 535BS' first such casualty in the course of 65 missions. It had been on charge since April and was maintained by M/Sgt. "Mouse" Davis's team. The crash site was near Rotenburg, about 20 miles east of Bremen, and of the nine men in Lt. Julius K. Levitoff's charge, only two failed to survive its loss.

Merseburg strikes Again

Fourteen further missions involving sharply-varying numbers of bombers would now be launched during the month, but the 1CBW's presence would add up to a group average of ten completed runs. The 381st and 398BGs went out on three missions and the 91st on two between 7 and 16 November, with oil refineries and marshalling yards attacked, along with two tactical thrusts; the latter were directed at enemy positions at Metz (9th) where Patton's 3rd U.S. Army was stalled in front of solid fortifications and between Eschweiler and Aachen (16th) in support of the 1st and 9th U.S. Armies. And then the latest assault against Merseburg came on hand. The previous one on the 8th had not involved the 1CBW, but it was present in full strength on this occasion. However, the 381BG ended up bombing a Target of Opportunity near Frankfurt, a lapse seemingly repeated by nearly half of the crews gaining mission "credit."

The other two groups, with the 91BG as Division Lead, were part of the overall force reaching the Primary, but by the day's end they shared the overall Wing loss of six crews MIA. (The initial tally was seven, with one bomber later turning up in astonishing circumstances after being abandoned in mid-air.) This time round it was the 398BG that bore the bulk of the punishment administered by a mix of flak and fighters. One victim of the ground gunners was probably 42-102600/N8: Z **Zoomeriago**, which separated from the formation after completing the bomb run; the final crash site near Erfurt was some 70 miles SW of the target, so the bomber's demise was clearly prolonged and not mirrored by other than Sgt. Marvin E. Clark (WG) on Lt. Frederick C. Wismer's crew.

The first evidence of fighter activity occurred several minutes after "bombs away" and took the form of a slashing attack from twelve o'clock. At least two of the other four losses were later attributed to this intervention, but the fact that the crash sites were similarly concentrated around Erfurt and the adjoining towns of Gotha and Eisenach to the west suggests that the dying agony of the B-17s, along with some of the nineteen crewmembers killed, was also prolonged.

Lt. Paul H. Rich's 42-107138/N7: T bore the title **Witka Tanka Ton**. This was Sioux Native American for "bird that lays big eggs," and after being so christened, the B-17 had been flown to Britain by Col. Hunter (Group CO). Following fighter strikes that set the starboard wing ablaze, it dropped out and down into the undercast. What was its 51st mission ended at Pferdingsleben, NE of Gotha, with the pilot and all but two of the other eight airmen losing their lives. The location was close to Zimmernsupra, where 43-38671/N7: F finally piled in; this time round, Lt. Robert W. Lehner (P) was lost, along with three of his crew. Trugleben lies on Gotha's western edge and accommodated the remains of 43-3147/N8: L **Fuddy Duddy**; only three airmen out of Lt. Charles E. Howell's (KIA) team survived.

The final MIA loss occurred SE of Eisenach, some 20 miles further west, and involved a PFF B-17 44-8348/K8: A **Nutty Hussy**, ironically received on 2 November—the day of the Merseburg massacre! Now she too had been consumed in combat, although of the ten-man crew just the pilot (Lt. Kenneth S. Hastings) failed to survive her destruction. Six further group aircraft diverted to Continental airfields and there was great anxiety experienced by the group personnel pending the full confirmation of this fact.

The 91BG was also short two crews at the day's end, but this statistic would soon be halved in a most amazing manner. **Fearless Fosdick** (43-37890/DF:) had put in over 40 missions since 11 July, but a flak strike on No. 3 engine during the bomb run set it on fire, whereupon it slipped into a steady descent in the hands of Lt. Charles Whitsell. Flak fragments had killed or fatally injured all but one of the five gunners; the exception was Sgt. Robert Matthes, but he was particularly fortunate to survive when the bomber exploded over Dobitzschen, some 30 miles south of the target; the four officers had just cleared the doomed aircraft and also reached the ground alive.

"Phantom" Myth

For the ground crew assigned to maintain 43-38545/DF:, its absence, along with Lt. Harold R. DeBolt's crew, was surely a psychological body blow. However, the sense of sadness at being permanently bereft of the B-17 into which they had poured so much detailed effort to ensure the best possible chance of salvation for the combat crew would be mollified a few days later when the DeBolt team turned up, albeit in a different bomber. However, what had transpired with the B-17 that had borne them aloft on the mission would create a mini-legend for the press at the time and storytellers long thereafter.

Problems had commenced on the bomb run when the aircraft stalled out and was exposed to a fighter pass. This was survived, but the inability to drop the bomb load was "solved" when a flak burst shook them free. Unfortunately, the blast effect also damaged one and totally disabled the other inboard engine. The homeward run was commenced, but all too soon, despite dumping all excess equipment, the steadily descending course impelled the pilots to head for Belgium. Once over Allied territory, the search for an airfield was made, but none was on hand by the time a bare 2,000ft altitude was on hand, so it was decided to bail out. After lowering the landing gear, the evacuation was safely completed and the last anyone saw of their charge was its steady downward progress towards destruction.

The members of a British Army AA unit must have assumed that the B-17 swooping in for a landing in an adjacent field was being properly handled, especially when a perfect three-point landing was made, the only marginal problem seeming to be the ground loop maneuver just before all momentum was lost. But their reaction on reaching the bomber, with its engines still roaring, followed by entering it after nobody emerged must have been stunning—because there was nobody there.

The unassisted and accident-free landing was the stuff of "tall tales," but what really raised the incident to "legendary" status was the discovery of parachutes; the soldiers would naturally be generally ignorant of the extra provision of packs in case any among the normal complement were rendered useless or destroyed. Thus, did the case of the "Phantom" Fortress become fostered as the tale was spread around to be picked up by the media. During the 1960s, a prominent aviation author recounted the incident in a book and alluded to it as being genuine in terms of its "phantom" background.

Month End Activities

Six missions would be launched by the 8AF before November ended, but the 1BD was not called upon for the first, again taking to the air on the 25th, when Merseburg was again targeted by both B-17 Divisions; it seemed almost a miracle that not a single victory was claimed, particularly by the normally efficient flak batteries, although nearly 700 bombers completed their bomb runs. On the other hand, weather over East Anglia was poor and several bombers crashed, one of which was 42-107014/N8: V **Lady Ella**, an "original" B-17.

The bomber struck trees while presumably seeking the airfield. Lt. V. A. Hansard regained enough control to climb his charge high enough for a safe bail out to be conducted; however, one of the six airmen did not survive the descent. Shortly after, the B-17 came down to the west of the airfield, along with Hansard and Lt. Robert Davis (CP), presumably having gone out of control and preventing either from following the others out. (The author recalls visiting the crash site at Reed Wood with a group of aviation researchers in 1975, one of whom—John Knights—unearthed a crewmember's watch with his name inscribed on the back.)

The ever-unpredictable nature of operations would ensure that this "clean slate" would be more than balanced out 24 hours later, when the bombers went after a mix of oil refineries and transportation locations, with the 1CBW heading for a railroad viaduct at Altenbecken, in between Dortmund and Hannover. The *Jagdwaffe* was aloft in sizeable numbers and by the day's end would contribute to the figure of thirty-four crews declared MIA. However, it was again a *Sturmgruppe*'s effect upon the 491BG in taking down fifteen B-24s that was a major factor in the statistic. Elsewhere, the 8FC bit deeply into their adversaries' ranks to take down over one hundred at minimal cost to themselves (nine).

The Wing did encounter fighter activity as it swung in over the German border in what amounted to a brief but somewhat costly assault. A large pack of Bf109s and Fw190s swept in unopposed by escort interference to dispatch three Bassingbourn B-17s in quick succession. **Seattle Sleeper** (43-37913/OR:) suffered heavy punishment that culminated in Lt. John Steven's charge descending several thousand feet before expiring in a vast balloon of flame and smoke. The witnesses at debriefing assumed nobody had survived, but in fact all nine on board escaped, albeit into captivity.

The fighters' second concentrated pass apparently sealed the fate of 42-31515/DF: J/N **The Wild Hare**, one of two squadron veterans to be so afflicted, having served at Bassingbourn since mid-January. This bomber suffered the same explosive fate at a lower altitude, but this time around only Lt. Robert Flint (P) and three other crewmembers survived the incident; the wreckage fell to earth west of Cloppenburg. **Dear Becky** (42-38128/DF: Z) was the other squadron veteran B-17, with over 80 missions flown. When last observed, the aircraft was falling away with No. 2 engine blazing. Neither Lt. Adolf Miller (P) nor Lt. Richard Prunty (CP) subsequently survived out of the nine-man team, but the circumstances of their deaths remained unclear.

Although a further four Wing bombers were lost, the cause of their demise was to other than the *Jagdwaffe*. The 398BG's effort was directed at Misburg's oil refining facilities within Hannover. Originally a 91BG PFF aircraft, 42-97740/K8: Q was received in July and was here being flown by Capt. Gene L. Douglas. A flak burst during the bomb run impacted with No. 2 engine and shortly after "bombs away" the B-17 was seen to dive steeply to port; the crippled aircraft was held aloft for some distance until approaching Detmold, on whose eastern fringe it finally fell to earth; by then all ten crewmembers had evacuated safely.

The other two group casualties were sustained on the return leg over Dutch soil. Lt Kermit R. Pope's 43-37846/N8: T **Phoney Express** was successfully crash landed some 17 miles east of Arnhem, where the nine-man team was promptly rounded up by Germans. A diametrically opposite fate overtook Lt. Benjamin G. Rolfe's crew on 42-102565/3O: M **The Ugly Duckling**. A flak strike near Zwolle culminated in a final descent into the waters of the Ijsselmeer that took the lives of the nine airmen. Ridgewell's single contribution to the overall loss figure involved 42-106994/VE: K **Little Guy**; having been a flak victim, it also came down on Dutch soil near Appeldoorn. Three members of Lt. Kyle S. Smith's crew, including the pilot, shared in their bomber's fate.

Two further 91BG B-17s were "written off," the first of which was 42-107069/LL: M **Round Trip Topsy**, flown by Lt. Warren

Smith and on its 70th mission. A litany of fighter-inflicted damage included jammed gun turrets, bomb doors sprung open, and a fire under one engine. Despite this, the B-17 was held in formation, although the bomb load had to be physically released, after which the pilots eased behind the group in order to prevent affecting other B-17s should the fire induce an explosion.

Amazingly, although the fire was never extinguished, neither did it develop to a lethal degree, and after crossing in over the coast a beeline was made for the first available airfield (Halesworth, 489BG). Ice accretion on the windshield and a damaged flap contributed to a swerving motion on landing and a final impact with several vehicles. It was fortunate that although the flames now took hold to reduce the airframe to ashes, all of the crew emerged unscathed.

A third 324BS bomber was "written off" after diverting into an airfield at Denain/Prouvy. Fighter shells had knocked out an engine and caused other damage that induced Lt. Thomas Martin to turn back after salvoing his bombs. Loss of a second engine added to control problems, but by then the airfield was in sight, upon which 44-8311/DF: P **Terry's Tigers**—named after the current group CO—was "bellied in." Unfortunately, the uncontrollable skidding motion that ensued prevented any prospect of avoiding a woman and child in its path, both being killed in the process; fifteen days later, the B-17 was declared "Category E."

Comment

The 381BG Group Bombardier Maj. Fullick made an acidic, albeit fairly relevant remark regarding the Altenbecken run: "I think we hit a field." Although the accuracy factor had been eroded by the need to bomb through a solid cloud formation, there would have been little better prospect of delivering a decisive blow even in visual conditions. The ribbon-like feature presented by a bridge left little latitude for the bomb loads veering off course to any extent. In addition, the solid construction of some of these structures could absorb the striking power of even the largest transportable USAAF bomb at 2,000lb gross—not explosive—weight. Examples of this target category would continue to be partially or even totally destroyed, but in a staccato and therefore not-guaranteed manner.

Marshalling yards and synthetic oil plants became the focus of Division attention for the month's final missions, but the 381BG remained behind for the 1CBW on the former occasion (27th). The first two runs proved to be free of loss, but the final one to Zeitz (30th) removed one crew each from the Bassingbourn and Nuthampstead formations. The 324BS' 43-38742/DF:, flown by Lt. Ralph E. Stolz, was hit and had barely completed the bomb run when it exploded, killing eight of the crew and blowing the navigator out to drift down. Capt. Iver O. Tufty's B-17 lost two engines, while both pilots and one gunner were wounded; the return flight ended with a successful crash landing in Belgium, although much equipment had to be jettisoned to keep the bomber in the air.

The 398BG's single loss out of 37 dispatched involved 43-38463/30: X, which was flak-afflicted between the IP and Primary and dived out of formation with one engine on fire; shortly after it exploded, scattering its remains at Grosloebichau, close to Jena's eastern fringes. Lt. Roger J. Wegum (P) was killed, along with five others, but of the three survivors, one was listed as evading capture. Presumably, he managed to reach the Czechoslovakian border roughly 50 to 60 miles distant from Jena and thereafter gain assistance from the population of that Nazi-occupied land.

Ardennes Setback

The final month of 1944 would witness an initial shocking reverse for the Anglo/American ground offensive that would be focused upon the latter nation's forces based in Luxembourg, while Mother Nature would add to the problem by blanketing the *Wehrmacht*/SS advance from the air for nearly seven days. Although the failure of Operation *Market Garden* during September had ensured the war in the West would carry on throughout the winter, all indications were that the enemy's ground resources in men and material were permanently spent; far from launching any counteroffensive, they were basically only capable of holding out until the Allied armies could enjoy better conditions in which to push further onwards.

Enter the "wild card" in this equation—Hitler—who despite the parlous situation on the Eastern Front had ordered a massing of Panzer and infantry strength with which to make a thrust towards Antwerp and effectively split the Allied Front. This achieved, he believed the Anglo/American governments would feel induced to enter into negotiations culminating in some form of armistice. The anticipated effect for Germany would be a mass re-deployment of resources with which to stem the burgeoning Soviet military tide.

Marshalling yards were focused upon on 2 and 4 December, although weather disrupted proceedings on the first occasion, which also saw a reduced 1BD force involved compared to eleven groups venturing out on the 4th. No MIA losses were incurred on either mission, but single B-17s from Bassingbourn and Nuthampstead diverted into Continental airfields on the latter occasion. The third mission involved the latest thrust at *Big B*, although the overall force was less than half the previous day's effort at 591 bombers. The city's Borsig panzer production plant was allotted to the 1BD sub-force of six groups. Flak was the principal destroyer among the formations, culling nine crews overall, one-third from the 91BG.

A direct strike on the No. 3 engine of 43-38234/LG: E **Easy Does It** that blew the propeller and most of the mount away threw the bomber into a dive. Reports that the pilots seemed to regain control held a degree of credence, since the listed crash site at Templin was some 40 miles due north of the Primary; seven of Lt. Donald R. Freer's team bailed out beforehand. **Bride of Mars** (43-38360/LG: D) three-month stint with the group was terminated after the flak gunners struck home prior to "bombs away." The B-17 eased off to one side and slowly descended until out of sight. This time round there were no fatalities among Lt. Ralph Blanton's crew before their charge crashed in the city's Spandau district adjacent to the Primary.

The final casualty was also a squadron machine: 43-389693/LG: C, flown by Lt. Howard L. Mitchell. At some stage it fell out of formation with a subsequent call received by the group Lead stating almost all power was gone. The bomber's agony was seemingly even more prolonged than the Freer-piloted B-17; the reported crash location at Talge/Wilsten was close to the Dutch/German border and their bomber's fate was sadly paralleled by the pilot and three of the crew.

The Wing's participation was not called upon (6th), even though the Primary was Merseburg—a fact the crews would have been very grateful for, even though no casualties were borne by the force dispatched. There then ensued a three-day period of non-activity for the bombers before the 1BD alone was sent to attack airfields and marshalling yards around Stuttgart, followed on the 11th by a full-scale 8AF assault on a series of marshalling yards and bridges ranging between Frankfurt and Mannheim. The Maximillian structure at the latter location was assigned to the 41CBW and the 381BG, while the other two groups headed for Frankfurt.

One of the Ridgewell crews was that of Lt. Leo I. Belskis, manning 43-38780/VE: J, who had Lt. Ross W. Perrin as his bombardier. Ross had recently sent a recorded message to his family, assuring them that all was well and he was doing fine—a natural but tragically premature act as events confirmed today. The *G-H* assisted bomb run was in progress, but the cloud cover provided no salvation from the flak barrage. A burst that tore away the No. 2 engine and caused flames to streak back in a long banner was swiftly followed by the entire port wing shearing off.

The vicious spinning motion that ensued held most of the survivors in place, although up to three crewmembers were reported coming out; as it was, only Sgts. Elvis A. McCoy (ROG) and Durward V. Suggs (WG) escaped the terminal fate of their seven colleagues. (In 2009 a relative, Ross Greene, who was named for his posthumous uncle and who had long researched the incident, as well as entering into correspondence with German researchers of the air war, went with his wife Lynne to Mannheim, where he met several eyewitnesses of the B-17's final moments.)

This was the second group loss in bombers within 48 hours, the previous casualty being 42-32060/MS: V **Boulder Buf**, in the hands of Lt. Clark. Four crewmembers were wounded, two of them seriously as a result of the flak strike (or strikes) that impelled the pilots to divert to France. A landing was finally made at Melun, but the B-17 over-shot and struck an obstacle that fortunately left the airframe largely intact. Sgts. Hallstrom and Rafael Larsen were urgently removed to hospital; in the former airmen's case, he was transferred to Paris, where the extent of damage to one leg necessitated its amputation. By then, his colleague in physical distress had expired on the 11th.

The latest foray against Merseburg (12th) that went to the 1BD again passed off in almost complete immunity from the defenses, with a solitary bomber being culled from among 337 dropping their loads. Nor was the mission three days later to assault Kassel's tank production plants any more harrowing, at least in terms of MIA losses; indeed, all crews completing their bomb runs regained British shores safely. However, no less than four B-17s were lost in "operational" crashes occurring either during Assembly, or in one case impacting with a pylon on approach to its airfield.

Unknown to the 8AF personnel, next morning was the launch of the Hitler-inspired offensive to drive through to Antwerp, with the epicenter for the assault directed through the Ardennes region, on Belgium's southern border with Germany. This was the same thickly-wooded and steep valley zone through which the German armor had begun its swiftly successful bid to divide the Anglo/French armies in May 1940. Over four years later, the German forces were expected to carry out a similar massive thrust, but this time around it would be conducted not in early summer, but during the onset of a particularly severe Winter.

However, the initial prospects for success were sound, given the paucity and combat-readiness of the American ground forces, being a mix of battle-weary units sent to what was (now wrongly) regarded as a quiet sector and the newly-arrived and accordingly "green" 106th Division. As already mentioned, the coincidental arrival of a sustained adverse weather pattern over much of Western Europe and Britain further aided the German forces in their endeavor.

The weather conditions notwithstanding, the 8AF was to launch three missions during the first four days of what was to be known as "The Battle of the Bulge," with the 1BD involved on two of the missions. The first was sent out on the 18th to interdict railroad communications, but the cloud patterns forced a "recall" of the 2BD and part of the other two Divisions. Next day, a reduced force that did not involve the 1CBW other than the 91BG—and whose records show the mission being "scrubbed"—went after tactical targets behind the enemy battle lines.

Then, all operations were totally thwarted by the blanketing effect of fog, leaving the Ardennes defenders basically dependent on their efforts to at least slow down the German advance, a duty that met with varying degrees of success, especially in denying the Panzer units access to key fuel dumps. Finally, the eighth day of the battle witnessed a vital change in the weather as a high-pressure front allowed the sun to break through and at least partially disperse the fog over Britain. Air operations were again on!

Concentration on tactical targets was again the priority, but although all three Divisions took part, the overall number of bombers was surprisingly limited to an overall figure of twelve. Once again, the 1CBW was not involved, but it was a vastly different situation next morning, when an equally vast force of just over 2,000 B-17s and B-24s rose in their usual stately and majestic manner and headed out to blast a veritable plethora of tactical locations, including airfields and communication centers. In the words of one Wing CO to his crews: "This will be a Xmas present our troops will never forget," although the soldiers would have to wait some time before they could really savor their airborne contemporaries' efforts on their behalf, the battle still being critically pitched this day.

Mother Nature Strikes

The fog's intensity level had hardly abated at Nuthampstead as Christmas Eve dawned and the atmosphere also still retained a heavy level of freezing frost. This in turn raised the danger of ice accretion adversely affecting the aircrafts' flight surfaces, especially during the take-off stage of the mission; loss of lift at this point could result in the bomber dropping out of the sky with an almost certain chance of it and its crew being consumed in the igniting of the fuel and bomb load. A countermeasure was the liberal application of anti-freeze to the wings and stabilizers, but requests from some crews for this to be acted on was reportedly denied. Whether this did contribute to the impending dual incident would neither be absolutely confirmed nor excluded from the minds of some personnel.

Take-off for the expanded force of 51 crews was conducted under "blind flying" conditions, with concentration on instruments as opposed to external visual reference. A bare handful of B-17s (two) had risen off the runway when the third one, a group "original" flown by Lt. Leland L. Zimmerman, suffered immediate aileron problems on taking to the air. The pilot took the immediate and potentially lethal decision to set 42-97374/K8: X **Madame X** back onto the fortunately flat area adjoining the airfield boundary. As it was, the B-17's contact with the ground did not result in an explosion, although fire did take hold, and even then the nine airmen had ample time to evacuate their positions.

A good number of following bombers got off safely before it was the turn of Lt. Donald D. Grinter to open the throttles on 42-102536/N8: C **Here's Hopin**, a title that was to fail two crewmembers within minutes. The aircraft's landing gear had just retracted when the initial indication of disaster was for the B-17 to develop a sharp bank to port; when counter-rudder/aileron action was taken, the result was a stall that brought it down at Chrishall Common, where it caught fire and exploded several minutes later. Although the pilot and six fellow crewmembers—one seriously injured—scrambled clear, the remaining two (Lt. Franklin D. Harrod [N] and S/Sgt. David V. Flores [WG]) were believed trapped within the fuselage and subsequently killed by the blast. It was somewhat of a miracle that so few fatalities were incurred in the circumstances, but no consolation for the individuals so affected or for their kin.

Turning the Aerial Screw

The Christmas Eve mission initiated a daily sequence of operations up to the month end, but the scale of assault was never to approach that day's level. In addition, the return of fog conditions over the Midlands ensured that much of the 1BD's force would divert to airfields further east and would not be assembled for a mission from their own bases until the 27th. Furthermore, the forces deployed by the other two Divisions in the interim spell would also experience disruption thanks to the weather.

As far as the 1CBW was concerned, it would first operate on the 28th, as well as the final three monthly runs, apart from the 381BG, which remained on the ground during the 29th, while the 91BG reportedly "scrubbed" the planned mission next day. The majority of the missions now witnessed concentration on targets further back, with marshalling yards spread across western and as far as central Germany a prominent feature; bridges were also focused upon. Four-figure numbers in bombers dispatched were also achieved on two of the missions.

These missions proved to be painful for the 398BG alone, with two crews lost on successive missions. On the 29th, 42-107188/K8: G **Ramp Rooster** was zeroing in on Bingen's marshalling yard complex but took a strike in No. 2 engine and fire caught hold. However, Lt. Mahion R. Erickson managed to steer his crippled bomber for some time on the return leg before it had to be abandoned; eight of the nine airmen survived, of which three evaded capture.

The other loss, also from the 602BS, was entered into the MIA category, but its demise was not thought to be due to enemy involvement. Instead, an RAF pilot operating near Beachy Head reported an aircraft exploding and tumbling into the Channel. This was 42-102610/K8: Y **Boomerang**, a 66-mission veteran; the bodies of three from Lt. Lyle J. Doerr's crew were subsequently picked up from the area by an ASR Launch guided there by the RAF pilot.

Los Angles City Limits is beautifully posed against a sun-lit but solid undercast. The 532BS B-17G commenced operations in April 1944 and won through to VE-Day; it survived a potentially lethal encounter with two Me163s on 7 October. Note the serial number's extension onto the rudder, a common practice with seven-figure examples.

T/Sgt. Gilbert Staats (Photo Section) and S/Sgt. Ray Ater (Engineering Section) are engaging one of a group of children in conversation while sitting in a church entrance within the vicinity of the airmen's Ridgewell airfield. Such encounters provided a degree of sanity in the midst of what was a protracted and bloody conflict.

Sgts. Simpson, Sopato, and Showgo, who are probably the maintenance crew for this "double entendre"-titled B-17G (43-38841/OR: L), are posed beneath her nose. She was assigned on 4 November 1944 and put in 45 missions prior to VE-Day. The B-26 in the right background is an early model with the extended "sting tail" turret cone and short wingspan.

Formation flying in combat or on practice flights was ever dangerous. On 5 December 1944, 42-107040/OR: K Shirley Jean was cast upward by prop wash and its upper fin impacted with a neighboring B-17. Lt. John Lindahl and his copilot were hard pressed to remain airborne, but finally landed safely. The fin was repaired and the bomber went on to complete 98 missions.

The destructive impact of flak is balanced out by the inherent aerodynamic strength of the B-17 in this picture. The Bassingbourn PFF machine is 44-8315/DF:, which returned to Bassingbourn despite the massive rent in the port side waist. The fate of any crewmember in this section at the time is not known. The censor has not blanked out the H2S radar pod.

The unintentional "villain" in the practice flight incident with OR: K was Lt. Tom Martin's 44-6151/DF: J Shure Shot, whose outer port stabilizer was similarly bent over to create an equally fraught control situation for the pilots. The damaged B-17 also landed safely and enjoyed a similar combat career by surviving 71 missions.

Col. Leber (fifth from right) is accompanied by two senior combat personnel among this returning crew. The Mae West-clad officer to the Colonel's left is Maj. Bill Fullick (group Bombardier), while flanking Leber on his right is Maj. Jim DeLano (group Navigator). This was taken on 12 December, when the Merseburg/Leuna's oil refinery complex was the Primary.

This B-17 assigned to the 602BS at Nuthampstead has suffered a collapsed tail wheel; a crane hook is being attached to a lug mounted in the center of the curved fin fairing. This is 44-8483/N8: T, which was currently equipped with H2X but was later adapted to Gee-H. The date of the incident was 2 December 1944.

This 323BS B-17G (44-6618/OR: U) was reportedly one of the relatively few Bassingbourn-based bombers not to bear some form of title. The port landing gear's collapse has resulted in bent propeller blades, but it is likely the aircraft will be restored to combat status within a short period.

A 91BG ambulance, often referred to in sardonic fashion as a "Blood wagon," holds position behind a B-17G bearing wounded or dead crewmembers. Bombers generally taxied with their outboard engines only on mission return. A line of P-51s dominates the left background. Photograph was taken during the winter of 1944/45.

The Ugly Duckling, a 398BG "original" assigned to the 601BS, bears an impressive three rows of mission "bombs"; note the practice of grouping the fuselage code letters and the thick outline to the triangle. Her luck would run out on 26 November 1944, along with Lt. Benjamin G. Rolfe's crew, when the aircraft descended into the Ijsselmeer.

This view of ground crew premises at Nuthampstead demonstrates the adaptability of the personnel. The solid structure on the left is typical of the facilities created by the men that enabled them to live out by their dispersals. The tented facility was a variation on the same theme, albeit not quite so comfortable in winter weather conditions.

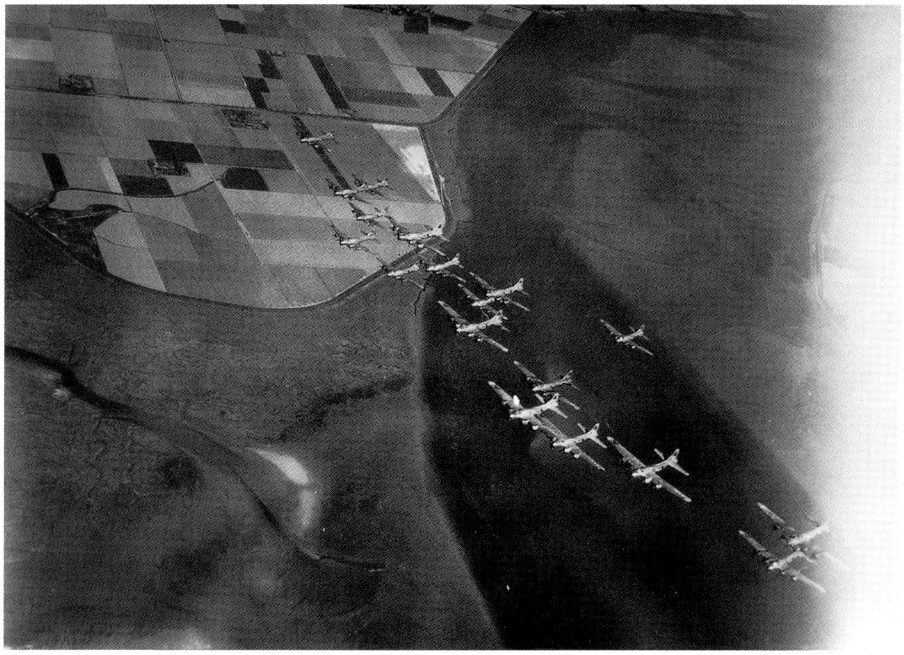

This view of part of a 381BG formation proves the value of close formation flying. The basic principles inherent in this procedure were to ensure maximum defensive firepower against enemy fighters and to equally ensure a tight bombing cluster on the Primary.

This distinctive Christmas tree fronted by a pictorial board has been set up at Ridgewell by 533BS personnel. The officer is George Shackley, an "original" group pilot who commanded the squadron at one stage of his operational career and ended up as group Air Executive. This picture was taken during December 1944.

Lt. Bill Dietrich (2nd right, kneeling) poses with his crew backed by the 91BG's legendary survivor; Sgt. Sam Cipalla (BT) stands on the left. Assigned during February 1944, 42 31909/ OR: R would complete 141 recorded missions. Her return stateside in June 1945 was equally and happily preceded by the nine airmen seen here.

The margins between physical security and serious injury or death during combat operations were ever infinitesimal. Sgt Nick Rotz a 535BS gunner is holding a flak fragment that sliced across the top and side of his flak helmet liner but left him unscathed. The wearing of a standard leather helmet would surely have produced a fatal outcome.

A vertical view of Nuthampstead includes the main concentrations of aircraft dispersals, as well as the hangars and support structures in the center. The main runway, with a B-17 ready for take-off, is aligned SW/NE, with the bomber facing the latter direction. The various technical and communal sites are largely grouped in the lower left quadrant of the picture.

The particularly severe winter of 1944/45 increased the already hazardous duty of operating under such conditions. These B-17s of the 398BG are hemmed in by snow that will probably have to be shovelled off the dispersals and their links with the perimeter track before operations can be initiated.

13/19) This late-War shot of the 91BG's 43-38755 Lewd Angel is equally interesting as regards the crew. By then B-17 crews normally comprised nine since one waist gunner was excluded in early 1944. The trio of officers suggests an NCO has assumed the bombardier's function as a 'togglier'. Presence of a seventh NCO also suggests he is probably charged with 'spot-jammer' or other electronic-disturbance equipment directed against the German ground-defence system.

Chapter Fourteen
En Route to Victory

Comment

New Year's Day 1945 opened with the German forces within the "Bulge" being steadily pushed back and under looming threat of being cut off by the twin pincers formed by the Allied armies on either side. As matters transpired, any repeat of the Falaise Gap massacre the previous August was to be cancelled out by Gen. Eisenhower's insistence on a full frontal advance as opposed to an encircling action, the result of which was a month-long campaign that succeeded only at a fairly high cost in American personnel.

As for the overall conduct of the war, any hope of bringing the European conflict to a close long before the year was out was currently in the hands of the Soviet armies alone. For the Western Allies to close in on the Nazi hinterland and squeeze the life out of the German military and industrial support resources in conjunction with the Russians, a major geographic barrier in the form of the River Rhine still had to be breached. That highly prized goal lay almost three months distant, however, since only the northern sector of the Allied Front was either at or within sight of its west bank.

The three Air Divisions (their new title introduced on 1 January) commenced the year by assaulting a variety of communications locations in the case of the other two sub-forces, while the 1AD went after Merseburg's oil production. However, two-thirds of the 451 crews ended up over the Secondary's marshalling yards at Kassel, with most of the remainder seeking out Targets of Opportunity. Today commenced a run of fourteen completed missions during the month for the 1CBW, with two further sorties "scrubbed" on the 16th and 27th, a scale of operations that generally applied across the entire 8AF ranks in the face of this particularly severe winter.

Nuthampstead's run of ill fortune since Christmas Eve continued as the formation was heading out for Kassel; Lt. Howard M. Pinner's 43-38895/N7: V suffered an engine fire. The B-17 turned back but never regained friendly shores, having to be "ditched." By then, the crew complement was reduced by one, as Lt. Warren L. King (N) elected to bail out when the incident occurred and ended up being swallowed by the sea. Two further crewmembers were lost in the "ditching," but the others got out, albeit confronted by a truly hostile environment formed by the frigid, winter waters. Two Vickers Warwick bombers bearing Lindholme motorized lifeboats reached the scene and the airmen came through the ordeal, but whether this was achieved by gaining access to the single example that did not break up on contact with the sea or by the subsequent arrival of an ASR Launch is not clear. Either way, they were lucky to survive death by hypothermia.

Ridgewell was also short one B-17 by the day's end, but the crew was safe, although one airman suffered a broken leg. Lt. Vincent Peters, flying 43-37553/ MS: Y **Feather Merchant II**, suffered the loss of both starboard engines during the bomb run and he and Lt. Nelson had to fight the asymmetric effect thus cast up that threatened to develop into a spin when attempting to hold level flight. The steadily downward course extended over 50 minutes before Allied lines near Metz were attained fortunately still left sufficient altitude for a bail out, however. All other than the pilot jumped clear, but Sgt. Robert B. Bolin (G) had to be rescued from a minefield, while Sgt. Charles F. Knaus (TG) was fired upon by GIs in a moving truck whose aim was fortunately poor. Peters managed to carry off a crash landing that left him intact but rendered the B-17 liable for "salvage" action. Both Sergeants would be KIA during March, as would Lt. Nelson.

The single contribution to the Wing loss statistic made by the 91BG was incurred right at mission start. **Heats On** (42-37911/LL: C) was on the point of celebrating a full year's presence at Bassingbourn, with ninety missions already completed. Shortly after take-off engine problems forced Lt. John Welch to head back, but the airfield he approached was near Steeple Morden (355FG). Whatever went wrong with the landing is uncertain, but the B-17 veered off the runway and straight into a group of P-51s. The impact resulted in the bomb and fuel load erupting, expunging the lives of all on board; one 355GF crew chief was seriously injured, but there were no fatalities otherwise among the ground crew.

Operations progressed on an almost continuous basis up to the 8th, with sizeable forces that exceeded 1,000 on four occasions being dispatched, only the 4th seeing no activity. The focus of attention involved communications stretching across western Germany. A marshalling yard at Gerolstein, SE of Koblenz, and a communications center at Prum directly behind the "Bulge" were attacked by the 381BG and 91BG, respectively (2nd), and next day, the full Wing headed for Köln to carry out a PFF-assisted attack on the city; a similar full-scale effort was directed at marshalling yards in Koblenz twenty-four hours later. All three missions had remained free from loss, but not the ensuing sortie, which returned to Köln to attack the major Rhine bridge at Deutz.

For whatever reason, single PFF aircraft flying with the 91BG and 398BG were actually B-17s from Kimbolton (379BG). The former example was 44-8501/LF: **Jeanie**, bearing Bassingbourn crewmembers other than Capt. McConnell (P) and the GH operator. The bridge was clouded over, so recourse was to again bomb the city. The flak gunners took their revenge by striking home against McConnell's bomber, hitting the No. 3 engine, which first began to smoke and then burst into flames; as the B-17 began its terminal descent, four of the ten-man crew lost their lives in the process. The *G-H* system was more sophisticated than *H2X* for example, but may well have not yet been applied to so many PFF-functioning bombers, hence the "borrowing" of the 379BG examples by the 1CBW on this occasion. However, 381BG records indicate two such specially equipped B-17s were already on hand, further confusing this issue.

Forty-eight hours elapsed before the 381st and 398BGs took off to attack separate targets: a railroad bridge at Alzey and Speyer marshalling yards, respectively; the latter unit again utilized two *G-H*-equipped B-17s from the 41CBW. The severe winter weather probably caused the latest break in operations next day, but it was back to business on the 10th, when the airfield at Köln/Ostheim was allotted to the Wing from among several airfields around that city attacked by the 1AD. One 398BG B-17 was involved in a collision with a truck that killed the driver and initially resulted in 44-8476/3O: X being declared "salvage"; however, the scale of damage was restricted enough for repair work and return to combat status to be carried out.

The bulk of the Wing managed to deposit their loads on the Primary in spite of the heavy, snow-laden cloud patterns, but two 381BG crews were fortunate to come through unscathed. The first was the group Lead bearing L/Col. Shackley (Group Air Executive). Loss of two engines when well into the outward leg forced an "abort," but the restricted visibility as the pilots sought any Belgian airfield on which to deposit their steadily sinking charge seemed doomed to failure. Then, with less than 1,000ft still on hand, Shackley sighted what looked like a strip and after making a pass that confirmed its status made a turn and headed down. The runway length was no more than adequate, even when free of any ice residue, but the landing was carried out perfectly, albeit involving the runway's complete length.

The companion bomber in distress had attained the target after assuming group Lead, but had suffered serious flak damage to the tail section. The B-17 in question was a *G-H* bomber "borrowed" from the 303BG and in Lt. Rouse's hands. Sgt. Hafner (WG) suffered a dreadful leg injury, with the limb being severed, and the fight was then on to save his life. The destruction of the rudder and elevator cables initially left Rouse and Lt. Crouse (CP) unable to deflect the B-17 from its easterly heading; the solution lay in juggling with the engine RPM levels, which resulted in a painfully protracted turn to starboard and final steadying on course for Belgium.

Two hours after the Shackley crew had clambered out of their aircraft, they gazed upon a second B-17 making its landing approach. On reaching the stationery machine, they were astounded at the sight of the Rouse-led team emerging! The critically-injured Sergeant was rushed to hospital, where the doctors succeeded in saving his life. Next day, both crews were flown back to Ridgewell; 42-97990/VE: F was subsequently repaired and reassigned to the 381BG on 23 February.

Not so fortunate were three members of Lt. John Martin's Bassingbourn crew. His B-17 (43-37988/DF: C **The BTO**) had suffered the loss of one engine and was similarly headed in the direction of Belgium. On reaching Brussels, the pilots made a landing approach for Evere, but the bomber's momentum was far from spent when it reached the end of the runway. The overshoot saw it impact with a C-47 before careening further into a hangar; only six of the nine on board emerged alive from the incident.

The weather "clamping down" ensured operations were suspended until the 13th, when only the 91BG remained behind, the other groups going out to a railroad bridge at Germersheim. Marshalling yards and bridges would feature almost exclusively in the Wing operational records for the rest of January. The next two completed missions saw the 91BG assaulting a key railroad bridge at Köln and the Ridgewell crews attacking a similar structure at Köln/Rodenkirchen close by (14th). Next day, the 91BG alone went out to Ingolstadt's marshalling yards; Nuthampstead records refer to a "scrubbed" briefing with no details on this occasion. An intended thrust at Berlin was "scrubbed" (16th) before the first full Wing effort since the 10th headed for marshalling yards at Paderborn.

During this spell, just one B-17 was declared MIA, with the 91BG's **Bull Session** (43-48911/OR:) the unlucky example. Lt. William E. Meyer's crew was on its fifth mission, but the men's Air Medal award would be earned posthumously by all but one out of the nine. Flying No. 2 in its element, the bomber was observed to literally fall apart following an apparent flak strike, with no explosive effect being seen by returning eyewitnesses. Both starboard engines became detached, followed by an eerie separation of both wings and finally, the fuselage breaking into three sections. Only Lt. James D. Buescher (B) managed to bail out before the final impact. The day previous (13th), Lt. Laurence DeLancey, whose crew had survived a devastating flak strike on 15 October, was directed to divert to RAF Woodbridge Emergency airfield, where he carried off a perfect crash landing in 42-102418/N8: M. The veteran "original" B-17's 65th mission was also its last, with "salvage" action ordered.

The latest enforced halt to 8AF operations lasted until the 20th, when the 1st and 2nd ADs dispensed the by-now regular punishment to Germany's marshalling yard complexes—in this case based around the upper-Rhine zone, with the 1CBW's effort directed against Mannheim's extensive facilities. Next day, it was the turn of Acshaffenburg's yards to feel the weight of the Wing's bomb loads. The enemy's oil production potential, although virtually strangled to death, was still being attacked, and Sterkrade, in the northern sector of the Ruehr, was targeted, although only a small proportion of the 1AD force, including the 91st and 398BG, got through to the Primary.

The Schaffenburg strike reduced the 91BG's aircraft establishment by one, although the crew were saved. The B-17G in question was 43-38083/OR: Q **Happy Valley Express**, which had put in 47 missions since arrival on 11 August. Two engines were crippled during the bomb run, but worse still was a steadily developing fire in the starboard wing, fortunately close to the juncture with the fuselage. S/Sgt. Stanbury cut through the bomb bay skin—a very risky action on his part—before successfully emptying the contents of a fire extinguisher on the flames. The crippled bomber was brought back to Metfield, in Suffolk, by Lt. Nelson Van Blarcom, but the scale of damage was deemed too great for restoration to combat status and "salvage" action was confirmed next day.

A Senior Casualty

Although all group COs were expected to fly missions on a regular basis, the overall casualty rate among this grade was surprisingly small during the entire time span of the Daylight Offensive. Col. Hunter had assumed command of the 398BG way back in March 1943 and had earned the respect of his men over the 22 months of the group's existence. On the 23rd, the briefing at Nuthampstead was for the group to join the 41CBW in carrying out a *G-H* assisted attack on marshalling yards at Neuss; the location was on the Rhine's west bank, opposite the Ruehr city of Düsseldorf.

The group was Force Lead and the Colonel, along with Lt. Federico Gonzales (P), was guiding 44-8224/DF: (a 91BG PFF aircraft) in on the bomb run when its progress was brutally halted. A flak shell impacted and excised the outer panel of the starboard wing. The aerodynamic imbalance cast the bomber into a roll to starboard that swiftly developed into a spinning motion. Lt. Gonzales recalled the Colonel's calm demeanor before he lost consciousness.

When his senses recovered, the Lieutenant was undoubtedly dumbfounded at realizing his surroundings—he was lying in the midst of the B-17's wreckage! Having been pulled out by German troops or civilians, he was later apprised of his CO's death, a fate shared by the other eight crewmembers. The incident again confirmed the extent to which dumb luck contributed to many a combat crewmember's survival or death.

Hunter's loss would cast a pall of gloom around the base and it would take some time for his successor, Col. Lewis Ensign, to stamp his authority on the personnel. There were rumors that Ensign's appointment might have been imminent even if Col. Hunter had not died; the latter officer's command was apparently regarded "Upstairs" as casual to the point of being counter-productive in maintaining discipline, whereas Col. Ensign's style was measurably more direct to the point of seeming ruthless.

Needless Tragedy

Forty-eight hours prior to Hunter's loss, his contemporary at Ridgewell, Col. Harry P. Leber, had returned from Aschaffenburg on what was the completion of his tenure of office at Ridgewell. He was later awarded the Silver Star by B/Gen. Gross (CG, 1CBW), but the pleasure at coming through his combat missions unscathed must have been tempered by the loss of eighteen airmen as the bombers entered the airfield circuit. Among the formation were two veteran B-17s: 42-97511/MS: K **Egg Haid** and 42-40011/GD: O **Schnozzle**, flown by F/O Nicholas Tauro and James E. Smith, respectively. At some stage in proceedings, one bomber made fatal contact with the other and the result was both plummeted to earth, leaving little chance for anybody to jump from the meager height of several hundred feet currently being flown; one tail gunner did survive for a short period within his position.

Left behind on the Continent was 43-38158/GD: G **Smashin' Time!**. Although the bomber had just been returned to combat status the previous night, problems with two engines on the way over impelled Lt. Robert E. Coates to turn for home. Matters went from bad to worse, with an inoperable ASI unit and ice accretion on the windshield among further difficulties as the ailing B-17 sank steadily through the undercast. When the pilots broke into the clear around 1,000ft Coates, who was on the point of ringing the bail out bell, instructed the bombardier to set the bomb fuses to "safe" before jettisoning them in case Allied territory was below. He sought out a suitable field in which to set his charge down for a successful crash landing.

The crew's problems were not over, however. The appearance of what appeared to be a hostile civilian crowd wielding farm implements happily presented no problem, since the location was in France (Sauverne), but when a U.S. Army truck also turned up the airmen's nerves were again stretched to breaking point when the driver yelled for them not to move, since they were in a mine field! The soldier managed to guide them out of their potentially perilous situation—although how he knew the exact disposition of the weapons is unclear—and drove them to nearby Luneville, from where repatriation to Ridgewell would subsequently commence.

On the ground, the German forces were in effect back on their original start lines as of 16 December, and moreover, would now face a steady drive by the Allied armies confronting them that would see the latter's advance to the Rhine largely accomplished by early March. The immediate priority for the 8AF was to maintain the pressure on the enemy rail transport system, as evidenced by the 1CBW's experience. However, the winter weather patterns ensured that the bombers would remain ground-bound until the 28th, when Köln's marshalling yards at Gremberg and the Hohenzollern Bridge drew the 1AD's attention. The Wing's final January run next day was to Niederlahnstein, opposite Koblenz, that also concluded with no losses in crews.

February 1945

Berlin Blues

The marshalling yard theme for the Division was maintained on 1 February, with a twin assault on facilities in Ludwigshafen and Mannheim, with the latter Primary involving the Wing; all crews returned, but 43-37509/3O: J—a 398BG bomber of eight-month service at Nuthampstead—was crash landed in Suffolk by Lt. James E. Koenig. **Julie Linda** (42-32102/MS: O) ran off the runway at Ridgewell after "aborting" the mission and smashed into several 533BS huts, breaking her fuselage in the process; the landing downwind on barely half power surely contributed to this failure, but did not save Lt. Kuhns from being downgraded to copilot, while his near eleven-month veteran B-17 was "written off."

Next day, a planned mission to Berlin was "scrubbed," but successfully resurrected twenty-four hours later—a result that would have sat badly with six crews within the Wing, however. The attack was conducted by the two B-17 Divisions, with the city's Tempelhof marshalling yards as the briefed Primary, with over 900 crews later recorded as striking home and a further thirteen bombing Gatow airfield as a Target of Opportunity. The weather provided crystal clear visibility and the flak barrage was as persistent and punishing as ever.

L/Col. Marvin D. Lord (91BG group Operations officer) had survived nearly two years in combat, having originally served with the 381BG as an "original" pilot and 532BS CO before transferring to Bassingbourn. Now today he was flying in the Lead B-17 42-97632 /DF: R with Lt. Frank L. Adams and an extremely experienced crew, three members of which had amassed a total of 268 missions between them. As ever, the Grim Reaper took no cognizance of this current survival factor because the group was seconds distant from "bombs away" when a shell struck the B-17's center section and blew the airframe in half; the gyrating nose section of the stricken machine provided little or no chance for any of the eleven airmen positioned therein to jump before the final impact, while the momentarily-level progress of the other section also saw no surviving crewmembers emerging.

The second group crew culled was led by Lt. George Miller and stationed as Lord's No. 3 in the Lead element. No sooner had the pilot observed the fate of the Lead B-17 when it was the turn of his (B-17 42-32085/DF: H **Yankee Belle**) to feel the wrath of the flak gunners. No. 3 and 4 engines were promptly disabled, followed shortly after by a third; worse still was the severing of control cables other than to the elevators and the automatic pilot. In spite of this parlous situation, the pilots managed to gain a degree of control during the bomber's gradual but inexorable downward path that culminated in a successful crash landing between Altentreptow and Neubrandenburg, around 80 miles north of *Big B*.

A duo of losses was experienced by the other two groups that was self imposed in the 398BG's case. The Wing was still some 100 miles short of Berlin when 43-38697/N7: M and 42-97387/K8: H came together in a fatal embrace. The former B-17, flown by Lt. Perry E. Powell, cut Lt. John R. McCormick's bomber in half and the separated parts of the 81-mission veteran spiralled down to their destruction SE of Uelzen; somehow, Sgt. William G. Logan (Togglier) cleared the aircraft safely. Powell's bomber also came down close by and again, just Sgt. Joseph D. Bancroft (TG) managed to survive, unlike the other sixteen airmen concerned in the tragic incident.

Ridgewell paralleled its companion units in loss scale during what was the group's first mission to *Big B* in seven months. The first MIA crew were on board 43-38898/GD: G **Hitler's Ho Do**, with Lt. Paul C. Pucylowski as pilot. This B-17 was yet another flak-afflicted aircraft, but its death throes appear to have been extended, judging by where it finally descended. Tutow lies near the Baltic coast and well distant from Berlin; all but one of the crew escaped their B-17's fate. Lt. John B. Anderson's 42-102873/VE: H **The Joker II** bore Sgt. Mike Medzie (BT), who

managed to operate his cramped position despite wearing his chest pack, a measure regarded as necessary following a previous mission with his regular pilot Lt. Ed Miller when the bomber was badly shot up. Mike had fallen behind his crew in missions and was "filling in" to make up this deficiency.

Mike would be grateful for his action in accommodating the parachute, however uncomfortable it must have been, after a port fuel tank on **Joker II** was set alight. The fire spread rapidly and the bail out signal was given, whereupon he simply released the turret door and fell out. He delayed opening his parachute until well towards the ground, but his pleasant descent ended with a problem when he got hung up in a large tree. Nothing daunted, he burnt some lines off the canopy, tied them together and weighted one end to form a crude "bolas" with which to gain a purchase on the tree trunk.

He then adopted a head-down attitude after releasing his harness that duly dropped away, and righting himself again swung down to the ground on the "bolas." Any bid at evading capture soon ended, but he was fortunate to escape from a rough manhandling by civilians as the soldiers marched him to Ebenswalde village. Several weeks later, he was reunited with his crew when he discovered that the pilot was the sole fatality. Then, while on a forced march, he was fortunate to survive a "friendly fire" incident when P-47s strafed the POW column, dealing out death to a number of personnel.

The Berlin mission was followed by the latest enforced break in operations extending up to the 5th, before three synthetic oil plants were briefed (6th). However, all remained inviolate thanks to weather, and in the 1AD's case, a number of greatly spread-out Targets of Opportunity were bombed, although no MIA losses were sustained. Three days later, following a recalled mission (8th), the Lutzkendorf refinery that escaped attention on the 6th was successfully reached by over two-thirds of the 1AD with just a single MIA casualty.

The staccato nature of February operations thanks to weather witnessed another four-day pause for the entire 8AF before a full-bodied thrust at marshalling yards and oil plants in Eastern Germany was launched on the 14th, when the 1AD's Primary was marshalling yards in Dresden. Once again, the 1CBW returned largely intact, other than for three 381BG and two 398BG crews who diverted to Continental airfields.

A fourth Ridgewell crew battled to bring their flak-afflicted B-17 42-40017/ MS: W **Me and my Gal** back; the 14-month veteran had originally been called **Assend**, but was changed thanks to Col. Leber's rather stuffy mind set on such titles. Progressive power loss finally induced Lt. Elmer B. Wulf to bail out his crew. He was unable to find his chest pack and with thick Belgian woodland below, his steadily-sinking bomber now appeared to be facing severe injury or death. At the last moment, a narrow treeless slope was encountered onto which the B-17 was desperately aimed with lowered gear.

The rocky surface literally ground the lower fuselage away after the gear collapsed, but left the cockpit compartment intact, out of which the pilot scrambled. Elsewhere, one of the diverting bombers (43-37657/GD: I **The Fox**) was similarly facing "salvage" action after eight months combat service; loss of two engines thanks to equal doses of mechanical failure and flak had culminated in one catching fire as the out-of-formation B-17 piloted by Lt. Anderson headed back at low altitude. All but the pilot jumped clear, leaving the latter to get his charge down safely.

The second half of the month commenced with a run of five missions in six days, although the 1AD's intention to attack Ruhland's oil production plant was thwarted by weather. However, similar facilities at Gelsenkirchen (16th) and Dortmund/Hoesch (19th) were attacked by the 1CBW, while in between an intended assault on a plant at Boehlen (17th) was recalled during Assembly. The seven missions flown by the Wing since Berlin had been loss free, but this run was broken on the 20th, during the protracted run to Nuremberg's marshalling yards.

The 91BG's 42-102490/OR: V **Wicked Witch** had regularly served as a Lead bomber during its ten-month tenure of service with 70 missions completed. Although the flak barrage was described as "meager," it was sufficient to claim two Division victims as the formations headed for the Rally point, one being OR: V. A strike under the forward fuselage started a fire and no parachutes were observed before the plunging B-17 disappeared; as it was, one-third of Lt. Edward Knight's crew did bail out, but the pilot was among the remaining six who were killed during what was their 11th mission in **Wicked Witch**.

The daily run of missions commenced on the 19th now extended to the month end, during which the overall MIA percentage was virtually nil at 17 out of over 8,000 completed sorties, although to these were added a number of incidents involving crews during Assembly or return to England. The 1CBW nearly achieved a perfect survival rate with the exception of a 398BG B-17 that was lost on the 22nd during a mission to Stendal. Lt. Hubert F. Beatty's 43-39128/N8: M was set on fire between the port side engines and swiftly blew apart. All three officers were killed, unlike the six Enlisted men, who parachuted down near Brome, NE of Brunswick.

The bomber's fate had been sealed by the latest and arguably most deadly weapon in the *Jagdwaffe's* armament—the jet-propelled Me262. The sleek twin-engine design with its rakish overall outline and shark-like fuselage had fortunately not even entered front line service until late 1944. Even so, the relatively few examples on hand could easily out-perform any Allied escort and make short shrift of any lumbering B-17 or B-24 falling foul of their standard 30mm cannon armament augmented sometimes by R4M rockets mounted under the wings.

The landing of a still fully-laden B-17 was ever hazardous, as the pilots on the 534BS' Ice Col' Katy discovered. The starboard main landing gear folded up and the crew were fortunate that the bomb load remained in place. As it was, the B-17G was brought back to operational status and returned home after VE-Day. The incident occurred on 30 November 1944.

The combat-scarred airframe of Egg Haid (42-97511/MS: K) is snapped as it participates in one of its many missions. The 535BS-assigned B-17G arrived at Ridgewell in February 1944 and soldiered on until the following 21 January, when all nine on Lt. James E. Smith's crew were lost in a tragically banal manner – a mid-air collision over the airfield circuit.

The 65th mission for 42-97061/LL: B General Ike could have ended in disaster following the "runaway" propeller on No. 3 engine that finally detached itself and slammed into the fuselage with this result. The copilot (Lt. Lewis Ellis) was particularly fortunate to escape injury or death; he and Lt. Will Carter (P) are among the personnel examining the damage.

On 1 February 1945, Lt. Kuhns "aborted" the mission, but his attempted landing in the veteran 535BS bomber Julie Linda went badly awry; the aircraft veered off the runway and flattened make-shift ground crew huts before grinding to a shattered halt. The pilot was reportedly reduced to copilot status.

The impressive array of mission symbols on this 602BS B-17 (42-102593) would grow to a final total of 108 by VE-Day, nearly matching the other group "centenarian" that amassed 116 missions. The absence of the chin turret on some 398BG aircraft was matched within the 1CBW's other two units, who selectively deleted ball turrets from their establishment.

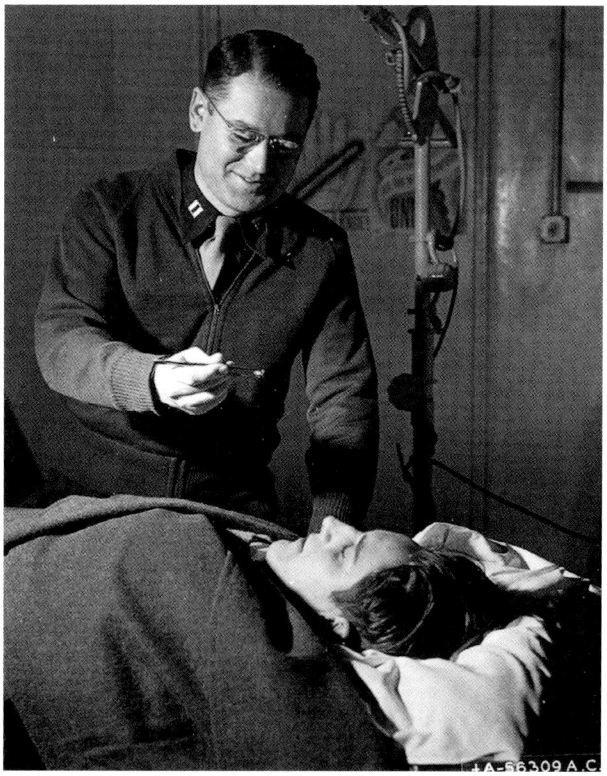

Capt. Paul F. Minor, a Flight Surgeon with the 91BG, holds the fragment of a flak shell that he just extracted from Sgt. Clarence Hing's (TG) left thigh. The high-velocity pace of such shards when impacting with the body all too often led to death or very serious injury.

Lt/Col. Emanuel J. Klette, 324BS CO is here flanked by Gen. Gross (CG, 1CBW) and Maj. Hudson (right). He originally flew in the 306BG, with whom he survived a horrendous crash that should have ended his combat days. He recovered and in fact put in 91 missions in all; KWH (44-8588/DF: E) served between late January and VE-Day.

The bulk of maintenance work on USAAF aircraft in Britain was conducted outdoors, but initially without the benefit of lights during nocturnal hours. The photograph of this flood-lit Ridgewell B-17 is clear evidence of a late-war period when the threat of Luftwaffe assaults had virtually disappeared.

The partially-concealed title of this B-17G from Bassingbourn is Blood n' Guts emblazoned across the forward fuselage; the words may be a reference to Gen. George Patton's nickname. The 401BS bomber served the group between September 1944 and VE-Day.

By early 1945, the virtual demise of the Jagdwaffe's strength in aircraft numbers combined with the equal reduction in its pilots' operational quality led to the 8AF hierarchy decreeing that bomber defensive capability could be reduced. The 381BG responded by removing the ball turrets on selected aircraft, as seen on 44-6625/GD: J of the 534BS.

K8: N arrived at Nuthampstead in late January and operated up to VE-Day, after which it joined hundreds of its contemporaries in heading home for ultimate "scrapping." The red wing tips and fin center section stand out, as does the large-scale aircraft letter on the fin.

Maj. Charles Hudson has every reason to be wearing a big grin, since he has just completed his final mission on 22 February 1945. He had served at Bassingbourn since October 1943, rising to the post of Group Bombardier as well as being awarded the DSC and DFC in the process.

Ramblin' Rebel (43-37540) arrived at Bassingbourn and commenced operations on the eve of D-Day. She was assigned to the 323BS, but changed her aircraft letter from B to Z in the course of the ensuing eleven months of the bombing campaign. She was finally abandoned on the Continent while flying repatriation missions following VE-Day.

An early February 1945 assignment to Nuthampstead and the 602BS, K8: H is caught unloading a string of 1,000-lb bombs. A runway over-shoot on 21 April witnessed its subsequent repair, although its services were by then probably redundant, with the Daylight Offensive's conclusion four days later. It was flown home two months later.

The reduction to "salvage" status for USAAF aircraft did not mean their immediate removal to a scrap yard. In this instance 43-38075, a 603BS B-17G that "nosed over" at Nuthampstead in early November, is serving as a "Hangar Queen" from which parts will be removed for inclusion on operational aircraft.

What is a beautiful but lethal scenario is being acted out over Berlin by the 91BG. The Lead B-17's target-marker flares exude their arcing smoke-trails and the twin visible bomb-loads are being salvoed to hopefully provide a solid strike-pattern upon the Primary. Silver-finish and Cheyenne tail gun positions are evident in this early 1945 picture.

Sgt. Howard Wilson holds the Meritorious Service-Unit shield awarded the 448th Sub-Depot—the very first to be gained within the European Theater of Operations. This achievement had been preceded by the sub-unit winning the 1BD's Stitt Trophy for proficiency three months in a row the previous Fall, along with permanent possession of the Cup! Picture is dated 20 February 1945 and Sgt. F. Kennedy is the other airmen on view.

Chapter Fifteen
"Killing the Cow"

March 1945

The daily mission run during late February was carried over into March as far as the 5th. The pusillanimous response of the German defenses to the aerial offensive was reflected even when the most fearsome Primaries were assaulted; for example Berlin, on 26 February, culled a mere three bomber crews out of nearly 800. No relaxation in effort either by the ground or air resources of the Allies could be assumed, however, since there was no indication of the Nazi hierarchy accepting the "unconditional surrender" terms first mooted at Casablanca in January 1943. The entire enemy hinterland would have to be occupied before that positive conclusion could be guaranteed to be reached.

Plans for the forging of the Rhine, which presented a massive fluid barrier to gaining unfettered access to central Germany for the Anglo/American armies, were well in hand, and by the month end would be fully and successfully implemented. Meanwhile, the enemy's oil production plants and transportation system, particularly marshalling yards, continued to merit top priority for attack.

March 1945 would witness 25 out of the 31 days having the 8AF launch missions with a Wing average of 22 aircraft utilized. The overall loss factor for all three Divisions continued to be statistically minimal on the 2nd, when the 1AD lost three out of fourteen MIA crews. The sporadic nature of *Jagdwaffe* intervention proved no consolation for all but one on Lt. Donald R. Christensen's 398BG crew this day.

B-17 44-6573/N7: K was lagging behind the formation, even after being forced to salvo its load in a bid to regain position, and was easy prey when pounced upon. The fighter's gunfire impacted with the rear fuselage and blew it away; the aerodynamic imbalance sent the main airframe out of control and resulted in none of the eight hapless occupants of the main fuselage section bailing out. Only Sgt. Selmer K. Haakensen, in the tail gun position, was fortunate enough to remain unscathed from the fusillade of fire as well as emerge from what was a potential tomb and deploy his parachute.

"Kick where you see a head"

On the 8th, the 1CBW headed for the August Viktoria oil plant at Huels, in the Ruehr, with 111 crews listed as striking the Primary. That figure should have been increased by one in the form of Lt. Charles "Hotrock" Carpenter and crew in 44-6883/MS: Q **RAFAAF**. This team had taken off in another B-17, but was forced to "abort" due to technical malfunction. After landing, they rushed over to their current mount and went aloft in the finally vain hope of catching up with the Ridgewell formation. This effort appeared to have borne fruit when a mass of fly-like specks were sighted at altitude, but on drawing within recognition range evolved not into B-17s, but as its mighty RAF contemporary, the Lancaster.

Nothing daunted and working on the principle that delivering the bomb load was the absolute priority, Carpenter linked up with his Allies and duly released on their assigned target at Köln. It appears that the RAF crews only then noticed their 8AF "buddy," but the return flight evolved into regular radio chatter while two Lancasters closed in to form a close "escort." On landing at Ridgewell, the pilot claimed that the aforementioned name was already marked up on the nose—a neat but probably the one apocryphal aspect of the incident. When asked why he took this option, he drily responded: "Daylight bombing is our forte, and I could not let the RAF think it could do better!"

The Wing had suffered one loss to date during what would be the penultimate month of combat operations, but the Grim Reaper struck again on the 9th, culling two crews during the mission to Kassel. The first half of the month would witness a niggling series of single losses at Nuthampstead, the second of which was 42-97810/K8: S, an "original" bomber. Whereas all but one of the Christensen crew had died, this time round only Lt. Gene F. Clinesmith (N) lost his life among Lt. Willard G. Jacobs's crew. The lagging B-17 was last observed with little apparent damage, and in fact was finally put down near Fritzlar, SW of the Primary. However, only seven of the survivors were apprehended, with Lt. Henry B. Hardenburg evading capture.

Ridgewell surrendered 43-39012/ VE: J **Miss Fortune** to the flak gunners. A burst around No. 3 engine saw fire taking an irresistible hold on the starboard inner wing and flames streamed back along the fuselage as the unfortunately-named aircraft sagged out of formation. Two parachutes were seen prior to the bomber's descent being peremptorily halted some 10,000ft lower by its disintegration; Lt. Paul J. Scherman joined his six other colleagues in a communion of death, with the wreckage littering the ground near Fritzlar.

The Wing was involved in three subsequent missions where no losses were incurred, but this respite from loss was short-lived, especially at Nuthampstead, where single casualties were incurred on two successive days beginning on the 14th. The group had been assigned to attack Osnabrueck and the now-standard force of 37 crews headed east. The bomb run was barely completed when the No. 3 engine on 43-37825/N7: J, a group veteran B-17, was hit by a flak shell. Fire was observed in the bomb bay as it fell away and shortly after it exploded. In that time, four on Lt. Richard F. Ellis's crew got clear either by jumping or being blown out into mid-air; the pilot and the remaining four on board were not so fortunate.

Oranienburg lies near Berlin's NW fringe and was targeted by the Wing and 351BG next day. The flak barrage over the town's marshalling yards succeeded in culling Lt. Andrew R. Thomas's 43-38562/ N7: L **Kitty, Kay and Katy**, one of the 145 bombers. One engine was disabled by the burst and the same steady descent and swift disintegration signalled the B-17's demise. Sgts. James B. Pettibone (Eng.) and Anthony J. Buddess (ROG) shared the fate of their pilot, but five other crewmembers succeeded in exiting safely.

Lt. "Hotrock" Carpenter was flying his 34th and penultimate mission with the 381BG, but he and his crew were fortunate to return home this day. The flak gunners landed a strike on 43-37561/VE: J that virtually demolished the radio room, although leaving its occupant alive. In contrast, Sgt. Walter Ahl (WG) was killed instantly by the blast, which also tore a 15-foot rent in the starboard fuselage and jammed all control cables to the rudder and elevators. There was no hope of bailing out all on board, as several packs had been destroyed or shredded.

In spite of this catalogue of disaster, the pilots managed to retain control and finally brought their charge back to the RAF Emergency airfield at Manston, on the Channel coast. The landing effort now went badly, albeit not fatally awry; no sooner had the wheels made contact with the runway then the landing gear collapsed and the resultant hard impact, coupled with the seriously fractured fuselage frame, saw the tail section detach completely; fire also erupted in two engines. As it was, all on board managed to scramble out; however, the pilot coolly insisted on carrying out a crew muster even as the nearby burning wreck was being attended to by several fire trucks!

Odds Ever Against

The odds against surviving a combat tour were by now tending to noticeably shorten, even compared with the latter part of 1944, and were immeasurably improved compared to the 1943 "Autumn Crisis" and the succeeding 1943/44 winter spell. But there was never a total guarantee of immunity from "Kriegydom" or the ultimate sanction of death, as would be evidenced during the 22 March mission to Dorsten and Feldhausen's military encampment sites.

Capt. George Stone, a 533BS Lead navigator, had amassed 49 missions and was on board the Lead bomber (44-8175/ VE: P) piloted by Lt. Robert D. Fawcett with Capt. Robert J. Gotthardt in the right seat as Air Commander. Also on board was Lt. Pete Kowalski, holder of the Silver Star, as well as another veteran Lt. Elbert W. Hiller flying as "Mickey" operator; a further two officers were part of the ten-man team.

The flak barrage during the bomb run was initially desultory, but ominously built up in force and accuracy as the target was looming. It was then that a shell impacted between the fuselage and No. 3 engine, setting the inner fuel tank on fire. The B-17 entered into a slow but constant spinning motion that placed increasing stress on the airframe and after several turns the inevitable fracturing of the airframe occurred.

The optimistic reports of up to six parachutes deploying proved tragically inaccurate and the MIA entry placed with each crewmember's record was confirmed as absolute by the following summer, with all ten listed as dead. The shock effect among the Ridgewell personnel was almost palpable and took some days to dissipate; Capts. Gotthardt and Stone in particular had been highly regarded even outside their squadron's ranks.

"Bouncing the Rhine"

Two days later, the anticipated breaching of the Rhine north of the Ruehr was commenced by the Anglo/American forces under Gen. Montgomery's overall command. The 2AD was called upon to attack a number of airfields or to drop supplies to the Allied parachute Divisions who were spearheading operation *Varsity*. The B-17 Divisions added to the range of airfields to be assaulted, with Achmer and Vechta feeling the 1CBW's effect during the first mission and Twente /Enschede in Holland struck on a second run. Even by nightfall on the 24th, it was clear that the onrush of armor with infantry/ artillery support was unrelenting, and was furthermore in no danger of being halted, let alone thrown back. The die was cast for the final demise of the Third Reich.

The day's first run had cost the 381BG one crew flying in 44-6478/VP: W and led by Lt. Robert Jankowiak. Flak demolished No. 4 engine and the wing erupted in flames. The bomb load was salvoed and a gentle dive initiated to hopefully extinguish the fire but this failed, in addition to which the bomber began to enter a spinning motion. A bail out was called for, and once the pilot was satisfied all other eight were gone he attempted to follow suit.

Emerging from the nose hatch, his body was slammed against the fuselage and his hand holding the ripcord pulled tight; the resultant deployment of the canopy saw it streaming back to anchor itself against some obstruction. The apparent lethal fate awaiting the pilot was miraculously stayed when an explosion snapped off the tail section and equally miraculously allowed the largely-intact canopy to detach itself and bear its human load to a safe if bumpy landing. The Lieutenant's fortune was sadly not matched by four of his crew.

Five further March missions would be completed by the 8AF, although adverse weather on the 25th restricted operations to the 2AD; the following two runs (26th and 28th) involved the two B-17 Divisions alone. In addition, only five 1AD groups went out to Zeitz on the first occasion, one of which was the 381BG, but it was a different matter two days later when the latest thrust at *Big B* was initiated. The full 1AD strength was dispatched, the bulk of which, including the 1CBW, attacked a munitions plant at Spandau, losing just two crews out of 318.

The mention of Bremen at any briefing had hitherto caused apprehension among the personnel, as it had ranked alongside Berlin and Hamburg in exacting a high price in bombers and crews. One of Ridgewell's teams sitting in the Briefing hut contained several members who had already survived the loss of their B-17 on 1 January, with all bailing out safely. However, Lt. Alexander D. Nelson, now CP on Lt. Robert A. Bennett's team, had vowed never to repeat the exercise, regardless of what might transpire. Their bomber today was the veteran 42-102590/MS: M **In Like Errol** that had operated since May 1944, and was now under the charge of S/Sgt. Dave Martin's ground crew.

Bennett's normal nine-man complement was increased by Sgt. Charles L. Majors, who was acting as "spot jammer" against enemy radio/radar signals. The clear visual conditions allowed for a sound bomb concentration on the city's submarine yards delivered by over 400 B-17s and all in the face of a flak barrage regarded as "inaccurate," if still quite heavy. Several hours later, all but one crew was safely ensconced in their debriefing rooms, although several unfortunate individuals were lying in a base morgue, having been struck by flak fragments. The one full crew exception was on board **Errol**.

During the bomb run, successive loss of two engines to the flak had resulted in a steady but controlled descent. Whatever the pilots' ultimate intention was, the situation was resolved in a brutal fashion by a Me262. The *Jagdwaffe* fighter made a pass from twelve o'clock that was delivered despite the belated intervention of a P-51 approaching from a roughly 9 o'clock angle in relation to the bomber and attempting to divert the German pilot. The 30mm cannon barrage delivered by the Me262 swiftly reduced the B-17 to a wreck and it began to go out of control; nine of the crew did manage to bail out, the exception being Lt. Nelson, who "went in" with the aircraft at Syke. Whether he had "frozen" at his station or been trapped by centrifugal forces is an eternally unanswered question.

Tragedy, with respective immediate and ultimate effect, came the way of two further airmen. Sgt. Charles F. Knaus (TG) had not survived, and for whatever reason it was generally regarded among most of the survivors that he had been stoned to death by civilians. In fact, Sgt. Majors, after being apprehended, was escorted over to his colleague's body, where he confirmed that his demise was caused by a parachute that did not deploy.

The other fatality was not destined to be confirmed for almost a decade. T/ Sgt. Chester M. Slomczenski (Eng.) was of Polish/American stock and had vowed to pass himself off as a "forced laborer" or similar non-German individual in the event of being shot down. No further word of his fate came to hand by VE-Day and his listing as MIA was confirmed. It was only in 1954 that his body was disinterred from a crude grave, thereby confirming that he had been one more among countless victims of "summary justice." The news meant that his family's torment of uncertainty had now been somewhat assuaged, albeit never totally extinguished—a fact stated to the author by Chester's younger brother, Frank, during a 381BGMA reunion.

The final monthly run was directed at German oil production that by now was virtually moribund; three Primaries around Merseburg/Leuna were targeted, but in the 1AD's case, its force had recourse to striking the Secondary, consisting of Halle's marshalling yards—an element of another enemy target category that had been battered into a similar state of virtual immobility.

April 1945

The Daylight Offensive was in almost measurable sight of completion as April was entered. The respective advances of the Soviet armies from the east and their Anglo/American contemporaries heading into Germany's rapidly-shrinking perimeters from the opposite direction were having an effect in terms of available strategic targets. The average of fifteen missions flown by the 1CBW during the month probably reflected this key factor in the campaign's prosecution; marshalling yards were the main target category that could be regarded as strategic, with airfields, munitions, and oil depots making up the bulk of the remaining selected Primaries.

The Wing's first mission (4th) was a strike on airfields at Fassberg and Reinsehlen, followed next day by a run to a munitions depot at Grafenwohr; a day's pause, and the bombers were in the air again to assault Fassberg and Kohlenbissen's airfields. All crews returned safely from this trio of missions, and indeed, 1AD losses overall were a mere two crews MIA. It had been 31 missions since the 91BG had suffered in this manner, so the briefing on the 8th for marshalling yards at Stendal, with the other two groups heading for an oil depot at Derben, was probably accepted in a calm if not blasé manner by the assembled personnel that included the crews led by Lts. Robert E. Fuller and Peter A. Pastras.

The former-named officer and his team were to fly aboard a true veteran B-17, 42-31333/LG: W **Wee Willie**. This bomber had arrived in late December 1943 and ploughed its way through the early period of 1944, when losses were still heavy; now, it was about to commence its 128th combat mission. The Pastras-crewed bomber was another long-term survivor from May 1944 (42-102504/LL: D **Times A-Wastin'**) that was now almost a centenarian in mission terms. The Reaper was ever lurking, however.

The Fuller crew had flown **Wee Willie** on the last four missions and was holding formation during the bomb run when a flak shell impacted around the juncture of the fuselage and port wing. The ignition of the inner fuel tank was followed almost at once by a huge explosion that excised the entire wing, causing it to flip up above the remainder of the airframe. The wreckage tumbled helplessly for several seconds before the main section in turn tore itself apart. In these circumstances, it was felt that none of the nine airmen could have survived the blast, a fact that held true for all. (A strike camera on board another bomber caught the tragic incident as it "fired off" pictures at several-second intervals.)

Fate was almost as comprehensively cruel in consuming all but two on Lt. Pastras's B-17 after flak dealt it a death blow. In this instance, the bomber caught fire, but was still being held in level flight, as up to five airmen were reported safely exiting and pulling their ripcords. Sadly, only T/Sgts. Lyle D. Jones (Eng.) and Robert A. Smith (ROG) were later found to have ended up in a POW camp; whether any of the other three were dealt with summarily once they were down is unclear. The remaining four were killed either by the flak strike, or after the bomber exploded when close to the ground.

The Nuthampstead contingent of 30 crews making the bomb run was short by one several hours later, while a second crew was lacking its tail gunner in horrendous circumstances for that hapless airman. The group was turning off the target at Derben when the final flak volley included a shell that impacted between the port side engines on 44-83276 /N8: N. A similar severance of the port wing as experienced by **Wee Willie** occurred, but in addition, the fuselage snapped off behind the ball turret; the ten occupants would have had little opportunity to make a wholesale exit in these circumstances and only Sgt. Robert A. Templeton (WG) alone out of Lt. William E. Wells, Jr.'s team was to be granted the precious gift of life.

Lt. Edwin B. Daily was piloting 44-8811/N8: G (a PFF B-17) as the Low squadron Lead when a flak burst blew off the entire rudder and tail gunner's position in line with the fixed portion of the fin, as well as badly shredding the elevators. In spite of this severe scale of damage, the bomber was kept aloft and brought all the way back for what must have been a potentially fraught but successful landing. What had been its first mission now proved to be its last, since the airframe was deemed fit only for salvage on the 10th! A second group B-17 was so badly damaged in terms of its control efficiency that the pilots were advised to divert to RAF Woodbridge after their landing approach to Nuthampstead proved to be potentially lethal in execution; the extra runway length there proved to be more than sufficient to accommodate a safe landing.

All three Wing units bore casualties today, which in the 381BG's case further heightened the sense of frustration at what was clearly a bombing result going badly awry. To date, the group had lost 130 crews declared MIA and unknown to all was that the final crew falling into this category was incurred here. **Miss Florala** (44-6173/GD: H), with Lt. Adelmeyer and crew, had suffered flak damage over the Primary, but remained in formation until approaching the region around Goettingen and Kassel. It was then that fire blossomed from No. 3 engine; the attempt to extinguish the flames by a controlled dive had the reverse effect of spreading the flames, followed by the wing spar giving way.

The B-17's plunge to destruction at Goettingen permitted only Sgts. Deward P. Houser (TG) and James H. Hayden (ROG) to scramble clear prior to impact; a third parachute was reported at debriefing, but without the same positive outcome for its bearer. The two airmen were quickly able to regain Allied lines, such was the proximity of the battlefront to where they descended. In this manner was Ridgewell's blood debt finally settled, albeit only in terms of combat operations, as events fifteen days later would confirm.

The third of five daily Wing missions proved to be free of loss, but the next day's run to Oranienburg left the 398BG short one crew, as well as setting up a three-mission sequence of MIA casualties for the group. The virtually eroded ranks of the *Jagdwaffe* did not prevent the pilots operating the Me262 from making their daunting presence felt and one of their victims was probably 43-38853/N8: L. Lt. James W. McAfee's B-17 was seen to drift out of formation after one pass and at some stage disintegrated in mid-air; four Enlisted men out of the ten-man crew emerged alive at some stage of their bomber's extinction.

Next day, a munitions plant at Kraiburg and Freihan's marshalling yards were targeted at the cost of a single B-17, the bomber in question being 43-38664/K8: P. A serious power loss during run-up to Kraiburg culminated in Lt. Arthur C. Shirk ordering his crew out as his charge began to fade away. Then, along with Lt. John F. Schmid (CP), he sought out a suitable site for crash landing, a bid that ended successfully, both airmen were apprehended; their luck was only shared by five of the other eight crewmembers, with the circumstances under which the trio of deaths occurred not clear.

RAFAAF's Luck

The 535BS' 44-6883/MS: Q **RAFAAF** had a somewhat eventful combat career during its seven-week sojourn at Ridgewell. Its involuntary involvement with the RAF on 9 March while in Lt. Carpenter's hands had been followed by a "runaway" propeller on No. 3 engine that ended with the errant unit separating and chewing up the forward cowling on 24 March. Today's mission to Freihan would test both aircraft and crew's courage and skill to the utmost, however.

The group was homeward bound and flying tight formation, but this operational factor would be the catalyst for a potentially fatal outcome. S/Sgt. Jack Prillaman, Tail Gunner to Lt. Turner Brashear, flew with their B-17 in No. 3 position to Capt. Garrett (squadron Lead) in 44-8826/MS: P. Suddenly, Garrett's bomber sagged downward, and although Prillaman and S/Sgt. Joe Norcom (WG) urgently informed the pilots of this wayward motion, no corrective action became possible before the other B-17's port wing tip impacted with **RAFAAF**'s starboard stabilizer. The effect was the same as a guillotine, because the entire sub-unit was sliced off at its juncture with the fuselage.

MS: P, although suffering bending of the outer aileron, managed to remain in level flight. Not so its "victim" that entered into a flat spin, tossing its crew around in the process. The pilots, for example, were pinned to the ceiling and Brashear recalled that he had to literally pull himself back down via the control column. Once in position, he and Lt. Robert Horn finally succeeded in arresting the spin motion, but this far from ended the crisis. The B-17's tendency to develop a nose up attitude soon proved to be a physical drag that had Brashear considering a bail out, an option that none on board accepted when it was then proposed.

The pilot had T/Sgt. "Red" Edwards (Eng.) utilize a length of cable that was passed through two instrument panel dials that were removed, then fed back around the control columns to make two loops. A square knot was formed and a crude turnbuckle created with the inclusion of a machine gun part. Rotation of the part permitted basic control of the port elevator, but the extreme pressure meant that the instrument panel was bowed out, although not finally giving way during the prolonged return leg that took upwards of four hours to complete.

Arrival over Ridgewell was followed by a series of circuits while the pilots decided how to bring their badly-crippled bomber down—not for a crash landing, but rather a conventional wheels down effort. Col. Hall (Group CO) advised Brashear to bail out the crew and abandon the B-17 over the coast in the same manner as the 534BS' **Whodat** one year previous. However, unlike the latter B-17, whose control surfaces were intact, the damagescale incurred here cast up the distinct likelihood of the pilots failing to get clear before **RAFAAF** snapped out of control. As it was, the crew again stuck with their decision to stay on board.

The inability to safely reduce airspeed below 140 ASI dictated a lengthy and flat approach to the runway, while the crude form of elevation control required the utmost of coordination between the pilots: Horn delicately manipulated the throttles while Brashear similarly manipulated the *ad hoc* controls. There was no question of an overshoot—it was all or nothing now, as the B-17 was painfully guided in towards the runway. As the threshold was over-flown, the copilot applied full flap while pulling back on the throttles.

The aircraft settled down on the runway, and although travelling at this greatly-increased rate was still brought to a halt before overshooting. **RAFAAF** had stood up to its most severe aerodynamic test, as well as providing full salvation for nine extremely grateful combat personnel! (MS: P had also returned to a safe landing, although the twisted aileron frame must have created a degree of difficulty in the process.)

Last Lap Fortunes

The Wing's full participation commenced on 4 April would continue for seven of the eight missions still to be flown prior to the Daylight Offensive's closure on the 25th. The first of these brought a particularly hard rebuff to the 398BG that moreover was self incurred. The bomb run over Neumunster's marshalling yards was being discharged in good order when one bombardier salvoed his load. What now transpired was a mighty explosion several hundred feet below the Lead squadron that was most likely caused by two or more of the closely-packed load coming into contact with one another.

The blast effect struck home in varying degrees among the sub-unit, most seriously against two bombers. The first was 43-39184/3O: U, containing Lt. Emil J. Martinek's eight-man crew. Lt. Theodore A. Kline (CP) and T/Sgt. Floyd R. Aaron (Eng.) lost their lives, while their more fortunate colleagues got clear before the B-17 piled in at Bad Oldesloe. The other crew, led by Lt. Samuel H. Palant, were more fortunate, in that not only did all ten safely evacuate from their fire-stricken bomber 44-8636/3O: X, but the pilot also evaded capture to quickly regain Allied lines. Four further B-17s were missing from the original 31-strong force on return, but news gradually filtered in that all had managed to remain airborne and seek airfields on the Continent. The Grim Reaper had largely stayed his hand among the Nuthampstead personnel, but was not yet finished, as two further crews would discover.

The Third Reich was clearly in its death throes as the Allied Armies squeezed the life out of the remaining national zones still under its control. The search for suitable targets upon which to focus the 8AF's "heavies" was almost at a redundant level and was switched over the ensuing 48 hours to a totally different region in the form of SW France, where the Germans were still holding out around Bordeaux. The 1CBW was excluded on the 14th, but 24 hours later was part of the overall force battering defensive sites at Royan, on the Gironde estuary. Railroad facilities at Regensburg and Landshut were assaulted next day, as were similar facilities at Dresden (17th). Whereas the previous two missions had left the 1AD intact, today saw six out of the 428 raiders going down.

The 91BG had been party to 196 crews falling into the MIA list since it commenced operations, and now this sorry account was closed with the demise of 44-6568 / DF: G **Skunkface III**. The first of its two predecessors had been lost in action, whereas its replacement had survived operations with the 95th and 379BG before serving at Bassingbourn as a radio relay machine. The present owner of the title had served for just over four months, during which it had amassed a figure of over 50 missions and was now in the hands of a veteran crew headed by Lt. Harry Camp.

The final remnants of the *Jagdwaffe* in the form of the Me262 were airborne, and several of this redoubtable fighter's pilots homed in on the group as the bomb run was commenced. The colossal disparity in performance between fighter and its prey allied with the need to fly a steady course from the IP ensured that the bombers were even more prone to lethal intervention, as proved to be the case for **Skunkface III**. However, the damage to its port wing, although sending the B-17 out of formation and down, did not totally align itself with the subsequent fact that only one out of the nine airmen—Sgt. Herman Evans (TG)—survived the incident: death from the gunfire fusillade; failure to bail out in the event of the B-17 going out of control; and "summary justice" from the enemy for any one of the other seven reaching the ground alive. None of these factors appears to have been either confirmed or eliminated from this ever-grim equation. Sufficient to say, that seven young Americans died for the immeasurable cause of freedom.

"Anonymous" Debacle

The ground crew at Ridgewell were typical of those serving within the 8AF, or any other airborne-based entity, in that they pursued their vital duties of maintaining the aircraft in top of the line order with little or none of the publicity directed towards the combat crews. The staff had borne the loss of sixteen personnel during preparations for the second group mission on 23 June 1943, when a 533BS bomber had obliterated their lives following the detonation of its bomb load. Now, an even greater human catastrophe was about to occur with the Daylight Campaign within two days of conclusion.

Capt. Charles E. Ackerman was a 534BS pilot who had survived one combat tour and was now engaged in his second. The squadron's 43-38856/GD: M was on hand on the 23rd for him to fly to Northern Ireland. Along with a "scratch crew" of four, he prepared the B-17 for the flight, which was to transport 26 group personnel on a Rest and Recreation visit. Among the number was Lt. Martin Matyas (N) and a close friend to his crew's "togglier," S/Sgt. Herb Kwart. The relatively clear visibility forecast over the Irish Sea promised a relaxed passage to their destination and the bomber duly lifted off and headed westward.

The Isle of Man lies between England and Ireland and is an undulating landmass; even so, there was no obvious reason why its highest level should have intervened to bring the B-17 into violent and fatal contact, along with its hapless human load. The news of the accident was received with stunned silence at the airfield, but Col. Hall, along with L/Col. Shackley, immediately flew over to the island. The task of bringing the corpses down from the high slopes proved to be protracted due to the lack of roads or even paths, but the RAF staff carried out the grim duty with efficiency. When asked how he wanted the bodies laid out, Col. Hall was reputed to have tersely said: "Three rows of ten and one over"—a seemingly insensitive comment that likely concealed the hurt inflicted on his mind. These broken remnants were "his men," for whom he held the highest respect, given their services in advancing the group's progress in overall operational efficiency.

The majority of the 31 airmen were ground personnel whose ultimate safe return to the states could have been anticipated. Danger had never been totally absent from the bulk of their service at Ridgewell, but now all that immediately awaited them was a collection of grave sites at Madingley Military Cemetery, outside Cambridge. The equally tragic events of 23 June 1943 were now paralleled in terms of human loss, and furthermore, had been cast up with the final 8AF mission barely 48 hours distant. There would be no newspaper headlines for these individuals despite their tremendous—if sadly unsung—contribution to a successful aerial campaign being of equal importance as their airborne contemporaries' efforts. Their only recognition would stem from the grief borne by their kin.

Last Pickings

The author can well remember 25 April 1945, because it was his seventh birthday on what was a brilliantly clear if chilly day in his home town; its Northern Scottish location was hundreds of miles distant from the 8AF airfields where briefings were being conducted at various 1st and 2nd AD locations; the 3AD was not included, and indeed, had unknowingly ended effective operations four days previous. The eight B-17 groups assigned to the mission were heading for a munitions plant and airfield at Pilsen, Czechoslovakia; a total of 307 crews were rostered and duly took off for what was anticipated as a physically draining run extending up to ten hours, but one that was not likely to encounter much enemy resistance.

The *Jagdwaffe's* presence had been virtually nil over the recent run of missions, but the German flak resources were far from ground down. This was the case as the formations finally commenced their bomb runs; although visibility was officially recorded as very good, the Nuthampstead 40-strong force ended up making two bomb runs, a factor that sealed the fate of two B-17s and their crews. The worst affected in terms of human loss was Lt. Allan H. Ferguson, Jr.'s team in 42-97265/K8: G **Godfathers Inc.**, an unfortunate reference to what we now regard as a term applied to the heads of the Mafia.

The fatal outcome for a number of these criminal characters over the decades was now (undeservedly) mirrored in respect of the pilot and five of his seven colleagues; the two survivors were seen to take to their parachutes as the bomber entered into a steep dive to crash near Lidice. The location was where the Nazis literally obliterated the village after shooting the male population and deporting the women and children; this was done in the wake of the assassination in mid-1942 of Reinhard Heydrich, the infamous "Protector" of Bohemia/Moravia. By contrast, only one of the eight airmen on board 43-38652/K8: V **Stinker, Jr.**, flown by Lt. Paul A. Coville, was killed; S/Sgt. Charles B. Walker (BT) was already dead when the other seven took to their parachutes before the flak-afflicted bomber went down.

The returning crews had unknowingly delivered their final blow against the Third Reich's structure; never again would the B-17s and B-24s rise off their airfields to strike at the heart of their obdurate and skilful adversary. The European conflict was destined to reach its long hoped-for conclusion in the Allies' favor within less than two weeks, when the Nazis' now leaderless authority would be sitting at the negotiating table opposite Gen. Eisenhower and his staff in Rheims, France.

Finis

The redeployment of the 8th Air Force from its British-based airfields was put into motion and largely completed within a matter of several weeks. A number of groups were retained for duties on the Continent, but the majority were dispatched back to the United States. In the case of the 1CBW, orders were issued for a return stateside that was activated during the last week of May regarding the aircraft; along with the combat crews went a more fortunate element of the ground crew and other support personnel. The remaining members of each Group's strength faced a more protracted journey homeward in terms of time and method of transport. It was only around the final week in June that the personnel wended their way by railroad transport to the Scottish port of Gourock, on the river Clyde. This was the very same location the "original" veterans among the Bassingbourn and Ridgewell contingents had arrived in Britain back in September 1942 and May 1943, respectively. Then, the likelihood of a swift return to the land of their birth must have seemed as far out of sight as the release date for a long-term prisoner.

As the vessel cleared the coastline of the island land mass with its unpredictable weather patterns that had been their detached "home" for upwards of three years, some would surely dwell on this period in their lives with the thought that their efforts in concert with the combat crews had brought about at least a degree of stability, if not sanity to a physically battered continent and its largely traumatized populations. To paraphrase some of Churchill's words uttered during the parlous months of 1940, the United States, in concert with its Allies, had restored the grounds for democracy and its principles to again launch Western Europe into the "broad, sunlit uplands" of tolerance and respect for one's fellow beings. This was, and will ever be, the priceless legacy gained at such human cost by the American airmen as part of the free nations' successful challenge to mindless and wicked autocracy.

The operational career of 43-38993, a 602BS aircraft, was relatively short and sweet while operating from Nuthampstead. Assigned on 3 January, it was participating in a mission to Chemnitz two calendar months later when it diverted into a Continental airfield, where it was abandoned.

This is the crew led by Lt. Charles "Hotrock" Carpenter who flew an "impromptu" mission with the RAF to Köln on 3 March 1945 in RAFAAF (44-6883/MS: Q). The picture date is quoted as also being 3 March, which would support the pilot's claim that the B-17 already bore the stated artwork; whether true or not, the anecdote is very interesting.

Lt. Hahn's B-17G/44-8811/N8: C has returned from bombing Derben's oil refinery, albeit minus its rudder, part of the starboard elevator, and the tail gun position. The hapless tail gunner was killed, and with severe loss of elevator control to add to the absent rudder, it was an uphill but finally successful effort by the pilots to land back at Nuthampstead.

This NMF B-17G arrived at Ridgewell on 18 January 1945 to be assigned to the 533BS as VP: V. Its operational career was relatively short; on 14 March, it was crash landed near Great Yeldham. Whether or not it was already on fire or caught alight on impact, the result was complete destruction of the main fuselage.

The Alamo (44-8228/MS: L) squats on her dispersal site that has a watery surface in comparison to its snow-covered surroundings at Ridgewell. Although she survived the campaign, she did not return to the USA; instead, she was assigned to the 306BG, which was dispatched to Germany on garrison duties and finished up being salvaged in that country during 1946.

These misshapen bundles on stretchers form a portion of 31 corpses. They are prepared for loading into the 381BG "hack" aircraft that ironically is a survivor from the very first 8AF heavy bomber mission back on 17 August 1942. Then she was Peggy D of the 97BG, but is now stripped of all armament and re-titled Little Rock-ette.

The burnt-out remnants of B-217G 43-38856/GD: M that bore Capt. Charles E. Ackerman (P), along with his scratch crew and their passengers, to their deaths lays strewn less than 100 feet from the highest point on the Isle of Man, into which the bomber impacted. Ackerman was in the process of carrying out a second combat tour with the 381BG.

Ms. Ella Prentice, a staff member of the 1CBW HQ at Bassingbourn, is about to christen B-17G 44-6975, which bears a reference to her name, on 15 April 1945; she is accompanied by Gen. Gross standing by the platform. The bomber, bereft of its chin turret, subsequently transferred to the 381BG, but then remained in Europe as a VIP transport.

Col. Hall (381BG CO) and L/Col. George Shackley (Group Air Executive, on the left) are seen in a deceptively casual pose. They are on the Isle of Man, where 31 of their personnel have been killed while transiting to Northern Ireland on 23 April. They will supervise the removal of their airmen's corpses back for burial at Madingley Military Cemetery.

There was never total security from injury or death while in flight, as is demonstrated here. One of the victims of the Isle of Man crash was S/Sgt.Albert M. Mata, a 535BS gunner. He was snapped during a practice mission in early 1945.

Rotherhithes Revenge (42-31761/VP:O) had been christened by that "Blitzed" London borough's Mayor back in February 1944 and had survived the conflict with some 120 missions to its credit. Now, on 13 May 1945, the Mayor's daughter (5th from right) celebrates this positive situation along with L/Col. Reed (3rd from right) and Maj. Karl Greenlee (right).

The European conflict was over nearly four weeks when this picture was taken outside the Officers Mess at Bassingbourn (4 June). The line-up of RAF and USAAF staff includes the 91BG's current CO, L/Col. Donald Sheeler, who is sitting on the right. This officer had served as the 322BS CO among other posts and had been with the group during the bulk of its time in Britain.

Appendix

Bomb Group Squadron	Codes	COs	Period of Service
91			
322	LG	Col. Stanley T Wray	15.5.42—1.5.43
323	OR	L/Col. William M Reid	1.5.43—23.5.43
324	DF	L/Col. Baskin R Lawrence	23.5.43—25.6.43
401	LL	L/Col. Clemens L Wurzbach	26.6.43—12.12.43
		Col. Claude E Putnam	13.12.43—16.5.44
		Col. Harry W Terry	14.12.44—30.5.45
		L/Col. Donald E Scheeler	31.5.45—June 45

Airfield Occupied
Kimbolton, (12.9.42-13.10.42)
Bassingbourn, Cambridgeshire (14.10. 42-23.6.45)

Bomb Group Squadron	Codes	COs	Period of Service
351			
508	YB	Col. William J Hatcher Jnr.	November 42—Dec. 43
509	RQ	Col. Eugene A Romig	1.1.44—Oct. 44
510	TU	Col. Robert W Burns	Oct. 44—30 Mar. 45
511	DS	Col. Merlin I Carter	30 Mar.—June 45

Airfield Occupied
Polebrook, Northants

Bomb Group Squadron	Codes	COs	Period of Service
381			
532	VE	L/Col. Joseph J Nazzaro	5.1.43—9.1.44
535	OQ/VP	L/Col. Harry P Leber	9.1.44—Jan 45
534	JZ/GD	L/Col. Conway S Hall	Jan 45—June 45
535	PL/MS		

Note Code letters for the 533rd, 534th and 535th revised during early July 1943

Airfield Occupied
Ridgewell, Essex (3.6.43—June 45)

Bomb Group Squadron	Codes	COs	Period of Service
398			
600	N8	Col. Frank P Hunter	1 Mar. 43—23 Jan. 45 (KIA)
601	3O	Col. Lewis P Ensign	29 Jan. 45—18 April 45
602	K8	L/Col. Arthur F Briggs	19 April 45—June 45
603	N7		

Bomb Wing/Division insignia (Introduced July 1943)
A triangle design was applied to fin center sections and starboard upper wing. White was used on camouflaged air frames and black on natural metal finish (NMF) airframes; the arrangement was not universal, since there was at least one exception within the 381BG where a black triangle was applied to the camouflaged wing surface. Group letters placed within the triangles were reversed in color and were as follows:

91BG-A 351BG - J 381BG—L 398BG- W

1CBW Color Markings (Introduced July 1944)
Red applied to stabilizers, fin center section, and wing tips.

Color Photo Gallery

The somewhat flimsy nature of a USAAF airfield's flag pole in no way diminishes the presence of "Old Glory" as it is fully unfurled by a typical East Anglian breeze. An Element of B-17s breaking into the circuit forms an appropriate background to the national emblem.

A party of Air Training Corps (ATC) cadets are visiting Ridgewell sometime in 1944. Their assigned officer guide (named as Charles R. McCarthy) is indicating a point of note with the inspected B-17. The cadets' ATC experience provided a sound base for many future RAF volunteers. (A Captain with the 381BG Group HQ bearing the foregoing name is listed as the sub-unit's Adjutant.)

The spiritual requirements for USAAF personnel were attended to by Chaplains. Father Ragan was the Catholic padre at Bassingbourn and is administering comfort to four combat crewmembers prior to their boarding a B-17.

"They're back!" would be the universal cry at 8AF bomber airfields as the waiting throng of airmen on the ground gained their initial sight of the group formation. This scene at Ridgewell catches the first B-17 out of the leading sub-force as it cants into a turn to port that will end with the pilots completing their landing.

Two fireman based at Bassingbourn are wearing the full fire fighting gear; the suits are asbestos-based fire-resistant equipment, while the head gear features rectangularly shaped apertures. A fire truck stands alongside the rear fuselage of 42-97880/DF: F Little Miss Mischief.

The unfortunately blurred face of M/Sgt. George Grose rides his unicycle past T/Sgt. Charles A. "Frenchy" Barbier at Ridgewell. Both were 448th Sub Deport personnel and the latter headed a team that worked for weeks to successfully restore Big Mike (42-39997 /VP: R) to operational condition, after which it was retitled Frenchys Folly!

Capt. Melvin R. Hecker is seen with his wife following his return stateside during 1944. He had served with the 381BG as an "original" pilot, first with the 535BS and subsequently with the 532BS, finishing his combat tour on 8 March 1944.

Sgt. Howard Van Hoozer attends to a waist gun on 42-30721 Sweet and Lovely, now retired from combat duties by mid-1944. Color bands were a visual recognition for the 381BG B-17F that was currently operating as a radio relay base for the 65th Fighter Wing and this unit's involvement in air-sea rescue operations.

The vast majority of maintenance work was outdoors; in this instance, the weather is unusually sunny and dry. A propeller has been removed from a 381BG bomber using a mobile triangular frame with an "endless chain" system. Propellers weighed in at around 450lbs.

Arguably one of the most hazardous aspects of ground crew functions was that "enjoyed" by the armorers. Here, a 2,000-lb bomb is being maneuvered onto a trolley alongside a companion weapon. The B-17's bomb bay could only accommodate this number of such calibre bombs.

Maj. Charles Hudson was assigned as a bombardier to the 91BG in the early autumn of 1943. Over the ensuing seventeen months up to VE-Day, he rose to the position of group Bombardier, in the course of which he was awarded the DSC and DFC.

Little Miss Mischief arrived at Bassingbourn in June 1944. Cpl. Charley Busa (top) and his colleagues are applying the final touches to the newly-introduced 1CBW color markings—fin, stabilizers, and wing tip surfaces sprayed in red. The wing was the first within the 1BD to apply the markings.

S/Sgt. Bill Kreska was an Engineer serving with the 91BG. He is posed alongside his top turret that bears the late-pattern frame with generous Plexiglas viewing panels compared to the original design that was not so well visually configured. Picture believed taken in mid- or late 1944.

Above: A mechanic sitting in the copilot's seat of a 91BG B-17G has just fired-up the No. 3 engine from which a heavy smoke cloud is exuding. In the foreground, his companion stands by with a fire extinguisher, ready to tackle the flames should any malfunction result in fire taking hold.

Left: The mottled shadow of the camouflage netting at Ridgewell's bomb dump casts itself over a bomb-laden trolley. The vehicle in the background is hitched up to a second laden trolley ready to be taken out onto the airfield.

This January 1945 picture is one of a sequence taken on a practice flight, rather than a combat mission. The clue lies in the photographer's B-17, which bears a red outlined Division triangle. The marking was applied to the 381BG "hack" aircraft 41-9043 Little Rock-ette, originally the 97BG's Peggy D; the title was a word play on Col. Hall's (Group CO) birthplace of Little Rock, Arkansas.

The much-battered Peacemaker 43-37552/LL: E) has just landed back at Bassingbourn from the costly mission to Leipzig. Lt. Jim Fletcher (CP) squats on the right as he and his fellow airmen inspect the shot-up port wing surface. The crew would complete their combat tour, but the B-17G would be lost during a "slow time" engine test on 12 April 1945.

Capt. Westwood is seen with a group of 91BG pilots. He is utilizing a set of model B-17s on metal rods that are arranged in formation pattern in order to demonstrate the basic principles behind proper control of the bombers in these circumstances.

The end of a ten-month operational career for 42-97880/DF: F Little Miss Mischief came on 4 April 1945. The landing with a full load following mission "abortion" culminated with the landing gear collapsing. The first view shows the "caterpillar" units under the fuselage with which to move the remains away. The second shot shows the removal of the port outer wing section using a mobile crane.

Above: The lady with the very trim figure ushering a flock of ducks across a Bassingbourn dispersal is an occupant of the farm, one of whose structures can be glimpsed in the right background through the trees. This pacific contrast with the aerial implement of war being worked on by two of its ground crew is very striking.

Left: M/Sgt. Herbert H. Roberts (wearing a reversed cap) is polishing the Plexiglas nose of a Bassingbourn B-17G. The "extra" propeller in the foreground belongs to an L4 Piper Cub observation aircraft whose diminutive frame is visually overwhelmed by its more combat-active contemporary!

In capturing this superb and evocative shot, the photographer has unconsciously pressed the button exactly as the fast-setting sun partially bisects the outline of a B-17G with the pilots "flaring out" their charge prior to making what should be a smooth landing.

Two members of a ground crew are carefully maneuvering a replacement oil tank into a B-17's No. 1 engine nacelle. The linking up of the various pipe and wire connections was no easy matter given the limited space, and was typical of the physical constraints placed upon the airmen tending to the ever-complicated intestines of a WWII aircraft.

The stocky figure of L/Col. Marvin D. Lord is directly below the letter P as he holds a post-flight discussion. The former 381BG pilot and squadron CO is now group Operations Officer with the 91BG, but he will not survive the conflict; he will be killed along with his crew over Berlin on 3 February 1945.

In January 1945, a 381BG formation carried out a publicity flight during which a series of pictures was taken, of which this is one. The 534BS' 44-6163/GD: P in the foreground is Passaic Warrior with a trio of 533BS B-17Gs in the background.

Index

A

Aaron, T/Sgt Floyd R (Eng.) 601BS, 398BG 225

Abbott, Lt. George A (P) 322BS, 91BG 160

Abbott, Sgt George E (T) 601BS, 398BG 183, 191

Abdo, Sgt Ed (BT) 324BS, 91BG 183, 190

Abernathy, Sgt (WG) 533BS, 381BG 131

Abramo, Sgt Nicholas (BT) 533BS, 381BG 72

Ackerman, Lt. Charles E (P) 534BS, 381BG 226, 230

Adams. Lt. Frank L (P) 324BS, 91BG 212

Adams, Lt. Robert W (P) 351BG 34

Adelmeyer, Lt. Harvey E (P) 534BS, 381BG 224

Ahl, Sgt Walter (WG) 535BS, 381BG 222

Alexander, Capt. Joe R (P) 532BS, 381BG 46

Allen, Sgt Charles E (TG) 401BS, 91BG 62

Alhadeff, Lt. Issac N (P) 600BS, 398BG 178

Ambrose, S/Sgt Tuite H (Eng.) 351BG 59

Ammann, Lt. Frank C (P) 401BS, 91BG 101, 140

Anataillia, Sgt Gerard C (BT) 398BG 164

Anders, Lt. (N) 322BS, 91BG 116

Anderson, Lt. (P) 534BS, 381BG 213

Anderson, Lt. Bill (P) 91BG 15

Anderson, Lt. John B (P) 534BS, 381BG 212

Anderson, Lt. John (N) 535BS, 381BG 100

Anderson, Lt. Julius D (P) 401 BS, 91BG 128

Anderson, Lt. Leonard F (P) 322BS, 91BG 99

Anderson, M/Gen. Fred Deputy CG, USSTAF56, 153

Anderson, Sgt Erling (WG) 532BS, 381BG 182

Anderson, S/Sgt Walter J (WG) 532BS, 381BG 48

Antaillia, Sgt Gerard C (BT) 600BS, 398BG 164

Arcaro, Lt. Anthony G (P) 323BS, 91BG 59

Archer, Lt. Randall (CP) 401 BS, 91BG 194

Arnold, Gen. Henry H "Hap" CG, USAAF 15

Arp, Lt. Elwood (P) 401BS, 91BG 71

Askins, Lt. John J (P) 401BS, 91BG 194

Ater, S/Sgt Ray C. Engineer, 381BG 95, 203

Atkinson, Lt. Challon P (P) 533BS, 381BG 59

Aycock, Maj. CO, 324BS, 91BG 40

Ayers, T/Sgt Charlie (C/C) 532BS, 381BG 137

B

Bader, S/Sgt Nathannie (BT) 351BG 29

Baer, Lt. Carl O (P) 535BS, 381BG 108, 111,118

Baer, Maj. Heinz Kommandeur, II/JG1 121

Bailey, Lt. Art (P) 532BS, 381BG 181, 182

Bailey, Lt. Arthur J (P) 533BS, 381BG 161

Baine, Lt. James (B) 324BS, 91BG 107

Baird, Lt. (P) 91BG 39

Baker, Lt. John M (P) 600BS, 398BG 178

Baker, Sgt (G) 532BS, 381BG 61

Baker, T/Sgt Louis T (Combat Crew) 351BG 29

Bakke, Sgt (GC) 534BS, 381BG 82

Ball, Lt. Bob (B) 91BG? 22

Ball, Maj. Clinton (P) 351BG 29, 66

Ballinger, Lt. Olaf M (P) 533BS, 381BG 42

Balmore, Sgt George (ROG) 533BS, 381BG 48, 104, 105

Baltrusaitus, Capt. Bill (P) 532BS, 381BG 41

Bancroft, Sgt Joseph D (TG) 602BS, 398BG 212

Bang, Sgt Charles F (BT) 535BS, 381BG 70

Barbier, M/Sgt Charles A. 448 Sub-depot, 381BG 135, 235

Bare, Lt. Donald K (P) 401BS, 91BG 164

Barker, Lt. Bill (B) 534BS, 381BG 196

Barnicle, Capt. Thomas (P) 535BS, 381BG 178

Barton, Lt. Bruce (P) 91BG 9

Basnight, Lt. Arvin (P) 323BS, 91BG 195

Baxley, Lt. Ed (P) 91BG 27

Beackley, Lt. R G (P) 535BS, 381BG 178

Beardsworth, Lt. Fred L (N) 534BS, 381BG 128
Beasley, Lt. Harold (P) 91BG 25
Beatty, Lt. Hubert F (P) 600BS, 398BG 213
Becker, Lt. (P) 535BS, 381BG 50
Beckman, Lt. Bernard E (P) 532BS, 381BG 136
Bell, Lt. JR (N) 324BS, 91BG 17
Bennett, Lt. Charles A (P) 323BS, 91BG 58
Bennett, Lt. John (P) 323BS, 91BG 43
Bennett, Lt. Robert A (P) 535BS, 381BG 223
Belskis, Lt. Leo I (P) 532BS, 381BG 200
Bennett, Sgt (G) 535BS, 381BG 109
Beran, Lt. John (CP) 323BS, 91BG 122
Berk, Sgt Matthew (WG) 535BS, 381BG 84, 85
Berry, Capt. Kearie L (P) 601BS, 398BG 163
Bettis, Sgt James A (BT) 322BS, 91BG 160
Biggs, Lt. Homer C Jnr, (P) 91BG 27
Birdsong, Lt. George (P) 323BS, 91BG 17, 22, 38, 41, 55, 57
Birlem, Maj. Keith (P) 351BG 28
Black, Lt. Bob (B) 535BS, 381BG 22, 84
Black, Louise, Wife of Lt. Bob Black 22
Blackmon , S/Sgt Bill (WG) 535BS, 381BG 142
Blanton, Lt. Ralph (P) 322BS, 91BG 200
Blaylock, Lt. Conrad H (N) 535BS, 381BG 120
Blaylock, Maj. John R (P) 351BG 84
Blog, Lt. Harold C (P) 532BS, 381BG 144
Bloodgood, Lt. William (P) 401BS, 91BG 10
Blyth, Lt. Donald H (N) 532BS, 381BG 146
Bobrow, Lt. Alan L (P) 91BG 16
Bobrow, Lt. Bob (P) 535BS, 381BG 163
Bohlen, Lt. Frank (B) 322BS, 91BG 180
Bolin, Sgt Robert B (G) 535BS, 381BG 210
Bond, Lt. Leslie A (P) 534BS, 381BG 141
Bone, S/Sgt Thomas S (WG) 91BG 73
Bonnett, Capt. Charles (B) 384BG 32
Borchers, Sgt Doyle C (WG) 602BS, 398BG 164
Borrego, Lt. Bill (CP) 532BS, 381BG 121
Bostick, Lt. Lunn I (CP) 401BS, 91BG 141
Bosley, Sgt Edwin B (WG) 533BS, 381BG 104
Boyd, Lt. Edwin S (P) 351BG 45
Bradford, Lt. Doyle P (P) 323BS, 91BG 126
Bradford, Sgt Joe W (TG) 322BS, 91BG 160
Brant, Lt. Dale E (P) 322BS, 91BG 194
Brashear, Lt. Turner (P) 535BS, 381BG 225
Braund, Lt. Cyril (P) 323BS, 91BG 165
Brazons, Lt. Donald (N) 322BS, 91BG 180
Briggs, Capt. Arthur F (P) 534BS, 381BG 47
Bream, Lt. Burt D (N) 601BS, 398BG 180
Brill, Lt. Allan (P) 91BG 17
Brinton, S/Sgt Charles W (WG) 533BS, 381BG 32
Brodin, Capt. Unite L (P) 603BS, 398BG 145
Brodnax, Lt. Edward T (P) 91BG 34
Broley, Lt. William (P) 322BS, 91BG 27
Brophy, David H (N) 532BS, 381BG 136
Brown, Capt. James G. Group Chaplain, 381BG 123
Brown, Lt. Erwin M (B) 533BS, 381BG 161
Brown, Lt. Hayden T (N/B?) 532BS, 381BG 98, 110
Brown, Lt. Kenneth L (P) 91BG 31
Brown, Lt. Russell H (P) 322BS, 91BG 195
Brown, Lt. Walter (B) 323BS, 91BG 57
Brown, Sgt Loren C (TG) 603BS, 398BG 164
Brummett, Lt. Dudley K (P) 534BS, 381BG 196
Bryan, Lt. George M (CP) 322BS, 91BG 59
Buddess, Sgt Anthony J (ROG) 603BS, 398BG 222
Buescher, Lt. James D (B) 91BG 211
Burch, Capt. Richard W (P) 324BS, 91BG 159
Burgasser, Sgt Herb (BT) 535BS, 381BG 120
Burkhead, Lt. Dale (P) 323BS, 91BG 181
Burne, Lt. Thomas P (P) 322BS, 91BG 195
Burnett, Lt. Paul (N) 322BS, 91BG 9
Burns, Col. Robert W. Deputy CO, 351BG 28, 82
Burns, Lt. Herbert W Jnr. (CP) 535BS, 381 BG 145
Burns, Sgt Wilbur Y (BT) 601BS, 398BG 180
Burton, Lt. Merrill O (P) 533BS, 381BG 146, 147
Burwick, Lt. Norman (P) 323BS, 91BG 148, 165
Busa, Cpl Charlie (GC) 324BS, 91BG 236
Buescher, Lt. James D (B) 323BS, 91BG 211
Butler, Lt. William (P) 532BS, 381BG 98, 110

C

Cahill, Lt. Rodney T (P) 532BS, 381BG 126
Calhoun, Capt. Bill (P) 303BG 73
Camp. Lt. Harry (P) 91BG 226
Campbell, Lt. Robert G (P) 603BS, 398BG 196

Campbell, Sgt Herbert A (WG) 324BS, 91BG 142
Canelake, Lt. Leo I (P) 534BS, 381BG 101
Cantrell, Lt. Theodore (RN) 324BS, 91BG 161
Cappel, Lt. Frank (B) 535BS, 381BG 43
Carah, Lt. John (CP) 533BS, 381BG 42
Carpenter, Lt. Charles "Hotrock" (P) 535BS, 381BG 221, 222, 225, 228
Carqueville, Lt. Herbert (P) 533BS, 381BG 48, 87
Carr, T/Sgt Don (Eng.) 534BS, 381BG 130
Carson, Sgt (G) 535BS, 381BG 109
Carter, Lt. Nigel B (P) 601BS, 398BG 178
Carter, Lt. William (P) 401BS, 91BG 215
Cater, Lt. James C (P) 324BS, 91BG 142
Caset, T/Sgt Percy (GC) 534BS, 381BG 82
Cavalieri, Sgt Rinaldo (WG) 532BS, 381BG 127
Chapin, Lt. Allen J (CP) 535BS, 381BG 60
Chapman, Lt. Frank (P) 535BS, 381BG 74, 108,118
Chase, Sgt (GC) 534BS, 381BG 82
Chason, Lt. Billy F (P) 533BS, 381BG 106
Chevraux, Sgt Raymond F (WG) 532BS, 381BG 103
Chouinard, Lt. Herbert (P) 401BS, 91BG 194
Christensen, Lt. Donald R (P) 603BS, 398BG 221
Christiensen, Lt. Harvey L (B) 535BS, 381BG 120
Christman, Lt. Lloyd A (P) 351BG 87
Churchill, Mary, Daughter of Winston 153
Churchill, Sir Winston S. British Prime Minister 7, 18, 227
Cipalla, S/Sgt Sam (BT) 323BS, 91BG 207
Clark, Lt. (P) 535BS, 381BG 200
Clark, Lt. Carl (P) 535BS, 381BG 70, 129, 157
Clark, Sgt Marvin E (WG) 600BS, 398BG 197
Claytor, Lt. Andrew G (P) 535BS, 381BG 142
Cliborn, Lt. Charles B (P) 91BG 8, 35, 36
Clinesmith, Lt. Gene F (N) 602BS, 398BG 221
Clore, Lt. Cecil (P) 532BS, 381BG 103
Coates, Lt. Robert E (CP) 532BS, 381BG 212
Coen, Lt. John A (P) 324BS, 91BG 18
Coffman, Lt. Alfred T (CP) 535BS, 381BG 120
Cogswell, Lt. Kirch (P) 532BS, 381BG 121
Coleman, Lt. Paris (P) 401BS, 91BG 125
Collett, Capt. Catholic Chaplain, 381BG 136
Collier, Lt. Zack C (P) 324BS, 91BG 147
Comer, Lt. Roger D (CP) 600BS, 398BG 144
Comer, T/Sgt John (Eng.) 533BS, 381BG 48, 71, 86, 87, 98, 104, 105
Connolly, Lt. Harry J (P) 602BS, 398BG 184
Conrow, Lt. Russell C (P) 601BS, 398BG 181
Considine, Lt. James R (P) 323BS, 91BG 122
Copeland, Lt. Derward R (P) 351BG 34
Copp, Sgt Eugene F (G/Ins.) 381BG 127
Corman, Lt. Nathan (P) 91BG 9
Cormany, Lt. Bill (P) 535BS, 381BG 50, 84
Cos, Lt. (P) 91BG 40
Corson, Lt. Dan W (P) 91BG 9
Corum, Sgt Howard L (BT) 532BS, 381BG 160
Cosendier, Sgt Paul G (ROG) 534BS, 91BG 162
Counce, Sgt Jim (WG) 533BS, 381BG 104, 105
Coville, Lt. Paul A (P) 602BS, 398BG 227
Cox, Lt. (P) 323BS, 91BG 76
Coyle, Lt. Richard (P) 533BS, 381BG 124, 125
Coyle, Sue, ARC, Ridgewell 130
Cranston, Lt. Lyman M (CP) 601BS, 398BG 181
Creska, T/Sgt Bill (Eng.) 91BG 236
Cress, Sgt Joseph A (ROG) 322BS, 91BG 194
Crisler, Lt. Robert R (CP) 534BS, 381BG 128
Cristman, Lt. Lloyd A (P) 351BG 87
Crismon, Lt. Oliver W (P) 351BG 89
Crosby, Bing, U.S. Entertainer 157
Crosson, Lt. Waldo B (P) 535BS, 381BG 100
Crouse, Lt. Fred L (CP) 533BS, 381BG 210
Crozier, Lt. Gordon (P) 533BS, 381BG 105
Crumm, Lt. Jack (P) 324BS, 91BG 16
Cytarzymski, Edward A (N) 532BS, 381BG 85

D

Daily, Lt. Edwin D (P) 600BS, 398BG 224
Darrow, Lt. George R (P) 532BS, 381BG 61
Dassault, Lt. Roger L (P) 381BG 160, 161
Dasselle, Capt. Dale (P) 91BG 7
Dasso, Lt. Carl H (P) 535BS, 381BG 145
Davis, Lt. Robert (CP) 600BS, 398BG 198
Davis, M/Sgt "Mouse" (C/C) 535BS, 381BG 197

DeBaum, Lt. Clyde (P) 324BS, 91BG 9, 36
DeBolt, Capt. Darrell (B) 534BS, 381BG 91, 104
DeBolt, Lt. Harold R (P) 324BS, 91BG 197
Deering, Lt. Robert P (P) 533BS, 381BG 107
Defenbaugh, Sgt Ross N (WG) 534BS, 381BG 106
DeLancey, Lt. Laurence (P) 601BS, 398BG 183, 189, 191, 211
DeLano, Maj. Jim (GN) 381BG 142, 205
Delchamp, Lt. (GC) 534BS, 381BG 82
DeLisle, Lt. Donald (P) 324BS, 91BG 164
Delp, Sgt Edgar (TG) 535BS, 381BG 100
Demara, Lt. Demarco (P)324BS, 91BG 107
Dennis, F/O George W (N) 532BS, 381 BG 144
Deshaw, Lt. Allen G (P) 322BS, 91BG 166
Devers, Gen. Jacob U.S. Army 30
Dietrich, Lt. William (P) 323BS, 91BG 207
Disbrow, Lt. Loren C (P) 535BS, 381BG 60
Disney, Lt. Frederick O (P) 384BG 32
Dittus, Lt. Carl (B) 535BS, 381BG 111
Dobbs, Lt. (B) 322BS, 91BG 116
Doenitz, Grand-Admiral Oberbefehlshaber, U-Boat *Dienst* 26
Doerfler, Lt. Joe (CP) 534BS, 381BG 84
Doerr, Lt. Lyle J (P) 602BS, 398BG 201
Doherty, Lt. Bill (CP) 535BS, 381BG 116, 138, 144
Donovan, Lt. John (N) 532BS, 381BG 103
Doolittle, L/Gen. James H "Jimmy" CG, 8AF 104, 121, 171
Douglas, Capt. Gene L (P) 602BS, 398BG 163, 177, 198
Douglas, Lt. Robert A (P) 534BS, 381BG 169
Downey, Lt. Charles W (P) 535BS, 381BG 123
Downey, Lt. Martin (P) 534BS, 381BG 91
Downing, Lt. Edgar C (P) 324BS, 91BG 128
Doyle, Lt. John B (P) 532BS, 381BG 159
Dreiseszun, Lt. Phil (N) 532BS, 381BG 45
Drosdek, S/Sgt Steve (GC) 532BS, 381BG 137
Duarte, Lt. Earl B (P) 535BS, 381BG 102
Dudley, Lt. Bayard (P) 324BS, 91BG 102
Duncan, Lt. Jason H (P) 532BS, 381BG 100
Dunkel, Lt. Mark R (P) 533BS, 381BG 159
Dunlap, Lt. John V (P) 322BS, 91BG 179
Dwyer, Lt. Wilbur S (P) 603BS, 398BG 167

E

Eaker, B/Gen. Ira A, CG, VIIIBC 6, 42, 112
Early. Lt. Charles L (P) 322BS, 91BG 99
Eason, Lt. Wilbert E (ROG) 533BS, 381BG 108
Eatinger, Lt. Norman C (P) 323BS, 91BG 74
Edwards, T/Sgt 'Red' (Eng.) 535BS, 381BG 225
Eisen, Lt. Charles K (B) 532BS, 381BG 146
Eisenhower, 5-Star Gen. Dwight David, (Supreme Commander, Allied Forces Europe) 139, 151, 158,
209, 227
Ellis, Lt. Eugene B (P) 91BG 16
Ellis, Lt. Lewis (CP) 401BS, 91BG 215
Ellis, Lt. Richard F (P) 603BS, 398BG 222
Elkins, Cpl. Goldmer E, 2021 Fire Platoon, 381BG 113
Elroy, Sgt, Bob S, Combat crew, 91BG 76
Englehardt, Sgt William H (WG) 603BS, 398BG 163
English, Lt. Robert S (P) 401BS, 91BG 9
Ensign, Col. Lewis, CO, 398BG 211
Erickson, Lt. Mahion R (P) 602BS, 398BG 201
Estrada, Sgt Amos F (TG) 322BS, 91BG 160
Evans, Lt. Fred G (P) 532BS, 381 BG 55
Evans, Lt. Rowland H (P) 535BS, 381BG 103, 123, 133
Evans, Lt. Sam L (P) 401BS, 91BG 141
Evans, Lt. W J (P) 602BS, 398BG 182
Evans, Sgt Herman (TG) 324BS, 91BG 226
Evers, Lt. Hilary 'Bud' (P) 401BS, 91BG 87
Evers, Pvt Joseph A (TG) 324BS, 91BG 160
Evertson, Lt. Bryce S (P) 322BS, 91BG 125
Eylens, T/Sgt John (Eng.) 533BS, 381BG 147
Ezzell, Lt. Clarence W (P) 532BS, 381BG 145

F

Fann, Sgt William A (BT) 322BS, 91BG 162
Farmer, Lt. John M (P) 602BS, 398BG 184
Faris, Lt. James E (P) 401BS, 91BG 195

Farmer, S/Sgt Arnold (TG) 535BS, 381 BG 138
Farr, Sgt John T (WG) 533BS, 381BG 124
Fastrup, Lt. Milton (P) 532BS, 381BG 125
Fawcett, Lt. Robert D (P) 533BS, 381BG 222
Fee, T/Sgt Edward (Eng.) 91BG 113
Felton, Lt. Ralph (P) 91BG 17
Ferguson, Lt. Alan H (P) 602BS, 398BG 227
Ferrin, Lt. (P) 533BS, 381BG 105
Fiegel, L/Col. Leland (P) Deputy CO, 381BG 41
Figie, Lt. Leonard (P) 322BS, 91BG 179
Fischer, Lt. Phillip (P) 91BG 15, 27
Fishburne, Maj. Paul (P) 91BG 17, 18, 23
Flaherty, Lt. Francis J (P) 532BS, 381BG 123
Fletcher, Lt. Jim (CP) 401BS, 91BG 166
Flint, Lt. Robert (P) 324BS, 91BG 198
Flores. S/Sgt David V (WG) 603BS, 398BG 201
Floyd, S/Sgt Fred, 448 Sub-depot, 381BG 138
Folger, Lt. Roger A (P) 600BS, 398BG 163
Follett, Lt. John R (P) 401BS, 91BG 160
Fonke, Lt. Vincent A (P) 324BS, 91BG 179
Forbes, Sgt James R (WG) 532BS, 381BG 85
Fore, F/O James W (P) 323BS, 91BG 163
Forkner, Lt. Hamden (P) 534BS, 381BG 58, 65
Forrest, Lt. Willard T (P) 351BG 29
Forsblad, Lt. Leland (P) 91BG 23, 43
Foster, Lt. Arthur G (N) 323BS, 91BG 89
Foster, Lt. Thomas K (P) 603,BS, 91BG 163, 164
Foumey, Lt. Ben (P) 323BS, 91BG 125
Fountain, Lt. Marcell E (P) 91BG 21, 31
Forsythe, Capt. William P (P) 351BG 28
Fox, Lt. Boyd C (CP) 534BS, 381BG 196
Freeman, Lt. Charles S (N) 533 BS, 381BG 178
Freer, Lt. Donald (P) 322BS, 91BG 199
French, T/Sgt Lifford, DSC (Eng.) 535BS, 381BG120
Fricks, Capt. Robert O (P) 534BS, 381BG 91
Fridgen, Lt. Francis (P) 533BS, 381BG 123, 131
Frost, Lt. Edwin (N) 535BS, 381BG 50
Frye, Lt. Wayne B (N) 401BS, 91BG 195
Frye, Sgt Bill, 7th Station Comp., 381BG 51
Fuller, Lt. Bob (N) 532BS, 381 BG 151
Fuller, Lt. Robert E (P) 322BS, 91BG 116, 151, 224
Fullick, Maj. Bill (GB) 381BG 189, 196, 199, 205
Fulton, Lt. Omar (P) 534BS, 381BG 137, 187
Fusco, Lt. Frank (P) 401BS, 91BG 166

G
Gable, Clark, U.S. film actor 28, 35, 36, 55, 73, 82
Gaffney, T/Sgt Jack (C/C) 91BG 166
Gaillard, Maj., HQ, 381BG 189
Gallagher, Lt. Raymond J (P) 603BS, 398BG 164
Galland, Hptm. "Wutz," Kommandeur III/JG26 32
Galland, Maj. Adolf (P) 32
Gamba, Sgt Eugene, (TG) 601BS, 398BG 180
Garcia, Lt. Jose G (P) 351BG 55
Gardon, Lt. Carl A (P) 534BS, 381BG 145
Garrett, Capt. Thomas S III (P) 535BS, 381BG 225
Gatewood, Lt. Jack W (P) 322BS, 91BG 59
Genz. S/Sgt Raymond, Silver Star (TG) 532BS, 381BG 58, 90
Germano, Lt. Ernest (P) 533BS, 381BG 181
Giambrone, M/Sgt Joe (C/C) 91BG 27, 94
Gibbons, Lt. William (P) 401BS, 91BG 77
Gildin, S/Sgt David (TG) 535BS, 381BG 134
Gill, Lt. Louis H (B) 533BS, 381BG 105
Ginder, Sgt Arthur G (Eng.) 322BS, 91BG 106
Girvan, T/Sgt Alexander M (Eng.) 535BS, 381BG 98
Glaze, Sgt Gerald D (BT) 322BS, 91BG 101
Gleichauf, Lt. Paul (P) 533BS, 381BG71, 86, 98, 104, 105, 125
Godwin, Lt. John C (P) 602BS, 398BG 163
Goebbels. Dr. Josef Nazi Propaganda Minister 147
Gomez, Lt. George (N or B) 532BS, 381BG 178
Gonzales, Lt Federico (CP) 398BG 211
Goodrich, Lt. Ferrall K (P) 322BS, 91BG 162
Gotthardt, Capt. Robert J (P) 533BS, 381BG 222, 223
Grant, Lt. Bill (P) 533BS, 381BG 32
Gray, Maj. Judson F (P) CO, 603BS, 398BG 145
Greco, Sgt Anthony F (TG) 534BS, 381BG 104
Green, Lt. John (P) 401BS, 91BG 166, 167
Greene, Lynne, Ross Greene's wife 200

Greene, Ross, Lt. Perrin's (381BG) nephew 200
Greenlee, Maj. Karl, Ground
Executive, HQ, 381BG 172, 232
Greer, Lt. Eldridge V (P) 32BS, 91BG 106, 114, 116
Greiner, Oblt. Hermann (P) IV/NJG1 125
Grinter, Lt. Donald D (P) 602BS, 398BG 201
Gromicki, Sgt Gregory G (TG) 602BS, 398BG 164
Gromicki, Sgt Gregory G (TG) 602BS, 398BG 164
Grose, M/Sgt George 448
Sub-depot, 381BG 235
Gross, Col. Bill (P) CO, 1PCBW 57, 109
Gross, B/Gen. Bill CG, 1CBW 132, 154, 161, 171, 175, 211, 216
Grube, Lt. James D (N) 401BS, 91BG 127
Guenther, Lt. Robert J (P) 401BS, 91BG 146
Guertin, Lt. Arthur L (N) 535BS, 381BG 142
Guinn, Lt. Charles (P) 401BS, 91BG 79, 99
Guinn, Sgt James M (ROG) 322BS, 91BG 102
Gunn, Lt. Tom (P) 324BS, 91BG 140, 141, 154
Gustafson, Lt. ( ) 322BS, 91BG 194
Gutta, Lt. Morris M (P) 323BS, 91BG 87
Gwinn, Lt. Lloyd W (B) 532BS, 381BG 60

H

Haakensen, Sgt Selmer K (TG) 602BS, 398BG 221
Hackstock, Lt. Charles R (CP) 322BS, 91BG 194
Hadges, Lt. Willard (P) 601BS, 398BG 159
Hafner, Sgt Arthur J (WG) 533 BS, 381BG 210
Hahn, Lt. J L (P) 398BG 228
Hainzer, Lt. Joe (P) 535BS, 381BG 169
Halberg, Lt. Chet (P) 20FG 128
Hall, Capt. Catholic Chaplain, 91BG, 36
Hall, Capt. Mitchell 448
Sub-depot, 381BG 149
Hall, Col. Conway S, Deputy CO, 381BG115, 132, 141, 159, 174, 175, 230, 238, 225, 226
Halligan, Sgt Tom HQ, 381BG 113
Hallstrom, S/Sgt Harold E (G) 535BS, 381BG 200
Halsey, Maj. Charles L (P) CO, 535BS, 381BG 153
Halsey, L/Col Charles L, CO, 535BS, 381BG 153, 161
Halter, Lt. Ralph L (P) 398BG 159
Hamilton, Lt. John (P) 322BS, 91BG 194
Hammer, Capt. Roy (P) 322BS, 91BG 194
Hammer, Sgt Ray (P) 322 BS, 91BG 194
Hammond, Sgt Robert J (WG) 533BS, 381BG 147
Hamor, Sgt William M (ROG) 602BS, 398BG 184
Hamory, Lt. Ashley (C)P) 534BS, 381BG 120
Hanninger, Sgt Edward W (TG) 351BG 55
Hans, Lt. Jerome T (CP) 603BS, 398BG 145
Hansard, Lt. V A (P) 600BS, 398BG 198
Hansen, Lt. Helmuth F (P) 351BG 59
Hansley, Sgt Richard (Eng.) 322BS, 91BG 102
Hanson, S/Sgt Floyd C (ROG) 535BS, 381BG 128
Hardenburg, Lt. Henry B ( ) 602BS, 398BG 222
Hardin, Lt. (P) 322BS, 91BG 8, 13
Harding, Lt. Douglas (P) 323BS, 91BG 125
Hardwick, Lt. Wayne T (N) 533BS, 381BG 144
Hare, Lt. Leroy R (P) 322BS, 91BG 195
Hargis, Lt. Jack (P) 322BS, 91BG 20, 46, 49, 56, 58
Harker, Sgt Charles E (ROG) 532BS, 381BG 159
Harland, Lt. Dick (B) ? 22
Harlick, Cpl. Joe (GC) 91BG 20
Harker, Sgt Charles E (ROG) 532BS, 381BG 159
Harness, S/Sgt Don (TG) 532BS, 381BG 151
Harper, Lt. Orton (CP) 322BS, 91BG 194
Harper, S/Sgt Hamilton (WG) 532BS, 381BG 151
Harris, Lt. Robert (P) 323BS, 91BG 195
Harrod, Lt. Franklin D (N) 602BS, 398BG 201
Hartje, Lt. James W (P) 533BS, 381BG 85
Hastings, Lt. Kenneth S (P) 602BS, 398BG 188, 197
Hatcher, Col. William, CO, 351BG 28, 39
Hathaway, Capt. Robert E (P) 351BG 71
Haushalter, Lt. Edward E (P) 534BS, 381BG 126
Havelaar, Lt. Marion (B) 401BS, 91BG 166, 174
Hawkins, Capt. Francis, Photo Officer, 381BG 80
Hawkins, Lt. Dallas A (P) 602BS, 398BG 164
Hawkins, Sgt Ed, 7th Station Comp., 381BG 51
Hayden, T/Sgt James H (ROG) 534BS, 381BG 224
Haynes, Lt. Kenneth T Jnr. (P) 532BS, 381BG 127
Haynes, Sgt Warren A (BT) 91BG 45
Hecker, Lt. Melvin R (P) 532/535BS, 381BG 43, 50, 132, 235
Hedglin, Lt. Warren D (P) 324BS, 91BG 101, 104
Hedin, Lt. Charles E (P) 533BS, 381BG 33, 43

Heimbach, Sgt Robert (WG) 401BS, 91BG 146
Heller, Lt. Robert (P) 401BS, 91BG 55
Henderson, Lt. Donald G (P) 534BS, 381BG 123
Henderson, Lt. Harold H (P) 91BG 17
Hendricks, Maj. Landon (P) CO, 533BS, 381BG 87
Hendrickson, Capt. William (P) 601BS, 398BG 181
Henry, Lt. Daniel C (P) 534BS, 381BG 128
Henslin, Lt. Harold F (P) 535BS, 381BG 112, 142
Herman, Lt. Maury (N) 401BS, 91BG 31
Hess, Lt. Warren C (P) 535BS, 381BG 77, 100
Hesse, Capt. Harvey (P) 324BS, 91BG 141
Hesse, Lt. Robert W (P) 534BS, 381BG 140
Heydrich, Reinhard, Nazi Reichs-protektor for Czechoslovakia 227
Higgins, Lt. Walter K (P) 535BS, 381BG 145
Hiller, Lt. Elbert W (RN) 533BS, 381BG 222
Hing, Sgt Clarence (TG) 91BG 216
Hittel, S/Sgt Bob (TG) 533BS, 381BG 147
Hoffman, Sgt Frank, 7th Station Comp., 381BG 51
Holdom, Lt. Robert L (P) 535BS, 381BG 43
Hollenbaugh, T/Sgt (Eng.) 401BS, 91BG 195
Hollenkamp, Lt. Bernard F (P) 532BS, 381BG 101
Holmes, Capt. Francis S (P) 324BS, 91BG 166
Homdrom, Lt. Theo (N) 535BS, 381BG106, 142, 161, 171
Hope, Bob U.S. Actor/Comedian 50
Hopkins, Capt. Robert L (P) 603BS, 398BG 178
Hopp, Lt. Donald K (P) 535BS, 381BG 98
Hopp, Lt. Raymond C (CP) 600BS, 398BG 163
Horn, Lt. Robert (CP) 535BS, 381BG 225
Horr, Lt. Earl R (P) 532BS, 381BG 32
Horsch, Sgt Frank (TG) 534BS, 381BG 196
Houck, Lt. James B (B) 532BS, 381BG 45
Houser, Sgt Edward P (TG) 534BS, 381BG 224
Houston, Lt. John (P) 534BS, 381BG 164, 173
Howland, Lt. John (N) 535BS, 381BG 101, 116, 129, 138, 144, 157, 158, 161, 165, 172
Howell, Lt. Charles E (P) 600BS, 398BG 197
Hudson, F/O James C (P) 533BS, 381BG 58
Hudson, Lt. Charles, DSC (B) 401BS, 91BG 85, 87, 88, 172
Hudson, Maj. Charles, DSC (GB) 91BG216, 218, 236
Huish, Lt. William L, 322BS, 91Bg 121
Hultin, Lt. Arthur (P) 401BS, 91BG 166
Humason, Lt. Gordon W (P) 532BS, 381BG 47
Hunter, B/Gen. "Monk," CG, VIIIFC 33, 39
Hunter, Col. Frank P, CO, 398BG 142, 155,177, 197, 211
Hustedt, Lt. Henry (P) 535BS, 381BG 123
Hylinski, Sgt Peter (WG) 533BS, 381BG 108
Hytenin, Lt. Harold H (P) 534BS, 381BG 100

I

Ingenhutt, Maj. Bill (P) 535BS, 381BG 84
Ingram, Lt. John W (P) 601BS, 398BG 145

J

Jackson, Lt. Robert W (P) 351BG 29
Jacobs, Lt. Willard G (P) 602BS, 398BG 222
James, Pvt. Leroy, 2021 Fire Platoon, 381BG 113
Jankowiak, Lt. Robert (P) 533BS, 381BG 223
Jarvis, Lt. Leo I (P) 532BS, 381BG 60
Jensen, Lt. Niel C (P) 323BS, 91BG 181
Jevons, Sgt Russell (Eng.) 535BS, 381BG 102
Jobe, Lt. Inman (P) 533BS, 381BG 32
Johnson, Lt. William J (B) 533BS, 381BG 115
Johnson, Sgt Alfred A (WG) 532BS, 381BG 85
Johnson, Sgt Stanley E (ROG) 401BS, 91BG 142
Jolicoeur, L/Col. Raymond, 432 Air Service Group, 381BG 149
Jones, Capt. Duane (P) 91BG 8
Jones, Lt. David R (N) 535BS, 381BG 60
Jones, Lt. Osce V (P) 535BS, 381BG 43, 44, 50, 126
Jones, Maj. Osce V (P) 535BS, 381BG 142
Jones, T/Sgt Lyle D (Eng.) 322BS, 91BG 224
Jowett, Lt. H M, Combat Crew 91BG 93
Judy, Lt. James (P) 322BS, 91BG 87, 88
Jukes, Capt. Elton D (P) 535BS, 381BG 84, 85

K

Kahl, Lt. Paul D (P) 91BG 31
Karch, Sgt Delmar (ROG) 323BS, 91BG 59
Karp, Lt. John K (P) 323BS, 91BG 85
Katsarelis, Sgt Peter A (WG) 533BS, 381BG 59

Kaufman, Lt. John C (P) 322BS, 91BG 34
Kelley, Lt. Ernest B (P) 322BS, 91BG 180
Kelley, Lt. Robert (P) 324BS, 91BG 138
Kellogg, Sgt (BT) 532BS, 381BG 90
Kelly, T/Sgt Paul M (Eng.) 322BS, 91BG 63
Kels, Lt. John (CP) 533BS, 381BG 86, 98
Kemp, Lt. Leslie A (P) 535BS, 381BG 85
Kennedy, Sgt Francis G, 448 Sub-depot, 381BG 220
Kenner, Lt. Everett L (P) 322BS, 91BG 59
Kepner, M/Gen Bill (CG, 8FC) 119
Kethley, Lt. Gerold (P) 323BS, 91BG 55
Keyes, Lt. David D (P) 532BS, 381BG 124, 132
Kidd, Lt. Ernest B (P) 322BS, 91BG 11, 121
Kimmel, Lt. Norman (CP) 324BS, 91BG 164
King George VI, British Monarch 38
King, Lt. Reinhard M (P) 534BS, 381BG 59
King, Lt. Warren L (N) 600BS, 398BG 209
King, Lt. William C (P) 351BG 33
Kious, Lt. Hal (N) 91BG 17
Kirkpatrick, Sgt Clifford K (WG) 91BG 120
Klein, Lt. Ed (B) 534BS, 381BG 103
Klein, Lt. Ernest M (P) 533BS, 381BG 105
Klette, L/Col. Emanuel J, CO, 324BS, 91BG 216
Kline, Lt. Theodore A (CP) 601BS, 398BG 225
Klotz, Lt. John (P) 324BS, 91BG 164
Knapp, Lt. Donald (P) 401BS, 91BG 166
Knaus, Sgt Charles F (TG) 535BS, 381BG 210, 223
Knight, Lt. Edward (P) 323BS, 91BG 213
Knights, John, British Civilian 198
Knoke, Oblt. Heinz, Staffelkapitaen, 5/JG11 18
Koenig, Lt. Orlando (P) 535BS, 381BG 62
Koenig, Lt. James E (P) 601BS, 398BG 212
Koll, Lt. Norbert (P) 91BG 27
Kolts, Lt. Frank (P) 323BS, 91BG 122
Kourie, Lt. Charles E (CP) 602BS, 398BG 183
Kovackjevich, Lt. Nenad (P) 323BS, 91BG 143
Kowalski, Lt. Pete (Silver Star) (B) 533BS, 381BG 222
Kozina, Lt. Joseph H (CP) 401BS, 91BG 143
Kralick, Sgt Joseph G (TG) 32BS, 381BG 45
Kramer, Sgt Arnold E (WG) 401BS, 91BG 194
Kraut, Lt. Irving (B) 532BS, 381BG 95, 103
Kucher, Sgt Peter (ROG) 534BS, 381BG 104, 110
Kuhns, Lt. (P) 535BS, 381BG 212, 215
Kuhl, Lt. John J (P) 534BS, 381BG 120
Kunkel, Lt/Col. David E, CO, 534BS, 381BG 109
Kurdevitz, S/Sgt (WG) 532BS, 381BG 151
Kurtz, S/Sgt Frank J (TG) 534BS, 381BG 128
Kwart, S/Sgt Herb (T) 534BS, 381BG 226

L

LaFontin, Lt. John E (P) 401BS, 91BG 141
Lamore, Sgt Tom (TG) 532BS, 381BG 127, 128
Lane, Lt. Dorman (P) 535BS, 381BG 100
Langford, Lt. Walter I (P) 401BS, 91BG 166, 167
Lantz, Sgt John R (WG) 533BS, 381 BG 104
Larsen, Lt. Austin A (P) 534BS, 381BG 106
Larsen, Sgt Rafael (G) 535BS, 381BG 200
Lawrence, L/Col. Baskin R, CO, 91BG 30
Lear, Lt. Paul T (CP) 534BS, 381BG 145, 156
Leavitt, Lt. Bernard S (B) 532BS, 381BG 159
Leber, Col. Harry P, CO, 381BG 123, 128, 132, 161, 171, 172, 174, 175, 205, 211, 213
LeDoux, Lt. Raymond (N) 601BS, 398BG 183
Lee, Maj. Charles (P) 324BS, 91BG 141
Legg, Sgt Raymond F (TG) 533BS, 381BG 125
Lehner, Lt. Robert W (P) 603BS, 398BG 197
Leigh, Vivian, British Actress 153
LeMay, Col. Curtis, CO, 305BG 14, 56
Leslie, Lt. John L (P) 324BS, 91BG 179
Leverett, Capt. Leroy (P) 323BS, 91BG 106
Levitoff. Lt. Julius K (P) 535BS, 381BG 197
Liddle, Lt. James R (P) 535BS, 381BG 128
Liekhus, Lt. John H (P) 323BS, 91BG 185, 195
Lilley, Lt. John A (B) 401BS, 91BG 88
Lindahl, Lt. John (P) 323BS, 91BG 203
Lindsay, Lt. Nathan (P) 91BG 25
Lindsey, Lt. Reece W (P) 324BS, 91BG 179
Lingberg, Sgt Evert (TG) 324BS, 91BG 31
Lishon, Capt. Dexter (P) 534BS, 381BG 72, 84, 85, 91, 105
Lockhart, Lt. Bill (B) 532BS, 381BG 60,
Lockhart, Lt. Eugene M (P) 401BS, 91BG 57, 60, 66
Loftin, Lt. James I (P) 534BS, 381BG 86

Logan, Sgt William G (T) 602BS, 398BG 212
London, Capt. Charles (P) 78FG 43
Long, Lt. Carlton (CP) 381BG 84
Long, Sgt Joe (G) 535BS, 381BG 111
Longfellow, B/Gen. Newton 7
Lord, Maj. Marvin D, Silver Star (P) 381BG 130
Lord. L/Col. Marvin D, Silver Star (P) 91BG 57, 61, 70, 212
Lorick, S/Sgt Arnold (G) 533BS, 381BG 33
Lovelace, Lt. Curtis D (P) 600BS, 398BG 163, 164
Lowry, Lt. Allen W (CP) 91BG 17
Lunt, Alfred, U.S. Politician 153
Lutz, Lt. James P (P) 324BS, 91BG 120

M
Mackay, Capt. Norman C (N) 532BS, 381BG 85
Majors, Lt. William (P) 324BS, 91BG 135
Majors, S/Sgt Charles L (S/J) 535BS, 381BG 223
Manchester, Lt. Edwin R (P) 381BG 22, 43
Manchester, Capt. Edwin R (P) 381BG 53, 84
Mangarpan, Lt. Joe (CP) 532BS, 381BG 62
Manion, Lt. James G (N) 534BS, 381BG 174
Mansfield, Lt. Robert W (P) 351BG 28
Marlowe, Hugh, U.S. film actor 15
Marpil, Lt. Louis C (P) 91BG 179
Martin, Capt. William R (CP) 401BS, 91BG 166
Martin, Lt. John (P) 324BS, 91BG 210
Martin, Lt. John L (P) 533BS, 381BG 32
Martin, Lt. John L (P) 381BG 32
Martin, Lt. Thomas (P) 324BS, 91BG 199, 204
Martin, S/Sgt Dave (C/C) 535BS, 381BG 223
Martinek, Lt. Emil J (P) 601BS, 398BG 225
Martyniak, Lt. Robert A (P) 534BS, 381BG 158, 159, 170
Maser, Lt. Howard G (P) 351BG 87
Mason, Lt. Clyde V (P) 401BS, 91BG 125
Mata, S/Sgt Albert M (WG) 535BS, 381BG 231
Matoni, Oblt. Walter (P) JG26 125
Matthes, S/Sgt Robert W (TG) 324BS, 91BG
Matyas, Lt. Martin (N) 534BS, 381BG 226
Matthews, Sgt Robert T (TG) 532BS, 381BG 159
Mayer, Hptm. Egon, Kommandeur, III/JG2 9, 10
Maziarz, Lt. Roman V (P) 323BS, 91BG 122
Medzie, S/Sgt Mike (BT) 532BS, 381BG 213
Meier, Sgt Elmer C (Eng.) 532BS, 381BG 161
Meli, Lt. Joseph A (P) 351BG 28
Melomo. Lt. Salvatore J (P) 533BS, 381BG 178
Mendelsohn, Lt. Stuart B (P) 324BS, 91BG 102, 112
Merkel, Lt. Ehud (CP) 323BSD, 91BG 122
Meyer, Lt. William E (P) 323BS, 91 BG 211
Meyers, Maj. Edward P (P) 91BG 10
Meyran, Lt. William L (CP) 602BS, 398BG 183
Mickow, Lt. Lawrence H (P) 534BS, 381BG 107, 117
Mikonis, Lt. Peter (P) 401BS, 91BG 154, 162, 172
Miles, Lt. Bob (P) 323 BS, 91BG 49
Miller, Lt. Adolf (P) 324BS, 91BG91BG 198
Miller, Lt. Bob (P) 534BS, 381BG 84
Miller, Lt. Ed (P) 534BS, 381BG 213
Miller, Lt. George (P) 324BS, 91BG 212
Miller, Lt. John H (P) 91BG 28
Miller, Sgt Wilfred L (TG) 532BS, 381BG 121
Miller, T/Sgt Earl F (Eng.) 381BG 85
Mills, Sgt John T (G) 535B, 381BG 109
Milton. L/Col. Theodore (P) 91BG 106
Minerich, Lt. Hal (P) 535BS, 381BG 85
Minor, Capt. Paul F, Flt. Surgeon, 91BG 216
Mitchell, Lt. Howard M (P) 322BS, 91BG 200
Mitchell, Millard, U.S. film actor 16
Moeller, Lt. John, Combat crew, 91BG 76
Mohnacky, Lt. Robert J (P) 534BS, 381BG 107
Mongrue, S/Sgt Carl A (ROG) 534BS, 381BG 128, 142
Monohan, Lt. John (P) 533BS, 381BG 147
Monohan, Sgt John (ROG) 324BS, 91BG 46
Moore, Lt. Bruce (N) 401BS, 91BG 87
Moore, Lt. Keith D (B) 381BG 84
Moore, Lt. William R (P) 532BS, 381BG 45
Morgan, Capt. Robert (P) 324BS, 91BG 35, 36
Morgan, Sgt James C (BT) 324BS, 91BG 17, 36
Morse, Lt. Harry B (P) 351BG 86
Mosley, Lt. William C (B) 534BS, 381BG 145
Moss, Lt. John M (P) 351BG 33
Mullane, Lt. James F (P) 535BS, 381BG 140
Mullins, Lt. Reece E (P) 323BS, 91BG 180

Munger, Lt. Bill (P) 91BG 59, 64
Murdock, Lt. Wayne (P) 324BS, 91BG 59, 104, 114
Murray, Capt. S2, 381BG 41
Myers, Sgt Edwin R (ROG) 535BS, 381BG 70, 74, 75
Myerscough, Lt. Sam (P) 535BS, 381BG 162

Mc
McAdams, Lt. Bill (P) 401BS, 91BG 98
McAfee, Lt. James W (P) 600BS, 398BG 224
McArthur, Lt. John S (P) 603BS, 398BG 178, 185
McBride, Lt. Fred (N) 323BS, 91BG 122
McCabe, Lt. Glenn A (CP) 535BS, 381BG 102
McCain, Lt. Walter (CP) 91BG 25
McCallum, Lt. Clyde (C)P) 401BS, 91BG 122
McCammon, Lt. Keene (P) 91BG 47
McCardle, Lt. Albert (P) 323BS, 91BG 143
McCarter, Sgt (BT) 401BS, 91BG 195
McCarthy, Capt. Martin W (P) 91BG 17
McCarthy. Lt. Charles R 234
McCarthy, Lt. Dave (N) 534BS, 381G 103
McCarty, Lt. David (P) 322BS, 91BG 180
McClellan, Capt. H C (P) 91BG 18
McConnell, Capt. (P) 379BG 210
McCook, S/Sgt Wade (TG) 535BS, 381BG 43, 84, 85
McCormick, Capt. Tom B (P) 91BG 8
McCormick, Lt. John R (P) 601BS, 398BG 212
McCoy, Capt. William P (P) CO, 510BS, 351BG 28
McCoy, Lt. Clifford J (P) 351BG 28
McCoy, Sgt Elvis A (ROG) 532BS, 381BG 200
McCrary, Capt. Tex, U.S. War Correspondent 31, 32, 56, 59, 67
McCallam, Lt. Clyde P (CP) 401BS, 91BG 122
McDowell, Lt. Paul (P) 324BS, 91BG 183, 190
McEvoy, Lt. Matthew J (P) 533BS, 381BG 104
McGee, Lt. Fewer R (P) 324BS, 91BG 120
McGoldrick, Sgt James C (BT) 533BS, 381BG 59
McGregor, Lt. Jack (P) 532BS, 381BG 164
McIntosh, Lt. George B (CP) 535BS, 381BG 44, 50, 126, 127
McLean, Sgt Charles B (TG) 603BS, 398BG 164

N
Naha, Sgt Emory Y (TG) 535BS, 381BG 128
Nalley, Sgt Floyd M (TG) 533BS, 381BG 145
Nason, Lt. Donald E (P) 533BS, 381BG 98, 104
Nauman, Lt. Daniel D (P) 351BG 84
Naumann, Hptm. Johannes, Staffelkapitaen 6/JG2 28
Navalle, Cpl. Billy GC, 91BG 20
Nazzaro, L/Col. Joseph CO, 381BG 30, 68, 109
Nazzaro, Col. Joseph J CO, 381BG 89
Nea, Lt. Kenneth C (CP) 533BS, 381BG 147
Nee, Lt. William F (P) 401BS, 91BG 146
Neel, Lt. Frederick T (N) 401BS, 91BG 146
Nelson, Capt. Robert, Silver Star (P) 532BS, 381BG 58, 90,
Nelson, Lt. Alexander B (CP) 535BS, 381BG210, 223
Neves, T/Sgt Ernie (ROG) 534BS, 381BG 130
Newman, Lt. Herbert H (P) 603BS, 398BG 196
Newton, Lt. Sam (P) 401BS, 91BG 160
Nickola, Lt. Ray L (CP) 401BS, 91BG 194
Niederitter, Lt. Richard (P) 534BS, 381BG 101
Nieswonger, Lt. Boyd A (P) 603BS, 398BG 163
Nisbet, Sgt Richard H (ROG) 534BS, 381BG103, 104
Noonan, Lt. John P (B) 535BS, 381BG 60
Norcom, Sgt. James F (WG) 534BS, 381BG 128
Norcom, S/Sgt Joseph (WG) 535BS, 381BG 225
Norris, Lt. Clarence F (P) 351BG 71
Norris, Sgt Harold (TG) 532BS, 381BG 178
Noxon, F/O Donald E (P) 535BS, 381BG 100
Nudell, Lt. Fred Engineer, 532BS 41
Nushy, S/Sgt John M (Eng.) 532BS, 381BG182, 183, 189

O
O’Bannon, Lt. Robert E (P) 322BS, 91BG 160
O’Black, Lt. Frank R (P) 533BS, 381BG 164
Oberlin, Sgt Richard D (WG) 534BS, 381BG 162
Obler, Lt. Clem (N) 381BG/91BG 57
Oblinski, Lt. Robert J (P) 384BG 32
Offman, Lt. Everett S (CP) 324BS, 91BG 107

Olivier, Laurence, British Actor 153
O'Loughlin, Lt. Edward T (B) 535BS, 381BG 62
Omohundro, Lt. Jack (P) 351BG 72, 73
O'Neal, Lt. Ira L (P) 600BS, 398BG 144
O'Neal, Sgt John S (TG) 534BS, 381BG 145
O'Neill, Lt. John O (P) 401BS, 91BG 195
O'Neill, Lt. Larry O (B) 323BS, 91BG 106
O'Neill, Capt. Oscar (P) 91BG 25
Osterberg, Lt. Spencer K (P) 323BS, 91BG 121, 129
Owens, Lt. Jack H (P) 532BS, 381BG 45
Owens, Sgt Harry E (WG) 534BS, 381BG 162

P
Padgett, Sgt J W (ROG) 535BS, 381BG 142
Page, Lt. J C (P) 322BS, 91BG 106, 115
Painter, Lt. Jack B (P) 532BS, 381BG 58, 90
Palant, Samuel H (P) 601BS, 398BG 225
Palenik, Lt. Frank (B) 535BS, 381BG 101, 116
Parks, T/Sgt George W (Eng.) 324BS, 91BG135, 140, 141, 154
Paskvan, Lt. Joseph P (P) 322BS, 91BG 160
Parsons, T/Sgt John (Eng.) 401BS, 91BG 122
Pastras, Lt. Peter A (P) 322BS, 91BG 224
Pastre, S/Sgt George (ROG) 532BS, 381BG 151
Patrick, Sgt Jack S (TG) 532BS, 381BG 178
Patton, M/Gen. George S CG, U.S. 3rd Army 217
Paul, Sgt Bob (ROG) 322BS, 91BG 17
Peak, Lt. Samuel L (P) 534BS, 381BG 162, 174
Pearson, Lt. Jack B (P) 533BS, 381BG 167
Peaslee, Col. "Bud" CO, 384BG 44
Peck, Gregory, U.S. film actor 15, 16
Peek, Lt. Buster (P) 401BS, 91BG 31, 39, 62
Pegram, Lt. Bill (P) 323BS, 91BG 71, 73, 74
Pendergist, Lt. Roy H (P) 534BS, 381BG 162
Perot, Lt. Wilfred R (P) 533BS, 381BG 104
Perrett, Lt. John M (P) 323BS, 91BG 74, 79
Perrin, Lt. Ross (B) 532BS, 381BG 200
Peters, Lt. Vincent (P) 535BS, 381BG 210
Peters, Lt. William F (P) 351BG 43
Peters, Sgt Belvin J (WG) 323BS, 91BG 74
Peterson, Capt. Tracey J (P) 601BS, 398BG 163
Peterson, Lt. Lloyd A (N) 533BS, 381BG 161, 169
Pettibone, Lt. Peter E (P) 603BS, 398BG 222
Phillips, Capt. Charles R (P) 401BS, 91BG 127
Piacentini, Lt. Irwin (P) 401BS, 91BG 121
Piatt, Lt. Forrest (N) 534BS, 381BG 156
Pickard, Lt. Walter M (P) 323BS, 91BG 124
Pilert, Lt. Marshal L (P) 324BS, 91BG 45
Pine, Sgt Frank, 7th Station Comp., 381BG 51
Pinkerton, Lt. Max A (P) 351BG 59
Pinner, Lt. Howard M (P) 603BS, 398BG 209
Pinning, Lt. Charles B (P) 322BS, 91BG 86
Pirtle, Lt. Thomas A (P) 532BS, 381BG 126
Pitts, Lt. Robert A (P) 323BS, 91BG 98
Plows, Sgt Arthur (TG) 532BS, 381BG 127
Pope, Lt. Kermit R (P) 600BS, 398BG 198
Porter, Capt George S2, 381BG 80
Post, Maj. Robert F (P) 532BS, 381BG 47
Potenza, Lt. Larry (B) 533BS, 381BG 32
Powell, Lt. Perry E (P) 603BS, 398BG 212
Prentice, Ms. Ella HQ, 1CBW 230
Pressey, Lt. Richard T (P) 401BS, 91BG 146
Price, Lt. Leslie A (B) 323BS, 91BG 122
Price, Sgt Thomas G (BT) 91BG 55
Prillaman, S/Sgt Jack (TG) 535BS, 381BG 225
Priller, Maj. "Pips" Kommodore, JG26 32
Prunty, Lt. Richard (CP) 324BS, 91BG 198
Pry, Lt. Jack S (P) 532BS, 381BG 85
Pryor, Lt. (P) 323BS, 91BG 167
Pucylowski, Lt. Paul C (P) 534BS, 381BG 212
Purdy, Lt. James F Jnr. (P) 322BS, 91BG 142
Purus, Lt. John (B) 533BS, 381BG 72
Putek, Lt. Henry (P) 535BS, 381BG 120, 142
Putman, Col. Claude E CO, 91BG 154, 172

Q
Quaresma, T/Sgt Sebastian (Eng.) 534BS, 381BG 128

R
Radener, Ltn. Waldimar. (P) 4/JG26 28
Ragan, Capt., Catholic Chaplain, 91BG 234
Ramirez, Sgt Rudy, 7th Station Comp., 381BG 51
Rand, Lt. Robert (P) 91BG 26, 35

Rautio, Lt. David R (CP) 532BS, 381BG182, 183, 189
Ray, Sgt Michael C (TG) 398BG 163
Rayburn, Lt. Robert W (P) 534BS, 381BG 141
Redman, Mrs Joyce, British civilian 101
Reed, L/Col. William, Gnd. Executive, 381BG 232
Reed, Lt. Russell E (P) 603BS, 398BG 196
Reed, Lt. Theo W (P) 351BG 84
Reid, Lt. Edwin (P) 323BS, 91BG 104
Reid, L/Col. William M CO, 91BG 30
Remmell, Sgt (Eng.) 323BS, 91BG 17
Rendall, Lt. James (P) 324BS, 91BG 46
Reseigh, Lt. Charles W (P) 532BS, 381BG 182, 183, 189
Retchen, Lt. Norman (P) 91BG 28
Rice, Lt. John (P) 534BS, 381BG 184
Rich, Lt. Paul H (P) 600BS, 398BG 197
Richards, F/O Richard H (N) 532BS, 381BG 159
Rickenbacker, Eddie, U. S. First World War "Ace"39
Rickerson, Lt. John A (P) 532BS, 381BG 127
Ridley, Lt. Bill (P) 535BS, 381BG 108, 111, 121
Ritter, Lt. W (CP) 602BS, 398BG 182
Rivera, Sgt Julius E (BT) 532BS, 381BG 95, 103
Roberts, M/Sgt Herbert H (GC) 91BG 15, 239
Robinson, Edward G, U.S. film actor 164,174
Robinson, Lt. Kenneth E (B) 533BS, 381BG 58
Robinson, S/Sgt (TG) 401BS, 91BG 195, 196
Rodman, Lt. Richard H (P) 323BS, 91BG 62
Rogers, Lt. Jess D (P) 322BS, 91BG 63, 68
Rogers, Lt. Robert H (P) 534BS, 381BG 124
Rohrer, Lt. Richard L (P) 324BS, 91BG 161
Rolfe, Lt. Benjamin G (P) 601BS, 398BG 198, 206
Rolfe, Lt. Frank O (N) 323BS, 91BG 74
Roling, Lt. Hal E (P) 533BS, 381BG 123
Rolla, Sgt Clarence (Eng.) 535BS, 381BG 162
Rolla, Sgt Clarence (Eng.) 535BS, 381BG 162
Romano, Tony, U.S. Musician 50
Romasco, Lt. Victor R (P) 534BS, 381BG 162, 169
Rosener, Maj. Maurice (P) 94BG 26
Ross, Sgt Jack R (TG) 534BS, 381BG 145
Ross, Sgt James (WG) 324BS, 91 BG 102
Rotz, Sgt. Nick (G) 535BS, 381BG 207
Rouse, Lt. (P) 533BS, 381BG 210
Rumberger, Sgt Fred (G) 534BS, 381BG 110
Russell, Colonel. J (P) 351BG 29
Rustand, Lt. Hanford (P) 323BS, 91BG 195
Rutledge, Karen, Niece to Harold Lt. Henslin 142
Rutledge, Lt. Kenneth B (P) 401BS, 91BG 98

S

Sabagh, Sgt Mike HQ, 381BG 113
Sample, Lt. Arthur A (P) 532BS, 381BG 81, 91
Samuels, S/Sgt Bob, 448 Sub-depot, 381BG 138
Saur, Lt. Robert V (P) 532BS, 381BG 104
Schaper, Lt. Lloyd S (P) 323BS, 91BG 71, 76, 83
Schaub, Lt. Henry S ( ) 324BS, 91BG 122
Scherman, Lt. Paul J (P) 532BS, 381BG 222
Schmid, Lt. John F (CP) 602BS, 398BG 225
Schneider, Lt. James A (B) 322BS, 91BG 102
Schneider, Lt. Lester (B) 534BS, 381BG 47
Schneider, S/Sgt Richard (TG) 533BS, 381BG 145, 178
Schaub, Lt. Henry S (N) 324BS, 91BG 122
Schrader, Lt. William K (P) 533BS, 381BG 33
Schulz, Lt. Eugene (P) 533BS, 381BG 124
Scott, Lt. Joe (N) 535BS, 381BG 128
Scroggins, Sgt Grover L (BT) 534BS, 381BG 162
Scruggs, Lt. William (CP) 534BS, 381BG 164, 173
Searl, Lt. Charles J (P) 600BS, 398BG 179
Sellars, Lt. Duncan A, DSC (CP) 535BS, 381BG 85, 112
Severson, T/Sgt Leo R (Eng.) 322BS, 91BG 87
Shackley, L/Col. George G, Air Executive, 381BG 45, 169, 171, 207, 210, 230
Sharp, Lt. Earl (P) 533BS, 381BG 144
Sheeler, Capt. Don (P) 324BS, 91BG 39
Sheeler, Lt/Col. Don, CO, 91BG 232
Sheeler, Maj. Don, CO, 322BS, 91BG 114
Sheely, Lt. Roy M Jnr. (P) 601BS, 398BG 184
Shenk, Capt. Martin (P) 533BS, 381BG 32
Sherrill, Lt. Halsted (P) 322BS, 91BG 179
Sherwood, Lt. T Paxton (CP) 535BS, 381BG123, 133, 140
Shirk, Lt. Arthur T (P) 600BS, 398BG 225
Showgo, Sgt (GC) 323BS, 91BG 203

Shutting, Lt. Carl (N) 533BS, 381BG 72
Siders, Sgt Harry (TG) 533BS, 381BG 181
Silvernale, Lt. John (P) 534BS, 381BG 130
Simmons, Lt. William (P) 401BS, 91BG 121, 122
Simpson, Lt. Weldon (P) 534BS, 381BG 58
Simpson, Sgt (GC) 323BS, 91BG 203
Sinclair, T/Sgt John, Silver Star (ROG) 533BS, 381BG 32
Skogland, Lt. Bill (P) 534BS, 381BG 162
Slane, Lt. Robert M (P) 91BG 93
Slattery, Lt. Joseph E (P) 324BS, 91BG 31
Slayton, Sgt Lowell (TG) 533BS, 381BG 123, 131
Sleaman, Lt. H J (P) 603BS, 398BG 163
Sloan, Sgt James F (TG) 381BG 32
Slomczenski, T/Sgt Chester M (Eng.) 535BS, 381BG 223
Smelser, Maj. Harold (P) 91BG 8
Smith, Lt. Beman E (P) 401BS, 91BG 16
Smith, Lt. Eldon J (P) 323BS, 91BG 56
Smith, Lt. Harry A (P) 534BS, 381BG 60, 169
Smith, Lt. Harry L (CP) 381BG 162
Smith, Lt. Harry M (P) 535BS, 381BG 60
Smith, Lt. James E (P) 532BS, 381BG 211, 214
Smith, Lt. Jim (P) 324BS, 91BG 31, 32, 37, 40
Smith, Lt. Kyle S (P) 532BS, 381BG 198
Smith, Lt. Lee W (P) 535BS, 381BG 123, 133
Smith, Lt. Marvin D (N) 535BS, 381BG 84
Smith, Lt. Thomas (P) 322BS, 91BG 179
Smith, Lt. Warren (P) 401BS, 91BG 198, 199
Smith, Mildred, ARC, Ridgewell 130
Smith, Sgt Claud J (TG) 323BS, 91BG 89
Smith, Sgt Irwin W (BT) 532BS, 381BG 85
Smith, S/Sgt Robert T (TG) 324BS, 91BG 154
Smith, T/Sgt Robert A (ROG) 322BS, 91BG 224
Snipes, Capt. Roy P (P) 351BG 28
Snow, Lt. Oscar (P) 322BS, 91BG 195
Soale, Lt. Don (P) 534BS, 381BG 169, 178
Soeder, Lt. Harlan D (P) 535BS, 381BG 140
Sopato, Sgt (GC) 323BS, 91BG 203
Spaatz, L/Gen. Carl "Tooey" CG, USSTAF 143
Spaulding, Sgt Donald F (TG) 401BS, 91 BG 146
Spellman, Cardinal, NY Prelate 71
Spika, Lt. Robert M (P) 351BG 71
Spivey, Lt. Len (N) 535BS, 381BG 62
Staats, T/Sgt Gilbert, Photo Sect., 381BG 95, 203
Stahlman, Lt. Phil (CP) 601BS, 398BG 183, 191
Stairs, Sgt Don C (ROG) 401BS, 91BG 127
Stanbury, S/Sgt (P) 323BS, 91BG 211
Stark, Lt. Lawrence J (P) 91G 27
Stayzak, T/Sgt Ray (GC) 534BS, 381BG 82
Stealey, Lt. Joseph E (P) 91BG 29
Steel, Lt. Edward M (P) 322BS, 91BG 101
Steele, Lt. Henry D (P) 533BS, 381BG 108
Steelhammer, Lt. Albert E (B) 323BS, 91BG 165
Stephens, Sgt Thomas A (ROG) 91BG 31
Stevens, Lt. Arthur L (P) 324BS, 91BG 177
Stevens, Lt. John (P) 323BS, 91BG 198
Stewart, Lt. Alexander W (P) 322BS, 91BG 87
Stewart, Lt. Ray L (N) 534BS, 381BG 162
Stewart, Maj. James T (P) 351BG 72
Stewart, S/Sgt Paul (ROG) 532BS, 381BG 165
Stiles, Lt. Bert (CP) 401BS, 91BG 155, 165, 166
Stoffel, Lt. Nicholas (P) 91BG 26
Stolz, Lt. Richard E (P) 324BS, 398BG 199
Stone, Capt. George (N) 533BS, 381BG 222, 223
Stone, Lt. Robert M (P) 323BS, 91BG 89
Stone, S/Sgt Ken (BT) 532BS, 381BG 57
Strednak, S/Sgt 'Whitey' (GC) 532BS, 381BG 137
Strong, Lt. Lucien E (P) 322BS, 91BG 166
Struble, Lt. Cleo C (P) 322BS, 91BG 73
Stull, Capt. Paul (Eng. officer) 534BS, 381BG 82
Stuart, Lt. Andrew A (P) 532BS, 381BG 146
Suggs, Sgt Durward V (WG) 532BS, 381BG 200
Suit, Lt. William J (P) 351BG 62
Sunde, Lt. Harlan V (P) 535BS, 381BG 100
Supchak, Lt. Harry W (P) 323BS, 91BG 167
Sutherland, Lt. Ken (P) 323bs, 91BG 122
Swais, Capt. John (P) 91BG 16
Swenumsen, Lt. Stan (P) 324BS, 91BG 141
Swinburne, F/O Bernard M (B) 324BS, 91BG 142

T

Tabor, Sgt Fred A (WG) 323BS, 91BG 122
Tamplin, Lt. Parke (B) 534BS, 381BG 156

Tarcyzinski, Sgt Thaddeus (BT) 535BS, 381BG 140
Tauro, F/O Nicholas (P) 381BG 211
Templeton, Sgt Robert A (WG) 600BS, 398BG 224
Terry, Col. Henry W CO 91BG 172
Theophilus, Lt. Henry L (P) 324BS, 91BG 126, 133
Thomas, Lt. Andrew R (P) 603BS, 398Bg 222
Thompson, Lt. Robert (P) 323BS, 91BG 55
Thompson, Lt. Thomas G (P) 600BS, 398BG 147
Thompson, Sgt Anthony S (Eng.) 532BS, 381BG 123
Tibbets, Lt. Robert (P) 323BS, 91BG 80, 98, 125
Tilson, Lt. Thomas G (P) 401BS, 91BG 142
Toler, S/Sgt Richard (WG) 534BS, 381BG 128
Tompson, Lt. Thomas P (P) 532BS, 381BG 127
Trapnell, Sgt Robert M Combat Crew, 381BG 124
Travis, B/Gen. 71
Tucker, Sgt Arthur L (BT) 535BS, 381BG 43
Tucker, Sgt Gerold (G) 322BS, 91BG 49
Tucker, Sgt Starr A (BT) 322BS, 91BG 58
Tufty, Capt. Iver O (P) 91BG 183, 199
Tull, Lt. Paul E` (B) 533BS, 381BG 33
Turgeon, Lt. Leo P (P) 351BG 31
Turk, Lt. Frank D (P) 401BS, 91BG 127
Turley, Lt. Joseph H (P) 351BG 87
Turner, Col. Howard M (P) Task Force CO 57, 60
Tyler, Lt. Marshal E (N) 535BS, 381BG 98
Tyson, Lt. James (P) 381BG/91BG 101,116, 128, 138, 158, 172
Tyson, Sgt Clayton O (WG) 324BS, 91BG 179

U
Uskala, Lt. Allen A (P) 324BS, 91 BG 105

V
Van Blarcom, Lt. Nelson (P) 91BG 166
Verinis, Lt. James (P) 324BS, 91BG, 35, 36, 37
Verrill, Lt. Earl (P) 401BS, 91BG 88
Van Ausdall, Lt. Charles (P) 401BS, 91BG 166
Van Blarcom, Lt. (P) 323BS, 91BG 185, 211
Van Buskirk, Lt. Bob (B) 532BS, 381BG 146, 151, 152
Van Hise, Lt. Malcolm (N) 535BS, 381BG 111
Van Hoozer, Sgt Howard (WG) 533BS, 381BG 235
Von der Heyde, Lt. Don (P) 91BG 22, 52, 57, 58, 64, 67
Von Kluge, Gen., CG, 7th Army, Wehrmacht 177

W
Wade, Lt. Warren J (P) 601BS, 398BG 180
Wade, T/Sgt Woodrow (WG) 322BS, 91BG 116, 122
Wagner, Capt. Meyer C (P) 603BS, 398BG 178
Wainwright, Lt. Clarence D (P) 533BS, 381BG 145
Walby, Lt. Charles T (P) 322BS, 91BG 166
Waldman, Lt. Ralph J (N) 532BS, 381BG 103
Walker, Lt. Robert B (P) 91BG 25
Walker, Lt. William C (B) 532BS, 381BG 103
Wallick, Capt. Ken (P) 322BS 9
Wallner, Lt. Edgar (N) 323BS, 91BG 143
Walsh, Lt. Thomas H (P) 323BS, 91BG 86
Walton, Sgt G (ROG) 322BS, 91BG 116
Ward, Lt. Neal P (P) 323BS, 91BG 122
Wardencki, Lt. John (P) 534BS, 381BG 145
Warkentin, Sgt Robert C (BT) 603BS, 398BG 164
Warner, Lt. Harry K (N) 323BS, 91BG 59
Warring, F/O William H (P) 351BG 87
Watkins, Sgt John M Jnr. (TG) 532BS, 381BG 45
Watson, Sgt (BT) 534BS, 381BG 196
Wattles, Lt. Fred M (N) 351BG 43
Webb, Lt. Allan (P) 532BS, 381BG 178
Webb, T/Sgt William (Eng.) 532BS, 381BG 151
Weber, Lt. Howard F (P) 401BS, 91BG 102
Weekley, Lt. Harold D (P) 601BS, 398BG 179
Weeks, Lt. Elburt (DSC) (P) 324BS, 91BG 180
Wegum, Lt. Roger J (P) 601BS, 398BG 199
Weibel, Maj. John C (P) 398BG 159
Weieneth, Lt. Arlyn A (P) 401BS, 91BG 59
Weitzenfeld, Capt. (P) 91BG 31, 39, 57
Weitzenfeld, Maj. (P) 91BG 156
Welch, Lt. John (B) 401BS, 91BG 151, 210
Welk, T/Sgt James F (ROG) 351BG 29
Wells, Lt. William E (P) 600BS, 398BG 224
Weltman, Lt. Nathan (N) 401BS, 91BG 71
Weniger, Lt. Robert L (CP) 535BS, 381BG 43, 84
Wendte, Lt. Dale G (CP) 532BS, 381BG 45

Weiby, Lt. Jens T (P) 323BS, 91BG 99
Wennerberg, Lt. John (P) 322BS, 91BG 99
Wertman, Sgt Rex (BT) 322BS, 91BG 121
Westwood, Capt., Gnd. Echelon, 91BG 238
Wheatley, S/Sgt Kyle B (BT) 534BS, 381BG 128
Wheeler, Lt. Bill (P) 91BG 40, 56, 59, 67
Whitehead, Lt. Sam (P) 534BS, 381BG 174
Whitsell, Lt. Charles (P) 324BS, 91BG 197
Widosh, Lt. Othmer (CP) 532BS, 381BG 146, 151
Wierman, Lt. John (CP) 533BS, 381BG 124, 125
Wilcock, Lt. John C (P) 534BS, 381BG 178
Wilkinson, Lt. Walter E (P) 323BS, 91BG 126, 134
Williams, Lt. (P) 534BS, 381BG 145, 156, 161
Williams, B/Gen. Robert, CG, 1BW/1BD 56, 57, 93
Williams, Lt. Claude M (P) 401BS, 91BG 126
Williams, Lt. George W (B) 533BS, 381BG 42
Williams, Sgt Durward J (WG) 532BS, 381BG 127
Willis, Lt. Gilbert (CP) 324BS, 91BG 180
Wilson, Lt. Arden D (P) 534BS, 381BG 103
Wilson, Lt. Donald M (CP) 532BS, 381BG 127
Wilson, Lt. George E (P) 601BS, 398BG 163
Wilson, Lt. John W (P) 91BG 10, 25
Wilson, Lt. Talmidge G (P) 401BS, 91BG 55
Wilson, S/Sgt James (BT) 532BS, 381BG 151
Wilson, Sgt Jesse, 7th Station Comp., 381BG 51, 58
Wilson, S/Sgt Howard, 448 Sub-depot, 381BG 138, 220
Windsor, Elizabeth, British Queen 38
Wing, Sgt Joseph O (Eng.) 91BG 28
Winicki, Lt. Maryan J (N) 532BS, 381BG 183
Winslow, Lt. Ted (N) 322BS, 91BG 49, 56
Winters, Capt. Doug (P) 532BS, 381BG 33, 81,136
Wismer, Lt. Frederick C (P) 600BS, 398BG 197
Wood, Sgt John (BT) 535BS, 381BG 85
Wood, Capt. Charles G (P) 532BS, 381BG 123
Wood, Lt. William D (P) 322BS, 91BG 116, 122
Wood, Lt. William D (P) 322BS, 91BG 116, 122
Woods, Lt. Laverne B (CP) 322BS, 91BG 102
Wray, Col. Stanley T CO, 91BG 7, 21, 23, 30
Wright, Lt. Neil N (P) 534BS, 381BG 58
Wright, Lt. Parke III (P) 602BS, 398BG 181
Wright, Sgt James W (G) 322BS, 91BG 34
Wroblicka, Lt. Bill (P) 534BS, 381BG 47, 55
Wulf, Lt. Elmer B (P) 535BS, 381BG 190, 213
Wurzbach, L/Col. Clemens CO, 91BG 30, 57, 154
Wyler, William, Hollywood Film Producer 29
Wylie, Lt. Robert S (P) 401BS, 91BG 144

Y

Yelle, Lt. Edgar (N) 323BS, 91BG 57
Yorba, Lt. Bernard (P) 534BS, 381BG 88, 89

Z

Zadnick, Lt. Robert (P) 532BS, 381BG 115
Zapinski, Lt. Leonard (P) 532BS, 381BG146, 151, 152
Zeman, Lt. Jack R (P) 532BS, 381BG 103
Zienowitz, Maj. Victor (P) 91BG 8
Zimmerman, Lt. Leland L (P) 602BS, 398BG 201
Zum, Lt, Benjamin (P) 535BS, 381BG 70, 74
Zwicky, Lt. Alfred (CP) 322BS, 91BG 195

Abbreviation Key (USAAF/Allied)

(B)	Bombardier
(CG)	Commanding General
(C-in-C)	Commander in Chief
(C/C)	Crew-chief
(CO)	Commanding Officer
(CP)	Co-pilot
(Eng.)	Engineer/top turret
(G)	Gunner
(GB)	Group-Bombardier
(GC)	Ground crew
(G/Int.)	German-language Interpreter
(G/Ins.)	Gunnery Instructor
(GN)	Group-Navigator
(N)	Navigator
(NT)	Nose turret
(P)	Pilot
(PN)	Pilotage navigator
(RN)	Radar-navigator
(RO)	Radar-operator
(ROG)	Radio operator/gunner
(S/J)	'Spot' jammer
(T)	Togglier
(TG)	Tail gunner
(VI)	Voice-interpreter (German-language)
(WG)	Waist gunner

Abbreviations (German Ranks)

Hptm	Hauptmann
Kommandeur	Gruppe CO
Kommodore	Geschwader (Wing) CO
Ltn.	Leutnant
Oblt.	Oberleutnant
Ogfr.	Obergefreiter
Staffelkapitaen	Staffel (Sqdn) CO